To Lee & Emily;
Aaron, Nikki, & Micah;
JP, Chelane, Pepper, & Bale;
& Carl & Mindy;
Thank you for being
my "other family" & for your
love & support. I hope that [illegible]il
see in the pages of this book wh[illegible]
great Friend you have in Jesus!
Love you all!
Nancy
Romans 8:18

Do not be discouraged, for the Lord your God will be with you wherever you go.

—Joshua 1:9, NIV

To order additional copies of *He's Got Your Back,*
by Nancy Canwell, **call 1-800-765-6955.**

Visit us at **www.reviewandherald.com** for information
on other Review and Herald® products.

Nancy Canwell | A Daily Devotional for Juniors / Earliteens

REVIEW AND HERALD® PUBLISHING ASSOCIATION
Since 1861 | www.reviewandherald.com

Published by Review and Herald® Publishing Association, Hagerstown, MD 21741-1119

Review and Herald® titles may be purchased in bulk for educational, business, fund-raising, or sales promotional use. For information, e-mail SpecialMarkets@reviewandherald.com.

The Review and Herald® Publishing Association publishes biblically based materials for spiritual, physical, and mental growth and Christian discipleship.

This book was
Edited by Rachel Cabose
Designed by Emily Ford / Review and Herald® Design Center
Cover art © Thinkstock.com
Typeset: Minion Pro 10.5/12.5

PRINTED IN U.S.A.

18 17 16 15 14 5 4 3 2 1

Library of Congress Cataloging-in-Publication Data
Canwell, Nancy.
He's got your back : a daily devotional for juniors / Nancy Canwell.
pages cm
ISBN 978-0-8280-2804-2
1. Preteens--Prayers and devotions--Juvenile literature. 2. Devotional calendars--Seventh-Day Adventists--Juvenile literature. I. Title.
BV4870.C35 2014
242'.63--dc23

2014017044

ISBN 978-0-8280-2804-2

DEDICATION

To Dad and Mom

I couldn't have asked for more loving, supportive parents than you two. You raised me well, setting an example by how you lived, and then you gave me the wings to fly.

Dad: I will always be thankful that you took that Bible down from the bookshelf, read it, gave your life to Jesus, and then led our family to Him, too. If you hadn't, my life would have taken an entirely different course, and this book would never have been written.

Mom: You have been my cheerleader throughout life. Whether I dreamed of being a veterinarian, a jockey, a pastor, or an author, you believed in me and encouraged me to never give up. Thank you for the framed verse from 1 Chronicles 28:20 that still sits on my writer's desk.

In loving memory of my big brother, Dan

When he was so sick with cancer, I promised Dan that I would write about the lessons I learned from his courage and unshakable faith in God. Some of those lessons are in this book, so his ministry as a youth pastor lives on. I can't wait to see him at the Second Coming. We'll have a lot of catching up to do!

And to Jesus, who every single day gives me something worth writing about.

"For I am not ashamed of the gospel,
because it is the power of God
that brings salvation to everyone who believes"
—Romans 1:16, NIV

ACKNOWLEDGMENTS

- **Thank you to the staff at Review and Herald® Publishing Association:**
  - Dwain Esmond, vice president for the Editorial Division, for asking me to write this book
  - Jeannette Johnson, former acquisitions editor, for walking me through my first book
  - Rachel Cabose, editor of this book, for her keen eye and kind heart
- **A special thank-you to the editors who have advanced my writing through the years. Some of the stories in this book were rewritten from articles in their magazines and Web sites:**
  - Linda DuBose, editor of *GraceNotes*: www.e-gracenotes.org
  - Rich DuBose, editor of *Answers for Me*: www.answersforme.org
  - Omar Miranda, editor of *Insight* magazine
  - Marvin Moore, editor of *Signs of the Times* magazine
  - Paul Richardson, director of the Center for Creative Ministry: www.creativeministry.org
  - Melody Tan, associate editor of *Signs of the Times* Australia magazine
- **A huge thank-you to the students at Rogers Adventist School and Walla Walla Valley Academy who shared their stories and suggested topic ideas. You are amazing!**
- **Loralee Thomas's fifth- and sixth-grade class**
- **Ralph Hogate's seventh- and eighth-grade Bible classes**
- **Daniel Perrin's academy Bible classes**
- **Additional thanks:**
  - Melanie Scherencel Bockmann, author of four books and the "best friend I've never met," who mentored me by phone and e-mails. You are much appreciated!
  - Brian Hernandez, founder of Vizual Graphix, for his Mac support when my computer crashed and I thought I'd lost two month's worth of devotionals!
  - My two families, the Snyders and the Canwells, for their love and support of my writing career.
- **And last, but certainly not least, my husband and daughter, whom I love so much:**
  - Keith: For the past eight years you have been my in-house proofreader for every article I've written, and you did the same for each devotional in this book. And to show your support you've often read my articles again after they were published. Thank you!
  - Christina: Thanks for letting me bounce ideas off you! You may be in college now, but I remember well when you were the age of these readers. You had, and still have, a commitment to God that inspires me.

INTRODUCTION

Dear Reader,

Life can be tough. There's no doubt about it. So I wanted to write this book to let you know that you are never alone. Someone is there for you. Someone is in your corner. Someone is willing to help you. It's Jesus—and *He's got your back.*

I became a Christian when I was the age of many of you readers. And now that I'm a grown-up, one thing I know for sure: if I could go back and choose Jesus again, I would. *In a heartbeat.*

Looking back on my life, I can clearly see that Jesus had my back so many times:

- when my three best friends dumped me after I was baptized
- when my dog got run over and killed
- when I was insecure about my acne
- when my family had to move to a different state
- when I had to start over in a new school
- when I got my heart broken
- when I faced a major surgery
- when I lost an election at school
- when my best friend chose a different best friend
- when my big brother got cancer and died

Through all those times Jesus was there—whether I realized it or not.

And He's there for you, too.

A lot of kids put their heads together to help me write this book by telling me their stories and giving me ideas. (I've changed some of their names.) Though you may not be facing every issue they faced, you may have a friend who is, or you may face something similar in the future. Whatever the case, no matter what comes, knowing Jesus is always the answer.

Want to read along with me? I'll be reading each day with you. Let's make a deal to not miss a day. Because every day that we take the time to read about Jesus and talk to Him is a good day!

—Pastor Nancy

JANUARY 1

Happy New Year!

Anyone who belongs to Christ is a new person. The past is forgotten, and everything is new. 2 Corinthians 5:17, CEV.

Five . . . four . . . three . . . two . . . one . . . Happy New Year! Did you stay up last night and count down the minutes to the new year? Or maybe you went to bed early and slept through it. Regardless, 2015 is here! A new year. A fresh start.

Sounds good, doesn't it? Especially if 2014 wasn't all that great. Maybe you're carrying a load of guilt from mistakes you made. Maybe you made some poor choices that can't be erased. Maybe you spoke words that can't be taken back.

Or maybe 2014 was a sad year for you. Did a good friend turn on you and now that friendship is history? Did your parents split up, or did one of them lose a job? Did someone you love die? Did you not make the sports team or win a school election?

Whatever may have made 2014 a bad year, a new one is waiting for you now. Imagine yourself in your dream car, sitting at a stop sign. You're in the driver's seat. The choice is yours. Which way will you go? You have two options: you can shift into reverse and relive all the bad memories of last year—or you can shift into drive and take off, never looking in the rearview mirror.

I hope that you choose to go forward. Life is waiting for you! I wonder what exciting things might lie ahead for you this year. Two things are for sure. The first is that this year will bring a mixture of good and bad, happy and sad. It would be great if we could see into the future and plan ahead for how we will handle the tough times. It would be even better if we knew what they were and could stop them. But we can't, and so we take life as it comes.

The second thing that is for sure is that you don't have to go through this year alone. Jesus will be with you. He saw you through last year; He'll see you through this year. You have Someone to talk to. You have Someone who will listen. You have Someone who cares. Someone who is in your corner cheering for you. Someone who loves you enough that He died for you. You are not alone.

He's got your back.

JANUARY 2

The Choice to Stand

Be on your guard; stand firm in the faith;
be courageous; be strong. 1 Corinthians 16:13, NIV.

I was hurrying to my elementary school homeroom with exciting news when I saw them walking toward me—and they didn't look happy. In fact, I had never seen such mean expressions on their faces. Cindy, Danielle, and Daisy had been my best friends since first grade. We were the Four Musketeers! We were inseparable. But now I felt like it was three against one.

I was 10 years old, and my family had recently become Christians. Just that weekend we had been baptized, and I couldn't wait to get back to my public school and share my excitement! But I didn't expect what happened next, as I stood face to face with my best friends.

"Were you baptized on Saturday?" one of them asked while the other two glared.

"Yes," I answered, "I was."

"Well, then, we're not your friends anymore!"

And they walked out of my life. I spent the morning recess crying in a bathroom stall.

That evening Dad told me, "Just hang on. Be kind to them even if they're mean to you. And stand up for what you believe."

That day was my first experience at choosing to stand up for what I believed. And it was a choice I decided to keep making as I grew up. One time I chose to leave the room at a party because some kids were about to watch a murder-horror movie. Another time I chose to walk away when a cute guy, whom I wasn't even dating, wanted to "make out." And I chose to say no when a classmate wanted both of us to cheat on a test. The more I practiced standing up for what I believed was right, the easier it got. And it can get easier for you, too.

It becomes easier when you realize just how much Jesus loves you—when you think of the disgrace and pain He gladly went through for you. You may get "dissed." You may even lose a friend. So is it worth it? Yes! It's been many years since my friends confronted me in the hallway at school. And to this day I have never regretted my decision to stand.

After awhile my three friends decided that being a Christian was actually pretty cool. They asked me to be their friend again and even started asking me questions about Jesus!

I hope you will make the choice to stand. Even if you look around and everyone else is making the wrong choice—stand.

JANUARY 3

New Year's Resolutions

But one thing I do: Forgetting what is behind and straining toward what is ahead, I press on toward the goal to win the prize for which God has called me heavenward in Christ Jesus. Philippians 3:13, 14, NIV.

So did you make any New Year's resolutions this year? I have an idea: what if you made resolutions you could keep by following advice from the Bible? Here are some ideas to get you started. You can find your own texts to personalize your own resolutions. You may also find it helpful to write them down in a journal and read them often.

Resolution: Be more kind and forgiving. "Be kind and compassionate to one another, forgiving each other, just as in Christ God forgave you" (Ephesians 4:32, NIV).

Resolution: Worry less by praying more. "Don't fret or worry. Instead of worrying, pray. Let petitions and praises shape your worries into prayers, letting God know your concerns. Before you know it, a sense of God's wholeness, everything coming together for good, will come and settle you down. It's wonderful what happens when Christ displaces worry at the center of your life" (Philippians 4:6, 7, Message).

Resolution: Fear less by trusting more. "Do not be afraid of sudden terror, nor of trouble from the wicked when it comes; for the Lord will be your confidence, and will keep your foot from being caught" (Proverbs 3:25, 26, NKJV).

Resolution: Think before I speak. "Everyone should be quick to listen, slow to speak and slow to become angry, because human anger does not produce the righteousness that God desires" (James 1:19, 20, NIV).

Resolution: Remember that I am never alone. "The Lord is there to rescue all who are discouraged and have given up hope" (Psalm 34:18, CEV).

Resolution: Remember that Jesus really is coming again. "I won't leave you like orphans. I will come back to you" (John 14:18, CEV).

Resolution: Believe that I can change and be a better person. "With man this is impossible, but with God all things are possible" (Matthew 19:26, NIV).

JANUARY 4

Kicking the Habit

So let God work his will in you. Yell a loud no to the Devil and watch him scamper. Say a quiet yes to God and he'll be there in no time. Quit dabbling in sin. Purify your inner life. Quit playing the field. Hit bottom, and cry your eyes out. The fun and games are over. Get serious, really serious. Get down on your knees before the Master; it's the only way you'll get on your feet. James 4:7, 8, Message.

Do you have a New Year's resolution to kick a bad habit? It may take work, but even the toughest of habits can be broken with God's help. My dad is living proof of this.

When Dad was 13 years old, he and a friend found a package of cigarettes. Curious about what it would feel like, they went behind a barn and smoked their first cigarette. "It made us so sick!" Dad told me. "But it was the cool thing to do, so I kept at it." By the time he was an adult, he was smoking more than a pack a day.

Dad wasn't a Christian, but when he married Mom and started having kids, he thought he should stop smoking. He tried many tricks, but none ever worked. For example, he tried flushing his cigarettes down the toilet, only to go out and buy more. He tried burying them in the backyard, only to dig them up and dry them out in the sun. Once during a family vacation he announced, "I'm throwing my cigarettes out the window!" only to turn back after 10 miles.

But then Dad became a Christian and realized that he didn't have to break his habit alone. He had Jesus on his side! First, Dad had to want to quit for the right reasons: his body now belonged to God, and he wanted to set a good example for his kids. Then he had to do his part and try. The first day, he failed. On the second day he prayed, "God, I want the world to see that You are real. Even if it kills me, I'll never smoke another cigarette!" And he never did.

If you want to kick a bad habit this year, here are some tips. First, start by admitting that it's not good for you. Next, sit down with paper and pen and list the reasons you want to change and the benefits you'll get from changing. Then decide whether you can stop it on your own or if you'll need outside help. There's nothing wrong with asking a school counselor, pastor, or doctor to help you. And finally, spend time with God every day in whatever way is meaningful for you. He is your greatest ally! He will give you strength and pick you up if you fall. And He will help you win your battle.

You're Never Alone

He heals the brokenhearted and binds up their wounds. Psalm 147:3, NIV.

After Kenny's dad died suddenly, he had to deal not only with his grief, but also with guilt. He and his dad hadn't gotten along for quite awhile. But instead of getting help with his grief and guilt, he let them consume him. He moped around the house during the day, watching TV and playing video games. In the evenings he hung out with friends but made sure they didn't talk about his dad. Worst of all, he stopped talking to God.

Kenny told me, "One night I was so fed up with the pain that I just had to get out of the house. Out in the darkness, some ugly thoughts came into my head: *Nobody cares about you . . . Your dad never was proud of you, or he would have told you . . . You'll never feel better . . .*

"I instantly realized that I was letting Satan fill my heart with bitterness toward God by believing that He had taken my dad away from me. And I was bitter toward myself because I thought I should have had a better relationship with my dad."

Kenny collapsed on the gravel on the side of the road and started crying. "I had felt so alone," he later told me. "But suddenly I felt like Someone was there. I immediately realized that the Someone was God. The best way I can describe it is that I felt a warm embrace.

"Right then I asked God to forgive me for abandoning Him—especially when I really needed Him the most. One thing I really admire about God is that you can try to push Him away, but when you see how much you need Him, you find out that He's been there all along."

If you ever feel the way Kenny felt that night—that you're all alone in your problems—don't stuff your feelings. Instead, take action to make your life better. Go find people who love you and are willing to help you. These may be your parents, siblings, friends, or teachers. And there are also trained professionals—counselors, doctors, and pastors—who can give you good advice. But they won't know what you need unless you tell them.

If you, like Kenny, are going through a tough time right now, know that life *can* get better with the right kind of help and new coping skills. And life will be better *forever* once you get to heaven! According to 1 Corinthians 2:9: "What God has planned for people who love him is more than eyes have seen or ears have heard. It has never even entered our minds!" (CEV). That day is coming! In the meantime, remember this: you are *never* alone.

JANUARY 6

A Picture of You

See what great love the Father has lavished on us, that we should be called children of God! And that is what we are! 1 John 3:1, NIV.

If you asked me to draw a picture of myself, you'd probably laugh at the result. Even though I'm a grown-up, I can draw only stick people.

I once asked a group of kids at our house for Bible study to draw me self-portraits. "Draw a picture of yourself that shows me what your self-worth is like," I asked. Jake drew a picture of his face dotted with acne. Sandi drew a picture of herself walking by a group of slender girls, and above them was a voice bubble that said, "She's fat!" Ricky drew a picture of himself holding a biology paper with a big D on it. Casey drew a picture of her large nose. Kathryn drew a picture of herself losing the class election, tears streaming down her face. Trevor drew a picture of himself as a weed about to be mowed down by a lawn mower. Shelly drew a picture of herself giving a speech in class, and no one was paying attention.

Their pictures made me sad, because when I looked at these kids, I saw them very differently. I saw kids of value. I saw sons and daughters of God.

What would your self-worth picture look like if I asked you to draw me one? Would you draw something you dislike about your looks? Would you draw how you think other kids see you? Or maybe how you think your parents or teachers view you? If you put yourself down in your drawing, I bet I'd look at it and say, "I don't see you this way. I see someone much more special than this picture shows."

But more important, I can imagine Jesus looking at your negative picture and saying, "Oh, this is all wrong! This isn't how I see you." Then He'd go on to tell you that He loved you even before you were born. He'd tell you that He's been there when you were sad, even though you couldn't see Him. That He's protected you, even when you didn't realize it. That He's heard and answered all your prayers, even if you didn't get the answers you wanted. That He sees the good in you—someone worth forgiving and giving a second chance. Someone worth dying for. He'd call you "daughter" or "son." And He'd tell you that He wants to spend eternity with you.

So the next time you picture yourself, see yourself through God's eyes. Then you'll see the real you. A beautiful picture of you.

JANUARY 7

Winter Blues

God keeps an eye on his friends,
his ears pick up every moan and groan. . . . Is anyone crying for help?
God is listening, ready to rescue you. Psalm 34:15-17, Message.

I always get kind of blue after the holidays," a friend told me. "You know, when it's all over and you want to bring the magic back." Maybe you feel this way now that Christmas is over. You've packed away the indoor and outdoor lights, and your world looks a little grayish. You've unwrapped all your gifts, and maybe you're even getting a little bored with them. You're done traveling, and you're back into the old routine of school and homework.

It's normal to feel a bit of a letdown after the holidays, but 15-year-old Leiloni felt something worse than that. She didn't have any energy and was sleepy all the time. There were days when she ate too much and other days when she ate too little. She withdrew from her friends and didn't even want to leave her house. But when spring came, her spirits started to lift.

This went on for three winters before Leiloni asked for help. She told her mom, who made an appointment for her to see a doctor. He diagnosed her as having something called SAD (seasonal affective disorder), which is basically winter depression. The doctor gave her advice, and she chose to follow it. She sat under a special light each morning. She started eating healthy meals and drinking plenty of water. She also exercised regularly. And she relied on her friends. They knew when she was having a tough time and would encourage her to do stuff with them.

Leiloni told me that the most important thing she did was to stay connected to Jesus. She knew that she needed Him during those dark times more than ever.

It's sometimes tempting to push God away when things are tough. Maybe you blame Him. Maybe you don't "feel" Him, so you think He's forgotten about you. Maybe you feel that reading your Bible and praying is just one more thing that you can't handle right now. God understands those feelings. But you really do need His help, so find a way to connect with Him that's not a burden, but actually a comfort. Maybe it's through listening to or playing music. Maybe it's walking out in nature in daylight. Maybe it's just sitting quietly in His company.

For Leiloni it was journaling. That's how she talked to God. "The whole time He was a constant in my life," she said. "I wouldn't have made it without Him."

JANUARY 8

How to Make a Team Work

You are better off to have a friend than to be all alone, because then you will get more enjoyment out of what you earn. If you fall, your friend can help you up. But if you fall without having a friend nearby, you are really in trouble. Ecclesiastes 4:9, 10, CEV.

The Knights' basketball season was off to a sad start. When their record was 0-6, their coach knew something needed to be done. They were a group of talented boys, but they weren't working as a team. It was as if each player was facing the opponent alone.

Isaiah, who played the wing position, told me, "We realized that we were taking too much of the responsibility of playing a good game and winning on our individual shoulders. We worked way too hard at practice and just never had fun playing basketball. That's when we decided that we could do better as a team than as individuals. We began to believe in each other." And that was the team's turning point.

They started enjoying the sport and stopped focusing on winning. If someone missed a shot, rather than getting heated, team members would say, "It's OK!" and later pass the ball to that player for another chance. They also listened to their coach's instructions more and communicated on the court. If they lost, their attitude was "The next game is a new game."

The Knights also began noticing how other teams functioned. Many of the teams they played were highly competitive among themselves. They also complained a lot to their coaches and didn't listen well to instructions.

Because of their change of attitude toward teamwork, the Knights started winning games! When the season was over, they left feeling confident and bonded as a team.

Whether it's a sports team, a music ensemble, a science lab group, or a drama club, sometimes it's hard to be a part of a team. If you're the one who gets passed by, or the one the rest of the team blames, it can be tough. And if you're the one who always takes charge and does all the hard work alone, that's no fun either. Today's text is right. Two are better than one. It's less stressful and more fun.

It's the same in your Christian life. To try to go it alone without Jesus just doesn't work. You need Him to be your Coach because He has knowledge and wisdom that you don't. So team up with Jesus, and you'll see what a difference that kind of teamwork can make!

JANUARY 9

Whiter Than Snow

"Come now, let us settle the matter," says the Lord.
"Though your sins are like scarlet, they shall be as white as snow;
though they are red as crimson, they shall be like wool." Isaiah 1:18, NIV.

I*t's snowing!* I'm sitting by our large living room window looking outside at a winter wonderland. Our backyard is covered in a blanket of white. The fir trees are flocked even though Christmas is over, and the birds are at the feeders eating breakfast.

Every time it snows I think of today's mind-blowing text. It's mind-blowing because when we sin, we are the ones who walk away from God. Yet it's God who calls us back! He's basically saying, "Come back, and I'll fix what you messed up by covering it with My forgiveness." Just as snow covers the mud, dead flowers, and bare branches of winter, His perfect life covers our ugly sins.

No matter how dirty a sin has made you feel, the promise is that you can be clean. White. *Even whiter than snow.* That's pretty awesome! I know a teenage girl who made some big mistakes in a relationship. Feeling used and disgraced, she went to Jesus for forgiveness—and her past is now whiter than snow. I know a teenage boy who robbed a store while high on drugs. Sitting in jail, he felt ashamed, so he went to Jesus for forgiveness—and his past, too, is now whiter than snow. And on a seemingly lesser scale, I've known liars, gossipers, cheaters, and people with bad tempers whose pasts are now whiter than snow—because of the miracle of forgiveness.

Do you think your past can't be covered white as snow? Remember the story of King David? He sinned big-time. He stole another man's wife and had her husband killed. Then he tried to cover it up by lying! After carrying a heavy load of guilt and shame, he finally accepted God's invitation to "come." And this was his prayer: "Generous in love—God, give grace! Huge in mercy —wipe out my bad record. Scrub away my guilt, soak out my sins in your laundry. I know how bad I've been; my sins are staring me down. . . . Soak me in your laundry and I'll come out clean, scrub me and I'll have a snow-white life" (Psalm 51:1-7, Message).

Jesus can hardly wait for you to come to Him so He can make your life whiter than snow! If you do accept His invitation, you won't be met with disgust, rejection, or blame. Instead, you'll find love, acceptance, and forgiveness.

JANUARY 10

Jesus Loves Kids

About this time the disciples came to Jesus and asked him who would be the greatest in the kingdom of heaven. Jesus called a child over and had the child stand near him. Then he said: "I promise you this. If you don't change and become like a child, you will never get into the kingdom of heaven." Matthew 18:1-3, CEV.

Do you ever feel that you're unloved? That no one values you? That no one stands up for you? The good news is that Jesus loves kids! He values them. He stands up for them. And I have Bible texts that prove it!

There's a chapter in the Bible, Matthew 18, that shows Jesus' *amazing* love for you. First there's the story of when the disciples asked Jesus who would be the greatest in heaven. He answered by calling a child over to Him. He used a child—a kid like you—as an example! He told the people that if they wanted to even enter heaven, they needed the faith, trust, and humility of a child.

In verse 6 Jesus speaks some of the strongest words quoted in the Bible. They show His fatherly sense of protection and the fate of those who might harm one of His kids: "Whoever causes one of these little ones who believe in Me to sin, it would be better for him if a millstone were hung around his neck, and he were drowned in the depth of the sea" (NKJV). Strong words of warning for sure. Talk about Jesus having your back!

Later, in verse 10, Jesus talks about heaven's view of kids: "Watch that you don't treat a single one of these childlike believers arrogantly. You realize, don't you, that their personal angels are constantly in touch with my Father in heaven?" (Message). How cool is that?

Then Jesus goes on to tell the well-known story of the lost sheep. But what some people overlook is that the lost sheep symbolizes a child. There is a shepherd who has 100 sheep, and one of them wanders off and gets lost. You'd think that the shepherd would say, "Oh, well, at least I have 99 left. I'll just stay and take care of them. It's that dumb sheep's fault that he left and got lost, anyway!" But surprisingly, he leaves all 99 to look for just one. When he finds it, he's happier about that one than all the 99! Then come Jesus' heartfelt words: "In the same way your Father in heaven is not willing that any of these little ones should perish" (verse 14, NIV).

And *that's* how much Jesus loves kids!

A Letter From God

Your word is a lamp for my feet, a light on my path. Psalm 119:105, NIV.

It's interesting how a bunch of pages bound together inside a white leather cover could mean so much to me, but my first Bible is a treasure. My parents gave it to me for my birthday the year our family became Christians. When I looked at it today, I wondered: Why does the Bible sometimes stop being our lamp and our light? Why do we sometimes take life into our own hands, make our own decisions, and get advice from everyone but God and His Word?

Although it was written thousands of years ago, the Bible is still today what it has always been: *the words of God Himself!* Words that teach us the right way to live; words that show us what Jesus is like; words that guarantee forgiveness and acceptance by God; words that comfort us when we're hurting; and words that give us hope for the future when we're fed up with this world.

There are different ways of studying the Bible. You can try what some kids have and read the entire Bible through from Genesis to Revelation every year. Or you can choose a particular word and use a concordance or online Bible to look up texts that use the same word. For instance, you could look up words such as hope, forgiveness, heaven, or peace.

You can also choose a single book to read. If you want to know more about what Jesus is like, read the book of John. The books of Galatians, Ephesians, Philippians, and Colossians will show you how to live like a Christian. In the book of Psalms you can read how David experienced many ups and downs yet always made it through praising God. There's also the option of studying the lives of different Bible characters such as Moses, Esther, Paul, and Mary. See how you relate to them and what you can learn from them. If you ever come across something you don't understand, dig deeper or ask for help from a more experienced Christian.

Some kids write their thoughts in a journal as they study. Others write favorite texts on their school notebook, where they see them all day, or on a note card that they hang by their bed or on their mirror. Many memorize texts that they can remember when they need them most.

One of the best things you can do with your time in this new year is to read your Bible every day. It will make a difference in your attitude toward school, friends, family, chores, and everything else! And it will give you the feeling that something is stable in this messed-up world.

JANUARY 12

Outstretched Arms

If your heart is broken, you'll find God right there; if you're kicked in the gut, he'll help you catch your breath. Psalm 34:18, Message.

Five years ago on this day, a massive 7.0 earthquake rocked the island of Haiti. It's been estimated that nearly 225,000 people died and more than a million were left homeless, many living in tent cities. Relief workers from around the world descended on Haiti to offer medical care, counseling, cleanup, and rebuilding. My husband was one of those relief workers.

During his two-week stay, he met a medical doctor from Spain who shared with him this sad yet beautiful story. The event happened just days after the earthquake:

"A Christian man with injuries to his lower body came in for treatment. As I treated him, the man began to tell me his story. His toddler son was lying on his lap when the quake hit. A wall fell on them, pinning them down. The boy was trapped between the wall and his father's lap—with his little arms outstretched. The father was unable to move to help his son. The gut-wrenching part is that they lay there helpless for three days as the father watched his son die.

"The imprints of his child's bones were still in this father's lap when I examined him. When I was finished, I told the man how very sorry I was that this tragedy had happened. I said, 'I cannot fully comprehend the pain you must feel. I've never lost a child.' But then I think God gave me the words to say next. I told him, 'But I know Someone who fully understands your pain. God Himself watched helplessly as His Son died—arms outstretched, too. He understands your pain very personally.' "

The doctor said the man's whole expression changed as he began to realize that God really did understand his grief. It was just what he needed to hear! He walked away realizing that he was not going through this heart-wrenching grief alone.

Do you ever feel that no one understands your pain? Do you feel that you're carrying it all alone, and sometimes it seems too much to handle? I can guarantee you that Jesus understands. While He lived on earth, He went through rejection, loss, disappointment, heartache, and all the other emotions you feel. So you *do* have Someone to talk to. Let it all out. Talk, scream, cry, or shout. He'll listen. He understands. His arms were outstretched on the cross for you.

JANUARY 13

Prayer and the Gumball Machine

Before they call I will answer;
while they are still speaking I will hear. Isaiah 65:24, NIV.

Would you please go find your little brother?" Mom asked my sister and me.

We were doing our weekly Friday shopping, and 3-year-old Davey had disappeared again. But we had a good idea where he might be: at the gumball machine. Mom always gave him pennies from her coin purse, and he would head for the machine. But he wasn't after the gum—he was hoping for the prize that might come out instead!

As my sister and I walked down the aisle, we saw a group of kids gathered around in a circle. When we got there, we saw why. Davey was kneeling down in front of the machine, praying every time he put in a penny that a prize would come out instead of a hard gumball. And it did! Time after time! You see, my family had just become Christians, and Dad had taught us that we could pray to Jesus about anything. So Davey did.

Now that we're all grown up, we recently talked about that little "miracle" in the grocery store and wondered why God seemed to answer such a simple request. Dad said that it was to strengthen a little boy's faith for what he would face in the years to come. And we've wondered what kind of lifelong impact it had on those kids who were watching.

I've made prayer a part of my daily life since I was 10. And for me it's truly like talking to my best Friend. Sometimes I pray silently; sometimes I pray out loud. Sometimes my eyes are closed; sometimes they're open. Sometimes I pray for a need, and sometimes I pray for a want. Sometimes I praise Him, and sometimes I question Him.

The most important part of prayer is that you and I are honest with God. If you're having a tough day, tell Him. What father wouldn't want to comfort his child? And if you're thankful for something, be sure and tell Him that, too.

There's no perfect time or place to pray. The time is anytime, and the place is anywhere.

Think of a friend who lives far away. If you didn't write letters, e-mails, or Facebook messages, after a while you'd feel like strangers. It's the same with Jesus. We need to talk to Him often to keep the friendship going. And if your prayers aren't answered just the way you hoped they would be, don't stop praying. It isn't that He wasn't listening, but He had a different plan because He can see the beginning from the end. And someday you'll understand.

JANUARY 14

An Eleventh Commandment?

A new command I give you: Love one another. As I have loved you, so you must love one another. John 13:34, NIV.

Just how does a kid follow this "new" commandment Jesus gave? How do you "love one another"? Here are some ideas from a fifth- and sixth-grade class I visited this week:

"Be nice to the younger kids at school. Don't pick on them."

"Respect your parents. Don't talk back. Do your chores without being asked."

"Invite a kid who is alone to sit with your group at lunch."

"Be polite to people in town by opening doors for them and carrying their groceries."

"Don't make a kid feel sad if they're on your team but you wish they weren't."

"Not everyone has to be your close friend, but you should be nice to everyone."

Loving each other is really important to Jesus. The night before He was going to die, He was having a special dinner with His disciples. He wanted them to know how much He loved them, so He called them "my children" and told them He would be with them only a little while longer. Then He gave them what some call the eleventh commandment: "A new command I give you: Love one another. As I have loved you, so you must love one another."

How were they supposed to love? The way He did. He touched. He accepted. He forgave. He listened. He cared.

Jesus went on to say something in verse 35 that's pretty intense: "By this everyone will know that you are my disciples, if you love one another" (NIV). Wow! Jesus isn't saying, "Everyone will know you're My disciples if you don't sin," or "Everyone will know that you're My disciples if you have perfect church attendance." No, He's saying "by *this*"—by *love*. And that's how people will know that you are His disciple, too.

What would your home be like if everyone loved each other? What would your classroom be like if every one loved each other? What would your sports team or music group be like if everyone loved each other? And here's an even better question: what if you were the one to start the love? It would be easy to start. Study Jesus' life. Read stories in Matthew, Mark, Luke, and John that show how He treated different kinds of people. Then go out and make a difference. Go out and change your world.

JANUARY 15

Wedding Invitation

"So be on your guard! You don't know when your Lord will come. Homeowners never know when a thief is coming, and they are always on guard to keep one from breaking in. Always be ready! You don't know when the Son of Man will come." Matthew 24:42-44, CEV.

Alexander pulled on the handle of the double doors, but they didn't open. He gave them a good yank and realized that they were locked!

It was the day of his cousin's evening wedding, and Alexander had put off getting ready all day long. He figured that he'd just wait till the last possible minute and then head out. When he finally did arrive, he was only five to 10 minutes late, but the wedding had begun and the doors were locked! He had missed the wedding, all because he hadn't made the wedding a high enough priority and hadn't gotten ready in time.

Alexander told me, "Missing that wedding taught me an important lesson. I thought of the parable of the 10 virgins and how I *don't* want to miss out on that wedding feast!"

Alexander was referring to a story that Jesus told in Matthew 25:1-13 to help His disciples remember to always be ready for His return.

There were 10 young women who were waiting for the groom to pass by on his way to the wedding. Five of them were wise and took extra oil for their lamps in case they had to wait a long while. But the other five were foolish and didn't take any extra oil.

Because the groom was late, they all got tired and fell asleep. Finally someone yelled, "Here's the groom! Come to meet him!" The girls grabbed their lamps, but the foolish five were out of oil. While they ran to town to get more, the groom came, and only those who were ready with their lamps got to go in to the wedding. When the others hurried back, the door was locked.

Jesus *is* coming again—no doubt about it! And He loves you enough that He has warned you: don't get tired of waiting and fall spiritually asleep. Instead, be ready so that whether He comes tomorrow or many years from now, it won't matter. You'll be waiting and ready.

How do you get ready? By giving your life to Jesus. By living in a constant friendship with Him. By taking anything out of your life that doesn't belong there. And by imitating Him.

Jesus is offering you the chance of a lifetime. He's offering you eternal life! Don't grow tired of waiting. He wants you at the wedding. It just wouldn't be the same without you.

JANUARY 16

Adoption Approved!

The Spirit you received does not make you slaves, so that you live in fear again; rather, the Spirit you received brought about your adoption to sonship. And by him we cry, "Abba, Father." Romans 8:15, NIV.

Nicole sometimes felt that she didn't belong. She wasn't part of a stable family, and she often felt lonesome. Her parents weren't married when she was born, and they split up for a while but later got back together. To make matters worse, Nicole's biological grandparents on both sides abandoned her. "They didn't approve of how I came into the world," she told me.

When Nicole was in fifth grade, she wanted more than anything to have grandparents like all the other kids. She always felt left out on grandparents' day at school, on Christmas day, and on her birthday. She told me, "One day I cried to God. I prayed and asked Him to send a grandparent into my life. The very next day my great-aunt called and said she wanted to take me to a restaurant. I was *so* excited!" Nicole is now 13, and that visit began an awesome grandma-granddaughter relationship that she still enjoys to this day.

Do you ever feel sad or lonely because your family isn't what the world calls "traditional"? Maybe your family is missing a mom or dad because both your parents don't live with you. Perhaps they're divorced or one has died. Did you know that God has the loving qualities of both a dad and a mom? Here are two texts that prove it: "I will be a Father to you, and you will be my sons and daughters, says the Lord Almighty" (2 Corinthians 6:18, NIV). "As a mother comforts her child, so will I comfort you" (Isaiah 66:13, NIV).

God can help fill the void of the people who are absent in your life or who have let you down. He's everything you've ever wanted in a dad or a mom. If you choose to, you can be one of His kids. Then you're a part of His big family—a family that will live together forever. But you don't have to wait till heaven. He's family to you now. And He'll never walk out on you. He's *promised:* "I'll never let you down, never walk off and leave you" (Hebrews 13:5, Message).

And in addition to His love, if you pray for someone to help fill the void, as Nicole did, I believe God will send someone your way. Be active and talk to your pastor about "adopting" someone in your church, and see what great things God has planned for you!

My Name Is Helen

Dear children, let us not love with words or speech but with actions and in truth. 1 John 3:18, NIV.

It was a cold, rainy day as I stood at the school door, looking outside. I really didn't feel like walking to the nearby nursing home on a day like this. But my teacher had assigned me to go visit for an hour and then write about my experience. So I tucked my notepad and pen inside my coat and headed out.

I checked in at the front desk, where the receptionist told me to feel free to walk around and observe. The first patient I saw was Helen. She was a woman probably in her 80s with black hair and green eyes, and she looked lost. As I walked past her, she grabbed me by the arm and pulled me toward her. Looking into my eyes, she smiled at me. Then she reached out her hand to touch my hair and face.

"You're pretty," she said slowly but clearly. "What's your name? My name is Helen." After I introduced myself, she took my hand and led me to her room, where we looked at pictures, cards, and flowers sent by her children and grandchildren.

I visited other rooms, and then my hour was up. As I reached for the bar on the exit door, I felt a firm grip on my arm. Quickly turning around, I saw Helen with a puzzled look on her face. "Where . . . where . . . you going?" she stuttered.

"I need to go back to school, Helen. I have a class."

Her expression turned sad. "You will come back . . . to visit?" she pleaded.

"Yes, Helen," I gently promised.

"Then we are friends?"

"Yes, Helen," I answered, squeezing her wrinkled hand. "We're friends."

Tears welled up in her eyes and began to fall down her face. She gave me a quick hug and a kiss on the cheek. Then, looking directly into my eyes, she said four words that made me realize that even though her mind wasn't clear, she had feelings like everyone else.

"I love you, Nancy," she said. Then she turned and walked down the hall.

As I headed back to school, I was glad it was still raining. No one would notice I'd been crying, too. My class assignment had turned out to be a lesson in acceptance and compassion.

JANUARY 18

He Had a Dream

After this I looked, and there before me was a great multitude that no one could count, from every nation, tribe, people and language, standing before the throne and before the Lamb. Revelation 7:9, NIV.

No school tomorrow! I bet you're excited about that! But what really makes tomorrow special is that it's the day we remember Martin Luther King, Jr. He had a dream that his children would grow up in a country where they would be judged by their character—not by the color of their skin. Isn't that what we all want? We don't want to be judged by the color of our skin, the brand of clothes we wear, the grades we get, or the car our parents drive. We want to be judged by who we are on the inside—by our hearts.

I grew up in a town that didn't have any African American residents. So I honestly didn't know what to think when I was a toddler and saw a Black person for the first time. I was at the grocery store with Mom when a man with dark skin walked down our aisle. Since one of my favorite pastimes was making mud pies, I looked at this man and said one innocent word: "Dirty!"

The man heard me. He approached us and kindly told me, "I'm not dirty. This is the color of my skin. See?" he said as he attempted to rub the black off his arm. Maybe it was the way he handled this situation that gave me an early start at a life without color or cultural barriers.

My friend Stephon is an African American. His stepfather calmly marched in a rally when Martin Luther King visited his hometown of Birmingham, Alabama. His grandmother was put in jail for peacefully boycotting a store that wouldn't hire Blacks. African Americans had to enter the store through the back door or were given their groceries while they waited outside.

Stephon told me, "I was very aware of racism, but Mother always helped me to believe in myself. If someone said I was no good, or that as a Black person I couldn't do this or that, she'd say to me, 'Stephon, you're an heir to God's throne! You're a child of the King!' When speaking of Jesus' great sacrifice for mankind she would say, 'The Lord bled for all of us, Stephon. His blood has no color.' "

So the question I wonder about is this: If Jesus views us all the same, regardless of the color of our skin, the slant of our eyes, or the language we speak . . . why can't we?

JANUARY 19

Don't Give Up on God

Blessed is the one who perseveres under trial because, having stood the test, that person will receive the crown of life that the Lord has promised to those who love him. James 1:12, NIV.

Today is my brother Dan's birthday. But there's no party. No balloons. No cake with candles. No singing the "Happy Birthday" song. Dan's not here to celebrate. He died of cancer several years ago. Yet today I still want to remember him and celebrate the years of life that he did have.

The way Dan lived after he was told he had incurable cancer was an inspiration to many—especially to me. Through it all he never blamed God. As hopeless as he felt, knowing that there was no medical cure, he once told me, "The devil doesn't want to just take away my health or my life. He wants to take away my joy. But I'm not going to let him!" And he didn't.

If you could have met Dan, you would have loved him. He was a youth pastor, a guy who liked to collect sports cards, who got a thrill out of playing practical jokes on people, and who loved contemporary Christian music. His sense of humor was unbeatable. He had a unique way of tilting his head back when he laughed, and if ever I needed cheering up, he'd do his Bucky Beaver face. He even did it for me just a few hours before he died.

Kneeling by his bed the day he died, I promised him: "I'm going to write your story so your ministry can live on." And I think that this is the part of the story he would want you to hear the most: *Don't give up on God*. You will have heartaches in this world, but you don't have to let them break you. Your prayers may seem to go unanswered, but the silence doesn't have to destroy your faith in God. You may ask "Why?" but your questioning doesn't have to lead to unbelief. The devil may try to steal your joy, but you don't have to let him take it.

Whatever pain you may face now or in the future, with God's help you can win the battle. The darkness of this world does seem unbearable at times, but a better world is coming! How do I know? God has promised, and I choose to believe Him. It's as simple as that. I'd be overcome with grief if I thought I'd never see my brother again.

Dan stayed faithful to the end.

So will I.

So can you.

JANUARY 20

Alien Attack!

Finally, my friends, keep your minds on whatever is true, pure, right, holy, friendly, and proper. Don't ever stop thinking about what is truly worthwhile and worthy of praise. Philippians 4:8, CEV.

Aaron tore down the dark alley toward home, still terrified by what he'd just watched on TV. Because his family didn't have a TV, he and his older brother would often go to the neighbor's to watch. Sometimes their mom gave them permission, and other times they just sneaked out. And too often they watched movies that weren't all that good for them.

On this particular night Aaron had been captivated by a movie about an alien invasion of Planet Earth. Flying saucers would appear in the sky and zap humans with a powerful beam of killer light. It seemed so real! When it was over, Aaron noticed that his brother had already gone home. That meant he would have to go down the alley, around the corner, and up their street all alone. *Or will I be alone?* he thought. *What if aliens are real?*

He raced home as if his life depended on it. He made it out of the alley, dashed around the corner, and started up the street toward home. Suddenly the street lit up with a bright light.

"Aliens!" he cried out. He was going to die, and no one would ever know what had happened to him. He sprinted for all he was worth, but the lights just got brighter. *Any minute now,* he thought. He glanced up at the sky, but it was dark. Then he looked back and saw them—two headlights on high beam coming down the street.

At first he felt relief. Then he began to feel really, really stupid. Safe at home, he thought it all over. *I guess it really* does *matter what I watch on TV.*

What do you think? Can you watch horror movies or murder mysteries and not feel anxious or afraid? Can you watch movies that show teens acting inappropriately with their boyfriend or girlfriend, doing drugs, or drinking and not be affected? You may think that you can, but actually everything you put into your mind stays right there, and after awhile you may become calloused and need more intense movies to hold your interest.

Your parents may or may not have rules for what you watch, but in the end the choice is really yours. My dad had a good rule I'd like to pass on to you to think about: Don't watch anything on TV or in a movie that you yourself wouldn't do.

JANUARY 21

Letting Go of the Past

Forget about what's happened; don't keep going over old history. Be alert, be present. I'm about to do something brand-new. It's bursting out! Don't you see it? Isaiah 43:18, 19, Message.

"Here," she said as she handed me the envelope. "I can't throw these away . . . but I can't keep them, either. Would you save them for me? And then someday, when I'm ready, I'll either ask for them back or ask you to burn them." The envelope was big and thick. It was stuffed full and had packaging tape holding the flap shut.

What was in that tightly sealed package? Letters. Letters from someone she cared deeply about, but now their friendship was over. Not by her choosing, but by his. And I guess she felt that if she threw away the letters, the friendship really would be over. Maybe keeping them gave her hope. So I put the envelope in a drawer in my file cabinet, expecting her to ask for them sometime soon. That was 20 years ago. I still have that envelope. It still sits in the same file drawer, unopened. And I still haven't heard from her.

Maybe you're holding onto a past hurt, too. Maybe it's not an envelope full of letters, or even anything you can see—but it's there. And it eats away at you a little every day. It's keeping you from being happy and feeling alive. If this is the case, know that you *can* heal from a hurtful past. Will the past always be there? Yes. But you don't need to let it consume you. Here are some helpful ideas for letting go of a hurtful past:

Talk to a trusted adult who will listen to your pain: a counselor, pastor, parent, or teacher. You may feel that you can get over it on your own, but if you can't, there's nothing embarrassing about asking for help. There are experienced people to help you, so why not use them?

Write in a journal about what happened and describe your feelings. This is a place where you can say whatever you want because the only person who will read it is you. So write, color, paint, or sketch your feelings.

Recruit a support group of friends, both kids and adults, who love you and believe in you.

Remember what Jesus thinks of you. He didn't cause this hurt. A human did. But He's on your side, and He thinks you're pretty special.

Getting over pain isn't about forgetting what happened. It's about letting go of it when the time is right. It's about healing and somehow coming away a stronger person because of it.

JANUARY 22

First Love

But I have this one thing against you. You do not love Me as you did at first. Remember how you once loved Me. Be sorry for your sin and love Me again as you did at first. Revelation 2:4, 5, NLT.

They had been married for many, many years. He was her first love, and she was his. When they first got married, they would sit together as close as they could in the car. It had a bench seat, and seat belts weren't mandatory back then, so she was glued to his side.

One morning, years later, they were driving to church in the same car. He was sitting at his usual place behind the steering wheel, but she was sitting way over by the passenger door.

She looked over at him and longingly said, "Honey, do you remember when we used to sit close and all snuggled up in the car?"

He stared straight ahead and answered, "Sweetheart, I haven't moved."

That story reminds me of today's text, because the same thing can happen with God and us. We can gradually begin to move away from Him, and before we know it, we've gone far. The other day I was visiting a junior high Bible class. For worship the teacher asked his students to pretend that they were little again. So they sang songs at the top of their lungs and went through all the motions. They answered Bible questions without being self-conscious. They were alive!

Watching them from the back of the room, I thought to myself, *At what age does it end? When does it become lame to sing out in Sabbath school? When is it not cool to know the answer to a Bible question? When does being actively involved in Sabbath school change into texting and whispering?* I don't know the answers to these questions, but I do know this: God hasn't moved. He's been in the same place your entire life. Take some time to look at your life and ask yourself: Am I still talking to Jesus every day? Am I still reading my Bible or a Christian book every day? Am I still listening to my pastor, trying to get something helpful out of his or her sermon? Do I still volunteer at church and keep involved?

Jesus pleads in today's verse, "Remember how you once loved Me." The words are sad ones, aren't they? But the solution to the problem of losing our first love for Him is simple: *Remember.* Remember and return to that place where Jesus was number one. Where He was your first love.

God Moments

You will seek Me and find Me when you search for Me with all your heart. Jeremiah 29:13, NASB.

Maria had been raised in a loving Christian home, but when she began junior high, she started wondering what God was *really* like. She wanted more than church once a week and Bible class at school every day. She'd grown up hearing stories about people who had a close connection with God, and she wondered what that would be like. What would it be like to have a difficult prayer answered? A miracle performed? Or one of those "God Moments?"

She found out one weekend when she attended a youth convention in a large city. The speaker said, "God would do anything in order to save you. No matter how many bad things you've done, or even if you've completely stopped believing in Him, He wants you to come home." Maria told me that the thought of that kind of love blew her away!

Then the speaker had an altar call for kids who wanted to give their lives to Jesus. Maria had never seen one of these and didn't know what to expect. At first a few kids shuffled down to the front, but then they started pouring out of the stands, some of them even running, as if they couldn't stay away from Jesus any longer! A few fell to their knees and cried out to God.

Maria said that there are two faces she'll never forget from that night. One is the face of a teenage boy who had crazy hair, lots of piercings, and weird clothes. Most people would be afraid of him. But there was a battle going on for his soul that night, and he came to Jesus. The other is the face of a girl who was crying harder than Maria had ever seen anyone cry before. Maria and her cousin walked forward to comfort the girl. The only words they could understand were, "I want Jesus." When Maria reached out to hug her, the girl clung to her and wouldn't let go. When she finally did let go, Maria's shirt was wet from the tears.

That night Maria experienced her "God moment." She saw God's Spirit move in a powerful way and save lost kids. You can have special moments with God, too. But as today's text says, you must seek Him. You have to go looking for Him through prayer and Bible study and time with other Christians. Some "God moments" are powerful, like Maria's. But the private and quiet ones are no less powerful. God is there. Waiting. Waiting to be found. By you.

JANUARY 24

Rules, Rules, Rules!

Jesus replied, "Anyone who loves me will obey my teaching. My Father will love them, and we will come to them and make our home with them." John 14:23, NIV.

A brand-new bike for his birthday! Max was beyond stoked! "Can I ride my new bike to school?" he asked his mom the next morning.

She hesitated. "Yes, on one condition: you can ride only straight there—no side trips."

That sounded easy enough, until Max met up with Gabe, who was also riding to school.

"Hey, Max! Sweet bike! I know a really fun hill we can race down that's just a few blocks away. We won't be late. Ya wanna go?" Gabe asked excitedly.

Max thought for a minute. "Yeah!" he answered. "Let's do it!"

Gabe went down the hill first. He went fast and made sure that he turned hard at the bottom in order to miss the big brick building there. "OK!" he hollered to Max. "Go for it!"

Max hesitated again. That hill was steep! But he finally took off. He had no idea his bike could go that fast! Faster and faster it went. Max froze, gripping the handlebars, too afraid to reach for the brakes. Gabe watched in horror, knowing Max was going too fast to make the turn at the bottom. There was a terrible crash as Max smashed into the building head-on.

A custodian inside heard the crash and came running out as Gabe rushed over. Max was barely conscious and was moaning. He was bleeding from his nose and mouth, and his forehead was rapidly swelling. His brand-new bike was a mangled mess. An ambulance took Max to the hospital, where he stayed for several days to recover from a severe concussion. He'd learned the hard way what can happen when you don't obey the rules.

Most kids don't like rules. And many kids think that the Bible is too full of them. They see the Bible as a bunch of "don'ts." But have you ever wondered why God gave us rules? Is it because He just likes to control us? Is it because He doesn't want us to have fun? No. The *real* reason is a positive one! God gave us rules simply because He loves us.

If you were to look up every command in the Bible, you'd discover that every single one is given by a Father who doesn't want His kids to get hurt. Every one protects either us or someone else. So maybe rules aren't so bad after all. And maybe we'd actually be happier if we followed them.

JANUARY 25

Sometimes . . .

Don't depend on things like fancy hairdos or gold jewelry or expensive clothes to make you look beautiful. Be beautiful in your heart by being gentle and quiet. This kind of beauty will last, and God considers it very special. 1 Peter 3:3, 4, CEV.

If you promise not to laugh, I'll share with you a bit of my private journal from when I was a teenager. I hadn't seen it for years, but recently I found it in a box in our storage unit. Maybe you won't laugh, because maybe, in its own way, it sounds a little bit like you. Here's my first entry:

Sometimes I stand in front of the mirror and feel a bit dissatisfied with my simple life. I wish I were somehow different. Something besides what I am. Something better.

Sometimes I wish I were famous—like an actress or singer. Everywhere I'd go people would stop me and say, "I just loved your latest movie! I saw it three times!" or "Your new song is going to be a real hit!" And I would sign autographs.

Sometimes I wish I were a real knockout. You know, the kind of beauty that would turn heads when I walked into a room. People would ask, "Who's that?" And guys would be knocking on my door, asking to take me out.

Sometimes I wish I were a scholar and my name would be listed among the intellects of the world. People would come to me for my opinion on important matters, and I would lean back in my chair and rattle off something profound.

And sometimes I wish I were some big, important executive sitting behind a large desk on the top floor of a large building. I would relax in my leather chair, look out at the city from my large picture window, and sign important papers that my secretaries would bring me.

But then I take a second look into the mirror and see me, Nancy. Maybe not a movie star, but I'd rather have Jesus than fame. Maybe not a knockout, but I'd rather have Jesus and be beautiful on the inside. Maybe not a scholar, but I'd rather have Jesus than all the brains in the world. And maybe not a big, important person in this world, but I'd rather have Jesus and be important to Him.

I'd rather have Jesus than anything this world can give, because someday it will all be gone. Only Jesus lasts. Only He matters.

JANUARY 26

One Day Closer

Do not let your hearts be troubled. You believe in God; believe also in me. My Father's house has many rooms; if that were not so, would I have told you that I am going there to prepare a place for you? And if I go and prepare a place for you, I will come back and take you to be with me that you also may be where I am. John 14:1-3, NIV.

Have you ever had to wait for something for a long time, and it seemed as though it was taking forever? A car trip to end, a package to come in the mail, the school bell to ring at the end of the day, your birthday, relatives arriving for vacation, or the Second Coming?

When I learned about the Second Coming as a new Christian at the age of 10, I was blown away! Imagine not knowing that heaven exists, and then having someone tell you that Jesus lives there and someday He'll come back to take you to a perfect world—and that you'll live forever!

The pictures I saw of the Second Coming fascinated me. One of my favorites was of Jesus coming down from heaven on His throne. The throne was sitting on billowy clouds with rays of light streaming from it. A rainbow arched overhead, and it looked like thousands of angels were surrounding Him. Below all that splendor stood people with outstretched arms, waiting to hug Him—people with smiling faces who looked like they knew Him, even though they were seeing Him for the first time.

Back then I looked forward to the Second Coming for some reasons that now seem kind of unimportant. In heaven I'd get to ride an elephant, live in a mansion, swim with dolphins, wear a crown, and own a herd of horses! I still think it will be pretty cool to do those things, but now that I've grown up, what I'm looking forward to the most is seeing Jesus for the first time. I just have this feeling that the moment I see Him, everything will be all right. As much as I enjoy this life and am pretty pumped most days, I'm tired of watching people I love hurt, and knowing hurt myself. And even though it seems I've waited a long time, I *know* He will come back!

The last words of Jesus recorded in the Bible are words meant to reassure you and give you hope: "Yes, I am coming soon" (Revelation 22:20, NIV). I believe that. I believe it with all my heart. Jesus' promise in today's text is very clear. He's preparing a place for *you*. He will come back for *you*. Today His coming is one day closer than yesterday—and tomorrow it will be one day closer than today.

JANUARY 27

Worship Through Music

Praise God with trumpets and all kinds of harps.
Praise him with tambourines and dancing,
with stringed instruments and woodwinds. Praise God with cymbals,
with clashing cymbals. Let every living creature praise the Lord.
Shout praises to the Lord! Psalm 150:3-6, CEV.

My daughter and I had driven four hours to attend a contemporary Christian concert that would be featuring five bands. As I looked around the coliseum packed with thousands of teenagers and college students, I thought, *These kids could be anywhere other than here tonight. They could be in a bar, at a party, or at the movies. But they chose to come here. Something here reaches them.* Kids I know tell me there are many reasons they listen to this kind of music: they can relate to the words, it brings them peace, it comforts them, it's positive, and it gives them hope. Here's what two of them told me:

Hannah: "Last school year was definitely a tough one for me, and I don't think I could have made it without my style of encouraging Christian music. Every time I felt like I was about to break down or just felt far away from God, I would turn on my favorite songs, and they would always bring me back to that special place with God. Once, when I was having a hard time, feeling like I didn't fit in, I turned on one of my favorites. Even though I didn't feel like I had many friends at that moment, I felt God close and vowed to trust Him no matter what."

Joel: "I've had the privilege of leading worship for tens of thousands of teenagers all around the country. The music is a contemporary style, but the words point kids toward a strong, intimate relationship with Jesus. It is an absolutely flooring moment for me to see young kids, sometimes 10 or 11 years old, connect with God in a way that they have never been able to do before. I've watched hardened kids with their arms stretched out toward heaven, singing songs of surrender. I've seen 12- and 13-year-old girls struggling with anorexia, cutting, or abuse at home, bawling their eyes out at an altar as they come to understand that they are beautiful in the eyes of God."

There's something about Christian music that connects us to God. So whether your style is the old hymns or some of the newer stuff, try to make music a part of your life and a part of your own worship. It can lift your spirits and give you hope.

JANUARY 28

Braving the Bullies

David said to the Philistine, "You come against me with sword and spear and javelin, but I come against you in the name of the Lord Almighty, the God of the armies of Israel, whom you have defied." 1 Samuel 17:45, NIV.

When you're so small that you have to be dropped off at junior high school in a booster seat, you're gonna get bullied," Timmy told me. "I was 4 feet 4 inches tall in the eighth grade. I was trying to be a teenager but was basically still the size of a child. And when you're bullied just because you're small, you learn a few things: you learn how to open a locker from the inside; you learn where to sit at lunch; and you learn to look over your shoulder."

It was tough for Timmy to be so small. No matter where he stood in the lunch line, every day he got pushed back to the end. He was called names like "Shrimp" and "Munchkin." And because he was so small, the other boys could pick him up and carry him wherever they wanted. Finally one day when Timmy got beat up, a teacher found him and asked what had happened. He decided to ask for help. Things started to get better after that day, and he even talked to the boy who had beaten him. "We're not like best friends," he told me. "But we're cool."

The future King David had a similar problem. Just like Timmy, David was at a disadvantage by being small, young, and inexperienced. There he stood in front of Goliath, who was 10 feet tall! And Goliath's armor weighed 126 pounds! That's more than most kids your age weigh! Goliath was definitely intimidating with his bronze helmet, bronze shin guards, and bronze spear. The Bible says that just the top of the spear alone weighed about 15 pounds.

Before him stood young David—with just a rod, a sling, and five small stones. But it took only one stone to bring the giant down! Because David wasn't fighting alone. God had his back. And He has yours.

Do you sometimes feel that you're at a disadvantage? Maybe you feel too small or too tall. Maybe you feel that everyone else learns more quickly than you. Maybe you're not the best in sports. Maybe you feel that you don't easily communicate. Regardless, there's nothing wrong with you. *You're OK.* Don't judge yourself by the world's standards. Who makes those, anyway? What's important is to accept yourself and find something you can be good at. For Timmy, it was music and acting. He found lots of opportunities to shine at both. And he grew taller!

JANUARY 29

What Love Really Is

Love is patient, love is kind. It does not envy,
it does not boast, it is not proud. It does not dishonor others,
it is not self-seeking, it is not easily angered, it keeps no record of wrongs.
Love does not delight in evil but rejoices with the truth. It always protects,
always trusts, always hopes, always perseveres. 1 Corinthians 13:4-7, NIV.

Although it's known as the "love chapter" and is often read at weddings, did you know that 1 Corinthians 13 can help you and your classmates get along better? It's true, because love's rules are basic, no matter what the circumstance. Here's how:

"Love is patient" when your teammate misses a shot and costs you the game, or when your science partner slows you down because they just don't understand.

"Love is kind" to everyone, regardless of what group they're in, what they look like, or where they buy their clothes.

"It does not envy" the girl with better looks who has the boys noticing her, the guy who's better in sports, or the student with higher grades.

"It does not boast" when you get straight A's, the newest iPod, or the most points in a sports game.

"It does not dishonor others" by casting a hateful look, shoving through a crowded door, or calling someone "Loser."

"It is not self-seeking" by always wanting to be first, wanting the biggest and best of what's being handed out, needing all the attention, or not celebrating another's success.

"It is not easily angered" even if the other kid gets mad first, even if you feel picked on, or even if you find out a friend has been talking behind your back.

"It keeps no record of wrongs" by reminding friends of how many times they've blown it with you.

"It does not delight in evil" when you hear a classmate has cheated, broken a school rule, or bullied someone, *"but rejoices in the truth."*

"It always protects, always trusts, always hopes, always perseveres." In other words, you've got your friend covered. She is safe with you. He knows he can depend on you.

JANUARY 30

The Green-eyed Monster

Whenever people are jealous or selfish, they cause trouble and do all sorts of cruel things. James 3:16, CEV.

Did you know that jealousy can kill? If left to get out of hand, it can ruin friendships, hurt someone's feelings, cause fights—and yes, even kill. I know because it happened to my grandma's sister.

The year was 1915, and "Pinky," as she was called, was 16 years old. She was a happy, friendly girl who loved the latest fashions and loved going to the drugstore with my grandma to get the best ice cream in town. While they were there one afternoon, Albert walked in. He was the boy all the girls wanted to date, and he had recently dated one of Pinky's friends. He walked over to Pinky and asked her out on a date. They hit it off immediately and dated for several months before he proposed to her. My great-grandma, Pinky's mother, said they were too young and would have to wait, and they said they would.

After their engagement Albert's former girlfriend was crazy jealous. Instead of being happy for Pinky and Albert and moving on with her own life, she let jealousy eat away at her, day after day. When the three would run into each other in public, she always made a scene. "I'm just going to kill you I'm so mad," she once screamed at Pinky. No one took her seriously—until one fateful night.

Pinky and Albert had gone to a play with my grandma. Afterward they came out of the building laughing and talking. Then they saw the jealous girl. She looked at Pinky and said, "If I can't have him, you can't have him." Then she fired three shots at Pinky.

Albert and Grandma rushed Pinky down the road to the town doctor while someone drove out to the farm to get their parents. But by the time they made it into town, she had died, my grandma by her side.

My mom grew up hearing this story, and Grandma would always end it by saying, "Jealousy will destroy you." It makes you unsatisfied with your own life. It makes you judge others. It can even turn to hate. And it can consume you. Don't let it! You can choose. You can choose to be content with what you have. There will always be someone who has less than you and more than you. And when someone has more, why waste your life wishing you were that person?

JANUARY 31

Your Foot in His Hand

Jesus knew that he had come from God and would go back to God. He also knew that the Father had given him complete power. So during the meal Jesus got up, removed his outer garment, and wrapped a towel around his waist. He put some water into a large bowl. Then he began washing his disciples' feet and drying them with the towel he was wearing. John 13:3-5, CEV.

It's my favorite place in town to sit. It's a bench near a life-size bronze sculpture by artist Alan Collins called *Jesus Among Us,* and it stands outside my church.

The sculpture has four figures. There are two young men and one young woman who are modern-day disciples. And then there is Jesus. With long hair and a beard, He looks the way many picture Him from Bible stories. Looking strong yet gentle, He's wearing an inner robe with a towel tied around His waist, and He's kneeling. In one hand He's holding a jar that has water trickling out of it into a basin below. The other hand is open, as if inviting.

Once, while I was sitting there after church, I couldn't help noticing a young girl about 6 years old studying the sculpture. She walked around to each of the three disciples, getting close to their faces and looking directly into their eyes.

Then she walked over and looked directly into Jesus' eyes. Almost reverently, she took off one of her sandals and placed her foot under the trickling water. Then she rested it in Jesus' open hand.

I was touched by how comfortable this little girl was with the statue portraying Jesus. She seemed to feel like the invitation for foot washing was extended to her personally. Apparently the God she knew made her feel comfortable enough to rest her foot in His hand.

Are you that comfortable with the God you know? Or have you spent too many days, weeks, or months without even talking to Him—till He seems like a stranger? Do you have too many wrong choices behind you to feel that comfortable in His presence?

The same Jesus who said, "Let the little children come to me, and do not hinder them, for the kingdom of heaven belongs to such as these" also said, "Whoever comes to me I will never drive away" (Matthew 19:14, NIV; John 6:37, NIV). He is warm and inviting. Accepting and gentle. Eager to have you feel comfortable enough to rest your foot in His hand. There you will find forgiveness and complete cleansing.

FEBRUARY 1

For the Love of the Game

But the Lord God keeps me from being disgraced. So I refuse to give up, because I know God will never let me down. Isaiah 50:7, CEV.

My nephew Davey was born to play football. Just today I looked at a picture from the Christmas when he was 2 years old. There he stood in front of the Christmas tree—not holding a new truck or sitting on a new tricycle—but wearing his new San Francisco 49ers football uniform, complete with helmet!

He started playing football in sixth grade, and from the first day he ran onto the field, everyone knew he had a gift. While he was still in junior high, high school coaches from nearby cities began courting him, offering him quarterback positions on their teams. But he chose to attend his local high school, and by the beginning of his sophomore year he was the starting quarterback. Every time Davey played, people in the stands were amazed at his talent, and his name often appeared in the local paper. I was a proud aunt! But I became even more proud later.

In the third game of the season during his senior year, he nailed a pass that gave his team the first touchdown. Little did Davey know that his next pass would be his last. Watching the opposing team pushing toward him, he drew his arm back for a pass. He was hit hard, and a defense player landed on his throwing arm. Davey felt a pop in his shoulder and excruciating pain. He was sent to the sidelines and iced. When the team doctor told him, "You're done for the day," Davey said, "I knew it was bad. My arm just hung like a flimsy piece of nothing."

The next day he had his shoulder X-rayed. "You have a bad tear in your AC joint," the doctor told him. "You'll be out for the rest of the season." But Davey refused to believe it. After two weeks of rest and physical therapy, he suited up for practice, but the pain was too much. Reality finally set in. His high school football days were over.

Davey had a choice to make. He could be angry and stay at home and sulk on game nights. Or he could choose something better. And that's what he did. He helped train his backup quarterback, a sophomore kid who was scared to death to take his place. "You have to step up," Davey told him. And he sat on the sidelines for every game, giving advice and support to his team. In spite of his disappointment, he chose to make something good come out of the bad. He showed true sportsmanship, which in the end will be remembered longer than the touchdowns.

The Promise

The Master himself will give the command. Archangel thunder! God's trumpet blast! He'll come down from heaven and the dead in Christ will rise—they'll go first. Then the rest of us who are still alive at the time will be caught up with them into the clouds to meet the Master. Oh, we'll be walking on air! And then there will be one huge family reunion with the Master. So reassure one another with these words. 1 Thessalonians 4:16, Message.

Today is Groundhog Day! You probably know about the folklore: when the groundhog comes out of hiding, if it's a cloudy day, he *won't* see his shadow, so spring will come early. But if it's a sunny day and he *does* see his shadow, then spring weather won't come for another six weeks.

Regardless of what the groundhog saw or didn't see today, I can't wait for spring! Last fall I planted a bunch of purple crocus bulbs outside our house, and when they bloom, I'll have dozens of beautiful spring flowers. But if you came to visit and looked at my flowerbed now, you wouldn't think that there are flowers waiting to grow and bloom. This winter a couple of inches of snow covered the dirt, and then on top of that a thick sheet of ice. It seemed impossible that something could be alive under that dark, frozen ground. Yet I know the bulbs are there because I planted them myself. It definitely takes a bit of faith in nature to plant bulbs and believe they'll survive the winter and bloom.

Waiting for spring flowers to come up is kind of like waiting for the resurrection. Maybe someone you love is buried in the ground. You know they're there because you watched as their casket was slowly lowered into a hole before it was covered with dirt. Maybe you've visited that grave when it's been covered with snow and ice. Sometimes it might seem surreal that the person you love is really there beneath the ground. And maybe at times you catch yourself being tempted to doubt that you'll ever see them again.

Well, there *is* a guarantee! Many Bible texts promise that the dead will be resurrected. One is in Isaiah 26:19: "And the earth shall cast out the dead" (NKJV). I love the power of this text! To cast something means to throw it with force. The resurrection of the dead will be a powerful experience because a God strong enough to conquer death will burst graves open!

But in the meantime, we wait. And we hope. Most of all, we hope.

FEBRUARY 3

Almost Arrested!

One who has unreliable friends soon comes to ruin,
but there is a friend who sticks closer than a brother. Proverbs 18:24, NIV.

"Put your hands on the wall!" Joe heard a voice behind him command. He turned to see a plain-clothes security guard. Joe began to laugh, thinking he'd been punked. But the man said sternly, "This is no joke."

Joe started freaking out! He knew he hadn't done anything wrong—he was just hanging out in the store with a friend. Sure, the guy was sketchy, but Joe needed someone to hang out with. They were looking at cell phone displays when his friend said, "Dude, these would be so easy to steal." Joe didn't think anything of it and told his friend he was going to look at CDs. The next thing he knew, his wrists were being zip-tied, and he was being taken upstairs to security.

When he got there, he saw his friend, but he still didn't know what was going on. His parents, as well as his friend's grandma, were called into the store. "We have evidence on camera that these boys were shoplifting," the security guard stated. "And it's a felony."

A felony! Joe knew he might end up in jail. He might have to leave home, leave his school, and drop out of the choir and drama group.

Joe and his parents sat dazed. All three knew that he wouldn't do anything like that. "Can we see the evidence?" his dad asked. The tape showed that after Joe had walked over to look at CDs, his friend took a phone off the rack and slipped it into his pocket. Just by being with this guy, Joe was considered an accomplice to the crime. For all they knew, he was involved in the lift when he went to another section, possibly to distract the cashier.

Somehow Joe was able to convince security that he had absolutely nothing to do with the shoplifting. When they reviewed the evidence and listened to Joe and his parents, they dropped the charges on him. He was able to go home, but his friend went to juvenile detention.

Later Joe told me, "It really *does* matter who your friends are. And it does matter who you hang out with. I guess a lot of times kids will make poor choices because they're lonely and don't think they can find another friend. Or they think it's cool to hang out with the sketchy kids, and they do it for status. Others do it just because they're bored. But after that day I began making better choices. There are a lot of great positive kids out there to be friends with."

FEBRUARY 4

You're Not a Failure

All those the Father gives me will come to me,
and whoever comes to me I will never drive away. John 6:37, NIV.

"What do you think God thinks of you?" I asked this question to a junior high classroom I was visiting and encouraged them to write down straightforward answers. When I got home and looked at their papers, I was happy to read positive answers such as these:

"I think that He loves me even though I've done some very bad things."

"He loves me and is trying to draw me closer to Him."

"He thinks of me as His child, even if I do make mistakes."

"I think He thinks I'm special and will do anything for me."

"He thinks I'm awesome."

"He sees me as a friend and someone who loves Him."

And then I read a different response—the one I couldn't get off my mind:

"He sees me as a failure."

My heart ached. I wished I knew which student had written this. It looked like a boy's handwriting, but the answers were anonymous. A lot questions filled my mind: Where did he get this view of God? Did someone tell him he was a failure? Has he done something that he thinks God won't forgive? Has he repeatedly failed at something?

If you ever feel that God thinks you're a failure, take out your Bible and read what King David—who had failed multiple times—said about God in Psalm 145:8: "You are merciful, Lord! You are kind and patient and always loving" (CEV).

To be a failure means you are unsuccessful at achieving your goals. Give yourself a break. You're still a kid with a lot of growing and maturing to do! Sure, you might mess up. You might even deliberately choose to mess up. But if you pick yourself up, learn from it, and make right what you can, you can start all over again.

So work at seeing yourself through God's eyes. When He looks at you, He doesn't see a failure. He sees one of His kids. A person He created and loves so much that He gave up His own life. A person worth giving a second chance.

You are not a failure to Him.

FEBRUARY 5

"I Am Here!"

They were all terrified when they saw him. But Jesus spoke to them at once. "Don't be afraid," he said. "Take courage! I am here!" Then he climbed into the boat, and the wind stopped. Mark 6:50, 51, NLT.

I couldn't believe the story Vera was telling me! It was one of those stories I'd only read about. While riding the city bus home from work, she accidentally got off at the wrong stop. It was already dark, and the street was empty. She had no choice but to start walking home.

Moments later a man drove by and yelled some crude words out his window. He drove up the street, circled back, and parked his car. Then he got out and started following her!

Vera walked faster. He walked faster. She started running. He started running. Not knowing what else to do, she stopped, turned to face the man, and cried out, "Jesus, help me!" The stranger got a terrified look on his face, ran back to his car, and sped away.

We'll never know till heaven what this man saw that scared him away. But Vera's story reminds me of another dark night when Jesus' disciples were terrified. Their boat was about to sink in a storm. If you read the whole story in verses 48-53, you'll learn some reassuring things about Jesus to remember when you're afraid.

The first is that Jesus is always watching out for you. Like a big brother, He's got your back. Even though He was on land and it was dark, the Bible says He *saw* His disciples. He knew they were in trouble. He always sees you, too. With the whole universe to watch over, He sees *you*.

The second is that Jesus always gives courage. When the disciples saw Him walking on the water, they were scared out of their wits! But His first words to them were *"Don't be afraid."* Courage for you may come from a Bible verse, a song, or something a friend says.

And finally, Jesus can calm your fears. What He told His disciples, He also tells you: "Take courage! I am here!" You don't need to fear the dark, death, loneliness, terrorism, sickness, tomorrow. Not because these things aren't sometimes frightening, but because Someone stronger than you is in control.

Between here and heaven we will face scary situations. But we don't have to live in constant fear. When we cry out to Jesus, this assurance is ours: *"Take courage! I'm here."*

FEBRUARY 6

Never Stop Singing

I will give thanks to the Lord with all my heart. I will tell of all the great things You have done. I will be glad and full of joy because of You. I will sing praise to Your name, O Most High. Psalm 9:1, 2, NLT.

"I wish my family had a nice car."
"Oh, no! Another pimple!"
"We lost our game—again!"
"My phone is just a basic phone, and it can't do anything fun."
"Man, I wish I had an iPod to listen to."
"My hair turned out terrible today!"

Sometimes we complain, don't we? At the time, that thing we're complaining about seems so big! It dominates everything else happening around us as we focus on our complaint.

You would have thought that Paul and Silas would have complained. They were trying to witness and do good for God, and they ended up in jail! They had prayed for a slave girl to be freed from an evil spirit, and she was. That made the girl's owners angry because she had brought them money by telling people's fortunes. So they dragged the two missionaries to the leaders of the town. They lied about them and said they were causing trouble. Soon a mob formed, and haters started joining in the accusations.

The leaders commanded that Paul and Silas be stripped naked in front of everyone and severely beaten. After they'd been hit again and again, they were thrown into jail with their feet placed in stocks. Now, their conversation could have gone something like this:

Silas: "Paul, are you OK?"

Paul: "Yes, but I'm in terrible pain!"

Silas: "I can't believe God let this happen! I mean, we were just trying to teach people about Him, and this is the thanks we get?"

Paul: "I know. I'm starting to think it's not worth all this. I'm about ready to give up. Why be Christians if we have to suffer?"

Silas: "I'm with you. Let's deny it the next time we're asked."

But they didn't. Do you know what they did? They sang hymns and prayed!

So the next time you feel like complaining, do what Paul and Silas did. Try singing and praying and see how much better you feel.

FEBRUARY 7

I Always Love You

What if I could speak all languages of humans and of angels?
If I did not love others, I would be nothing more than a noisy gong
or a clanging cymbal. . . . Love is always supportive, loyal, hopeful,
and trusting. Love never fails! 1 Corinthians 13:1-8, CEV.

"I don't know what to do! I don't know what to do!" Anthony kept repeating out loud.

While his mom attended a life skills class for former homeless people, Anthony attended the kids' program. Lynn, the director, had asked the kids to write their mom or dad a Valentine's letter. Although he didn't know where his dad was, Anthony chose to write to him. But with severe ADD (attention deficit disorder), he was having a hard time writing his thoughts.

"How about I be your secretary?" Lynn asked cheerfully. "You tell me what you want to say, and I'll write it for you." With a faraway look in his eyes, this is what Anthony said:

Dear Dad,

Happy Valentine's Day, Dad. I wish I could spend some time with you this summer, if I knew where you lived. Do you live in the mountains up high? Do you live by a river so if I came we could go fishing? I've always wanted to fish.

Dad, do you always wish you had a son? If you want me to come this summer, tell my mom where you live. I always love you.

Your son,
Anthony

His sad letter got me to thinking. Is there someone in your life who needs to know that you love them? Like Anthony, are they aching to hear it from you? Maybe it's someone who lives far away, and you've been out of touch for a while. Or maybe it's someone you live with every day. Maybe it's a friend, parent, sibling, grandparent, or teacher.

Valentine's Day is just a week away. It's not just a day for people who are "in love," you know. It's a day to show love to anyone you want to. So if this thought brings someone to mind, I hope you'll write a letter or send a card—whichever you're comfortable with. Let the "Anthony" in your life know that you love them. Don't leave them aching to hear it.

Get Your Armor On!

Stay alert! Watch out for your great enemy, the devil. He prowls around like a roaring lion, looking for someone to devour. 1 Peter 5:8, NLT.

It was a sunny February morning. The light snow that had been on the ground was melting, and my husband and I decided to walk around a lake near our house. We were the only ones there so early on that winter morning. Well, at least we *thought* we were alone.

At the end of the hike, we decided to rest on a bench and look at the lake. "Stay on the bench and let me take a picture from behind of you and the lake," Keith said.

After taking the picture, he walked up behind me and said, "Honey! Look at this!" There behind the bench in the melting snow and mud was a fresh cougar track! And we hadn't even been on the lookout. Had we been there earlier, he could have sneaked up behind us.

Later that morning I thought about today's text. It sounds kind of alarming, doesn't it? But it's true. There's a battle going on—a war—that you and I can't even see. Just as you can't see that Jesus is always there with you, you can't see that your enemy, the devil, is on this earth, too. What are God and Satan fighting over? *You and me.* And we have to choose whose side we're going to be on.

Ephesians 6:12 says, "For we are not fighting against human beings but against the wicked spiritual forces in the heavenly world, the rulers, authorities, and cosmic powers of this dark age" (TEV). But you don't need to fear the enemy, because the Bible says, "He who is in you is greater than he who is in the world" (1 John 4:4, NKJV). *Jesus is stronger!* He always has been. That's why He was able to defy death and burst from the tomb.

So what part do you have in fighting this battle? Ephesians 6:11 says, "Put on all of God's armor so that you will be able to stand firm against all strategies of the devil" (NLT). What is God's armor? "God's Word is an *indispensable* weapon. In the same way, prayer is essential in this ongoing warfare" (Ephesians 6:17, 18, Message). Those are the two weapons you need: your Bible and prayer. Spending time with God through these two each day will give you strength, courage, and hope.

The Bible has told us how this war will turn out. God will win! We already know the end of that big story. How your story will end is up to you.

Here I Am, Lord!

Commit your way to the Lord, trust also in Him, and He shall bring it to pass. Psalm 37:5, NKJV.

It was the last day of Week of Prayer at Columbia Adventist Academy, and the pastor was having an altar call. But it was a different kind of call. He said, "If any of you young men feel called to be a pastor, come forward at this time." Well, this was the conversation that was going on in my mind:

"He's talking about you! You have to go forward!"

"No, you can't go forward. It would cause a scene."

"But you know that's what God is calling you to do!"

"But he said 'young men'—not 'young women.' Just stay seated and do it in your heart."

Since my baptism day when I was 10, I knew what I was supposed to do with my life. I was supposed to be a pastor. But at that time women pastors were unheard-of. I remember asking Dad after my baptism, "Is there any way a woman can be a pastor?" He looked at me lovingly, stroked my hair, and answered sadly, "I don't think so, Nancy."

Now it was eight years later, and I watched as a handful of boys went forward. I wanted *so badly* to go! Not to prove a point. Not to make a scene. But because I felt I was supposed to. So I decided to sit there and commit to the ministry from my seat. Until the speaker gave the invitation a second time. And as if someone was helping me, I found myself standing up and walking humbly to the front of the church. The speaker immediately said, "Oh! And if there are any young women who feel God is calling them to ministry, you can come, too!"

I went on to study theology at Walla Walla University, but I didn't get a pastoring job after graduation. Some conference presidents did say, "If you were a young man, we'd hire you in a heartbeat. But right now we just can't. We're sorry." Even though it took time, seven years after graduating I was hired to be a full-time pastor!

What do you think God wants you to do with your life? You're not too young to be thinking about it, or to pray and ask Him to show you. I believe that He's very interested in what you will do for a career. And whatever that dream is, don't give up. If God is calling you to it, I believe it will happen!

FEBRUARY 10

A Rug, a Cake, and a Lot of Love

If you give to others, you will be given a full amount in return.
It will be packed down, shaken together, and spilling over into your lap.
The way you treat others is the way you will be treated. Luke 6:38, CEV.

We never expected to receive anything in return. But now that I think back, it's quite clear to me that even without expecting, we did receive. And this is how it all happened.

Dad was driving to work one cold, icy winter morning. Up ahead on the side of the road he saw an old woman down in a ditch, breaking the ice and dipping water out with a bucket.

All day long Dad was troubled by what he'd seen. On the way home something made him stop at the little house by the ditch. He knocked on the door, and when it opened, there stood the old woman, skinny, bent over, and dressed for the outdoors while inside.

Dad didn't know why he'd stopped. He didn't even know what to say. "I saw you getting water out of the ditch this morning. Is there anything I can do for you?" That's what came out.

"Well, yes," she answered. "There's some wood out back that needs to be split."

After a full day's work, Dad not only chopped her pile of wood, but he brought some into her house so she could build a fire. She tried to pay him a little bit of money, but Dad told her he couldn't take it. "I'm a Christian," he said. "And I chopped your wood so you would know that Jesus loves you and is watching out for you."

During their conversation he found out that the woman's name was Mrs. Bolger, and that she'd soon be turning 92! When Dad told the story to our youth group, we didn't just say, "Oh, that's a nice story." We began planning. We would give Mrs. Bolger a surprise birthday party!

Dad had mentioned that her floor was bare, cold wood. So for a gift we kids made her a large hand-woven rug to go under her rocker. We made her a cake and put as many candles on it as we could. We also planned the entertainment—we would bring our guitars and sing some old hymns she might recognize. Mrs. Bolger surprised us by going into the back room and coming out with a fiddle, which she played along with us.

What I remember most about that night is how happy she was—and how happy we were. How the light from the birthday cake candles danced in her eyes, and how our eyes filled with tears. How her little house was so cold, and a group of teenagers warmed it with love.

For All to See

Once again he bent over and began writing on the ground. The people left one by one, beginning with the oldest. Finally, Jesus and the woman were there alone. Jesus stood up and asked her, "Where is everyone? Isn't there anyone left to accuse you?" "No sir," the woman answered. Then Jesus told her, "I am not going to accuse you either. You may go now, but don't sin anymore." John 8:8-11, CEV.

Think of a sin. You know, *that* sin you hope no one ever finds out about. Now imagine that someone in your school catches you in the very act of committing that sin. They drag you out in front of the whole student body and tell everyone what you have done. Your principal, teachers, and classmates are all glaring at you. Now your parents show up, shocked, disappointed, and angry. How would you feel? This is basically what happened to the woman whose story is found in John 8. I can imagine her telling her story like this:

"I was caught in the act when a group of men burst through the door and dragged me out into the street. They shoved me in front of Jesus and reminded Him that according to the Law of Moses, I should be stoned to death. Except for my trembling, I was paralyzed by fear. My life was now in the hands of this Man. If He said, 'Stone her!' it would be only seconds before the angry crowd would rain stones on me. And I would feel the pain of every single rock until death came.

"But Jesus didn't say that. In fact, He didn't say anything at all. Instead, He bent down and began writing with His finger in the dust. Then He stood up and said, 'If any of you have never sinned, then go ahead and throw the first stone at her!' Once more He bent down and began writing. I watched in amazement as people in the crowd began dropping their stones and walking away.

"Finally, only Jesus and I were left there in the dusty street. I kept my head bowed, too ashamed to look up at Him. He knew what I had done, and I felt worthless—dirty. But He spoke gently. 'Where is everyone?' He asked me. 'Isn't there anyone left to accuse you?' I answered, 'No sir.' And then He spoke the words of freedom I will never forget: 'I am not going to accuse you either. You may go now, but don't sin anymore.' I was forgiven!"

And so are you.

FEBRUARY 12

Anna's Forever Love

I have loved you with a love that lasts forever. So I have helped you come to Me with loving-kindness. Jeremiah 31:3, NLT.

For Anna, the ideal life included belonging to a picture-perfect family. She grew up watching TV shows of happy families that gave her what she calls a "warm and fuzzy" feeling. She thought, *This is the way families are supposed to be. With happy love-you-forever endings.* But when Anna reached her teenage years, her family became anything but happy. As she watched her parents' marriage fall apart, she slowly lost her self-worth and security.

Is this what marriage is like? she asked herself. *Can vows be so easily broken?* She also wondered why God had let this happen. Looking toward her own future, she questioned whether or not she could trust any man enough to marry him.

How did she cope? Much of the time she withdrew into herself, not wanting to step out and risk adding more pain to her life by getting too close to anyone.

Anna recently told me: "It wasn't until many years later, when I turned to God for answers, that I began to realize He had been there with me all along. As I read my Bible, the effects of this sinful world became clear. God told me that He loved me. He showed me that the pain I went through was not in His plan for me. I was a victim of human nature. He told me that He understood feelings of pain and rejection, because He'd felt them, too. He showed me a promise to take away my sadness and make a way for me to live with Him for eternity. He let me know that He loved me and will continue to love me forever."

If your parents have gone through divorce, I'm sorry. I *really* am. And I want to let you know that it's OK to feel whatever you might be feeling—anger, betrayal, fear, anxiety, or sadness. It's normal to have strong feelings right now. But a feeling I don't want you to have is guilt. The divorce was not your fault. It wasn't even your decision. And rather than keeping your feelings hidden as Anna did, I hope you'll find someone to talk to. Friends, grandparents, aunts and uncles, pastors, and teachers are some possible people you can lean on. You can also express your feelings through writing them in a journal, through artwork, and through music.

And you always, always have Jesus to lean on. He hurts with you. And He's preparing a better world for you to live in. A world in which nothing will ever disappoint you or make you sad.

FEBRUARY 13

He Will Be

Turn to the Lord! He can still be found.
Call out to God! He is near. Isaiah 55:6, CEV.

Do you ever wish you had someone in your life that could always, without a doubt, meet all your needs? Through reading my Bible, I have discovered that Jesus is that someone for me. He's just not lacking in anything! And the neat thing is, He can be everything for you, too.

I love to spread good news! And the good news today is that the Bible gives you texts that prove Jesus can meet your needs. Here's what He will be to you:

He will be your *Comforter*—when your heart aches from sadness: "The Lord is close to the brokenhearted; he rescues those whose spirits are crushed" (Psalm 34:18, NLT).

He will be your *Peace*—when you wake up in the middle of the night with anxious thoughts: "Don't fret or worry. Instead of worrying, pray. Let petitions and praises shape your worries into prayers, letting God know your concerns. Before you know it, a sense of God's wholeness, everything coming together for good, will come and settle you down. It's wonderful what happens when Christ displaces worry at the center of your life" (Philippians 4:6, 7, Message).

He will be your *Helper*—when you don't know what to do or which choice is best: "God is our refuge and strength, an ever-present help in trouble" (Psalm 46:1, NIV).

He will be your *Strength*—when you feel helpless because you can't change the way things are: "He gives strength to the weary and increases the power of the weak" (Isaiah 40:29, NIV).

He will be your *Hope*—when you forget to take your eyes off all the problems of this world and look up: "I would have lost heart, unless I had believed that I would see the goodness of the Lord in the land of the living" (Psalm 27:13, NKJV).

He will be your *Conqueror*—once and for all, someday: "He will wipe every tear from their eyes. There will be no more death or mourning or crying or pain, for the old order of things has passed away" (Revelation 21:4, NIV).

He will be your *Anchor*—when your world feels like it's being turned upside down: "Jesus Christ is the same yesterday and today and forever" (Hebrews 13:8, NIV).

Whatever you go through now or in the future, Jesus is and will be what you need.

Future Valentine

Many waters cannot quench love, nor can rivers drown it.
If a man tried to buy love with all his wealth,
his offer would be utterly scorned. Song of Solomon 8:7, NLT.

You may not be old enough to date yet, but you are old enough to start thinking about the kind of person you want to date someday and the kinds of things you want to do on those dates. Your age limit for dating is a discussion you and your parents will need to have. My parents had set an age for me, so I was pretty disappointed when Roger—one of the "cool guys" in our youth group—asked me out to the county fair. But since he was a longtime family friend, my parents said OK, *if* we double-dated with my older sister, Debi, and her boyfriend, Kevin. So Roger picked me up on his 350 Honda motorcycle, and we followed them to the fair.

I think Roger was trying to impress me that night, because he bought me popcorn, cotton candy, a caramel apple, pop, a donut, and candy bar.

And then he took me on a ride called The Hammer.

During the ride Roger looked at me and yelled, "YOU LOOK GREEN!" He hollered for the operator to stop the ride, and I ran out to a field and upchucked it all. We decided to leave early because I couldn't quit throwing up. The boys took a shortcut home on a curvy road, and I had to ask Roger to stop so I could run into the woods and throw up again. I vomited so hard that my nose started bleeding! The only rag for my nose was an oil rag from Kevin's car trunk. I spent the rest of the trip home nauseated and bleeding in the back seat of his car.

Roger never asked me out again . . .

Throughout academy and college I met some nice guys. Some dates were for just one afternoon or evening, while there were a couple of boys I went out with for several months.

But then came that day in July. When people ask how I met my husband, I tell them, "Our eyes met across a crowded room." In the days, weeks, and months that followed, I found myself attracted to him for all the right reasons. Sure, he was cute, and I loved the sound of his voice, the twinkle in his eyes, and his physical strength. But the two things that attracted me the most were the way he treated people and his love for God. He was the type of man I'd dreamed of marrying when I was your age. Now that we've been married for many years, I'm glad I waited. I'm glad I waited emotionally and physically for my future valentine. I hope you do, too.

FEBRUARY 15

Four Hundred and Ninety Forgivenesses

Then Peter came to Him and said, "Lord, how often shall my brother sin against me, and I forgive him? Up to seven times?" Jesus said to him, "I do not say to you, up to seven times, but up to seventy times seven." Matthew 18:21, 22, NKJV.

Rachel had been planning this for more than three years. Ever since fifth grade, she'd dreamed of running for class president of her eighth-grade class. So had her friend Emily.

Rachel worked hard on her campaign speech. Her motto for the class was "Be the change you want to see in the world." She promised that as president she would work with the other officers to plan activities that would help the class get closer to each other and to God.

A few days before she was to give her campaign speech, Rachel noticed some of the kids giving her mean looks. Others were huddled and glancing over at her, acting like they were talking about her. A few of them walked up to her and said, "I can't believe you'd do that to Emily," and just walked away. Now she was even more confused. So she asked her best friend, Mallory, "What's wrong with everyone? Why are people being mean to me?"

Mallory told her what she'd heard. Emily had been doing some campaigning of her own by making up lies. She'd told some of their classmates that Rachel had told her, "I don't want to lose and am going to find a way to win the election by somehow rigging the votes." Rachel couldn't believe it! They were supposed to be friends! She felt a whole bunch of emotions: anger, hurt, betrayal, resentment, confusion—and maybe even some hate.

With the help of some of her true friends, they went around and told everyone they could find that the rumor wasn't true. Unfortunately, not everyone believed them. And Emily won the election.

"At least I lost honestly," Rachel later told me. "And I felt good about myself—that I didn't choose to lie in order to make kids like me and vote for me. It made me stronger."

"Did you forgive Emily when she finally apologized?" I asked.

"Yeah, I did. It took about six months to get over the whole thing, but I forgave her because she asked, and I felt sorry for her. Obviously, she had self-worth issues if she would lie."

Did Emily ever hurt Rachel again? Unfortunately, she did. But she always asked for forgiveness. And 490 forgivenesses go a long way in a friendship!

FEBRUARY 16

"We're Going to Crash!"

The cords of death entangled me, the anguish of the grave came over me; I was overcome by distress and sorrow. Then I called on the name of the Lord: "Lord, save me!" Psalm 116:3, 4, NIV.

My friend Lynn was working as a junior high youth pastor when an accident happened that changed his life forever. It made him question God and wonder if he even wanted to live.

Lynn and some of his youth group kids were on a mission trip in Mexico to help build a church. They also planned on giving dental aid to the Huichol Indian tribe in the mountains. But Lynn and four others never made it to the mountain village. They had barely taken off in a Piper Cherokee 6 plane when the engine began to sputter and cough. They were in trouble. The copilot turned around and yelled, "Tighten your seatbelts! We're going to crash!"

Lynn said his first thoughts were, *Not us! Not me!* And then suddenly peace flowed over him. He got the strong impression that he would be OK. "I felt like I was being cradled in God's arms," he told me. The plane hit hard, flipped, and landed upside down. Lynn released his seatbelt but discovered that he couldn't move his legs! He was in terrible pain. His legs felt like they were on fire.

Miraculously, all five were alive when help finally arrived. Lynn was taken to a nearby clinic, and the next day an Air Evac team from San Diego, California, picked him up and brought him back to the U.S. He lay in a coma for one week.

It was his mom who told him, "Lynn, you're paralyzed. You may never walk again."

"What do you mean?" he asked in shock. "I have things to do!"

Several weeks later he was flown to Oregon, where he started rehab treatments. "My spirit was broken in rehab," he said. "It didn't help that one of the aides told me, 'You'll never walk again.' I made it through nine long months in a plastic body cast by putting my whole trust in God."

If someone had the right to be bitter, it would be Lynn, don't you think? There he was, on a mission trip for God, and he comes home paralyzed! And if that weren't enough, another tragedy struck while he was in rehab. But you'll have to wait until tomorrow to find out what that was!

FEBRUARY 17

Double Trouble

For you, Lord, have delivered me from death, my eyes from tears, my feet from stumbling, that I may walk before the Lord in the land of the living. Psalm 116:8, 9, NIV.

One day while in rehab, Lynn began seeing double. An X-ray showed he had a tumor in his brain. He would have to have a risky surgery to save his life. But before he agreed to the surgery, he asked to be anointed. (That's when a pastor and elders pray for you and place oil on your head—a special service that's taught in James 5:13-16.) Immediately afterward, Lynn could see to read! No double vision! "Do You work that fast?" he asked God. He went back to the doctor, who took another X-ray. The tumor had stopped growing, and surgery was no longer needed.

But seven months later Lynn woke up to severe double vision again. The tumor had started growing. "I was angry!" he told me. "I thought God was playing with me. I said to Him, 'Why did You save me from a plane crash just to let me die of a brain tumor? *What is with You?*' " But no sooner had he said those words than he cried to God, "But I need You!" A peace came over him. The same peaceful feeling that came when the plane was going down. And he strongly felt that God was telling him, "My grace is sufficient for you . . ." Those are words from 2 Corinthians 12:9 (NIV).

After being anointed again, Lynn had the risky surgery in which a surgeon attempted to remove the tumor from his brain stem. In preparation, the doctor told him that after the surgery he would be in a coma anywhere from two days to two months. The thought of that would freak most people out, but Lynn felt God asking him, "Will you just trust Me?" He answered God by saying, "I'm tired of struggling. If I die, I know there's a resurrection. I'll just trust You." The moment he prayed that prayer of surrender, that same beautiful peace flooded over him.

"The plane crash and brain cancer have made me who I am," Lynn says today. "And I wouldn't want to change anything. I would go through it again if I had to because I'm now closer to Jesus. Why would I want to change that relationship? There is a man who is also God. He understands your pain because He's gone through everything you have. Tell Him your feelings. He understands. He is aware of *you*!"

FEBRUARY 18

What's the Difference?

A thief is only there to steal and kill and destroy.
I came so they can have real and eternal life, more and better life than they ever dreamed of. John 10:10, Message.

It's a question that I've been asked more than once: "Why be a Christian? If you have to struggle through life as much as any non-Christian, then why bother? What's the difference?" My answer is simple: the difference is *Jesus*. Jesus in my past, Jesus in my present, and Jesus in my future.

I have Jesus to take care of my past. Even though I try to live right, I sometimes mess up. But when I do, I know that I can go to Jesus and pour my heart out. I can tell Him that I'm sorry and know—without a doubt—that He forgives me. First John 1:9 promises: "But if we confess our sins to God, he can always be trusted to forgive us and take away our sins" (CEV). And I'll repeat that text to myself if the guilty feelings try to come back.

I have Jesus to take care of my present. He is here for me now. *Today*. When I'm afraid, worried, or sad, I can go to Him and talk about it. Philippians 4:6, 7 says: "Don't worry about anything, but pray about everything. With thankful hearts offer up your prayers and requests to God. Then, because you belong to Christ Jesus, God will bless you with peace that no one can completely understand. And this peace will control the way you think and feel" (CEV).

And I have Jesus to take care of my future. Someday the pain, suffering, and unfairness of this world will be over: "He will wipe all tears from their eyes, and there will be no more death, suffering, crying, or pain. These things of the past are gone forever" (Revelation 21:4, CEV).

Being a Christian *does* make a difference: a difference in my past, my present, and my future. Sure, even though I'm a Christian I'll still get sick, people I love will die, and at times I'll be worried about how messed up this world is. God doesn't play favorites. Matthew 5:45 says: "He makes the sun rise on both good and bad people. And he sends rain for the ones who do right and for the ones who do wrong" (CEV). It wouldn't be fair if He blessed only the Christians. He loves all His children—the believers and the nonbelievers alike. But through all of life's uncertainties, I have a Forgiver. I have a Provider. I have a Hope.

And *that's* the difference.

FEBRUARY 19

Fire!

When you pass through the waters,
I will be with you; and through the rivers, they shall not overflow you.
When you walk through the fire, you shall not be burned,
nor shall the flame scorch you. Isaiah 43:2, NKJV.

It was my second home. During the summers of my teen years I worked as a girls' counselor at Big Lake Youth Camp near Bend, Oregon. I loved everything about it. The smell of the wood chips, the sound of the wind in the pine trees, the beautiful view of the lake, and the feeling that God was there. Maybe you have a summer camp that you love to attend. How would you feel if you thought your camp might burn down? And with campers on the grounds? Well, that happened to us one summer.

It was an ordinary day at camp when Kevin yelled to Terry, "Come quick! I think we've got ourselves a fire! I saw smoke near the slopes of Mt. Washington!" They raced down to the dock, where Bruce had a ski boat waiting. They sped to the middle of the lake and looked around. A gray column of smoke was rising from the thick forest of pine and fir trees about three fourths of a mile from camp.

Terry, who loved Big Lake Youth Camp as if it were his own, shouted to Bruce, "Take me to the shore and drop me off! Then grab some of the staff and firefighting equipment and meet me up at the fire!" Bruce took the boat as close as he could to the shoreline, and Terry hopped out. *I wished I'd had time to grab my compass,* he thought as he ran into the woods.

He finally reached the Pacific Crest Trail, but the trees were so thick it was hard for him to navigate. "Lord," he prayed, "I need some help. Especially if You need me to get to that fire soon!" As soon as he finished praying, he heard a plane overhead. It was a forest service plane! The pilot had spotted Terry's bright orange staff T-shirt and guided him to the fire.

Terry could tell that the fire was a result of careless campers who hadn't put out their campfire. Hot coals had ignited the dry ground, and the campfire had turned into a big ring of fire. So there was Terry, alone on the ground, facing a fire that could quickly spread not only through the forest but also to our camp with 200 campers. "Lord . . . I need help!" he cried out.

Did God help Terry? You'll have to wait until tomorrow to find out!

FEBRUARY 20

An Idea That Worked

If any of you lacks wisdom, you should ask God, who gives generously to all without finding fault, and it will be given to you. James 1:5, NIV.

Where do I begin? Terry asked himself. The odds were not in his favor. It was one young man against the beginnings of a forest fire. But Terry wasn't alone. And he knew it. He kept his head about him and surveyed the situation. The greatest threat was the flames that were climbing a 12-foot-tall white fir tree whose branches were low enough to catch on fire. If those flames continued to climb, nearby trees would catch fire, too. It's called a "crown fire" because the fire jumps from tree to tree ahead of the fire on the ground. A story he had heard too many times flashed through his mind: the infamous "Big Lake Airstrip Fire" had burned more than 4,000 acres!

Because Terry had left camp in a hurry, he didn't have any firefighting equipment. "I did the only thing that was left to do," he later told me. "I found all the burning branches of that tree that were within arm's reach. One by one I circled my fingers around the branches and began running my hands out to the end of each branch, hoping to put out the fire. It worked! And I ran my hands so fast that I didn't get burned."

Next Terry turned his attention to the ground. The fire was spreading, and flames were dangerously close to other smaller trees. He had on thick leather boots that day, so he began making a narrow firebreak around the flaming area and pulling pine needles away from low-hanging trees. Just then he heard a welcoming voice booming through the woods. "Terry!" It was Bruce's voice. He had returned with a crew of Big Lake staff workers with shovels and tools in hand. Within a half hour the fire was completely out.

Why do you think Kevin saw that smoke? Why do you think the forest service pilot spotted Terry's orange shirt? Why do you think God impressed Terry with just the right thing to do? We all believed it was for the kids. Because God loves kids! He wanted to protect Big Lake Youth Camp so that through the years thousands might come to know Him better. As Terry said, "We were all exhausted by the end of that day, but we were thankful. Thankful for a Creator God who enjoys summer camp with His kids!"

FEBRUARY 21

You'd Better Be Good!

When the Son of Man comes in His shining greatness, He will sit down on His throne of greatness. All the angels will be with Him. All the nations of the earth will be gathered before Him. He will divide them from each other as a shepherd divides the sheep from the goats. He will put the sheep on His right side, but the goats He will put on His left side. Matthew 25:31-33, NLV.

"You'd better be good, or you won't make it to heaven!"
"If you sin too many times, Jesus will stop forgiving you."
"God gets mad when you do things like that."
"You're going to hell if you keep living that way!"

I know people who were told statements like these when they were teenagers. Adults in their lives tried to get them to be "good" and thought that maybe if they could strike some fear in these teens, they'd shape up. But wouldn't they be shaping up for the wrong reasons?

Today's text is talking about the judgment. It says that when Jesus comes, He'll divide the sheep from the goats—the saved from the unsaved. Does the thought of that frighten you? Do you fear judgment day because you know you've sinned? Do you fear it because you don't think you can measure up to what God expects?

One day I was the guest at an elementary school and had to sign out at the front desk before I left. I could see the principal's office from there. He was standing in the doorway talking to a boy. With one hand on the boy's shoulder, I heard him say, "You can't keep hurting people. If you hit people, someday the police are going to come and get you. They're going to put handcuffs on you and take you away to kids' prison." The boy stood there listening, wide-eyed. Obviously, the principal was trying to get him to fear his potential future if he didn't change.

But you don't have to fear your future on judgment day. Do you know why? *Because your Judge is also your Savior.* The One who will judge you is the same One who died for you! John 3:17 says: "For God did not send his Son into the world to condemn the world, but to save the world through him" (NIV). And while you can't take advantage of His death by acting any way you want because you know He'll forgive you, you can think about the judgment with peace. It's not something to fear, because Jesus has your back!

Angel in the Tree

For he will order his angels to protect you wherever you go. Psalm 91:11, NLT.

Hallie feels that she got just a taste of what it would be like to be a guardian angel. Once, when she was in the fifth grade, she was having a bummer of a day. Things got worse that evening when she got into an argument with her parents. Hallie felt that she just had to get away and be alone. So she ran out the back door and climbed up a tree. It was about an hour till sundown, and she sat there for a long time, crying and praying. She began to wonder if God even knew who she was in this big world, and if He cared. "If You're really there," Hallie prayed out loud, "please show me."

It was dark now, and Hallie watched as a white truck drove up and down her street several times. Then it parked in front of her house. Two teenage boys got out and started taking stuff from her yard! Hallie yelled out from the tree, "Hey! Drop that! I'm calling the police!" Imagine how startled those boys were when they heard a voice coming from the tree, ordering them to stop! They ran to their truck, and Hallie ran into the house to tell her parents.

Later that night she realized that Jesus had answered her prayer by using her! "I wondered if God was there, and He showed me He was by using me up in the tree," she told me. He showed her that He cared about her and her family. "I felt like an angel in a tree," Hallie said.

Wouldn't it be neat if we could see heaven's angels? If there were some kind of X-ray angel glasses we could put on? I wonder what we would see?

What does the Bible teach us about angels? Well, we know from today's text that God asks them to look out for us. We know that they announced Jesus' birth to the shepherds. We know that they ministered to Jesus when He spent 40 days in the desert preparing for His earthly ministry. We know that they're powerful—they rolled the stone away from Jesus' tomb! We know that one will sound a trumpet to announce the second coming of Jesus.

But do you know my favorite Bible text that describes what angels do? It's something Jesus said in Luke 15:10: "Likewise, I say to you, there is joy in the presence of the angels of God over one sinner who repents" (NKJV).

So you see, you have a heavenly team watching you and cheering for you! Jesus isn't the only one who has your back. There are angels surrounding you, and they have your back too!

FEBRUARY 23

Like Any Other Girl

People look at the outward appearance, but the Lord looks at the heart. 1 Samuel 16:7, NIV.

The moment my friend Patsy gave birth to her daughter, she knew something was terribly wrong. Although the doctor tried to beat around the bush, Patsy knew in her heart what it was: her daughter had Down syndrome—a birth defect that causes both physical and intellectual handicaps. Among other signs, Down babies' eyes and facial features look different from those of other babies. Did the way her newborn looked change Patsy's love for her? Not at all! She told me, "When I looked at her, she was perfect. She just had Down syndrome."

But the rest of the world hasn't always been so accepting. "I wish people would have seen her as a baby first," Patsy told me. "But they didn't. They saw her as a disabled baby first." And then there were the looks and whispers from strangers. "I remember one day in church there was a little boy sitting in front of us with his grandma. He kept staring at Tiffany. Finally he asked his grandma, 'What's wrong with that girl?' Rather than answer him, she ignored us and jerked him around to face the front."

Why do we sometimes judge and even make fun of kids who look or act different? The boy with a face full of pimples; the girl who is overweight; the boy who flunks math; the girl who wears thick glasses; the boy who can't shoot a basket; the girl who wears hand-me-down clothes; the boy who walks funny; the girl who can't pronounce her R's correctly. All these are wide open to be laughed at, whispered about, and then ignored.

Tiffany is now 18 and a typical teenager. "She's like any other teenage girl," Patsy says. "She's gone through all the classic stages girls do. She just learns at a slower speed." Tiffany has a huge smile and a great sense of humor. She loves to listen to music and knows the words to most of the songs in the church hymnal—all stanzas too! She enjoys the same movies other teens do and has a celebrity crush. Her bedroom walls are plastered with teen posters.

I recently asked Patsy how she wishes kids would react to disabled children. She said: "Treat them like any other children. Realize that there is no limit to what they can learn. Know they have feelings—it's just harder for them to communicate." So the next time you meet a kid who's "different," take time to really *see* them. Why not try to follow God's example in today's text? Don't look at their outward appearance, but rather their heart.

Blindly Following Jesus

"My grace is enough; it's all you need. My strength comes into its own in your weakness." Once I heard that, I was glad to let it happen. I quit focusing on the handicap and began appreciating the gift. 2 Corinthians 12:9, Message.

Jared is part of a music, drama, and preaching ministry team that tours the United States, holding weekend conferences for teens. A stop on his first tour was an arena in Sacramento, California. It was Friday night, and the message was titled "Leaving the Trash Behind." He told me the following story about that night:

"I was asked to help up front with the altar call. I was in the bowl area when I looked up into the stands and saw a teenage boy start to make his way down the steps and to the front.

"But something was different about this kid. A friend was helping him maneuver the steps, and he was walking with a cane. Once he was down the steps and had a straight line to the front, he began walking alone. When he reached the front, he dropped to his knees, set his cane on the ground, looked straight up to heaven, and started bawling.

"It was then that I realized: this guy was fully blind!

"The cool thing was that he wasn't looking around at the other kids, wondering who saw him walk to the front—wondering if people were impressed by his being there. Because he couldn't see what was going on around him, he was focusing totally on the Lord.

"As I watched him in awe, I thought to myself, *This is full surrender.* It was a struggle for him to get to the altar, but he knew there was something bigger waiting for him. He knew there was something greater waiting for him at the altar, and all he wanted to do was get down there. He could have surrendered his life to Jesus from his seat. He could have sat there and prayed, but he wanted to make the effort toward his commitment. He wanted to give Jesus *complete* surrender.

"Those of us who can see and walk need to have that kind of burning desire. We don't have an excuse. It gave me a different outlook on my life. I need to fully surrender to the Lord no matter what my situation is.

"His eyes weren't healed that day, but his heart was. And he taught me that God is worth more. God's worth more than the bad things that have happened to you, so leave them behind."

FEBRUARY 25

Peace Out!

Do not be afraid of sudden terror, nor of trouble from the wicked when it comes; for the Lord will be your confidence, and will keep your foot from being caught. Proverbs 3:25, 26, NKJV.

What are you afraid of? Don't be afraid to admit it! You have to be afraid of something. Here's a list of some of the things that I feared when I was a kid: dogs that had rabies (although I never saw one); the dark (although I always survived it); black widow spiders (although one never bit me); bogeymen under my bed or in my closet (although every time I looked, they weren't there); and mountain lions (although I only saw them on TV).

Maybe you have fears like these that never amount to anything. But there are also bigger fears that kids face today. Just watching the news or reading the paper can make you feel afraid. War, terrorism, natural disasters, gangs, superbugs, and crime fill the headlines.

For me, the only way to feel peace in a messed-up world is to believe that Someone is in control. *The Creator of the world is also the one who controls the world.* Remember the song "He's Got the Whole World in His Hands"? And since His children live here, He won't turn His back on it. Here are two texts to memorize and repeat when you're feeling afraid.

The first is Isaiah 26:3: "You will keep him in perfect peace, whose mind is stayed on You, because he trusts in You" (NKJV). Ever heard that you can't think of two things at once? That's what this text is saying. If your mind stays on God, it can't dwell on fearful thoughts.

How do you keep your mind on God? The second text, Philippians 4:5-7, teaches how: "The Lord is near. Do not be anxious about anything, but in every situation, by prayer and petition, with thanksgiving, present your requests to God. And the peace of God, which transcends all understanding, will guard your hearts and your minds in Christ Jesus" (NIV).

This text suggests three steps: 1. Remember that God is near. You may not always feel Him near, but trust that He is because He's promised to be. 2. Replace anxious thoughts with prayer. Take your requests to Him. He's promised to listen. 3. Thank Him for all the times He's heard and answered your prayers. He then promises peace that's beyond human understanding!

Sometimes it's a struggle. Sometimes feelings can mess with our faith. But believe that God is in control. He loves you. And if you had supernatural vision, you'd look and see that He's always with you.

FEBRUARY 26

Don't Let Your Bones Dry Up!

A joyful heart is good medicine,
but a broken spirit dries up the bones. Proverbs 17:22, NASB.

I wake up happy! Every morning I just wake up happy—even on dark, cold February mornings. Sometimes this slightly annoys other people in my house. They need some time to raise their happiness factor. But a joyful heart is something that was passed down to me, I guess. Grandma raised Mom with it, Mom raised me with it, and I'm doing my best to raise my daughter with it. Call it seeing our cups as half full, finding the best in every situation, or looking on the bright side. It's a great way to look at life!

When Mom was a young girl, the smell of homemade biscuits baking in the oven and freshly gathered eggs frying in the skillet would wake her up each morning. And before she even opened her eyes, she'd hear the sound of Grandma humming in the kitchen. "Good morning, my sweetheart!" was the greeting she'd get when she walked out. "It's going to be a great day today!"

Grandma had some good advice for Mom when she was a kid. Positive mottoes such as:

"Put worries on the back burner until they become a reality."

"Worrying today takes away a fun day."

"Enjoy the day and let it be a great one, because you can't relive today."

I remember one summer when we were visiting Granny, and we had a full day of outdoor fun planned. But when we stepped out onto the front porch, the sky was cloudy. "Oh, no, it's going to rain today!" my brother said.

But Granny wouldn't have that kind of talk. She said, "Danny Boy, don't worry about those clouds—it's going to be a good day regardless of the weather! So we're not going to make it bad, are we? Wipe that gloomy look off your face—if it rains we'll bake cookies!"

Every morning when you wake up, you have a choice to make that only *you* can make: to live the day with a joyful heart or with a broken spirit. You can gather all the bad stuff that happened yesterday and worry about what might happen tomorrow. Or you can make a deliberate choice to have a joyful heart. You can mumble and grumble—which, according to our text, can even make you sick—or you can choose to look on the bright side. If Granny were still alive, she'd say to you, "And that's plum good medicine for whatever ails ya!"

FEBRUARY 27

Sticks and Stones

A good man brings good things out of the good stored up in his heart, and an evil man brings evil things out of the evil stored up in his heart. For the mouth speaks what the heart is full of. Luke 6:45, NIV.

Have you ever had a broken bone? If so, the doctor probably X-rayed it and then put a cast on whichever limb was broken. In time your bone healed, and your cast came off. Before long you were back to doing the things you love to do.

There's an old saying that goes like this: "Sticks and stones may break my bones, but words can never hurt me." But that's not true, is it? Words *do* hurt. In fact, broken bones will heal, but wounds caused by words can last a very long time. Even a lifetime.

I remember a time when words embarrassed and hurt me. I was probably in the fifth grade and was walking home from school when the junior high bus carrying the football team passed me. One of the boys stuck his head out the window and yelled, "Hello, Dreamboat!" Blushing, I turned and smiled. *He's talking to me!* I thought. But as soon as the bus passed, he looked back and yelled even louder, "Not you, Shipwreck!" Ouch. Looking back, I know it was a joke—a play on words. But back then it hurt so bad that I cried.

Jesus said in today's text that what comes out of our mouth is really what's in our hearts. That makes me stop and think. If I talk trash about someone, does that mean there's trash in my heart? If I hate-talk about someone, does that mean there's hate in my heart? If I talk critically about someone, does that mean there's criticism in my heart? According to Jesus, yes. And the cure? Having *Him* in my heart. There's not room for Him and the other stuff, too.

But what if you're the one who was hurt by someone's words? First, you can talk to the person. You can say, "What you said hurt me. Please stop talking to me that way." The second thing you can do is this: *choose not to let it get to you.* If it gets to you, then the person who hurt you has control over your feelings. But if you stay strong, then you are the one in control!

When your heart and head try to believe the ugly name someone called you or the cruel things they said about you, *stop*. Stop and see yourself through God's eyes and the eyes of your closest family and friends who love you. You're no shipwreck to them. And neither am I.

I'm in Charge!

Therefore put on the full armor of God, so that when the day of evil comes, you may be able to stand your ground, and after you have done everything, to stand. Ephesians 6:13, NIV.

Do you ever get tired of people telling you what to do? Maybe you feel like every adult in your life bosses you around. Maybe you want to feel more grown up and be able to make more decisions on your own. Let's imagine for a minute. What if you were in charge for a day? What would it be like?

What if you were "Principal for a Day"? Your rules might be like these rules:

1. Come to school only after you've slept in as long as you want.
2. Every student is allowed one day a week to stay home to play video games.
3. Pizza, veggie burgers, french fries, ice cream, and unlimited soda are available at lunch.

What if you were "Parent for a Day"? Consider these rules, and add your own:

1. Stay up as late as you want.
2. Don't make your bed in the morning.
3. Eat whatever you want, as much as you want, whenever you want.

Your "rules" might seem fun for a while, but they're not very realistic, are they? And they're not very responsible. As a kid, you can't be in charge as an adult can. But did you know there's one thing you *can* be in charge of? You can begin to be in charge of YOU!

You can choose when to say yes—and no—at the right time. That's what being in charge is all about. You can say yes to obeying your parents. You can say yes to doing something kind for someone. You can say yes to choosing healthy food and drink to put into your body. You can say yes to doing your homework without being told. You can say yes to doing your chores.

And then there are times when being in charge of you means saying no. You can say no to cheating in school. You can say no to talking back to your parents. You can say no to lying. You can say no to cigarettes. You can say no to alcohol. You can say no to that inappropriate kiss.

Someday you'll be a grown-up in charge. But for now you can be in charge of your own actions. That in itself actually makes you feel more grown up. Because every time you say yes or no at just the right time, you become a stronger person—a person in charge!

MARCH 1

A Broken Heart

Then Jesus made a circuit of all the towns and villages.
He taught in their meeting places, reported kingdom news,
and healed their diseased bodies, healed their bruised and hurt lives.
When he looked out over the crowds, his heart broke.
So confused and aimless they were, like sheep with no shepherd.
"What a huge harvest!" he said to his disciples. "How few workers!
On your knees and pray for harvest hands!" Matthew 9:35-38, Message.

Do you know what I wish for you? I wish for you a heart that breaks. Not from a broken relationship or from what someone says about you or does to you. I wish for your heart to break the way Jesus' heart did. When you see someone hurt, lonely, sick, or sad, I wish for you to have so much of Jesus in your heart that your heart breaks for him or her.

When you see a kid sitting alone at lunch, I wish for your heart to break. And then for you to invite that kid to sit at your table.

When you're at the grocery story and see an elderly woman struggle to reach a box on the top shelf, I wish for your heart to break. And then for you to reach up and take it down for her.

When you hear about a tsunami, earthquake, or hurricane in some far country that doesn't affect you, I wish for your heart to break. And then for you and your friends to brainstorm on ways to help the victims.

When you see a kid getting bullied at school, I wish for your heart to break. And then for you to tell the bullies, "Hey, come on, guys—stop it!" And then for you to walk away with the victim.

When you hear that someone in your neighborhood has been very sick, I wish for your heart to break. And then for you and your family to make a big pot of soup or a batch of cookies to take them.

I wish for your heart to break for the poor, the hungry, the outcasts—the forgotten ones. Why? Because I want your heart to be like Jesus' heart. He felt a whole bunch of emotions for people in need: pity, compassion, love, and sorrow. Today's text says that the workers are few. Volunteer to be a worker for Jesus! Look for ways to help people in need. Don't just live for yourself. What if Jesus had done that? What if He had just lived for Himself? Then we'd all be in trouble.

MARCH 2

You're an Example

About this time the disciples came to Jesus
and asked him who would be the greatest in the kingdom of heaven.
Jesus called a child over and had the child stand near him. Then he said:
"I promise you this. If you don't change and become like a child,
you will never get into the kingdom of heaven." Matthew 18:1-3, CEV.

What do you think of today's text? Jesus used a kid like you to answer a question the disciples had asked! They wanted to know which of them would be the greatest in heaven. And Jesus' answer was pretty straightforward: He told them to become like kids in humbleness and simple faith.

Years ago my dad was giving a worship talk to a classroom full of fifth graders. For an illustration he put three cups of water on a table in the front of the room. He told the kids, "In one of these cups is an odorless, colorless substance that could kill a person in a matter of minutes. Is there anyone brave enough to come up here, choose a cup, and drink what's in it?"

Brave Jeff raised his hand and walked up to the front. But as he studied the cups, he stopped looking so brave. With fear in his eyes and shaking hands, he reached for the middle cup. Now Dad started to feel terrible! He didn't think the illustration would be taken so seriously. But Jeff raised the cup to his trembling lips and drank all of it. Then he looked up at Dad, who quickly assured him and the class, "You chose the right cup! In fact, all the cups are right. The odorless, colorless substance is water. And just a few inches of water can kill a person if they breathe it in."

Jeff was relieved! Before he sat down, Dad asked him, "Why did you drink any of the cups if you thought the contents of one of them could kill you?" Jeff answered, "Because, Pastor Dave, I knew you wouldn't let me die." He had faith in Dad, because he knew Dad loved him.

Jeff and kids like him are an example of the kind of faith adults need. Faith that tells Jesus what you need, believing He'll take care of you. Faith that is confident that He's coming back, even though you've waited a long time. Faith that Jesus is listening when you pray, even though you can't hear His reply. Faith that He's there, even though you can't see Him. This is why, according to Jesus, grown-ups must change and become like kids. So keep it up! Your faith is an example!

MARCH 3

Surrounded by Talons

But you will receive power when the Holy Spirit comes into your life. You will tell about Me in the city of Jerusalem and over all the countries of Judea and Samaria and to the ends of the earth. Acts 1:8, CEV.

Riley was outnumbered. The ratio was 20 to 1. Twenty gang members to one Christian. *What have I gotten myself into here?* he wondered. Then he prayed, *God, I'm trusting You . . .*

Riley was on a mission trip to a faraway country. On his day off he decided to explore the city, so he put his backpack on and headed out. After walking about a mile, a local teenage boy came out of a house across the street and started walking Riley's way. Riley motioned for him to come over. The boy knew some English, so they began talking.

"Are you in a gang in America?" the boy asked.

"Noo," Riley answered with a laugh. "Wait. Are *you* in a gang?"

The boy got very excited. "Yeah!" he said. "We are called the Talons!" He went on to tell Riley that his favorite game to play was Snooker and asked Riley if he wanted to play a game with him. When Riley accepted the invitation, the boy said, "We can go to my club. That's where the Talons play." Riley felt his heart skip a beat.

They soon entered a small doorway that led to a narrow set of stairs. When Riley entered the clubroom, all 20 guys stood up and stared at him. The room was silent except for the loud beating of Riley's heart. Then they all rushed over to him to shake his hand and say hello.

They showed Riley how to play Snooker, which is basically a pool game. During the game one gang member offered him alcohol. Another offered him drugs. When he turned those down, they offered him guns—and even their sisters! At that point Riley asked God, *Who in the world have You put me with?*

When they discovered Riley was hungry, they were good hosts and prepared a meal that they ate together on the roof. He asked them about their religion, which they eagerly talked about. When they were finished, he asked if he could share his beliefs. He got to tell the gang members about Jesus! And they listened! Before he left, Riley asked, "Can I pray with you?" Surprised, they all looked at each other and then agreed. So there in the clubroom, surrounded by Talons, Riley prayed. Then he walked out the door, amazed at what God had just done!

MARCH 4

Forgive and Forget

And when you stand praying, if you hold anything against anyone, forgive them, so that your Father in heaven may forgive you your sins. Mark 11:25, NIV.

I can still picture him racing out the door. My little brother and I were scrapping about something when he took it up a notch and called me a bad name. He knew that wasn't allowed in our house, and that Mom had heard. So he turned and ran as fast as he could out the front door. I ran after him, stood in the doorway, and yelled, "I'LL FORGIVE YOU FOR WHAT YOU CALLED ME, BUT I'LL NEVER FORGET IT!"

Not a very good way to forgive, was it? True forgiveness isn't remembering—it's *forgetting*. Jesus gives a good example in Isaiah 45:23: "But I wipe away your sins because of who I am. And so, I will forget the wrongs you have done" (CEV). That's such great news! Picture your sins written on the whiteboard at school. Now imagine them being wiped off. That's what Jesus does for us. A clean board every time we ask! Then He goes a step further—He forgets what was written there. Obviously He can remember if He chooses to, but He doesn't. He chooses to forget.

What are some things that are hard for you to forgive and forget? Being talked about behind your back? Being lied to? Being yelled at by your parents? Being embarrassed by a teacher? Being made fun of during PE class? Being called a name? Being shoved around?

Forgiving and forgetting doesn't mean that you'll never think about the hurt someone has caused you. But it *does* mean that once you've dealt with the hurt, and it tries to come back to hurt you again, you choose to push it out of your mind.

Some hurts are easier to forgive and forget than others. Hurts caused by physical or emotional abuse might need the help of a counselor or trained pastor for you to feel free. That's OK. In fact, getting help is often the first step toward healing. At some point you'll discover that you've healed enough to leave the hurt as history. For lesser hurts it's a matter of choice: to hold on, or to let go. To replay the hurts over and over in your mind, or to hit the eject button.

There's a simple one-sentence verse in Isaiah 43:18 that offers some good advice. I like the way *The Message* Bible says it: "Forget about what's happened; don't keep going over old history." Jesus doesn't. Why should we?

MARCH 5

Lexi Was Lost

Then Jesus told them this story: If any of you has a hundred sheep, and one of them gets lost, what will you do? Won't you leave the ninety-nine in the field and go look for the lost sheep until you find it? And when you find it, you will be so glad that you will put it on your shoulder and carry it home. Then you will call in your friends and neighbors and say, "Let's celebrate! I've found my lost sheep." Jesus said, "In the same way there is more happiness in heaven because of one sinner who turns to God than over ninety-nine good people who don't need to." Luke 15:3-7, CEV.

If you've ever had to move to a new city or state, you know how tough it is. You have to say goodbye to your house, your friends, your favorite places, and a lot of memories.

When Lexi was 14, her dad took a new job far away. And that meant a new school for her—a place where she was a stranger and didn't know a single soul. As with any school, there were kids who had it together and kids who didn't. Lexi was so lonely for friendship that she began hanging out with anyone who'd invite her.

Before she knew it, she was hanging out with the wrong crowd. Then she started making poor choices just to be accepted. Before long she'd pushed God right out of her life. She didn't talk to Him or read her Bible anymore, and she went to church only because her family attended.

One night while she was lying on her bed, Lexi found herself lonely again. Her new friends weren't really friends at all and only got her into trouble. She also felt lost. That's when she saw her Bible on the dresser. She thought, *I'm so far away from God right now. And I know I'm not making good choices.*

I can imagine Jesus in Lexi's room with her. I can imagine Him speaking to her heart and saying, *Come back, Lexi! You haven't gone so far that My grace can't reach you. Start over. I'll help you!*

But Lexi kept struggling until one day at church when the pastor preached, "God loves you no matter what. When you sin, He doesn't love what you've done, but He does love *you*."

She needed to hear those words! Lexi was never the same after that day. She finally realized how much God loved her—in spite of her actions. She became reacquainted with her old Friend, Jesus, who helped her find new and true friends at school. And now life is good again!

MARCH 6

Breaking the Cycle

So here's what I want you to do, God helping you: Take your everyday, ordinary life—your sleeping, eating, going-to-work, and walking-around life—and place it before God as an offering. Embracing what God does for you is the best thing you can do for him. Don't become so well-adjusted to your culture that you fit into it without even thinking. Instead, fix your attention on God. You'll be changed from the inside out. Readily recognize what he wants from you, and quickly respond to it. Unlike the culture around you, always dragging you down to its level of immaturity, God brings the best out of you, develops well-formed maturity in you. Romans 12:1, 2, Message.

My friend Kayla hated her home life when she was a teenager. Her parents fought all the time, her friends were messed up, and she often felt depressed and alone. Things got so bad that she tried to take her own life in order to escape the pain. When that didn't work, she vowed never to get married and never to have children. She didn't want another kid to live the life she felt forced to live.

But that was before she knew Jesus. After she became a Christian, Kayla realized that she didn't have to live the way her family had. She could break the cycle! She could decide to live differently—better. Today she's an adult who's happily married and has three children.

Even though you're still a kid, you can break unhealthy cycles too. Although you need to respect your family, you don't have to choose the same lifestyle if it's wrong or harmful. You can break the cycle! Here are some suggestions to show you what I mean:

If people in your family yell when they're angry, you can choose to talk calmly. You can learn how to express your feelings with confidence, but without anger.

If no one in your family goes to church, you can choose to go yourself. Call your pastor and ask if someone can give you a ride each Sabbath.

If your family isn't interested in having worship every night, you can choose to have your own worship.

And who knows? Maybe the changes you make to break the cycle will be a witness to the rest of your family. Maybe they will see that there are better choices to make and will join you. Sometimes the greatest witness you can be is a witness in your own home.

MARCH 7

Uncle Tarzan

Now that we know what we have—Jesus, this great High Priest with ready access to God—let's not let it slip through our fingers. We don't have a priest who is out of touch with our reality. He's been through weakness and testing, experienced it all—all but the sin. So let's walk right up to him and get what he is so ready to give. Take the mercy, accept the help. Hebrews 4:14-16, Message.

Although his name was Clarence, I called him Tarzan. When I'd ask him, he'd show me his big bicep, or he'd beat on his chest and give the Tarzan call: "Aaaaah-ah-ah-ah-aaaah-ah-ah-ah-aaaah!" He was definitely my favorite uncle. My mom, his sister, loved him too.

After my family became Christians, Mom couldn't get her mind off Uncle Clarence. She strongly felt that she needed to go and talk to him about Jesus, and the feeling just wouldn't go away. When she told Dad, they decided we should all make the trip to visit Uncle Clarence, even though he lived nine hours away. When we got there, he was standing in the front yard looking at some flowers. The rest of us gave him a hug and went into the house, while Mom stayed outside.

She told him, "Clarence, I don't know where you are with God. And I want you to give your life to Him, if you haven't. I plan on being in heaven, and I want you there, too."

He put his hand on her shoulder and said, "Come back and see me when I'm old enough to be in a rocking chair."

Two weeks later Uncle Tarzan died unexpectedly. "I believe that God led me there to talk to him," Mom later told me. "I hope he had time to remember what I said before he died. I hope I'll see him in heaven."

Mom wanted me to share this story with you because she and I don't want you to wait until it's too late. You're not guaranteed tomorrow. I'm not saying that to scare you. It's just a fact. We don't know what the future will bring. To hold out on becoming a Christian until you're older so you can have more fun now would be a mistake. Not only because you don't know the future, but also because you'd miss out on being a Christian now.

I became a Christian at the age of 10, and I haven't missed out on any fun! In fact, life is much more fun with Jesus in it. I hate to think what it would be like if I hadn't given my life to Him.

MARCH 8

An Hour Lost

Teach us to number our days,
that we may gain a heart of wisdom. Psalm 90:12, NIV.

At 2:00 this morning, while you and I were sound asleep (hopefully!), daylight saving time began. I've never understood why it happens at 2:00 a.m. Who gets up at that hour and changes their clock? I always change our clocks the night before. Then when we wake up, we're looking at the right time.

Although it's great to have an extra hour of daylight, the fact is, we lost an hour of sleep early this morning. An hour of life is gone that we can't get back till fall. And that got me to thinking . . . how do we spend our days?

Let's do a checkup. I'll ask some questions, and you answer to yourself: How much time do you spend watching TV every day? How much time do you spend playing video games every day? How much time do you spend reading teen magazines or novels every day? How much time do you spend surfing the Web every day? How much time do you spend texting every day?

I'm not trying to spoil your fun. And I'm not judging you. I'm just asking you to think about how you spend your free time. Chances are, if your parents work, you have a fair bit of time to yourself. And with no one watching, you get to choose what you do with your time. Some kids I know do some great things with their free time:

- Renee spends her free time practicing guitar and piano.
- Mike spends his free time coaching younger kids in sports.
- Tami spends her free time taking pictures of friends that make them smile.
- Carl spends his free time visiting with his grandma, who lives alone.
- Jonathan spends his free time working at a local mission.
- Meagan spends her free time volunteering at a local animal shelter.
- Darcy spends her free time baking desserts and delivering them to people.

When my brother first found out he had terminal cancer, he told me that he wished for five more years. Later he wished for just one. And the day he died, if he'd had the choice, I'm sure he'd have wished for just one more hour with us.

Take a look at how you spend your free time. Do you need to make any changes? I trust your good judgment!

MARCH 9

Too Embarrassed to Pray

Then he said to them all: "Whoever wants to be my disciple must deny themselves and take up their cross daily and follow me." Luke 9:23, NIV.

Steve sat alone in a restaurant at lunchtime. When the server brought him his food, without even thinking he bowed his head to thank God for his meal. He'd been doing that his whole life. But then it hit him. What if the other people in the restaurant were watching him? What if they thought he was some kind of religious freak or something?

Keeping his head bowed, Steve adjusted and readjusted the napkin on his lap, hoping it would look like he was doing something other than praying. Finally he decided to take a peek at all the people he was sure were staring at him. But when he looked up, he discovered that not even one person was looking in his direction! And then he felt ashamed. Ashamed that he was embarrassed about talking to God in public.

Suddenly he didn't feel like Steve anymore. He felt like Peter—Peter, the disciple who betrayed Jesus. Jesus had told Peter at the Last Supper, " 'This very night, before the rooster crows up the dawn, you will deny me three times.' Peter protested, 'Even if I had to die with you, I would never deny you.' All the others said the same thing" (Matthew 26:34, 35, Message).

But Peter did deny Jesus—three times in one night. After he had spent three years living with Jesus, watching Him heal the sick, cast out demons, and raise the dead, he denied that he even knew Him. "I don't know what you're talking about" is what he told a servant girl who recognized him as one who had been with Jesus. "I swear, I never laid eyes on the man" is what he said when another person recognized him. And "I don't know the man!" is what he said when another confronted him directly (Matthew 26:70, 72, 74, Message).

The other disciples didn't do any better. They all scattered when Jesus was arrested.

That got Steve to thinking. It was God who gave him life! He was alive because God had created him. And he was a son of the King of the universe! All of a sudden he *wished* that someone had seen him praying and would come up and talk to him about Jesus.

You don't have to make the mistake Steve and the disciples made. You can say with pride that you know Jesus! You can pray without being embarrassed. You can be proud that you're one of God's kids, talking to your Father.

MARCH 10

The Storm Within Me

God's a safe-house for the battered, a sanctuary during bad times. The moment you arrive, you relax; you're never sorry you knocked. Psalm 9:9, 10, Message.

Derek had made some pretty bad choices. Although he'd hoped no one would find out, before long his parents, friends, and school discovered what he'd done. Everyone seemed to have an opinion about what the truth was and what his punishment should be. Kids at school took sides and began to argue with each other. It was just one big mess.

Only his parents and a few friends remained faithful. They saw good in Derek even though he'd made a bad choice. And although he'd been living disconnected from God for a while, Derek discovered that God had remained faithful, too. When friends turned on him and the school expelled him, God became his anchor. One day he showed me a poem that he had written:

Anchor of my soul
Keeps me grounded
When life is out of control
I am surrounded
When life gets confusing
God anchors me
When I am left choosing
God puts me on my knee

What's the purpose of an anchor? I have a friend who skippers boats. He tells me that when a boat is docked in the harbor, it doesn't need an anchor because it's safely tied to the dock. But when it's out on the open sea, an anchor can literally be a lifesaver. An anchor holds the boat steady in a storm. It keeps the boat from drifting out to sea or crashing on the rocks.

Maybe you've made some bad choices like Derek. Maybe friends or even some family members have turned on you. If so, hold on to those who still support you. Don't let the haters make you feel that your life is one big mess. You have an Anchor, if you want Him. He'll keep your ship safe. How? If you connect with Him every day by praying and reading His Word, you'll become a stronger person to face what storms come your way. And the next time one hits hard, you won't let it throw you around, because you now have an Anchor that holds you steady.

MARCH 11

Don't Forget to Wear Your Mouth Guard!

Set a guard over my mouth, Lord;
keep watch over the door of my lips. Psalm 141:3, NIV.

I need a mouth guard sometimes. How about you? I don't mean the kind you wear to protect your teeth and gums when you're playing a sport. I'm talking about having God guard your mouth from saying something that might hurt someone else.

When I was in the sixth grade, I had a friend named Brett. He didn't have very many friends. He was a nice kid, but he was kind of simple, and he struggled in school. Yet I tried to always be nice to him and talk to him when I could. I think he trusted me and knew I was his friend. But I destroyed his trust one day when I briefly let my mouth go unguarded.

It was the week of class elections, and I was running for sixth grade secretary of a large class of about 60 kids. Brett was running for president—against the most popular boy in our class. One morning I was hanging out with the cool kids at recess. We were standing in a circle and talking about the elections. One of the boys said, "Can you believe Brett running for president? Ha! He doesn't even stand a chance!"

I had a choice to make at that moment. A choice to guard my mouth or to join the Brett-bashing conversation. I made the wrong choice. Rather than standing up for my friend, or even just being quiet, I said in a sarcastic tone, "Yeah, can you believe that?"

When I turned to walk away, I was face to face with Brett. I'll never forget the look on his face. A look of confusion. A look of shock and then hurt. He walked away, and I followed him. I immediately told him I was sorry and tried to explain that I didn't mean what I'd said.

He forgave me, but things were never quite the same between us. And I'll never forget what it felt like to diss someone and then discover that they'd heard it. And to see the look of hurt on their face . . .

A sports mouth guard is used to protect you—to make sure you don't get hurt. Today's text is a prayer about God being a guard over our mouths so that we don't hurt others. And in a way, protecting others from hurt protects us from hurt, because whether or not we want to admit it, it doesn't feel good to hurt someone with our words. Believe me, I know. So let's ask God to guard our mouths. Then, when we're tempted to say something mean, we'll hear that voice inside that says, *Don't say that. Just keep quiet instead.* And we'll be glad we listened!

MARCH 12

The Day I Ran Away

Where can I go from Your Spirit? Or where can I run away from where You are? If I go up to heaven, You are there! If I make my bed in the place of the dead, You are there! If I take the wings of the morning or live in the farthest part of the sea, even there Your hand will lead me and Your right hand will hold me. Psalm 139:7-10, NLT.

I decided that I wanted to run away from home when I was about 5 years old! Kind of young, wasn't it? But I was having a hard day. There were some rules I didn't like, and my older brother and sister were picking on me. "I'm running away from home!" I announced.

Mom didn't take me seriously, but when she saw me pull out my little red suitcase, she realized I was serious. That's when she and Dad decided to give me some space and see if I would really leave.

With suitcase packed, my pillow under one arm, and my stuffed dog under the other, I told everyone goodbye and marched out the door. Dad and Mom stood looking out the window, watching to make sure I was safe and didn't go too far. Three times I stopped and looked back at our house. I didn't really want to leave.

When I got to the end of our street, I was already homesick. I raced back to the house, my suitcase banging against my legs. Dad and Mom were already outside by the time I got there. The three of us hugged tight and started crying. What was I thinking? Home was where I belonged. It was where I was safe. It was where I was loved.

Like David in today's text, have you ever tried to run away from God? Maybe you're unhappy with His rules. Maybe you don't like the way other Christians are treating you. So you leave—for a little while or for a long while. But you know what? *He leaves with you.* Just as my parents watched me out the window, He watches you. He loves you too much to let you get completely lost. So even though He doesn't force you to come back, He does watch and wait.

I'm sure my parents were anxious as they waited at the window. And I can see God anxiously waiting, too—wondering how far you'll go before you get homesick for Him and run back to Him. If you do choose to run back, He won't shame you. He won't say, "OK, I'll take you back this time, but don't you ever leave again!" No, He opens His arms and says, "Welcome back! Let's forget about what happened. You're home now."

MARCH 13

A Second Chance

But you, the Lord God, are kind and merciful. You don't easily get angry, and your love can always be trusted. Psalm 86:15, CEV.

Does your classroom get a little crazy the last few days of school before summer vacation? Last year I was asked to sub a fifth- and sixth-grade classroom just three days before school got out. Even before the morning bell rang, I knew I was in for a challenge. The kids were hyper! Their teacher had warned me about this, and we had made a plan. I told the class, "Your teacher said that if you stay focused and get all your work done, there might be time for an extra recess!" The kids cheered and sat in their seats like little angels. The plan worked—for about 10 minutes. Then they were pumped again.

I wanted them to have a fun day, but they also needed to get their work done. After a few warnings, they were still noisy. It was time for consequences. "I'm sorry," I told them. "You're not cooperating, so there won't be an extra recess." You would have thought that I had just told them school would last all summer! They lowered their heads and looked sad as I passed out the history quiz. I had no intention of changing my mind until a thought from God came to me: *Use this as a learning experience to teach them about Me and how I give second chances.*

I couldn't ignore that. So I said to the class, "Actually, I've changed my mind. I was just thinking about how many times Jesus has given me a second chance when I've messed up, and I want to give you one, too. If you will focus on your work, and if you get each assignment done, then we will have an extra recess." Their eyes lit up, and they were amazing for the rest of the day. They worked hard and even helped each other stay focused.

They got their extra recess, and at the end of the day I told them, "I want you to remember today. Because someday, as you're growing up, you may make a big mistake and wonder whether or not God can possibly forgive you. If that happens, I want you to remember that when you were in grade school, there was a substitute teacher who told you that God gives second chances. And then you'll remember that you can be forgiven."

Will they remember? I don't know. But there is a second chance waiting for them, for you, and for me. And the best part? It's there even though we certainly don't deserve it.

Game Over!

I've told you all this so that trusting me, you will be unshakable and assured, deeply at peace. In this godless world you will continue to experience difficulties. But take heart! I've conquered the world. John 16:33, Message.

I'm not very good at playing video games. In fact, my teenage daughter beats me every time. Choose your game, and you'd probably beat me, too! So since I'm not that great at winning, you have no idea how glad I am that Jesus is a conqueror—that He wins the battles in life for me.

The last night that Jesus was with His disciples, only He knew that He would soon be killed. Since He was leaving, He wanted to assure them and comfort them. He knew that they would have some tough days ahead. That very night Peter would deny Him three times. And later they would be persecuted for believing in Him. Some would even face a martyr's death.

Jesus had an important message for them that night. In dying, He was about to face and win over our greatest enemy, Satan, once and for all! And since He would surely conquer, they could surely conquer, too. So He spoke the words of today's text to them. He speaks them to you, too. Jesus' final words to His disciples are a promise. They're *your* promise.

Are you struggling with a problem that's too big for you to handle?

"I've conquered the world."

Does life have too many temptations that cause you to stumble and fall every day?

"I've conquered the world."

Do you sometimes feel like life's too hard and you just can't take it anymore?

"I've conquered the world."

Are you tired of bullies pushing you around emotionally and physically?

"I've conquered the world."

In other words, He's already won the big battle for the world, and He will help you win your battles. How does He do that? By giving you strength when you need it. By giving you peace when you ask for it. And by giving you a reason to live when you search for it.

We can't be conquerors without Him. But with Him there isn't a single battle we cannot win. Jesus said, "I've conquered the world." In other words, "I've got your back."

MARCH 15

But I Want It My Way!

This is the confidence we have in approaching God: that if we ask anything according to his will, he hears us. And if we know that he hears us—whatever we ask—we know that we have what we asked of him. 1 John 5:14, 15, NIV.

Today's Bible verse makes it sound like a sure thing that all of our prayers will be answered, doesn't it? But have you ever prayed for something and felt like your prayer wasn't answered? Did it make you feel that God didn't hear you? Did it discourage you from praying? Did you think, *What's the use?* It can be discouraging, I know. Not all of my prayers have been answered the way I'd hoped. And to be honest, sometimes it puzzles me when God says yes to a small request and no to a very important one.

My biggest disappointment was when my brother Dan was diagnosed with terminal cancer. I prayed with a faith-that-can-move-mountains type of prayer. I knew that God had the power to heal my brother. There wasn't a doubt in my mind that He was able. But five months later my brother died. Why? Why didn't God heal Dan? I wasn't angry with Him, but neither did I understand it.

Then one day I realized: God *did* hear my prayer, and my prayer *was* answered. God answered with "No, not now." When our prayers don't get answered right away, or answered in the way we want, we tend to assume that God didn't hear. But I believe He does hear—always. And He does answer—always. I also realized that someday my prayer will be answered with "Yes!" Because Dan will live again!

Throughout this year I'm going to tell some stories about answers to prayer when God said, "Yes." I want to share them because I believe in miracles. I want to share them because I think that Jesus wants us to ask Him for things. Just because His answer is sometimes a "No" or "Not now" doesn't mean we should forget about praying. It's important to remember that God sees the bigger picture. He sees your life from beginning to end. And if He chooses to answer your prayer with a "No" or "Not now," then there's a very good reason.

If He loved you enough to die for you, He loves you enough to hear and answer all your prayers. Trust Him. He doesn't make mistakes. When you have a small or big need, you can tell Him, knowing that He's listening and will answer in the best way for you.

MARCH 16

Jesus Freak

If with heart and soul you're doing good, do you think you can be stopped? Even if you suffer for it, you're still better off. Don't give the opposition a second thought. Through thick and thin, keep your hearts at attention, in adoration before Christ, your Master. Be ready to speak up and tell anyone who asks why you're living the way you are, and always with the utmost courtesy. Keep a clear conscience before God so that when people throw mud at you, none of it will stick. They'll end up realizing that they're the ones who need a bath. It's better to suffer for doing good, if that's what God wants, than to be punished for doing bad. 1 Peter 3:15-17, Message.

Quinn was an outgoing girl who had lots of friends. Everyone in her seventh-grade class knew that she was a strong Christian, and most respected her for it. But there were two boys who liked to give her a hard time about her faith. It got especially bad whenever she went to a Christian event, such as a concert or conference. They would make fun of the event and tell her it was lame. Then one day one of the boys called her a name. "You're a Jesus freak!" he said.

Quinn was devastated! After school she called a friend who was like a big brother to her. Crying, she told Jared what had happened. And he started laughing! But then he quickly said, "Quinn! Do you realize what happened? Being called a 'Jesus freak' is an honor! It means that kids can see Jesus in you. Don't cry. Be happy that you were called such a name!"

When you stop and think about it, there are lots of people in the Bible who would have been considered "Jesus freaks"—people who stood up for what they believed and who were known for being followers of God. In the Old Testament there's Daniel, who was thrown into a den of lions because he prayed to God. Then there are Shadrach, Meshach, and Abednego, who were thrown into a fiery furnace because they wouldn't worship a statue. There's also Noah, who was laughed at and mocked as he built the ark.

In the New Testament there's John the Baptist, whose head was cut off and presented on a platter because he preached about Jesus. Paul and Silas were beaten and thrown into prison for evangelizing. And Stephen was stoned to death for witnessing about Jesus.

So if anyone ever makes fun of you for your faith, or even calls you a name, don't let it get to you. It's an honor! Don't feel tempted to keep your faith quiet, or worse, to give it up. As you can see, you're in very good company.

MARCH 17

Don't Wear Green!

You shall not covet your neighbor's house. You shall not covet your neighbor's wife, or his male or female servant, his ox or donkey, or anything that belongs to your neighbor. Exodus 20:17, NIV.

Today's the day when some people play the game that you must wear the color green. Because if you don't, you'll be pinched! We couldn't play this game at our school, and you probably can't at yours, either. But that didn't stop my brothers and sister from pinching me if I forgot to wear green on March 17!

Have you ever heard of the term "green with envy"? That term isn't talking about wearing green but about having envy in your heart—and that's where you *don't* want to wear the color green. It's the same thing as coveting, which is the tenth commandment and today's text.

It's sometimes hard not to be envious over what other kids have. Maybe someone has a better bike than yours, an expensive brand-name skateboard, or a nice pair of skis. Or maybe someone has designer clothes, a bigger bedroom, or a backyard pool. Maybe some family has a nicer house, a boat, or an expensive car. But what's so bad about being envious over something that someone else has? Why is it such a big deal—so big that God made "Don't covet" one of the Ten Commandments?

For one thing, when you covet you hurt yourself. Comparing your life to another kid's can make yours seem boring. And you begin to live your life in what I call "if only"s. If only I had a wakeboard like Brad's; if only I had a pair of jeans like Serena's; if only I had a dirt bike like Cody's; if only I had a bedroom like Brittany's. And before you know it, your whole focus is on what you *don't* have. What you do have just doesn't seem to count anymore.

I like the way the Message Bible says the last part of today's text: "Don't set your heart on anything that is your neighbor's." Why? Matthew 6:19-21 gives the answer: "Don't hoard treasure down here where it gets eaten by moths and corroded by rust or—worse!—stolen by burglars. Stockpile treasure in heaven, where it's safe from moth and rust and burglars. It's obvious, isn't it? The place where your treasure is, is the place you will most want to be, and end up being" (Message).

Elaborate possessions here on earth won't last forever. But heaven will.

MARCH 18

Twenty-five Reasons to Live

"For I know the plans I have for you," declares the Lord, "plans to prosper you and not to harm you, plans to give you hope and a future." Jeremiah 29:11, NIV.

"What would a kid miss out on if they chose to end their life?" I asked a group of junior high students who were at our house. They immediately started talking and gave me these 25 reasons to live:

1. Getting your diploma. 2. Your next birthday. 3. Hanging out with friends. 4. Your first kiss. 5. The smell of the ocean. 6. Building a snowman. 7. Talking to God. 8. Knowing what your face looks like without acne. 9. Going to college. 10. Being proposed to. 11. Having her say, "YES!" 12. Watching a sunset. 13. Getting your driver's license. 14. Being too old to get grounded. 15. Becoming a parent. 16. Getting your first full-time job. 17. Having facial hair. 18. Watching the autumn leaves change color. 19. Riding your longboard. 20. Getting your first car. 21. Your wedding day. 22. Hugs. 23. Hearing "I love you" for the first time. 24. Tomorrow. 25. The day after tomorrow . . .

That's quite a list, isn't it? Who would want to miss out on this and so much more? Kids contemplate suicide because they feel there is no hope. When they look ahead into the future, they can't see how the pain they're feeling now will ever go away. *But there is always hope!*

My husband's cousin works as a nighttime emergency room nurse at a large hospital. She's seen her share of suicide attempts on her shift. I asked her, "When a patient's suicide attempt fails, are they ever glad the next morning that they're still alive?" She answered, "Almost always." For the people who make it, they have a second chance. But what about those who don't? Suicide is irreversible. There's no changing your mind once it's done.

Today's text says that God has plans for your life. And part of those plans is to give you a future and a hope. A hope that life can get better here, and a hope that one day He'll take you to a new world where you will feel only peace and happiness forever!

If you've ever thought about ending your life, DON'T! Don't make that irreversible decision. Instead, get help for the pain. Find tools to cope and ways to make life better. Talk to your parents, pastor, counselor—someone you trust. Or call one of these two numbers: 1-800-SUICIDE (1-800-784-2433) or 1-800-273-TALK (1-800-273-8255). Don't give up. Choose life!

MARCH 19

Mirror, Mirror on the Wall

It is not fancy hair, gold jewelry, or fine clothes
that should make you beautiful. No, your beauty should come
from within you—the beauty of a gentle and quiet spirit that will never be
destroyed and is very precious to God. 1 Peter 3:3, 4, NCV.

Taylor sat on the examination table, her hands shaking with fear as she held the phone. "Daddy?" her voice quivered. "If something happens to me, just know that I love you . . ."

Her family was in the middle of a major move when Taylor became sick with flulike symptoms. *No big deal,* she thought. *Just the flu. I'll feel better in a few days.* But after a week had gone by, her symptoms grew worse. A doctor diagnosed her with a severe sinus infection, but three days later she lost control of the muscles on the left side of her face. "Am I having a stroke?" she wondered in fear.

As she anxiously waited on the table for the doctor to come in, all sorts of thoughts were going through her head. When the doctor arrived, she gave a diagnosis: Taylor had Bell's palsy at the age of 17. Taylor told me, "I never truly realized how much I needed the left side of my face until I lost the use of it. There were so many things I'd taken for granted. I couldn't smile, blink, speak clearly, or even drink water. I had to relearn it all, and that was hard!"

Along with the relearning came humiliating reactions from strangers and even friends who saw her face. One particular friend saw her and quickly turned away, not knowing what to say or do. "It hurt me deeply," Taylor said. "Wasn't I the same person on the inside? Did my outer appearance matter that much?" She knew herself, and she certainly hadn't changed on the inside. And she knew what mattered most was that her heart had stayed the same.

How about you? Do you value yourself based on how you look? When you look in the mirror, do you always look for flaws—pimples, crooked teeth, flat hair, undeveloped muscles, weight gain, or something else negative? Whether you're a girl or a guy, check out today's text. It's not saying, "Don't try to look your best." But it *is* saying not to depend on your looks to make yourself beautiful or handsome. The kind of attractiveness that lasts comes from the inside.

Think about the people you love the most. I bet you love each of them for the kind of people they are, not for what they look like. And that's what people will love you for, too. So why not focus on the inside—your character? That's what lasts!

MARCH 20

Taking Out the Trash

Wash and make yourselves clean. Take your evil deeds out of my sight; stop doing wrong. Isaiah 1:16, NIV.

Happy first day of spring! What do you have planned for the day? Spring-cleaning your room, maybe? Whatever you do, I'd like to make a suggestion: while we're cleaning things, how about spring-cleaning our lives? How about taking a look at the things in our minds and hearts that don't belong there, getting rid of them, and replacing them with better things?

Listed below are some areas inside our lives that we can take a look at to see if they need spring cleaning. They're not meant to judge. In fact, I'll ask myself these questions as I write them here. Each is followed by a Bible text that shows why it's so important to clean up these areas in our lives:

Clean up your mouth: Do you often talk trash about other people? Do you start rumors or gossip about others? *"Watch your talk! No bad words should be coming from your mouth. Say what is good. Your words should help others grow as Christians"* (Ephesians 4:29, NLT).

Clean up your thoughts: Do you find yourself thinking thoughts that you know are wrong? *"Finally, my friends, keep your minds on whatever is true, pure, right, holy, friendly, and proper. Don't ever stop thinking about what is truly worthwhile and worthy of praise"* (Philippians 4:8, CEV).

Clean up your anger: Do you blow up at people easily? Do you find it hard to discuss a problem without getting mad? *"Controlling your temper is better than being a hero who captures a city"* (Proverbs 16:32, CEV).

Clean up your pride: Do you sometimes think that you're better than other people? *"First pride, then the crash—the bigger the ego, the harder the fall"* (Proverbs 16:18, Message).

Clean up your complaining: Do you complain and whine a lot? *"Do everything without complaining and arguing, so that no one can criticize you. Live clean, innocent lives as children of God, shining like bright lights in a world full of crooked and perverse people"* (Philippians 2:14, 15, NLT).

Spring cleaning on the inside can feel so good! And we can keep our inside clean by staying close to Jesus and living our lives the way He lived His.

MARCH 21

Come Out Blooming

You have accepted Christ Jesus as your Lord. Now keep on following him. Plant your roots in Christ and let him be the foundation for your life. Be strong in your faith, just as you were taught. And be grateful. Colossians 2:6, 7, CEV.

Have you ever been surprised by a springtime snowstorm? We were one spring day, and I was so excited! Until I remembered that I'd planted some pansies. They're my favorite spring flower, and I usually plant a few dozen around our house every year. I thought I was safe in planting them because I'd checked the forecast—and snow wasn't a part of it.

As I watched the large snowflakes come down, I wondered how my flowers could possibly survive. The snow fell on top of them until I couldn't see them anymore. You wouldn't have even known that there were flowers in the ground. "Oh, well," I said. "Looks like I'll be buying more pansies to plant."

After the storm was over, I went outside to take a look. I first went to the pot that contained my favorite purple and yellow pansies, figuring that the heavy snow and cold temperature had killed them. But as I gently moved aside the snow with my fingers, a bloom popped out! Then another . . . and another. My plants had survived!

Later that day I thought to myself, *I want to be like those flowers. Whatever life dumps on me, I want to come out blooming.* It's a choice that you and I get to make whenever life gets tough. We can stay covered in darkness under the heavy load, or we can choose to break through and keep blooming.

What's making life tough for you? Your parents' divorce? Getting behind in school? Feeling that you don't have any friends? Not making the sports team? The death of someone you love? The key to making it through these tough times is in today's text: "Plant your roots in Christ."

How do you do that? Through spending time with Him every single day. Through reading and memorizing Scripture and talking to Him often. Through listening to uplifting Christian music and hanging out with Christian friends. Through going to church and attending youth group events. These things will help "root" you. They'll give you strength to face whatever comes. Then when life dumps unexpected trouble on you, you can come out blooming.

MARCH 22

Say What?

This is the day which the Lord has made;
let us rejoice and be glad in it. Psalm 118:24, NASB.

What if you woke up on a school morning and said this text out loud? Your parents would probably check to see if you were delirious with fever!

Like most kids, my siblings and I sometimes weren't too excited about getting up for school. We used some of the traditional tricks (please don't try them!), but Mom was always too wise to believe us. Once Dan pretended that he couldn't see well enough to go to school. When Mom didn't go for that, he started limping, complaining that his leg hurt. His last-ditch effort? He went into the bathroom and held the thermometer near a light. But when Mom saw that his temp was 106 degrees, she thought it odd that his skin was still cool. So off to school he went!

My sister, Debi, and I thought we'd get the measles by taking a red marker and placing dots on our faces and arms. But of course Mom knew the difference. And the dots didn't wash off for several days.

When 13-year-old Pixie went on a mission trip to El Salvador, she and her friends visited refugee camps. She told me this story: "I had so many eye-opening experiences, but this one hit me the hardest. One afternoon while I was sitting in the shade with some local kids, a boy came up to me. He was about 11, and he asked me to write down the alphabet. Then he showed me how he'd learned to do fractions at the refugee camp school. That started an amazing afternoon of teaching and learning! The kids wanted to learn so badly, and it touched my heart.

"For me, school is a drag. But for them, school is everything! Without school they have almost no hope for any future beyond the refugee camps. They reminded me how blessed I am for the chance to go not only to school, but to college as well. They probably won't get the chance to go to college—to be what they want to be—and that breaks my heart. They showed me that I needed to value learning and be everything I can be. And I'm trying, thanks to those amazing little kids living in a refugee camp, so excited about learning."

Maybe a way to have a better attitude about school is to imagine life without it. As fun as it might seem to sleep in every day, play video games all day, or go shopping at the mall day after day, you'd probably get tired of it and want some purpose in your life. Besides, if you don't go to school, how can you become the amazing grown-up God has planned for you to be?

MARCH 23

A Place for You

But as it is written: "Eye has not seen, nor ear heard, nor have entered into the heart of man the things which God has prepared for those who love Him." 1 Corinthians 2:9, NKJV.

Have you ever had a dream about heaven? I did once. I was probably close to your age when I dreamed that I was sitting outside on a swing. It was an old-fashioned swing with a wooden seat and rope handles. Suddenly the sky above me opened and a bright light came shining down. My swing started lifting up into the air as if someone was pulling on the ropes. I was on my way to heaven! But I woke up before I got there. And I was disappointed because I wondered what heaven would look like, even in a dream.

What do you think heaven looks like? What are you most looking forward to doing there? When I was younger and thought about heaven, I thought about how cool it would be to have my own herd of horses and go riding bareback on one of them while the herd ran alongside me. I also imagined swimming with an orca whale and making friends with all the wild animals I'd seen at the zoo. And I thought about how amazing it would be to actually talk to some of my Bible heroes, such as Noah, Moses, Mary, and Peter.

All these things will be great, that's for sure! But now that I've lived more of life and have experienced disappointments and sadness, the thing I look forward to most is that in heaven Jesus will make all the wrongs right—in my life and in yours. Everything that's broken, wounded, missing, or messed up here will be fixed in heaven.

The day our daughter was born, my husband held her and said, "I'm really sorry, sweetie, that I don't have a better world to bring you into. But Jesus is working on that, and someday He'll make it all better."

Jesus *is* working it! He promises in John 14:1-4: "Do not let your hearts be troubled. You believe in God; believe also in me. My Father's house has many rooms; if that were not so, would I have told you that I am going there to prepare a place for you? And if I go and prepare a place for you, I will come back and take you to be with me that you also may be where I am. You know the way to the place where I am going" (NIV). The way is through Jesus. Through accepting His gift of salvation and not holding on to the things of this earth. Don't miss out. He's preparing a place for you. *For you!* Wow! He must love you a lot!

MARCH 24

This Little Light of Mine

You are the light of the world. A town built on a hill cannot be hidden. Neither do people light a lamp and put it under a bowl. Instead they put it on its stand, and it gives light to everyone in the house. In the same way, let your light shine before others, that they may see your good deeds and glorify your Father in heaven. Matthew 5:14-16, NIV.

Do you remember singing the song "This Little Light of Mine" when you were little? You'd hold your finger up as your light and do all the motions to the song. As you sang, you promised that you wouldn't let Satan blow your light out, and you committed to shining your light all around the neighborhood until Jesus comes.

I've read today's text many times, but today that first sentence stood out in a new way. "You are the light of the world." *You.* Yes, you! That's quite an honor! It means that Jesus is counting on you to reflect what He's like to the world. And He seems to be talking about doing it through the way you live, because He says, "Let your light so shine before others, that they may see your good deeds." So shining your light means doing whatever good you can. It's living out the fruits of the Spirit mentioned in Galatians 5:22, 23: "Love, joy, peace, patience, kindness, goodness, faithfulness, gentleness, and self-control" (NLT).

Several years ago we took our daughter to a four-day Christian music event. After the last concert of the final night, all the outdoor lights were turned off. Candles had been given to each of the 20,000 people gathered. At the front of the stage, one single candle was lit. From up on the hill, with our daughter by our side, we could see the light gradually spreading until our candles were lit, too. You could have heard a pin drop as the speaker challenged us to let our lights shine, to recommit our lives to God, and to leave there as changed people.

The sight of all the candles was an amazing one—a very spiritual moment. That's when our daughter leaned over and said in my ear, "Look, Mom. The devil just lost 20,000 people!"

This world can be a dark place at times. It needs light. It needs *your* light. When you're a light, the devil loses and God wins. Satan will try to blow your light out through sadness, tough times, and temptations, but don't let him. Shine even brighter when these things happen. Shine till Jesus comes. And who knows? Maybe your light will help someone else become a light . . . who helps someone else become a light . . . who helps someone else become a light . . .

MARCH 25

Sons and Daughters of God

Then Jesus called for the children and said to the disciples, "Let the children come to me. Don't stop them! For the Kingdom of God belongs to those who are like these children." Luke 18:16, NLT.

Some of Jesus' greatest miracles involved kids. One day a man named Jairus came to Jesus in terrible grief and desperation. He fell at Jesus' feet, pleading for Him to come to his house. His only daughter—a girl about 12—was dying. But when Jesus got there, the girl was already dead. Jesus told the people wailing and mourning outside the house to stop. Then He walked inside and said to the dead girl, "My child, get up!" And the dead girl came back to life (Luke 8:40-56, NIV)!

Another time a royal official, whose son was terribly sick, came to Jesus. He too asked Jesus to come to his house and heal his child. But Jesus healed the boy without going! He told the father, "Go, your son will live." So the man left on his two-day journey home. The next day his servants met him with great news. His son was healed! He asked when the miracle had happened. It had happened at the exact time when Jesus pronounced his son well (John 4:46-54)!

Then there was the desperate mother of a girl who was possessed by an evil spirit. The mother fell at Jesus' feet, begging Him to drive the demon out. Jesus simply told her that the demon had left. And sure enough, when she got home she found her daughter absolutely whole again (Mark 7:24-30)!

And one day, as Jesus was entering the city of Nain, He met a funeral procession. A widow's only son had died. First her husband, and now her son. "When the Lord saw her, his heart overflowed with compassion. 'Don't cry!' he said. Then he walked over to the coffin and touched it, and the bearers stopped. 'Young man,' he said, 'I tell you, get up.' Then the dead boy sat up and began to talk! And Jesus gave him back to his mother" (Luke 7:11-17, NLT).

Don't you love these miracle stories? They show that Jesus has the power to heal. They show that He is stronger than the devil. They show that He can conquer death! And they show that kids are very important to Him. *You* are very important to Him. God tells you, "I will be a Father to you, and you will be my sons and daughters, says the Lord Almighty" (1 Corinthians 6:18, NIV).

MARCH 26

Adventist or "Badventist"?

My dear friends, stand firm and don't be shaken. Always keep busy working for the Lord. You know that everything you do for him is worthwhile. 1 Corinthians 15:58, CEV.

Jessica was born a fish. Well, not really a fish! But she was born to swim, and she's good at it. Bath time was her favorite time of day when she was a toddler, and she began swimming lessons when she was about 4. Then when she was 9 years old, she tried out for the local YMCA swim team. After watching her swim a lap, the coach said, "You're in!"

The joy of being a part of the team came with its challenges. Most of the Y's swim meets were Friday through Sunday, and Jessica and her family are Seventh-day Adventists. She didn't feel that it would be honoring God's special day to compete on Saturdays. Instead she chose to go to church with her family, have a special lunch together, spend time outdoors in God's creation, and be with Christian friends.

But things changed when Jessica went to academy. Pursuing her love of swimming, she tried out for the local high school swim team—and made it! When she shared her beliefs with her coach, he was very understanding. He told her that she could opt out of the weekly Saturday practices. And at the district coaches' meetings, he'd say, "I have a girl on my swim team who worships on Saturday. Can we do our best to respect that and try to schedule as many meets as possible during the week?" They all agreed, although Jessica still missed out on quite a few.

She found the girls on her team to be supportive, too—although she did have to endure some teasing. They were never mean about it, but they would say things like, "We have a meet this Saturday. Can't you be a 'Badventist' just this once? God won't care. He's not going to condemn you for that." But Jessica stayed strong in what she believed.

She told me, "I think that my junior high years were the hardest. When you're little, your parents tell you what's right and what's wrong. But then you start making your own decisions. You have to decide what's important to you—what you're going to stand for."

Jessica is now a college student, and I recently asked her, "How do you feel about that decision you made back when you were 9?"

"I feel proud that I stuck to what I believed in," she said, "because that's really what helped form me into who I am today. I have no regrets."

MARCH 27

Prison Break

Don't fool yourselves. Bad friends will destroy you. 1 Corinthians 15:33, CEV.

"Everybody at this school is in a clique or a group," Faith and Leah told me. They had each been in separate groups, but their groups turned out to be not as cool as they looked. The kids in Faith's group were smoking and drinking, and there was a lot of drama and fighting. Faith stopped caring about school and started goofing off in class rather than paying attention, and her grades showed it. So she finally made up her mind to leave the clique.

Leah left her group because they were picking on other kids and calling them names, and she didn't like that. Sometimes they would even be mean to her and would punch her when the drama got intense. But the next day they would apologize for it and want her back.

Between the two groups there was a lot of cyberbullying and bullying through text messages and phone calls. Faith and Leah had had enough. They both walked away and started hanging out with each other and another nice girl they met. But leaving wasn't easy. Leah got shoved into a corner, and they both got yelled at. The girls in the cliques called them names and pointed out all their flaws.

"Are you happier now that you're not a part of those groups?" I asked them.

"Yes!" they answered together. "A lot happier! There's less drama and less stress, and we can focus on our schoolwork more."

"Do you have fewer or more friends now that you've left your groups?" I was curious.

"More!" they told me. "It's actually the kids in the cliques who have fewer friends."

"You know what?" I told them. "You girls are incredible for doing what you did! It's hard to stand up for yourself and walk away. Very, very hard. Especially with the pressure. But it's so great to see you smiling now and to hear you say that you're happier. What would you tell other kids who are in a clique but want to get out?"

"Just back off," they told me. "Back away. Never just stick with one group. Be friends with a lot of people. God helped us back away. We prayed to Him and asked Him to give us strength. And He did!"

"Wise friends make you wise, but you hurt yourself by going around with fools" (Proverbs 13:20, CEV).

MARCH 28

Being the Opposite

Do you want to live and enjoy a long life?
Then don't say cruel things and don't tell lies. Psalm 34:12, 13, CEV.

He's the kind of kid you just like having around. He's funny, positive, and full of energy. But most of all, he's kind—to everyone. His name is Cougar. And yes, that's his real name!

One of Cougar's life's goals is to be kind to everyone he comes in contact with and to make each person feel good about themselves. I've been to gatherings and have watched him work his way through the crowd. He'll visit with the "popular" kids who think that he's pretty cool. But then he'll go talk with those kids who are shy or maybe don't feel like they fit in. He'll have something positive to say to them, usually giving a compliment. He makes them feel like they belong.

One evening as we were sitting around a small campfire in our backyard, he told me why he tries his best to be kind to everyone.

"When I was in middle school and junior high, some kids treated me pretty badly," he said. "Because I wasn't involved in sports and I liked singing and performing in plays, some of the guys made fun of me and called me names. Just because I was different and not your 'typical' guy, they put me down. My dad gave me permission to hit the bullies, but I never did. Because I was grounded in God—because I knew how *He* saw me—I was able not to let their words get me down. And I worked at being the opposite of what the bullies were.

"All they were good at was making fun of people, while I became good at making people feel good about themselves. I've developed this as my life motto: *If I can go to bed every night knowing that another person isn't going to bed hurt because of something that I said or did, then it was a successful day—no matter what else happened.* I can't control what happens in other people's lives, but I can control how I treat them."

Isn't this how Jesus treated people? He called short Zacchaeus down from the tree and went to his house. He spoke to the Samaritan woman at the well when religious law said He shouldn't. He touched the leper whom society rejected. He ate a meal with tax collectors and sinners. He made a difference in the lives of everyone He came in contact with.

The choice is yours: make fun of people, or make them feel good about themselves.

MARCH 29

In a Blink

Jesus then said, "I am the one who raises the dead to life! Everyone who has faith in me will live, even if they die." John 11:25, CEV.

With Easter just a week away, I want us to spend the next several days thinking about the incredible gift of life Jesus gave us by giving up His life.

Today I'm thinking about His resurrection and the resurrection of the dead at the Second Coming. By this stage in your life you probably know someone who has died. Maybe it was even a close family member or a friend. I didn't think much about death when I was your age. Except for my grandpa and a friend of my parents, I wasn't affected by death. But the older I got, the more people I knew started dying from illness, accident, or old age. The fact is, between now and when Jesus returns, people we know and love will die.

Since you know that people will die, it's important to know what God says about death. Then, although their death may be heartbreaking, you can know—*without a doubt*—that you will see them again!

A few years ago I attended the funeral of a friend who died after a courageous two-year battle with cancer. She left behind a husband and two teenage boys—right before the holidays.

Standing by her casket with her husband, I looked him in the eye and said, "She's not staying in there, Paul."

He replied with quiet confidence, "I know."

You see, Paul knew that even though Marla had lost her battle with cancer, she'd win the ultimate battle against death and be resurrected at Jesus' second coming! This life is not the end for those who believe in Jesus, because *His* resurrection guarantees *our* resurrection.

Whether we are alive when Jesus returns or whether we rise from the grave, on that day we will be changed. Take a moment to blink your eyes once. That was fast, wasn't it? Now read what 1 Corinthians 15:52 promises: "It will happen suddenly, quicker than the blink of an eye. At the sound of the last trumpet the dead will be raised. We will all be changed, so that we will never die again" (CEV).

This is the hope we need to hold on to until Jesus comes back for us. Because He rose, we will rise!

MARCH 30

Whoever . . .

For God so loved the world that he gave
his one and only Son, that whoever believes in him shall not perish
but have eternal life. John 3:16, NIV.

You've probably read today's text many times and even memorized it at church or in school. What's your favorite word in John 3:16? Is it the word "loved"? Is it "gave"? Or is it "eternal"? Until recently, for me, it was the word "loved." It's because God *loved* us so much that He gave. That's why we won't perish, and why we'll have eternal life. But then I read something by author and speaker Max Lucado that made me consider a different word in this verse: "whoever."

"Whoever" means that *anyone* who believes can be saved! Notice that the text doesn't say that the perfect shall not perish but have eternal life. It doesn't say that eternal life is a reward to those who work hard enough and obey all the rules. It doesn't even say it's offered only to those who have been lifelong Christians. And it doesn't say that God plays favorites and is giving eternal life only to people who have been evangelists or missionaries. No, the word is definitely "whoever." Whoever believes in Him.

Today I was thinking of all the "whoevers" I've met through my years:

The girl who cheated on her midterm exam. She's a *whoever.*

The boy who stole a pair of jeans and hid the truth from his parents. He's a *whoever.*

The boy who secretly played violent video games. He's a *whoever.*

The girl who couldn't control her temper. She's a *whoever.*

The girl who constantly mouthed off to her teachers. She's a *whoever.*

The boy who sneaked a porn magazine under his bed. Yep, he's a *whoever*, too.

And then there are those other two *whoevers.* There's you. And there's me.

I have always known that God loves and forgives everyone who comes to Him. But now that I've focused on the word "whoever," I can't help but stand in awe of such love.

"Now, most people would not be willing to die for an upright person, though someone might perhaps be willing to die for a person who is especially good. But God showed his great love for us by sending Christ to die for us while we were still sinners" (Romans 5:7, 8, NLT).

"For God so loved the world . . ." For God so loved *you*. That's what Easter is about.

MARCH 31

Losing Shannon

The angel said to the women, "Do not be afraid, for I know that you are looking for Jesus, who was crucified. He is not here; he has risen, just as he said." Matthew 28:5, 6, NIV.

Nancy!" a voice cried into the phone. "Shannon has been murdered!" The phone slowly slipped from my hand, and I nearly fell to my knees in shock and grief.

Shannon had been a faithful member of my youth group. She was the kind of young person a youth pastor could count on—always attending every function, always coming early to help set up, and always staying behind to help clean up. She was one of the kindest people I knew, our daughter's first babysitter, and a true servant who lived her life for others. But now, through one brutal act, she was gone from our lives.

I don't remember the rest of that phone call. I just remember feeling numb. I was in such shock that when I told my husband and 3-year-old daughter, Christina, I didn't even cry. But later that day, while we were eating dinner, the tears finally came.

"What's wrong, Mommy?" Christina asked, her brow wrinkled with concern.

"Sweetie, I'm crying because I'm sad. Shannon was hurt so badly that the doctors couldn't make her well, and she died."

"Don't cry, Mommy," she said in a hopeful tone. "You know that when Jesus comes back He'll bring Shannon out of her tomb!" It was matter-of-fact to her. No doubts. He'd promised, and someday He'd do it.

When Easter came around that year, Christina drew me a picture that I put in our family scrapbook. If you looked at the picture, it might look like circles, lines, and scribbles. But to me it looks just like what Christina said it was: the sun shining brightly, an angel in the sky, a smiling Mary, and Jesus standing next to an empty tomb. To me it speaks of the faith of a little child who simply believes this: that just as Jesus promised He would rise—and He did—He promises to raise those we love—and He will.

"Jesus said to her, 'I am the resurrection and the life. He who believes in Me, though he may die, he shall live. And whoever lives and believes in Me shall never die. Do you believe this?' " (John 11:25, 26, NKJV).

Yes! I do! Believe with me! When it comes to the resurrection, He's got your back.

April Fools!

Finally, be strong in the Lord and in his mighty power.
Put on the full armor of God so that you can take your stand
against the devil's schemes. For our struggle is not against flesh and blood,
but against the rulers, against the authorities, against the powers
of this dark world and against the spiritual forces of evil
in the heavenly realms. Ephesians 6:10-12, NIV.

It was the best April Fools joke ever! At least we thought so when we were kids. When I was growing up, my siblings and I bought some small toys that we had endless fun with. They were plastic ice cubes that had fake insects inside. They came with a spider, fly, or beetle. And of course, we bought one of each. When they were placed in a glass of water with real ice cubes, no one could tell the difference.

One April first Debi and I offered to bring Mom a glass of cold ice water, while Dan was in the kitchen preparing it. He poured the water and then put in a few ice cubes, along with the plastic one with a beetle inside. Mom gladly took the glass and started to drink. Then we saw her suddenly look cross-eyed into the glass as she saw the beetle floating around. She let out a shriek, and the glass, water, ice cubes, and beetle went flying across the room! We laughed so hard! But Mom didn't seem to think it was quite so funny.

It can be fun to play harmless pranks on people. Especially on days like today. But when it comes to the devil trying to fool us, it's no laughing matter. Even though Jesus won the war with the devil when He died and rose again, Satan is still trying to fool God's people. He hopes to be the last one standing after the Second Coming.

What does he want? He wants *you*. He wants you to follow him and not Jesus. He wants you to believe you're not good enough for Jesus to love. He wants you to get discouraged when your prayers aren't answered the way you want. He wants you to live a selfish life. He wants you to think that being a Christian is boring. He wants you to think that God's rules are too strict. He wants you to think that God is too busy for you. He wants you to give in to temptation and sin.

Don't let the devil fool you! It's Jesus—not Satan—who loves you. It's Jesus who gave His very life for you! It's Jesus who's preparing a place for you. The devil hasn't done a single thing for you—except to bring you temptations, heartaches, pain, and hopelessness. Jesus has done *everything* for you. He's not out to destroy you, but to save you. And I'm not foolin'!

APRIL 2

Me First!

Then he said, "Do you understand what I have done to you? You address me as 'Teacher' and 'Master,' and rightly so. That is what I am. So if I, the Master and Teacher, washed your feet, you must now wash each other's feet. I've laid down a pattern for you. What I've done, you do. I'm only pointing out the obvious. A servant is not ranked above his master; an employee doesn't give orders to the employer. If you understand what I'm telling you, act like it—and live a blessed life." John 13:12-17, Message.

It was the evening of the Passover feast. Ever since the Israelites were freed from slavery, believers had remembered and celebrated with this special meal. Little did the disciples know that the One who was about to free the entire world was right there!

They were with Jesus in an upstairs room of a home. On the table before them were the traditional bread and grape juice—what would become symbols of Jesus' blood and body to be sacrificed for us.

But something was missing. There wasn't a servant to wash the dust and grit off their feet. It would be unthinkable for any one of them to volunteer! They'd just been arguing about who would be the greatest in the kingdom of heaven. It wouldn't do to be second, or even third! Each was determined to be first.

Maybe you know a kid like that. She has to get the best test score in the class, or she cries. He has to play the most minutes in a game, or he gets angry. She always has to be chosen first by the teacher. He has to be first in line at lunch. She has to win. He can never lose.

Imagine the disciples sitting there, tense, awkward, wondering who will stoop low enough to take on the role of a servant. And who steps up to the plate? *The Son of God!* They watch in amazement as He stands up, wraps a towel around His waist, gets a basin and pitcher, and gets down on His knees. What kind of emotions do you think they felt as Jesus washed the dust and dirt off their feet? Embarrassment. Shame. Guilt. *And overwhelming love.*

It's so easy to fall into a trap of thinking that we always have to be first in order to be somebody. Jesus did a servant's job, and He definitely *was* somebody! Even better than always being "top dog" is being a kid who is willing to sometimes take out the trash, scrub the floor, wash the dirty clothes, pull the weeds, and yes, even clean the toilet!

The Sacrifice

And He took bread, gave thanks and broke it, and gave it to them, saying, "This is My body which is given for you; do this in remembrance of Me." Likewise He also took the cup after supper, saying, "This cup is the new covenant in My blood, which is shed for you." Luke 22:19, 20, NKJV.

I think the speaker was trying to get us to see Communion in a new light, but it just didn't seem right. I sat at a long table with the rest of my friends in Bible class. But instead of the traditional bread and grape juice, our speaker brought pizza and root beer! Somehow that wasn't special to me. And as I looked around at my classmates, I don't think it was special to them, either. It seemed more like a Saturday night party than a reflection of Jesus' great sacrifice.

Why did Jesus ask us to eat bread and drink grape juice in remembrance of Him? It's because He wanted us to remember the sacrifice He made to save us. Here's a glimpse of His great sacrifice for you and me:

Traditionally, before the Romans executed a criminal, they would strip the prisoner of his clothes and tie his hands to a post. Then as he stood there soldiers would repeatedly whip him with all their might. The whip was especially cruel. It had leather strips with sharp pieces of sheep bones or iron balls braided in. The sharp objects would cut to the bone, and soldiers would whip the prisoner just short of killing him. They did this to Jesus.

Then Jesus was paraded in front of a whole group of soldiers that had gathered. They tore off His clothes again and draped a red robe on Him. Then they twisted thorn branches into the shape of a crown and shoved it on His head. They placed a staff in His hand and knelt down in front of Him in mock worship of His royalty. They spit on Him and took the rod and hit Him on the head over and over.

And finally they crucified Him—a death usually saved for the worst criminals. Soldiers hammered large spikes into Jesus' wrists and feet, nailing Him to a cross, and then stood it up for all to see. There He died an agonized death—so that you and I could live forever.

The next time you take part in Communion—when you eat the bread that is a symbol of His body broken for you and drink the juice that is a symbol of His blood shed for you—*remember*. Remember what He did for you. Remember how much He loves you.

APRIL 4

Sometimes, Empty Is Good

Now on the first day of the week Mary Magdalene went to the tomb early, while it was still dark, and saw that the stone had been taken away from the tomb. . . . Then Simon Peter came, following him, and went into the tomb; and he saw the linen cloths lying there, and the handkerchief that had been around His head, not lying with the linen cloths, but folded together in a place by itself. Then the other disciple, who came to the tomb first, went in also; and he saw and believed. John 20:1-8, NKJV.

When you think of something that's empty, it's usually a negative thought: an empty cookie jar, an empty piggy bank, an empty bag of candy, or an empty inbox. But every Easter I'm reminded of something else that's empty—and I'm glad it is: *the empty tomb*. The fact that Jesus' tomb is empty gives me a lot of hope! The emptiness of His tomb provides the promise that someday the new earth will be empty too—empty of heartache, crying, pain, suffering, and death.

Dane's life felt empty. He couldn't quite put a finger on the problem, but he knew that something was wrong. He'd left home when he was 14 years old in search of a better life, but he never found it. The alcohol was only a temporary fix for his sadness. The cigarettes were only a temporary fix for his anxiety. And the clubs were only a temporary fix for his loneliness.

If I could introduce you to Dane, he'd tell you that without a doubt the best day of his life was the day he found Jesus. Through praying and reading his Bible, his life started to make sense. He realized he'd been looking for happiness in the wrong places. The drinking, smoking, and partying now seemed so shallow compared to what he'd found—and he quit them all.

Even though he quit the things he'd thought helped him cope, he didn't feel empty. Not by any means! His life was now full! Full of hope, full of purpose, full of service, and full of a joy no one could take away—not even some family members and friends who thought he was nuts for making the choice to become a Christian.

The fact that Jesus' tomb is now empty means that He won the battle against the devil. What did He win? He won the power over sin. He won the power over death.

And He won *you*.

You are His prize.

He's Alive!

And behold, there was a great earthquake; for an angel of the Lord descended from heaven, and came and rolled back the stone from the door, and sat on it. Matthew 28:2, NKJV.

Heaven held its breath. The angels waited in anticipation while most of the earth slept—unaware of what was about to take place. Some who were awake had spent the night crying. Others tossed and turned, their minds filled with questions and doubts. Some sat and stared, while a few hid the night away in fear.

They had forgotten the promise. The promise Jesus made when He repeated this prophecy: "For He will be delivered to the Gentiles and will be mocked and insulted and spit upon. They will scourge Him and kill Him. And the third day He will rise again" (Luke 18:32, 33, NKJV).

Jesus kept that promise. In spite of the fact that the chief priests and Pharisees asked Pilate to secure His tomb; in spite of the fact that Pilate had a seal placed on the heavy stone that blocked its entrance; in spite of the fact that guards were appointed to watch it; in spite of the fact that Satan used all the power he possessed—*nothing* could keep Jesus in the grave!

When the disciples first heard the news, they didn't believe it. So Peter and John raced to the tomb to see for themselves. It wasn't until they saw it empty that they believed.

Many today don't believe, either. They think the resurrection story is a fairytale, not a fact. But in a way, you too can see the empty tomb. You can see it by reading the Bible story. You'll find a written account by those who were there. But the same enemy who tried to keep Jesus in the grave tempts you to doubt. Doubt that Scripture is accurate. Doubt that such a miracle could even happen. Yet you and I have the opportunity to be the people Jesus talked about when He said, "Blessed are those who believe without seeing me" (John 20:29, NLT).

I believe this Bible story, and wish I could have been there on that resurrection morning to feel the earth shake beneath my feet, to hear the heavy stone being rolled away by an angel sent from heaven, and to shade my eyes from the brilliance of Jesus' form as He appeared at the entrance of the tomb! The earth had never before felt such power. It was the power of our God, who is strong enough to conquer death.

The best news anyone could ever give you is this: He's alive! *Believe it.*

April 6

What If?

He went a little farther and fell on His face, and prayed, saying, "O My Father, if it is possible, let this cup pass from Me; nevertheless, not as I will, but as You will." Matthew 26:39, NKJV.

What if Jesus hadn't conquered the grave? What if He had decided at the last minute that He wanted to back out of dying? What if Jesus had lost and Satan had won? Just imagine how frightening and hopeless this world would be.

If Jesus hadn't won the battle, there would have been no disciples or apostles to write the New Testament. All of those beautiful books from Matthew to John that tell us what Jesus was like would not have been written. Paul's letters that show us how to live a Christian life wouldn't have been written. And the book of Revelation, which tells us what to expect at the end of time, wouldn't have been written, because there would be no predictable end of time. Humankind would just live on and on without a Savior, becoming more and more evil.

If Jesus hadn't won the battle, there would be no rules to live by. The Ten Commandments wouldn't matter anymore. People would freely steal, murder, lie, and disrespect God. The world would be worse than it was during the time of Noah, when only one family believed God enough to be saved. You wouldn't even feel safe walking down the street.

If Jesus hadn't won the battle, there would be no forgiveness of sin. Even if you somehow felt guilty for what you'd done, there wouldn't be anyone to wipe your slate clean so you could start all over.

If Jesus hadn't won the battle, there would be no resurrection from the dead. When someone you love died, you would bury them knowing that you'd never, ever see them, talk to them, or hold them again.

And if Jesus hadn't won the battle, there would be no Second Coming and no heaven. This life would be it, without any hope. No hope of a world without war, poverty, and famine. No hope of living a life without physical or emotional pain. No hope of someday having pure, sinless bodies. No hope of seeing our deceased loved ones again. No hope of living forever.

But He *did* choose to die. And then He rose! He has risen! This one fact changes earth's history. This one fact can change *your* history. Someday Jesus will burst through the sky just as He burst from the tomb. And nothing will hold Him back. He'll be coming for *you!*

APRIL 7

The Road to Emmaus

As they were talking and thinking about what had happened, Jesus came near and started walking along beside them. But they did not know who he was. Luke 24:14-16, CEV.

There's a painting hanging in my dad's office that has been there as long as I can remember. It's a picture of two men walking down a road. Walking between them is Jesus. On the frame is the picture's title: *The Road to Emmaus.*

That painting meant a lot to me when I was your age. Whenever I would visit Dad's office, I was somehow drawn to it. I often stood and stared at it, reliving the story in my mind. It's really the completion to the Easter story. Here's what happened on that road.

It was resurrection Sunday. Two women had gone to Jesus' tomb and found it empty. All they'd hoped for had come true! They raced back to tell the disciples, but the disciples didn't believe. The two men walking the road to Emmaus didn't believe, either.

Maybe you can remember finding out that your parents were the Tooth Fairy or that the Santa at the mall was really a dressed-up grandpa, doing his job. Do you remember how you felt? Did you feel cheated, disappointed, or angry? Did you feel that you'd been lied to? Imagine how these men felt. They thought Jesus was the *Messiah*—but they'd watched Him die.

The Bible says that as they walked along, they talked about everything that had happened. They were focused on the past. Their talk was not of hope that this was the third day and that Jesus was somewhere alive. As far as they knew, their hopes were dead and buried.

It's hard for us to imagine that the men didn't recognize Jesus when He started walking beside them. It wasn't until they had reached Emmaus and Jesus was eating with them that they finally realized who their Companion really was. Imagine their excitement! He had kept His promise! Good news had come from the bad! Hope was alive!

I think that at times we're like those two men. When we're bummed out, we walk along with our heads down. We think only of the past and all the bad things that happened. We don't have any hope for the future. And our sadness makes us blind to the fact that we're not walking through the tough times alone. But Jesus is walking right beside us! How do I know? Because He promised us thousands of years ago: "I will never leave you nor forsake you" (Hebrews 13:5, NKJV). In other words, on your road of life, He's got your back.

APRIL 8

Midnight Celebration

For the Son of Man came to seek and to save the lost. Luke 19:10, NIV.

My dad has always said that Mom was the nicest atheist he'd ever met! She just couldn't be convinced that there really was a God.

"I'd been around too many 'weird' Christians," she once told me. "I attended a church once with my older sister. At the end of the sermon, I was basically dragged up to the altar by two women and told I must repent, because if I got in a car wreck and died, I would go to hell!"

When Dad became a Christian, and then we kids, too, Mom thought she'd lost us to something she could never be a part of. I'd never heard her speak an unkind word in my life, so I was shocked when I heard her tell Dad, "You live with God on your side of the house, and I'll live without Him on mine."

What did we do? We prayed! And we set the best example we could of what a Christian is like. I was 10 at the time, my sister 12, and my brother 14. We lived our lives as a witness to Mom. Don't ever think you're too young to make a difference for God. The way you live your life does matter!

We didn't know it at the time, but just as today's verse says, Jesus was out to seek and save my lost mom. She noticed such a big difference in us—especially in Dad—that she began to wonder if she was missing out on something. We weren't "weird" at all! We were happy and had given up our bad habits. So when Dad went to work and we went to school, she would open Dad's Bible and read it.

One night a few months later, after we'd all gone to bed, Mom couldn't sleep. She tossed and turned. She actually felt the presence of Jesus in their bedroom, and He was knocking on her heart's door. She fought it for some time, but then she awakened Dad and said, "I want to pray." Dad bolted up and said, "What?" She repeated herself, and then they knelt across the bed from each other for about 30 minutes. Dad doesn't know what Mom said to God, but when she got up off her knees, she was a changed woman.

They woke us up, crying. I can still see their tear-streaked faces and hear Dad saying, "Your mom just gave her life to Jesus!" Dad built a fire in the family room fireplace, Mom made hot chocolate, and we celebrated! Our family now felt whole.

APRIL 9

Help Is on the Way

I know what it is to be in need, and I know what it is to have plenty. I have learned the secret of being content in any and every situation, whether well fed or hungry, whether living in plenty or in want. I can do all this through him who gives me strength. Philippians 4:12, 13, NIV.

I mentioned back in January that my husband went to Haiti after a devastating earthquake in 2010. Some of you might remember seeing it on the news. I remember feeling helpless as I watched. So many people had lost their family, friends, home, business, and all they called their own.

The earthquake had killed nearly 225,000 people and left more than a million homeless! Imagine everything you cared about turned into rubble. Imagine not being able to drive to an emergency room for your injuries, but having to wait in line outside a makeshift clinic. Imagine having your stomach ache with hunger, but having no food to eat. Imagine the smell of death as truckload after truckload of corpses is driven down the street, headed for mass graves.

The news story that troubled me most was the story of a woman who was grieving. The news didn't mention her name but just said that she was wearing an orange dress. Five days after the quake, she was seen walking the streets downtown where corpses were being burned. Pulling out a copy of the Bible from her dress pocket, she flung it into the fire.

When I heard this story, I thought, *The Haitians are very much like us. We both have a choice when tragedy strikes. We can blame God, or we can trust Him. We can run from God, or we can run to Him. We can hate God, or we can love Him.*

To say there is no God is to say there is no plan or purpose. To fling your Bible into the flames is to throw away the very words that bring hope. But to hold on to God and the promise of heaven will not only help you make it through this life, it will take you on to eternal life. A place where God has promised, "I, the Lord, will be your everlasting light, and your days of sorrow will come to an end" (Isaiah 60:20, CEV).

You can't choose which tough things come your way, but you *can* choose the outcome. You can choose whom you blame, what you learn, and what you do with God. The best choice is to hold on to the One who will someday come to your rescue and end your days of sadness, loneliness, and loss. Don't give up now! Help is on its way in the form of the Second Coming.

APRIL 10

The Woman in the Orange Dress

And this gospel of the kingdom will be preached in all the world as a witness to all the nations, and then the end will come. Matthew 24:14, NKJV.

If you read yesterday's devotional, you read the story about the woman in the orange dress. That story troubled me for days. I wanted so badly to go to Haiti and find her. I wanted to listen to the reasons she threw her Bible into the fire of burning corpses. Whom or what had she lost? Was God now dead to her, too? Did she no longer believe His Word, so she burned it?

If I could find her, I would first listen to her, and then I would give her *hope*. I would explain to her that the earthquake was not an act of God, and that He is preparing a better place for her where earthquakes will never happen.

But I couldn't go, so I did the next-best thing. I decided to send something with my husband, Keith, when he went for his two-week mission trip. Knowing he didn't speak their language, I bought several little cards with a picture of Jesus on them. Jesus' face looked kind and gentle. I gave them to Keith on the day he left and asked, "If any women wearing an orange dress come to your clinics, *please* give them one of these pictures. I know it's a shot in the dark, but just maybe one of them will be the woman who threw her Bible in the fire." So off they went to Haiti, with a prayer from me that the woman would come.

Whenever Keith was able to call home during those weeks, I'd anxiously ask him, "Has a woman wearing an orange dress come to the clinic yet?" But each time the answer was no. And when he finally came home, the cards came with him.

I still have those cards with the picture of Jesus on them today. I'm not sure what to do with them, so I'll keep them until I know. In the meantime, they're a reminder to me. A reminder that there are many people out there in the world—and in my own little world—who need to know that God is kind, caring, and compassionate.

Today's text says that the gospel of the kingdom needs to be preached everywhere—including at your school. What is the gospel? It's the good news! In its simplicity, it's this: Sin came into the world, and the world needed to be rescued. Jesus rescued it by dying for everyone. He returned to heaven to build us new homes and will someday come back to get us.

So there *is* hope. And Jesus needs you to pass it on!

My Hero

I think about you before I go to sleep, and my thoughts turn to you during the night. You have helped me, and I sing happy songs in the shadow of your wings. I stay close to you, and your powerful arm supports me. Psalm 63:6-8, CEV.

This devotional book is dedicated in memory of my brother, Dan. I'm thinking about him today because he died of cancer on this date. Although it's been eight years, I still miss him so much! It's not as rough now as it was those first few years, but I still sometimes ache when I think of him.

Today's text was one of Dan's favorites when he was sick. Nights were especially tough for him, so this text meant a lot. The way Dan lived the final months of his life was an inspiration to many—especially to me. And I wanted to tell him so. Near the end he became so weak that we had to take him to the emergency room. Alone with him there, I took his hand.

"Dan, I have something to tell you, and I really need you to hear me, OK?"

"OK," he said in a weak voice.

"You're an inspiration to me," I said. "You've gone through so much, and yet you don't complain. You never give up. Watching you go through this makes me feel that I can face whatever tough things might come my way. *You're my hero.*"

"Thanks, Nanc," he said, with tears in his eyes.

Dan fought his battle with cancer emotionally by choosing to dwell on the positive and thinking of others. Whenever negative thoughts haunted him, he rejected them for positive ones. And he fought spiritually in a powerful way. He began each new day of life with God, thankful to be alive. His strength came from choosing—choosing to read his Bible, choosing to fill his home with worship music, and choosing to pray. He shared his most private and personal thoughts with God—his fears, his worries about leaving his wife and kids, his pain—yet he never blamed God. He knew that the enemy had caused this, not God.

Today's text also saw him through his final moments. Even on his deathbed he remembered God, and God's powerful arm did support him. When Dan could no longer speak, our dad leaned over and said, "Dan, we'll meet in heaven."

And Dan nodded. He knew the final outcome. Praise God, he knew!

APRIL 12

The Hope Card

Yet what we suffer now is nothing compared
to the glory he will reveal to us later. Romans 8:18, NLT.

When the first-year anniversary of my brother's death got closer, I began dreading it. Our family had just completed our year of "firsts" without him. Maybe your family knows what that's like after having someone you love die. The first Thanksgiving. The first Christmas. The first birthday. The first graduation. The first family barbecue. Now I was dreading that one-year mark. The images of his final day were still so vivid in my mind, and the last thing I wanted to do was sit and relive them.

So I made the choice to do something different with that day. Something better. Something that would encourage the rest of my close-knit family.

I bought a set of blank cards, one for each member of our family. On the outside of the card was just one word—HOPE. Inside each card I wrote these words:

April 11, 2007 — April 11, 2008
We're one year closer to seeing Dan again!
Then our family will be together forever!
"For the Lord himself shall descend from heaven, with a shout,
with the voice of the archangel, and with the trump of God:
and the dead in Christ shall rise first; then we that are alive,
that are left, shall together with them be caught up in the clouds,
to meet the Lord in the air: and so shall we ever be with the Lord.
Wherefore comfort one another with these words"
(1 Thessalonians 4:16-18, ASV).

It was a deliberate choice on my part to view the one-year anniversary in a hopeful way. I could have been consumed by the thought that it had been one long year since I'd seen my brother. But instead I chose to focus on the fact that I was one year closer to the second coming of Jesus and seeing Dan again!

Did I miss him on that one-year anniversary? Oh, yes! Did I cry? A bucket of tears! Yet at the same time I had a steady sense of hope that was even stronger than my grief, because the One who conquered death has promised a resurrection. And I believe with all my heart that it will someday be a reality for me and my family—and for you and your family, too.

APRIL 13

Hugs From God

The eternal God is our hiding place;
he carries us in his arms. Deuteronomy 33:27, CEV.

A few weeks ago I was at a Christian gathering for teens, their families, and their youth groups. There were quite a few kids walking around wearing T-shirts that read, "Free Hugs." I was surprised at how many kids walked up to other kids they didn't even know to get a quick hug. I guess a lot of kids feel the need for a hug once in awhile.

Do you ever feel the need to be hugged? When you're sad or lonely, do you wish that someone would come and just wrap their arms around you? Then you'd feel safe and loved, protected and cared for.

When I read today's text, it actually brought tears to my eyes. To imagine Jesus wrapping His arms around you and me and carrying us in His arms was a heartwarming thought. And even though Jesus can't be there to physically hug you when you're hurting, He's done the next best thing. He's written you a letter full of "word hugs." It's your Bible. Here are just a few of the words He has to say to you today:

"I give you peace, the kind of peace that only I can give. It isn't like the peace that this world can give. So don't be worried or afraid" (John 14:27, CEV).

"This is how God showed his love for us: God sent his only Son into the world so we might live through him. This is the kind of love we are talking about—not that we once upon a time loved God, but that he loved us and sent his Son as a sacrifice to clear away our sins and the damage they've done to our relationship with God" (1 John 4:9, 10, Message).

"For the Lord your God is living among you. He is a mighty savior. He will take delight in you with gladness. With his love, he will calm all your fears. He will rejoice over you with joyful songs" (Zephaniah 3:17, NLT).

"Give all your worries and cares to God, for he cares about you" (1 Peter 5:7, NLT).

"See how very much our Father loves us, for he calls us his children, and that is what we are!" (1 John 3:1, NLT).

"I love all who love me. Those who search will surely find me" (Proverbs 8:17, NLT).

These are just a few of the *thousands* of texts in the Bible that feel like hugs from God. Go searching for more. I promise that you won't be disappointed!

APRIL 14

Choking on Cherries

Quit dabbling in sin. Purify your inner life. Quit playing the field. Hit bottom, and cry your eyes out. The fun and games are over. Get serious, really serious. Get down on your knees before the Master; it's the only way you'll get on your feet. James 4:8-10, Message.

It was a warm summer day, and 10-year-old Allen was home alone, bored. So he went outside to use his imagination. He noticed that the door to the shed was open. The forbidden shed! Mom had told him never to go inside because that's where she kept all her canned food in glass jars. Walking closer to the shed, he saw the sun sparkling on jars of juicy, plump cherries. His favorite!

As he walked closer, he thought, *I'll just close the door.* When he got to the door, he thought, *I'll just go inside and take a look.* When he got inside, he thought, *I'll just take down one jar and eat a few cherries, then put it back. Mom won't even notice.*

So he took a jar and climbed up on the roof of the shed. He lay there in the sun and started eating those delicious cherries. Before he knew it, almost half of the jar was gone. *Oh, no!* Allen thought. *Mom will notice for sure now!* But before putting them back, he decided to have just one more. So he plopped one last cherry into his mouth. But it got stuck in his throat. He couldn't breathe!

Allen panicked and jumped off the shed. *I'm going to die!* he thought, because he knew no one was home to help him. He raced toward the house, ran up the steps, opened the door . . . and ran smack into his mom! She had just gotten home and had seen the look on Allen's face as he ran toward the house. She knew something was wrong. So she bent him over and gave him a hard whack on the back, and the cherry popped out.

Temptation is like that, isn't it? We see something that we think looks good, and we decide it won't hurt just to take a look. Then we think, *I'll do this just once, and no one will ever find out.* But we do it again and again until we're hooked. Then we realize what we're doing and think, *Just once more . . .* And that's the time we choke.

Is God there when we're choking and gasping for breath? Yes. But wouldn't it be better not to even let it get that far? Wouldn't it be better to walk away when we first see that the shed door is open? I think so.

Welcome Home!

Who dares accuse us whom God has chosen for his own? No one—for God himself has given us right standing with himself. Who then will condemn us? No one—for Christ Jesus died for us and was raised to life for us, and he is sitting in the place of honor at God's right hand, pleading for us. Romans 8:33, 34, NLT.

What would you do if you received a letter in the mail today telling you that someone had left you an inheritance? And what if that inheritance was *thousands of dollars*? I can hear you thinking! Would you go to Disneyland every year for the rest of your life? Would you buy a Wii and all the games the system offers? Would you grab all the designer clothes and shoes you want? Would you purchase a red Mustang convertible and garage it till you're 16?

One of my favorite stories in the Bible is the story of the prodigal son. He asks his dad for his inheritance ahead of time and leaves home for what he thinks will be an exciting life. But he wastes every last penny on partying. And the only job he can find is working on a farm, feeding pigs. He gets so desperate and hungry that even the pigs' food looks good to him! Have you ever seen or smelled pigs' food? Just imagine a week's worth of leftovers all mixed together!

Finally, the son decides to go home to see if his dad will give him a job as a servant. Even that would be better than his life now. So he heads home. And then comes the awesome part of the story: "When he was still a long way off, his father saw him. His heart pounding, he ran out, embraced him, and kissed him. The son started his speech: 'Father, I've sinned against God, I've sinned before you; I don't deserve to be called your son ever again.' But the father wasn't listening. He was calling to the servants, 'Quick. Bring a clean set of clothes and dress him. Put the family ring on his finger and sandals on his feet' " (Luke 15:20-22, Message).

Jesus told this story because we are like the son. We sometimes think that life without God would be more exciting. We could party all we want without any rules. But we'd soon learn what the son learned. It's not better. It's worse. It's lonely. And it's full of guilt.

When we decide to return, God is like the dad in this story. He's been waiting, and He comes to meet us! He doesn't yell, "Where have you been? You're going to have to pay for this!" No, He lovingly says, "Welcome home! You're forgiven. And I've already forgotten what you did wrong."

APRIL 16

A Free Ride

Would any of you give your hungry child a stone, if the child asked for some bread? Would you give your child a snake if the child asked for a fish? As bad as you are, you still know how to give good gifts to your children. But your heavenly Father is even more ready to give good things to people who ask. Matthew 7:9-11, CEV.

I was driving on a dark, rainy Tuesday night with a carful of junior high kids. It was a weekly routine for me. I would crisscross our town, picking up kids who wanted to go to our church's youth group. The kids all knew that I was a willing taxi driver and would often call our daughter and ask, "Can you guys pick me up and take me to the church tonight?" No matter how far we had to drive, we always said yes unless we had a full car. On this particular night two kids who called had to stay home because we were full.

I had been praying that God would somehow provide me with a vehicle large enough to take more kids to youth group—and I even prayed that it would be free! I knew we couldn't afford one. Only my husband, daughter, mom, and one prayer-warrior teenage boy knew what I had been asking of God.

As I was driving along that night, my cell phone rang. My sister, who lives nine hours away, was calling me out of the blue. "Hey," she said. "Would you by any chance want our van? We have a newer car now, and I don't know why, but something urged me to call you and offer our van for free."

"Did Mom talk to you?" I asked in shock.

"No. Why?" she asked.

I was overwhelmed! It was exactly what I'd prayed for! "I can't talk now," I told her as I choked back the tears. "I'll call you as soon as I get home."

One week later a friend of theirs delivered the van. A van that seated eight people! For free! The kids were ecstatic and treated it like they owned it. And in a way, they did. Week after week I'd drive around town and out in the country to pick up kids for youth group.

Why did Jesus answer my prayer? Why did He impress my sister to offer me the van for free? The answer has always been a simple one for me: *Jesus loves kids!* And He wanted all those kids to make it to youth group so they could get closer to Him.

APRIL 17

Worth the Wait

God wants you to be holy. You must keep away from sex sins. God wants each of you to use his body in the right way by keeping it holy and by respecting it. You should not use it to please your own desires like the people who do not know God. 1 Thessalonians 4:3-5, NLT.

I didn't know Andrew and Cate when they first came to my office for an appointment, but I instantly liked both of them. I also ached for both of them. They were older teenagers who had been dating for a few months, and they were both concerned because they felt their relationship was going too far too fast. Things were getting way too intense physically.

Since their relationship began as a physical one, I suggested that they back off and become friends. They needed to get to know each other's minds and hearts—not each other's bodies.

They impressed me by setting up a list of dating rules that covered a 10-week period. They would spend their dates getting to know each other on a heart level. In time they would add appropriate physical contact but never allow themselves to go as far as they had gone before. They actually wrote this out as a contract, and each signed it in front of me.

Did it work? They broke the contract in the first week! I'm sharing their story with you because even though you're not quite old enough to go out on dates yet, before you know it, that time will come. It's a fun and exciting time! But it's also a time that you need to prepare for.

Now is the time to ask yourself questions like: What are my own personal standards going to be when I go out on dates? Am I going to be a guy who respects girls, or uses them? Am I going to be a girl who flirts her way into a shallow physical relationship, or respect myself enough to let my values be known? How far do I want to go physically before I get married?

As Andrew and Cate learned, once you get all physical in a relationship and go too far, it's pretty hard to back up and start over. My wish for you is that you think ahead and plan ahead when it comes to dating. Then, when you find just the right guy or girl to marry someday, you won't have regrets from past relationships.

Will you be missing out on some fun during your teen years? No, it will be worth the wait! I've never met an adult who said, "I wish I had fooled around more before marriage. I really feel I missed out!" But I've lost count of the ones who've said, "I wish I hadn't . . ."

APRIL 18

If at First You Don't Succeed . . .

Keep on being brave! It will bring you great rewards. Learn to be patient, so that you will please God and be given what he has promised. As the Scriptures say, "God is coming soon! It won't be very long!" Hebrews 10:35-37, CEV.

My dad put me on a horse when I was just 2 years old, and that's all it took. I've been a horse lover all my life! He bought me my first pony when I was 7—a little brown-and-white Shetland pony named Muffin. She was a spirited and stubborn pony, and I shed many tears out of frustration because of that, but I loved her. When I was 10, we sold Muffin and bought me a bigger pony named Princess. And it was Princess who taught me how to be a good rider. She was a great horse and would do whatever I asked. But I outgrew her, so when I was 13, Dad bought me a half quarter horse, half thoroughbred filly I named Lady Taro—in honor of her sire.

I spent hours on long summer days, and even after school, riding and training my horses. But it wasn't always easy. I've been kicked, bitten, bucked off, butted, thrown, and stepped on. But each time I started to fear horses, Dad told me that I needed to get back on and keep riding. The longer I waited, the harder it was to get back in the saddle. If I had quit riding out of fear, I would have missed out on years of fun and adventure!

Have you ever tried something that didn't go quite right, and you were tempted to give up? Maybe you got smacked in the face by a spiked volleyball. Maybe you fell and twisted your ankle ice-skating. Maybe you crashed your dirt bike and got skinned up pretty bad. Or maybe you fell water skiing and drank half the lake! The important thing to do is to get up, straighten your back, and try again. You may be scared to death, but it feels so good when you conquer your fear and reach your goal!

Even more important than succeeding at sports is never to give up on your friendship with Jesus. I've met people who have given up. They give their lives to Him, but then they give in to temptation again and again, and they just give up. They say, "What's the use? I keep on failing. I've probably done too many bad things to come back to God." Nothing could be further from the truth! God isn't sitting up in heaven keeping score of the number of times we mess up. He doesn't tally them and say, "Well, that's it! You might as well not try again, because you'll never make it to heaven!" Instead, He wants us to get back in the saddle and try again.

Modern-Day Mary

"Then neither do I condemn you," Jesus declared. "Go now and leave your life of sin." John 8:11, NIV.

She was like a modern-day Mary Magdalene. Most kids in Allison's class knew what kind of life she'd been living. So when she was asked to give the baccalaureate graduation talk, she decided to be honest and lay her life out before them. Most of us listening sat there with tears in our eyes at the wonder of how Jesus can change a life. Here's some of what she said that day:

"I started struggling with everyday life. I fell into a deep depression that I couldn't escape. I wouldn't accept help, which made everything and everyone slip away. The worst part is that I let go of God. I acted out and did whatever I felt like doing. I made some horrible choices and ignored all the help people tried to give me. I was doing things that I knew were wrong. I felt God trying to reach me again and again. It was as if He was saying, 'What are you doing?'

"But instead of listening, I started taking advantage of God. I would say to myself, 'He'll forgive me later.' It's sad for me now that I have to look back on this year of my life and not be proud of my choices. There are so many things I wish I could change, and so many people I wish I could say 'I'm sorry' to. But what's done is done. I cannot change the past.

"God appeared when I hit rock bottom. I had no one. Secrets were out, and my mistakes were now catching up with me. But then I stopped. I stopped and thought about what I was doing. Why wasn't I happy anymore? I used to be. And I realized it was because I'd let God slip from my life. Something told me that I needed to run back into His arms. I told myself I was done hiding. Just last week I told myself that hiding from God was not helping, and I realized that I'd been so much happier when God was a part of my life.

"It was hard accepting God's love again. But I realized that He knows we're going to make mistakes. He even knows what mistakes we're going to make before we make them! And despite all this, His love will always be there. He is holding us, and He will never let go."

Allison wanted me to share her story because for you it's not too late. You're not quite teenagers yet or are just beginning your teen years. You don't have to get to your senior year and look back with regrets. *Right now, that past is still your future.* And you get to write it! Choose now how you want to feel when you look back from your senior year. Choose Jesus.

APRIL 20

From Scarecrow to Crow

Whenever people are jealous or selfish,
they cause trouble and do all sorts of cruel things. James 3:16, CEV.

Brady loved acting! He had devoted the past eight years of his spare time to plays and musicals. He and his two best friends were expected to get the lead roles in the next musical.

"We were top dog," Brady proudly told me. "We practiced and knew our lines really well. We were *so* swag."

He'd hoped for the part of the scarecrow in the musical, and everyone just assumed he'd get it, because he was perfect for the part.

The day after auditions, he and his two friends went to check the board at school to see if they'd made the first callback list. His friends' names were on the list—but Brady's wasn't. This was the first time in eight years that his name wasn't listed! *Maybe the director just forgot to put my name down,* he rationalized to himself. But a few days later his name wasn't on the second callback list, either. And the names that were on the list weren't even experienced actors!

When the final list of cast members was posted, Brady's name was *finally* on the list. But he didn't get the lead as the scarecrow. He got the part of a crow! Even though he was an experienced actor and singer, his only lines in the play were, "Caw, caw!" while he flapped his wings on stage.

"I had a sourpuss attitude," he later told me. "Everyone expected me to get the big part. Some kids teased me by saying things like 'Well, at least you can fly!' I was pretty hard on myself. I kept asking myself questions like 'What did I do wrong? Am I even good at acting?'

"The green-eyed monster of jealousy took over," Brady admitted. "I started acting up in drama class and was disrespectful to the teacher. And I hoped like everything that the guy who got the part of the scarecrow would somehow mess up on opening night.

"Then I found out from our teacher that the kid who got my part was going through a tough time. His parents were getting a divorce, and he felt like his world was falling apart. The teacher told me that I could be a good influence on this younger kid by supporting him.

"On opening night the scarecrow did a great job. He gave it his all, and I decided to give it my all, too—even though my only job was to flap my wings and call out, 'Caw, caw!' "

APRIL 21

The Evangelist

But you are the ones chosen by God, chosen for the high calling of priestly work, chosen to be a holy people, God's instruments to do his work and speak out for him, to tell others of the night-and-day difference he made for you—from nothing to something, from rejected to accepted. 1 Peter 2:9,10, Message.

I remember how excited I was to go to church that night. An evangelist was coming to tell his conversion story. The lights lowered as he stepped up to the pulpit to preach.

"Sometimes you have to lose everything to gain something. I used to think I had everything I needed to be happy," he said. "There was a time in my life when I felt I had arrived. I had it all: a family, a great job, a nice house, and social status in the community. But one night, returning home from a party in our expensive car, I turned to my wife and said, 'I don't know what it is, but something isn't right. Something is wrong with my life. Something is missing.'

"While driving to work the next morning, I cursed the world. It had promised me something it couldn't give. I felt like there was a hole in my soul, and nothing was filling it. For the next several days I felt confused and depressed.

"In desperation to find peace, late one night I opened a Bible that a relative had accidentally left at our house. I said to God, 'All right, God, I'll give You 30 days. I'm going to read this book of Yours and check You out—to see what You're all about.'

"God never forces Himself on anyone. He lets us choose, even if we make the wrong choice. But as I read night after night, it was as if He was saying, 'Here's home if you want it.'

"My wife was watching me very closely, and my kids were wondering what was happening to Dad. A change was taking place. Jesus was making His way into my heart, and I wasn't trying to stop Him! My friends were amazed at the change in me. But even more amazed was my family. I tossed my cigarettes, stopped cursing, and spent my evenings reading the Bible.

"Late one night I put my Bible aside and went to my knees. The next morning I woke up a new man. When I walked into the office, I couldn't keep the good news to myself! I told my friends that I had made the decision to become a Christian. And my life was forever changed."

The man behind the pulpit turned blurry as tears filled my eyes. His story had touched my heart and changed my life forever. And that's understandable. The evangelist was my dad.

APRIL 22

Save the Worms!

Then God said, "Let the waters swarm with fish and other life. Let the skies be filled with birds of every kind." So God created great sea creatures and every living thing that scurries and swarms in the water, and every sort of bird—each producing offspring of the same kind. And God saw that it was good. Genesis 1:20, 21, NLT.

This story would be humorous if it weren't so touching.

My husband, Keith, and I were walking the track at an athletic field in our town. It had rained throughout the day, and there were worms *everywhere* on the track! People jogging or walking before us had smashed some, but many were still alive. They had crawled out of the grass and onto the track to keep from drowning during the heavy rain.

As we walked, we noticed an elderly man who kept bending over and picking up things off the track. Then he'd walk into the grassy area, bend over again, and then go back to the track. As we got closer to him, Keith said, "He's picking up worms!"

Sure enough, we watched him rescue one worm after another. We watched from a distance as he picked up a long earthworm with a stick and gently laid it in his hand. Then he walked to the grass, parted the blades, and laid the worm down. We saw his lips moving, and Keith said, "He's talking to the worm!"

That did it for me! I thought about those of you reading this book and told Keith, "I need to talk to that man!" So we walked over to where he was.

"Quite a few worms out here to save, aren't there?" Keith asked him.

"Yes, there are," he answered. "I try give as many as I can a second chance at life."

"How long have you been doing this?" I asked. "How many worms have you saved?"

"Oh, I've been coming here for years. I suppose I've saved hundreds."

I had to ask, "What do you say to them when you put them back in the grass?"

"I tell them, 'Now you're safe. Have a good life.' And you know, sometimes a worm will raise its head and look at me as if to say, 'Thank you.' "

Today is Earth Day, and God created this earth for you to take care of and enjoy. Look around you—at your school, your home, your community. What might you save?

APRIL 23

No Green Grass

For a day in Your house is better than a thousand outside.
I would rather be the one who opens the door of the house of my God,
than to live in the tents of the sinful. Psalm 84:10, NLV.

Have you ever wondered what's "out there"? If the grass really *is* greener on the other side of the fence? Rich wondered as a teenager. He thought he could find happiness and meaning without God in the picture. He felt that God was overrated and that he didn't really need Him. Being a Christian was getting in his way. He didn't want rules—he wanted freedom! Besides, when he looked at people in the church, there were too many hypocrites. So he removed himself as far away as he could from his Christian family and his church.

By the time Rich was 17, he was lead singer of a rock band based in California. Their manager had them working on a project in a recording studio, and plans were in the works for a European debut. Sounds like an exciting life, doesn't it? But the excitement didn't last long.

One gig his band landed is especially memorable to Rich. They were invited to play at a high-profile celebrity party, and some of the biggest names in Hollywood would be there. An awesome opportunity! But while Rich was there, he saw some things that caused him to question where he was headed. The "famous" people that the world thought of so highly seemed so fragile. They had a vacant, hungry longing in their eyes.

During a break in the concert, Rich went outside to get some fresh air and noticed one of the celebrities leaning against a tree, vomiting. He was obviously wasted. Most of the people at the party had been drinking or smoking pot all evening. And then it struck him: many of these people weren't happy. Some of the successful actors, musicians, and producers he'd met on his journey weren't happy, either. They were miserable! The grass really wasn't greener on the other side of the fence. Rich had experienced that firsthand, and now he felt empty, too.

Several weeks after that party, Rich realized that he'd made a terrible mistake in thinking that fame and fortune could bring him happiness. *Maybe I should give God another chance,* he thought. *Maybe my view of God and Christianity has been twisted.* It dawned on him that Christians aren't perfect. The church isn't perfect. But Jesus is! Suddenly he realized that Jesus had everything he'd ever needed. He wouldn't need to go searching anymore. What he was looking for was right there in front of him. And it's right there in front of you, too.

APRIL 24

Cure for Bullying

God is sheer mercy and grace; not easily angered,
he's rich in love. He doesn't endlessly nag and scold,
nor hold grudges forever. He doesn't treat us as our sins deserve,
nor pay us back in full for our wrongs. Psalm 103:8-10, Message.

The day was *not* going the way I'd planned. I was so excited to be substitute teaching in a fifth- and sixth-grade classroom for a friend of mine. She would be gone for a few days, and I envisioned wonderful, peaceful days full of kids learning and feeling like one big happy family. But Jake changed all that.

Seriously, I'd never seen a kid be such a bully! He picked on everyone, it seemed, and especially the girls. He made fun of them. He poked them. He called them names. One girl came to me in tears because of something he'd said. Telling him to stop and even threatening in-school detention didn't help one bit. I wondered how I was ever going to get through to him.

Finally during the afternoon recess break he crossed the line when he shoved another kid in the hallway.

"Jake!" I called his name, exasperated. "You can't treat people that way!"

"Why shouldn't I?" he challenged me.

I blurted out without even thinking, "Because Jesus wouldn't treat people that way, and you want to be just like Him!"

Jake looked at me for a long while, almost confused. Then he turned around and walked away. He didn't cause any more problems that day, or any other day, and we became friends.

It's true. Jesus wouldn't bully other people. Which brings me to the question How *did* Jesus treat people? He treated the social outcast, a leper, with compassion when He reached out and touched him. He treated the town sinner, a woman caught in the act of sinning, with forgiveness when the crowd wanted to stone her to death. He treated the little guy, Zacchaeus, with acceptance when He went to his house for a visit. He treated a friend, Peter, with love even when he betrayed Jesus three times. And He treated the slow to learn, the Israelites, with patience when it took them 40 years to make it to the Promised Land.

That's how Jesus treated people—with compassion, forgiveness, acceptance, love, and patience. And that's how we should treat people, too.

APRIL 25

Give 'Em a Break

Keep on loving each other as brothers and sisters. Don't forget to show hospitality to strangers, for some who have done this have entertained angels without realizing it! Hebrews 13:1, 2, NLT.

I pass by it every time I go to the grocery store. There's a funeral home on the right-hand side of the road about halfway into town. When the parking lot is full, I know that a funeral is going on. When I see one or two cars there, I figure a family has gathered to make funeral arrangements. I usually see just cars there, not people.

But one day when I was driving into town, I noticed a car pulling out of the lot. A middle-aged woman was driving, and an elderly, hunched-over man sat in the passenger seat. My guess was that they had just made funeral arrangements for his wife, and her mom.

What struck me was how very sad they looked. Sad and tired. And I thought, *Whatever strangers they encounter today, no one will know what they're going through.* If she drives too slow and gets honked at, the irritated driver won't know that she's exhausted, or why. If he goes into a store and a group of teenagers rush by him, bumping into him, they won't know to stop and make sure that he's OK.

I have a friend who's an elementary school teacher, and she has a neat sign hanging in her classroom. It's a reminder to her students that they should always treat people with kindness. The quote says: "Be kind, for everyone you meet is fighting a hard battle." There's a lot of truth to that, isn't there? Although everyone's battle may not be hard right now, we all have battles to fight at one time or another. And since we don't always know what's going on in other people's lives, shouldn't we always treat them with kindness, just in case?

That girl who wasn't watching where she was going in the hall and knocked your books out of your arms? Her parents are getting a divorce. That boy who snapped at you during recess? His dad just lost his job. That elderly woman who was too slow at the grocery checkout when you were in a hurry? She has arthritis, and every movement hurts. Your teacher who seemed a bit cranky today? His mom was diagnosed with a terminal disease.

So don't they deserve a break? Don't they deserve our kindness? Yes, I believe they do. They deserve it because when we're hurting, we want to be treated with kindness, too. And they deserve it because they're also God's children.

APRIL 26

Clipping Toenails

They came to Capernaum. When he was in the house, he asked them, "What were you arguing about on the road?" But they kept quiet because on the way they had argued about who was the greatest. Sitting down, Jesus called the Twelve and said, "Anyone who wants to be first must be the very last, and the servant of all." Mark 9:33-35, NIV.

I did *not* want to do it, but there was no way out. It's not that I thought I was too good for the job. But honestly, I just thought it was . . . well . . . gross.

The summer when I was 15, a friend of my parents hired me to work at her classy retirement home. I would do odd jobs when needed. The first few weeks I served meals, did some grocery shopping, combed residents' hair, and visited with them.

Then one day the owner said, "Nancy, Mrs. Whipple needs her toenails clipped. She can't bend over far enough to do it herself. Would you please take care of that for me?"

What could I say? I had to say yes. I was an employee and couldn't pick and choose which jobs I wanted.

I walked into Mrs. Whipple's room. She was a pleasant woman with long white hair and sparkling blue eyes. As I took off her slippers and put her foot in my hand, I noticed that her toenails were long and yellow. I wished for a pair of gloves. *Well, here goes,* I said to myself.

As I started clipping, something changed inside me. I saw Mrs. Whipple as a person. A person who needed my help. I took my mind off myself and my dislike for long, yellow toenails, and put it on her. And that made *all* the difference.

Are there some jobs that you have to do at home or school that you dislike? Maybe you don't like to take out the stinky garbage. Maybe you don't like to clean the toilet. Maybe you don't like getting dirt under your fingernails when you weed the garden. Maybe you don't like putting away the smelly basketball gear. Maybe you don't like wiping another kid's food off the cafeteria table.

If ever I start thinking about jobs I don't like, I often stop and think about Jesus. He left perfect heaven to come to this messed-up world, and His whole life was about giving to others. He lived the life of a servant. I realized that day that I was clipping toenails what it feels like to serve. And you know what? It feels pretty good!

APRIL 27

Kirk's Wilderness Temptation

I often think of the heavens your hands have made, and of the moon and stars you put in place. Then I ask, "Why do you care about us humans? Why are you concerned for us weaklings?" Psalm 8:3, 4, CEV.

How could someone who was raised in a Christian home and was attending a Christian school decide to become an atheist? Sounds impossible, doesn't it? But that's just what happened to Kirk while he was on a solo backpack trip. He was hiking up a trail toward an alpine lake when, unexpectedly, doubts about God's existence flooded his mind. Suddenly he wanted proof! But since he thought he didn't have proof, he decided right then and there to stop believing in God. But his unbelief didn't last very long.

A few hours later, as Kirk hiked down toward his campsite, he began to notice his body in motion. His mind began to wander, and he thought about his digestive system—how it could somehow turn food into fuel for his body. He thought about his circulatory system—he could feel his blood pulsing in his hands as he hiked. He thought about his respiratory system—how his lungs filled with mountain air without him having to tell them to. He thought about his lymphatic system—how his white blood cells defended him against deadly germs. He thought about his brain—how it not only coordinates all the functions of his body, but how it could also reason intelligently. He thought about the amazing reproductive system—the miracle of being put together inside his mom's body. Kirk found himself awestruck at the incredible complexity of his body!

Then he began to look around him. The trees and grass produced the oxygen he breathed. He passed a stream and marveled that his own body was at least 60 percent water. From there his mind wandered to the vastness of the oceans and all the creatures living there. He looked up at the blue sky and remembered how it had been full of thousands of stars the night before. He thought about the earth itself, how it faithfully circles the sun at just the right distance, and how it's just one of billions of planets in the universe.

"Why is there such a deliberate and complex, life-supporting system?" he asked. "Who is behind it? Somebody simply has to be. There must be a God!" In that moment he began to believe again, and he has believed in God ever since. The proof had been there all along.

APRIL 28

Advice From Kindergarten

Then he said, "I tell you the truth, unless you turn from your sins and become like little children, you will never get into the Kingdom of heaven. So anyone who becomes as humble as this little child is the greatest in the Kingdom of heaven." Matthew 18:3, 4, NLT.

I had such a fun afternoon today! I helped out in a kindergarten Bible class. When the 5- and 6-year-olds found out that I was writing a book for "big kids," they were so excited and wanted to be a part of it. So I asked them a few questions, and here is your advice from kindergarten:

What should a big kid do if a friend tries to get them to do something that's wrong?

"Don't even *think* about doing it."

"Say, 'I don't want to do that.' "

"Say, 'Please stop trying to get me to do that.' "

"Just don't listen to them."

"Just walk away."

What should a big kid do if someone asks them to drink alcohol?

"Say, 'No!' "

"Don't, because you can get drunk."

"Don't, because it can make you sick and you can get a tummy ache and you can die."

"If you get in a car and drive, you'd be a crazy driver and could get in a car accident."

"It makes your mind not work well."

"It makes you not smart."

Don't you love their answers? Funny thing is, they're good ones! Their answers were so simple, yet such good advice: don't do it; say no; just walk away.

There was a time when it was that simple for you, too. Do you remember? Do you remember knowing a clear difference between right and wrong? Jesus said that we need to turn from our sins and become like little kids. And after talking with them today, I can see why.

God's Stain Remover

"Although you wash yourself with soap and use an abundance of cleansing powder, the stain of your guilt is still before me," declares the Sovereign Lord. Jeremiah 2:22, NIV.

I was so excited to wear my new blue top! Mom had bought it for me, and I loved it so much that I was careful not to get it dirty. Until dinner—when we had spaghetti. My brother was teasing me and bumped my elbow right when a forkful of spaghetti was almost in my mouth. It fell off my fork and landed on my beautiful blue top instead.

My brother felt so bad that he offered to help me get the stain out. "I know what to do!" he declared. "I've seen Mom take out stains with bleach."

So he took me to the laundry room, and we poured a bunch of bleach right on the stain. What he and I didn't realize is that you can use bleach only on white clothes. When I took my beautiful blue top out of the washer, the stain had turned into a white blob.

Sometimes things other than clothes get stained. Our minds get stained when we think unkind thoughts about someone. Our lips get stained when we speak words that hurt. Our eyes get stained when we watch bad movies or read books or magazines that aren't good for us. Our ears get stained when we listen to something that goes against the way we should live. And our hearts get stained when we choose our own selfish ways over God's.

When my friend Robyn was younger, she felt like her life was one big stain. She'd made a terrible mistake that she couldn't undo. She started drinking and smoking pot to try to numb the pain inside. She felt that God hated her, and she hated herself. Robyn had been carrying around that guilt and shame for *10 years* before I met her and told her that she didn't need to carry it anymore. I told her to stop punishing herself and let Jesus love her and forgive her.

Today Robyn says: "I thank God for His love and forgiveness. There are still days when the devil tries to bring back those feelings of worthlessness, and I have to remind myself that if God can forgive me, how can I not forgive myself? And if He loves me, how can I not love me?"

Jesus removed your sin stains 2,000 years ago. His stain remover was His own blood. Because He died on the cross in your place, He can make this promise: "If your sins are blood-red, they'll be snow-white. If they're red like crimson, they'll be like wool" (Isaiah 1:18, Message).

APRIL 30

It's Too Heavy!

Help each other in troubles and problems.
This is the kind of law Christ asks us to obey. Galatians 6:2, NLT.

I was sitting at a round table with a group of sixth graders when I asked this question: "What's hard about being a sixth grader?" Here were some of their answers:

"Having someone hit you."

"Having your mom yell at you."

"My sister telling me that I don't have a brain."

"My brother breaking his promise to me."

"Having your mom smoke."

"When my friends are mean to me."

Several weeks later I was in a junior high classroom speaking for morning worship and decided to ask them the same question: "What makes life hard for you?"

"Being overweight."

"Trying to be accepted."

"When my dad doesn't listen to me."

"My parents fighting."

"Trying to fit in is always hard."

"Adults being judgmental."

"My dad yelling at me."

"Divorce."

"When my mom died."

"Life itself . . ."

Who knew that when these kids walked into school that morning, they were carrying such heavy loads? They mask their pain with laughter, bad behavior, or withdrawn silence.

Today's text tells us to help each other out. How do you do that? By simply being there for someone. By helping them see that they're not alone. By being kind and supportive. By showing patience and compassion. By being like Jesus.

MAY 1

Why Pray?

But do not forget this one thing, dear friends: With the Lord
a day is like a thousand years, and a thousand years are like a day.
The Lord is not slow in keeping his promise, as some understand slowness.
Instead he is patient with you, not wanting anyone to perish,
but everyone to come to repentance. 2 Peter 3:8, 9, NIV.

Does it do any good to pray for people to come back to God? I mean, if everyone is given a free choice whether or not to accept Jesus, and they choose not to, what good could prayer do? I believe it does a lot of good! And so does Jazlynn. The day I met her, she told me this story of how prayer worked to bring her big sister back home and back to God:

"When my older sister turned 13, she gave her life to Jesus and was baptized. Things were going well for her until there was a death in our family, and we had to move. The move was tough on my sister, and she didn't make many friends in our new town. The friends she did make were either school dropouts or older kids who were already finished with school. Most of them were into drugs and other bad habits. When my family found out some of the things she was doing, we were all devastated! My sister withdrew from us and was usually out with friends or downstairs in her room, alone.

"My parents and I talked about how to help her, but we didn't know what to do. She was out of control, and no one could get through to her. Then one of us came up with an idea: we would pray for my sister! But not just once in a while. We would pray for her *every night*.

"At first nothing happened. My sister ran away a few times, and it really scared me. I would wonder if she was OK—even or if she was still alive. I worried that I might never see her again. When she finally returned home, she was deep into drugs, drinking, and wild parties.

"But then one day it happened. My sister realized that she'd better get her act together. That day she flushed all her drugs and alcohol down the toilet and started a new life. She came back to God and is going to church now, and she lives at home! Our family is together again."

Today's text says that one of the reasons Jesus hasn't come back yet is that He's waiting. He doesn't want anyone to miss out on heaven! He died for the person you're praying for. And He will do everything within His power to bring them back. So don't give up! Love, don't judge. Love, don't preach. God is working in a powerful way, even if you can't see it.

MAY 2

You Hypocrite!

Woe to you, teachers of the law and Pharisees, you hypocrites! You are like whitewashed tombs, which look beautiful on the outside but on the inside are full of the bones of the dead and everything unclean. Matthew 23:27, NIV.

Whoa! Those are some pretty strong words Jesus said to the teachers of the law and the Pharisees! But it made Him unhappy that they were being hypocrites—people who look like followers of God on the outside but are full of sin on the inside. Hypocrites made Sarah angry too. So angry that she decided to leave the church and God.

Sarah had grown up going to church. In fact, her dad was a pastor. She had the opportunity to see a lot of "behind the scenes" stuff that sometimes goes on at church. "I saw people who claimed to be Christians—even church leaders—living their lives opposite of what the Bible teaches," she told me. "It was like they didn't even read it, or they'd made up their own version of it, trying to justify themselves. Seeing that, I made the decision that I was going to hate Christians. They were all hypocrites. And that led to hating God. I was mad at God because I thought, *If people who know Him act like this, then He can't be all that great!*

"My junior high years were really, really bad years for me. I wouldn't let anyone get close to me because I figured that if I didn't let them in, I wouldn't get hurt. But that wasn't the answer. I was searching and searching . . .

"One day, when I happened to be sitting in a church, I finally let God in. The pastor was talking about forgiveness and how we need to forgive and let go, because if we don't, we'll never be able to move on with life. I finally broke down and forgave the people who had hurt me. I realized that everyone messes up. The people who claimed to be Christians were either people who were *truly* Christians and made mistakes, or they were people who were Christians in name only. I realized that you can never rely on humans. You can rely only on God."

How true that is! We can't judge the church or Christianity by the way people act. We're all puny humans. The only One we can look to with full confidence is Jesus. And He *is* perfect! He offers forgiveness when Christians fail, and He shows us an example of the right way to live.

MAY 3

Look! There's a Bear!

Don't panic. I'm with you.
There's no need to fear for I'm your God.
I'll give you strength. I'll help you. I'll hold you steady,
keep a firm grip on you. Isaiah 41:10, Message.

If only I hadn't watched that movie! That's what I said to myself during a Sabbath afternoon hike in May with my husband and daughter. Sure, I was a grown-up now. But when I was 10 years old, I'd watched a movie called *The Night of the Grizzly*. It was terrifying! And I'd feared bears from that day on.

We were hiking along a narrow, remote logging road, and I felt unsettled. The left side dropped down into a deep ravine, and the right side was covered in thick brush. I was leading the way when suddenly I saw some kind of animal race across the road and scramble up a tall fir tree. It was only about 50 feet away, but it moved so fast that I couldn't tell exactly what it was. Then another one ran across the road and up the tree. Now I stopped, and my husband walked up behind me. That's when a third one darted across the road and scampered up the tree.

"That was a bear cub!" my husband exclaimed.

"Well, I just saw two others run up the tree," I said. "So if those are cubs, then the mother bear must be . . ." But I didn't get to finish my sentence. Right then the mother bear came out of the brush. She was jet-black, and she was big! Even though she was on all fours, her head was higher than my waist! I froze and stared at her. She froze and stared at me. Several long seconds passed. Then with a huff she ducked back into the thick brush and was gone.

The three of us backed away nervously, watching the brush for the mother bear, until we were completely out of danger. I couldn't believe what had just happened! I'd faced my biggest fear since childhood—and I had survived!

After we had backed our way around the ravine and were at a very safe distance, my husband took out his binoculars, and we watched the cubs playing in the tree. I couldn't believe how cute they were! Then I saw bears in a whole new light. An animal to be respected, that's for sure. But I also saw how neat it was that the mama bear sent her cubs safely up the tree. How she studied me to make sure I wasn't going to hurt them. How she ducked into the bushes after she realized we weren't a threat. Bears are a part of God's creation that will be gentle in heaven.

What are you afraid of? Tomorrow we'll talk more about fear and how to handle it.

MAY 4

The Fear Factor

The angel of the Lord encamps around those who fear him, and he delivers them. Psalm 34:7, NIV.

As you know from yesterday's story, I used to be afraid of bears. I still have a healthy respect for them, but I no longer fear them the way I used to.

What are you afraid of? Are you afraid of the dark or of thunderstorms? Are you afraid of spiders or snakes? Are you afraid of heights or deep water? These things do call for caution, but you don't need to live in fear of them. You'll probably outgrow many of your fears in time. But with the right help, you can begin to conquer them now.

Here are some helpful things you can try if you have a specific fear, or if you tend to be a fearful person in general:

1. Decide whether your fears are valid or not. When our daughter was younger, for some reason she was afraid that something might be in her closet at night. Specifically, a skeleton with glowing, green eyes! We would open her closet door and show her that nothing was there. And that helped her see that her fear wasn't based on reality.

2. Think about what you watch and read. Scary movies and books *will* make you scared!

3. Read Bible texts that calm you. My favorite one when I was a kid is today's verse. And I still like that text! I like to picture angels surrounding me when I'm afraid. Another favorite is yesterday's text, Isaiah 41:10. Picture God being right there with you when you're afraid—because He really is! Even though you can't see Him, He always has your back.

4. Listen to calming music. Have some on your iPod, or set your radio to Christian music.

5. Talk about your fears. Talk to a parent, grandparent, teacher, pastor, school counselor—someone you trust. They can help you.

6. Talk to Jesus. He understands your fears better than anyone else, so talk to Him about them. Ask Him to heal you of fearful thoughts. Ask Him to be your Protector. Remember: He's got your back!

The best thing to do with fear is to take action. Face your fears head-on in a safe way, with adult input, if needed. You can defeat your fears! And when you do, you'll feel a little stronger, a little more grown-up, and a lot more confident!

MAY 5

Speaking the Same Language

There is neither Jew nor Gentile, neither slave nor free, nor is there male and female, for you are all one in Christ Jesus. Galatians 3:28, NIV.

Happy Cinco de Mayo to my Mexican friends! If you're not familiar with today's holiday, it's a day to celebrate Mexican heritage and pride all across America.

When our daughter was growing up, one of her best friends was a neighborhood girl named Nicole. Nicole moved from Mexico to the U.S. when she was 5 years old. She had great fun teaching us Spanish words and songs, and we had fun introducing her to certain American foods she'd never tasted. Her favorite was vegetarian hot dogs! Since she was a minority in our neighborhood, we made sure she always felt welcome and made new friends.

There was one day when I felt like I was the minority. I was attending the funeral of a Hispanic teenage boy in which the sermon, prayer, and music were all presented in Spanish. I carefully watched the faces of those presenting, trying to make sense of their language.

Partway through the service, my careful listening was interrupted by a different language—the sounds of crying, sniffling, and quiet moaning. It was the language of grief. I personally knew these sounds all too well, because I'd made them myself. I realized at that moment that even though I couldn't understand their particular language, grief sounds the same the world over. Why? Because from the United States to Uganda, from Bangladesh to Brazil, from Finland to Fiji, we all speak the same language of the heart.

So this is what I'm thinking: if we grieve the same for those we've lost, we must love the same. And if we love the same, we must be children of the same loving Father, which makes us brothers and sisters regardless of language, skin color, dress, or customs. And since we have the same Father, someday He'll take *all* His children home! The apostle John was lucky enough to actually see a vision of that day: "After this I looked, and there before me was a great multitude that no one could count, from every nation, tribe, people and language, standing before the throne and before the Lamb" (Revelation 7:9, NIV).

The world may try to separate us by nationalities, but according to today's text, in heaven we'll all speak the same language. It will be the language of love and unity. We might as well start speaking it now.

MAY 6

The Better Choice

I know what it is to be in need, and I know what it is to have plenty. I have learned the secret of being content in any and every situation, whether well fed or hungry, whether living in plenty or in want. I can do all this through him who gives me strength. Philippians 4:12, 13, NIV.

You know the feeling. You want something so bad that you can taste it! *Everyone* seems to have one, and you won't be happy until you get one, too. What is it for you? A certain skateboard? That brand of designer jeans? A particular bike? A well-known brand of popular shoes? But when you told your parents how much you wanted it, did they tell you: "Just be content with what you have"? If they did, that might have made you angry. But you know what? Their advice was actually good! And it's the apostle Paul's advice in today's text, too.

I think the key to contentment is found when he said that he has *learned* the secret of being content in any and every situation. Contentment doesn't come easy—it's something to be learned. Paul learned it by realizing that he could make it through anything because God would give him the strength he needed. He didn't say that he was thrilled about every situation or happy about every outcome. But he had learned to be content.

I know it's hard to want something and not be able to have it. When our family moved into a house less than half the size of the one we'd been living in, it was tough on me. A lot of what we owned had to go in boxes and off to a storage unit. I felt sorry for myself for a few days, and then I realized that I had wasted several days of life wishing for something that wasn't going to happen, at least for a while.

I realized that I had a choice. I could waste my days pouting about where I lived, or I could learn to be content by practicing a positive attitude, by looking for the good in this house, and by not letting it stop me from doing the things that make our family happy. So I decided to make the better choice. I didn't want to someday look back on our time here and realize that I'd thrown away days that could have built memories. So we still have company over for dinner, even though we don't have a formal dining room. We still put up a large Christmas tree and find places for *every* decoration. We still have out-of-town family come to visit, spreading cousins in sleeping bags across the floor. And our daughter still has large groups of friends over.

I've learned to be content. You can, too!

MAY 7

Get a Life

Trust God from the bottom of your heart; don't try to figure out everything on your own. Listen for God's voice in everything you do, everywhere you go; he's the one who will keep you on track. Proverbs 3:5, 6, Message.

You're really fortunate—did you know that? You're old enough to think for yourself as to what kind of future you want, yet young enough that you don't have a lot of regrets. So you get to decide now what the motto—the theme—of your life will be.

A few years ago I had the chance to meet Christian author and inspirational speaker Bob Lenz. He travels the country speaking to thousands of teenagers each year. He told me that he lives by several mottoes for his life. One is "No regrets," which is written on his dad's grave marker. Another is "Love well," which is written on his mom's grave marker. Yet another is John 17:3, which is written on his brother's grave marker. The text says, "This is eternal life, that they may know You, the only true God, and Jesus Christ whom You have sent" (NASB).

"What is life?" he asked me. "It's not hockey. It's not tennis. It's not fishing. It's not shopping. It's not the success of this world. John 17:3 tells us what life really is. *This* is life—it's to know Jesus! If you live your life for anything except for Jesus, it comes up empty. If hockey is life, the rest is just false teeth. If shopping is life, the rest is just credit card debt. If football is life, the rest is just bad knees.

"If you put your life in anything but Jesus, it can be taken away. Put it in Christ for salvation. Then how do you live your life? You live it with no regrets. If you've made mistakes in the past, you ask for forgiveness. Then you fulfill your destiny. How do you do that? You love well. The end isn't just saying 'yes' to Jesus. *It's then living it out.*"

Bob went on to say that it's not too late for kids who have messed up their lives to turn them around. "I met a girl just yesterday who was a 16-year-old recovering heroin addict," he said. "Her family was broken, so she turned to the popular kids at school. Then to the destructive things to find life. Christ took away her regrets and gave her hope and a plan for the future."

Are you ever confused, wondering what life is all about? *This* is life—to know Jesus. He makes life worthwhile. He makes sense of things.

MAY 8

Punched in the Gut

So you have sorrow now, but I will see you again; then you will rejoice, and no one can rob you of that joy. John 16:22, NLT.

I call them "gut-punchers." Here's how they happen. You can be going about an otherwise happy day when you see or hear something that reminds you of a loss. And it feels like you've been punched in the gut. There are many different scenarios for gut-punchers:

You tried so hard to make the basketball team, but the coach said you just didn't cut it. As you sit there watching a game, one of your friends makes a basket, and the crowd cheers. And you feel like you've been punched in the gut.

Your parents are going through a divorce, and one of them has moved out. At church you sit behind a family with both parents, and they all look so happy. And you feel like you've been punched in the gut.

It's grandparents' day at school, and you're having an OK day until lunchtime. You see all the other kids with grandparents, but yours aren't there because they have died. And you feel like you've been punched in the gut.

Your former best friend is mad at you. She won't even speak to you anymore. She passes you in the hall, laughing with her new friends. And you feel like you've been punched in the gut.

I've experienced my own gut-punchers. We all have them, although you may have a different name for yours. The question is, what do we do with them when they happen?

When I experience these moments, I acknowledge the pain. I don't think it's healthy to ignore pain by pushing it away. I might even cry a bit. But the most important thing is this: *I don't stay there.* Gut-punchers come from things we once held dear in our past, and we can't heal by dwelling on them. We have to look toward the future. And that's what I do.

I look forward to my new home in heaven. Revelation 21:4 says, "He will wipe all tears from their eyes, and there will be no more death, suffering, crying, or pain. These things of the past are gone forever" (CEV).

Wait. *Gone forever?* No more tears, death, suffering, crying, or pain? No more gut-punchers? Now that's something to look forward to!

The Red Ribbon

Many who are first will be last.
Many who are last will be first. Matthew 19:30, NLT.

I was going through my memory box the other day and pulled out a red ribbon. I held the now-wrinkled silk in my hand, remembering the valuable lesson it taught me . . .

It was Campus Day, and I had signed up to run the 50-yard dash. In preparation for the race, I asked my big brother to train and clock me. I ate well and got my sleep. My goal was to win—to bring home the prized blue ribbon and hang it on my bedroom wall above my bed.

I stood at the starting line on that warm, sunny morning. Mom was standing to my right in the crowd of parents, students, and teachers. To my left with the other runners stood my competition—Sandra. She was fast, and I knew it.

"On your mark," the judge hollered, "get set . . . GO!" I took off, my legs moving as fast as they could. Near the finish line, I realized that I was in the lead! I was winning! But then I made the mistake that any runner knows you don't make. *I glanced back.* I glanced back to see where Sandra was. She was just inches behind me, her long black hair blowing in the wind.

I honestly don't know who crossed the finish line first—Sandra or me. The judges argued about it for a moment until one of them marched over to Sandra, raised her arm up in the air, and declared, "Here's our first-place winner!" So she received the first-place ribbon, and I was given the second-place one—the red ribbon I still have today.

That day was the beginning of many times when I didn't come in first. My trio didn't win at the school talent show. My volleyball team didn't win in our region. And I didn't even place in the one horse show I entered. But you know what? I lived through those disappointments.

Who says you and I always have to be first? Or that being first is even always best? In fact, the Bible talks about another kind of winning. It seems that heaven has a different view on being first. Jesus said that whoever sacrifices here on earth in order to follow Him will receive a hundred times as much in heaven—plus eternal life! He then spoke the words in today's verse.

The last will be first? How can that be? Because God's kingdom is different from this world's. The world might say that following Jesus puts you in last place. But in heaven you'll receive the blue ribbon.

MAY 10

Lessons Mom Taught Me

Honor your father and your mother, so that you may live long in the land the Lord your God is giving you. Exodus 20:12, NIV.

I could probably write a book titled *Lessons Mom Taught Me.* I couldn't have written it when I was a child, or even a teenager. But now that I'm a mom, I realize that my mom's example taught me all along, and that I stored lessons in my head and heart that I'd later remember and use.

Mom taught me how to let kids be kids—which came in handy when I was a youth pastor and a substitute teacher for grades K-12. When I was a kid, I got to make mud pies and bring them inside. I even tasted one (without permission). Mom also let me bring outdoor treasures inside: bees in jars and crickets, ladybugs, frogs, and earthworms in shoeboxes got to spend the night in my room. And Mom was only slightly annoyed the day she found my pony standing in the living room. That particular pet didn't spend the night inside!

When I was a teenager, Mom taught me a lot about patience. Not so much by words, but by her actions. Like the time she showed patience when I insisted that I could give her hair a nice trim, and it turned out too short and lopsided.

But the greatest lesson Mom taught me was how to know God's love through a mother's love. To help us better understand His love, God likened it to a mother's: "As a mother comforts her child, so will I comfort you" (Isaiah 66:13, Message). I know the warm feeling of that kind of love. Mom was great at comforting me when my knee hurt because I'd skinned it; when my teeth hurt because I'd gotten braces; when my foot hurt because my horse had stepped on it; or when my heart hurt because someone had been unkind.

What lessons did your mom teach you? Today on Mother's Day why not remember some of them with her? If she has died, then remember with a sibling or other relative. If most of the memories of your mom are painful ones, think of what Psalm 27:10 says: "Even if my father and mother abandon me, the Lord will hold me close" (NLT). Moms and dads may sometimes disappoint us. After all, they're human. But God will always be the perfect parent. And in spite of your parents' flaws, in today's text God still asks us to honor them—to respect them. So honor your mom somehow today, and watch a smile come across her face.

MAY 11

Taming Your Tongue

If a person thinks he is religious,
but does not keep his tongue from speaking bad things,
he is fooling himself. His religion is worth nothing. James 1:26, NLT.

Ouch! Read today's text again. Wow! Really? If I don't keep my tongue from saying bad things, I'm fooling myself, and my religion is worth nothing? How can this be? Well, here's what I think.

Sometimes we misuse our tongues. We criticize. We judge. And we gossip about what we criticize and judge. But we don't have to be this way. It's a choice, really. We can choose what comes out of our mouths. No one else controls our words—we do.

So why would it be important to get in the habit of speaking well of others? Because according to Jesus, if we have a tongue problem, the diagnosis is that we really have a heart problem. He says in Matthew 12:34: "For the mouth speaks what the heart is full of" (NIV). The Message Bible makes it a little more direct: "It's your heart, not the dictionary, that gives meaning to your words."

Why is this? Because who we are—who we really are in our hearts—will come out of our mouths. So rather than just biting our tongue, what we need to do is to work on softening our hearts. And that comes by spending time with Jesus and imitating Him.

Here are some steps you can take to begin speaking well of others:

Step 1: Strive to be like Jesus. Daily read and think about how accepting, gentle, and loving He is. Read about how patient He was—even with the worst of sinners.

Step 2: Practice speaking well of others. When tempted to criticize, find something positive to say instead.

Step 3: Train yourself to look for the good qualities in people. Overlook their flaws the way you want others to overlook yours.

Step 4: Serve others. It's easier to have a critical tongue when you're living a self-centered life, and harder when your life is focused outside yourself.

Step 5: Pray this prayer at the beginning of every day: "Set a guard over my mouth, Lord; keep watch over the door of my lips" (Psalm 141:3, NIV).

Practice these steps, and you will be well on your way to taming your tongue!

MAY 12

Dying Wish

Stay on good terms with each other, held together by love. Hebrews 13:1, Message.

If you knew that you were going to die, and you could have one wish, what would it be? Would you wish to go to Disneyland? to be able to drive your own sports car? to swim with dolphins? to throw the first pitch at a major-league baseball game?

The night before Jesus died, He had a wish. But His wish wasn't for Himself. Of course it wouldn't have been. He'd spent His whole earthly life living for others.

That night He prayed a lengthy prayer to God the Father. You can read it in John 17. One of the things He prayed for touches me every time I read it, because He prayed for us—for you and me. After He prayed for His disciples He said, "I am not praying just for these followers. I am also praying for everyone else who will have faith because of what my followers will say about me." (That's us!) "I want all of them to be one with each other, just as I am one with you and you are one with me. I also want them to be one with us. Then the people of this world will believe that you sent me" (John 17:20, 21, CEV).

Of *all* the things that were on His mind that night, we were also on His mind. One of His dying wishes was that we would be one—that we would, as His children, be a loving family. And not only this, but that we might be one in the same manner that Jesus and God the Father are one. What a big challenge! But it must be doable, or He wouldn't have prayed for it.

I want us to help make Jesus' wish become a reality. To love each other. To get along. To treat everyone as an equal. To not judge. To not bully. To be close like Jesus and God are.

I've always said that if you expect to be in heaven, and the person you don't get along with expects to be there, you'd better start getting along now! Unity doesn't appear somewhere between earth and heaven at the Second Coming. You won't begin getting along with someone as you're riding the clouds toward heaven! It begins now. It begins today. It begins with you and I making that phone call, knocking on that door, or writing that letter to the person we're not getting along with. It's swallowing our pride and saying, "I'm sorry. I was wrong." It's saying, "I forgive you," when they ask for our forgiveness.

And by doing this, we can help make Jesus' wish come true.

Why Go to Church?

Some people have gotten out of the habit of meeting for worship, but we must not do that. We should keep on encouraging each other, especially since you know that the day of the Lord's coming is getting closer. Hebrews 10:25, CEV.

Doug was on his way to church with his family, just as he was every Sabbath. Then he dropped a bombshell: "I don't want to go to church anymore," he told his parents and siblings. "It's boring, it's full of old people, and it's just not fun." His family was shocked and hurt.

As it turned out, Doug needed a different view of church. He needed to see it as a place to worship, to share his talents, and to enjoy time with other Christians. Not just as a place to be entertained.

A few years ago, my husband was working on a project and decided to visit our church school to ask kids in grades four through six two questions. Here are some of their answers.

Question 1: What is a bad reason for going to church?

"To read the *Guide* magazine during the sermon."

"To get some sleep."

"To show off your clothes."

"To whisper with friends."

"To go out of fear that if you don't, you'll go to hell."

Question 2: What are some good reasons for going to church?

"To learn something."

"To get answers."

"To give *and* get a blessing."

"Because you *want* to."

"To thank God for all He's done for you."

Why do *you* go to church? Take some time today to think about it. You're old enough to go for all the right reasons. You're old enough to make the choice to find something useful in the sermons and songs. Next time you go to church, make it a goal to look for at least one thing that's positive—something that was said, sung, or read that brought you closer to Jesus. Then the next week, look for two, then three, and then four . . . It will grow on you!

MAY 14

Closed on Saturdays

So He came to Nazareth, where He had been brought up. And as His custom was, He went into the synagogue on the Sabbath day, and stood up to read. Luke 4:16, NKJV.

"I don't want to go to church anymore." That's what Doug told his parents in yesterday's story. What a contrast to our family friend Jim.

Jim had been attending evangelistic meetings that my dad was holding, and he was convinced that Saturday is the Sabbath. The proof was there in the Bible—he couldn't ignore that. And he wanted to start attending church. But there was a problem. Jim owned a gas station that was open seven days a week. He told Dad, "I want to start coming to church, but it makes me nervous to shut down on Saturdays. What if people take their business elsewhere?" Dad assured Jim that if he obeyed God, God would take care of him.

Dad was thrilled when he drove by the station on his way to church the next Sabbath and saw a sign in the window that read: CLOSED ON SATURDAYS. Jim did what he knew was right. He obeyed, and he obeyed out of love for God, not out of fear. And guess what? His decision didn't hurt his business—it actually grew! More customers came in six days than seven!

When I think of what Jim was willing to do in order to attend church, I think of all the excuses some give for *not* attending. See if any sound familiar: you're too tired; it's been a rough week; the pastor's sermons are boring; you don't like the style of music; you need to do homework; your favorite cartoons air on Saturday mornings; no one talks to you; the church is full of old, judgmental people; none of your friends go . . . and the list goes on.

I wonder what God thinks of all our lame excuses? Do they make Him mad? Actually, I think they make Him sad. Think of it this way: let's say you've planned an event at your house and you've invited all your friends to come. The day arrives, and you wait patiently for the clock to hit the very minute it's supposed to start. But you stand there alone in your house, waiting. No one comes. When you call and ask if they're coming, they all have excuses.

The church is God's house. And you're invited to an event at least once a week. It's a time to give back to God as we worship Him, to get encouragement from other Christians, and to give back to others as we serve—even by just saying an encouraging word. Plus, going to church can be something solid through all the ups and downs of growing up.

Snickers, the Indescribable Mutt

He'll wipe every tear from their eyes. Death is gone for good—tears gone, crying gone, pain gone—all the first order of things gone. Revelation 21:4, Message.

The night my dog Snickers died, I thought my heart would break. He somehow got free from the backyard and ran out into the road. A car hit him, and he died instantly.

I called him "Snickers, the Indescribable Mutt" because there were no words to describe him. I couldn't describe him as intelligent, because at night he'd sit out in the field and howl at the moon. I couldn't describe him as a dog with manners, because he'd eat a vegetarian hotdog in one swallow! I couldn't describe him as a refined dog, because he would come home from an adventure covered in mud or smelling like something dead. And I couldn't describe him as a dog with a good bloodline, because he was a mutt with no papers. But I loved him!

Snickers was like a best friend when I was a kid. I'd talk to him about my problems, take him on walks as he followed me while I was riding my horse, and sneak him into the family room on cold days when Mom wasn't watching. It was such a shock the night he died. We didn't know he'd escaped from the backyard. He was only trying to follow my brother, who was riding his dirt bike across the road.

Dad and I buried Snickers that night by flashlight beneath a tall fir tree that I could see from my bedroom window. And since Dad was a pastor, he gave a funeral talk. He also gave me his best white church shirt to wrap around Snickers. Before I laid him in the hole Dad had dug, I took off his dog collar, which I still have today. It was so very hard to say goodbye!

The next morning I asked Dad the big question: "Will Snickers be in heaven?"

Dad didn't even have to think about his answer. He said, "In heaven you won't be disappointed. Everything will be perfect. You won't cry, and you won't be sad. You'll always be happy. So if Jesus thinks you couldn't be happy in heaven without Snickers, then he'll be there." That answer was good enough for me!

Take another look at today's text. What do you look forward to the most about heaven? Is it seeing a pet that has died? Or bigger yet, a person who has died? Is it never feeling sadness again? Is it never having a reason to cry or feeling any kind of pain? These things will be gone—forever! Like Dad said, when you get to heaven, you won't be disappointed!

MAY 16

Guts for God

Be on guard. Stand firm in the faith.
Be courageous. Be strong. 1 Corinthians 16:13, NLT.

Have you ever done something really brave and someone praised you by saying, "Wow! That took guts!" It felt good, didn't it? They were basically saying that you're tough. You have a strong backbone. You have real courage.

So what if people said that about you and what you do for God? What if someone said, "Wow! You have guts for God!" Here are some examples of when it takes guts to be a Christian:

It takes guts for God to say, "I'm sorry. Please forgive me."

It takes guts for God to stand up for someone when they're being bullied.

It takes guts for God to walk away from a group that's gossiping.

It takes guts for God not to laugh at a dirty joke.

It takes guts for God not to look at inappropriate pictures in a magazine or online.

It takes guts for God to click the TV remote to a better channel.

It takes guts for God to turn the radio knob when you hear a song with bad lyrics.

It takes guts for God not to copy your friend's homework.

It takes guts for God not to lie.

It takes guts for God to explain why you're not attending a certain event on Sabbath.

It takes guts for God not to steal, no matter how badly you want something.

It takes guts for God to stand up for Him when most everyone else is sitting.

I believe that God is calling you today. Yes, *you*! He's calling you to stand for Him—for truth, for purity, for honesty—in a world where a lot of kids are weak and don't really stand for much.

Anyone can follow the crowd. That's easy. But *you* can be different. You can be like Esther, who had guts for God and stood up for her people in the presence of King Xerxes. You can be like Shadrach, Meshach, and Abednego, who had guts for God when they refused to bow down to an idol. You can be like Mary, who had guts for God when she surrendered her life's plans to become the mother of Jesus. It's a choice you can make. And I hope you will.

MAY 17

The Worst Nightmare Ever

Carry each other's burdens,
and in this way you will fulfill the law of Christ. Galatians 6:2, NIV.

It was a nightmare that my husband, Keith, will never forget. Not just because it was terrible, but because of the valuable lesson it taught him. A lesson on what it's like to truly empathize with someone.

Most of us do OK at sympathizing with someone—feeling sorry for them when they're going through a tough time. But to *empathize* with someone is different. When you empathize, you understand their emotions very well because you've been there yourself.

Back in 2004, Banda Aceh, Indonesia, had a massive earthquake that registered 9.1 on the Richter scale. It was the third strongest earthquake recorded in history. It triggered a tsunami that brought a 30- to 90-foot wall of water from the ocean onto the shore. Within minutes 125,000 people died in that one city alone. An organization Keith work for asked if he would go and spend a month there, working with a dentist to help survivors who had abscessed teeth. He jumped at the chance to go!

Two nights after he arrived, he bought a DVD that contained two hours of tsunami news—scenes that were too graphic to show on TV. He watched the unbelievable scenes at bedtime and then went to sleep.

That night he had a dream that our then 11-year-old daughter, Christina, and I were in Indonesia with him. Christina and I were in another part of town when an earthquake struck. After it was over, Keith went frantically searching for us. Finally he saw me walking toward him down a crowded street—alone.

"Where's Christina?" he asked me anxiously.

I was in shock as I answered, "I'm sorry . . . she didn't make it. But she's peaceful."

"No! No! No!" he shouted. "That can't be!" He ran, searching for Christina, and found her lying in a makeshift morgue with many other bodies. He knelt beside her to feel for a pulse in her neck, but there was none.

Thankfully, his nightmare was just that—a nightmare. And as terrible as it was, it was a gift to him. *Now he knew exactly how the Indonesians felt.* Tomorrow I'll share a story of how this nightmare helped Keith minister to a woman who had lost a child, and much more.

MAY 18

Three Taps on the Heart

For we do not have a high priest who is unable to empathize with our weaknesses, but we have one who has been tempted in every way, just as we are—yet he did not sin. Hebrews 4:15, NIV.

Keith woke up from his nightmare with a jolt and realized with sweet relief that it had been only a bad dream! Christina and I were safe, half a world away, where it was now daytime.

A few days later a woman stood in line at one of Keith's clinics, waiting to have her aching tooth pulled. Pointing to the woman, Keith's interpreter said to him, "See that woman in line? She lost *everything* in the tsunami—her home, her husband, and all of her children." And because of his nightmare—because it had seemed so real—Keith better understood what this woman must be feeling.

He looked at her, and their eyes met. All he could see was sadness. Deep sadness. *I was able to wake up from my nightmare,* he thought, *but she will never be able to wake up from hers.*

The woman must have somehow sensed the compassion Keith was feeling for her, because she slowly raised her hand and tapped gently three times over her heart, then just held her hand there. Keith nodded to say he understood, and then tears blurred his vision. He later told me, "Since that dream, when I hear sad news about people's lives, I try to put myself in their place."

What about you? Are there other kids you know who are going through a tough or traumatic time and need your compassion? Maybe you understand a bit of what they're going through because you've gone through something similar. Are there ways you can help them?

Maybe you're the one going through pain. If you are, and you feel that no one understands, Jesus does. That's not just an overused statement. He *does* understand! He was bullied; His friends ditched Him; He was physically abused; He was called names; He was misunderstood; He was yelled at; He was lonely; He was tempted; He cried; and He felt God had forgotten about Him.

Jesus could have come from heaven and died for your sins in one day. But He chose to live here so that He could empathize with you. Talk to Him. He's there, tapping on His heart.

MAY 19

Quick, Slow, and Slow

My dear brothers and sisters, take note of this: Everyone should be quick to listen, slow to speak and slow to become angry. James 1:19, NIV.

Stop and think about it. Isn't it usually words that hurt a relationship? I hate you . . . I don't want to be your friend . . . You're stupid . . . Leave me alone . . . You're a loser.

Today's Bible text holds the key to healthy, respectful relationships. I call it the "Quick, Slow, Slow" method. If you can remember this method, you'll find out that your relationships with your friends, family, and teachers will be a lot happier and less stressful. And who doesn't want that? Here are some ways that we can apply these three skills:

Quick to listen. We need to be sincerely eager to hear what the other person has to say, and to listen with our hearts. That means that when they're talking, we shouldn't be planning our response, and then start talking as soon as they finish their sentence. To really listen means to put ourselves in the other person's place.

Slow to speak. How many times have you wished you could take back your words as soon as they left your mouth? Being slow to speak means thinking about what we're going to say *before* we say it. We need to consider how it will sound and how it will make the listener feel.

Slow to become angry. Don't we all need this one? Too often we quickly blow up, and once that happens, resolving the conflict gets harder and harder.

Imagine what our homes would be like if every family member was "quick to listen, slow to speak and slow to become angry." Kids would respect their parents. Brothers and sisters wouldn't fight. There would be no physical or verbal abuse.

Imagine what our schools would be like if every kid was "quick to listen, slow to speak and slow to become angry." There would be no bullying, gossiping, or disrespect.

Imagine what our friendships would be like if every friend was "quick to listen, slow to speak and slow to become angry." Friendships wouldn't have conflicts, because if a problem came up, both sides would listen and speak gently.

James 1:19 holds the key to relationships that are helpful instead of hurtful. I like the way *The Message* Bible puts this text: "Lead with your ears, follow up with your tongue, and let anger straggle along in the rear."

MAY 20

But It Hurts!

If a fellow believer hurts you, go and tell him—work it out between the two of you. If he listens, you've made a friend. Matthew 18:15, Message.

Yesterday we talked about how to listen, speak, and act so that we don't hurt people. But what if you're on the receiving end of hurtful words? What if you're the subject of someone's cruel words or gossip? I'd like to suggest that you *act* instead of *react*. Here are some steps you can take. I know they work, because I've tried them!

Step 1: Pray for the person who has hurt you. It might be hard at first, but it's actually something Jesus asks of you. He said in Matthew 5:43, 44: "You have heard people say, 'Love your neighbors and hate your enemies.' But I tell you to love your enemies and pray for anyone who mistreats you" (CEV). That prayer isn't meant to be a prayer that God's wrath will come down upon them! Pray that He will heal their hurts, soften their hearts, and heal the relationship.

Step 2: Pray for yourself. Ask God for help not to dwell on the hurtful words. Ask Him to help you forgive *and* forget. Ask Him to help you love that person.

Step 3: Don't return hurt for hurt. Follow yesterday's advice from James 1:19: "Everyone should be quick to listen, slow to speak and slow to become angry" (NIV).

Step 4: Place yourself in their shoes. I have come to believe that there is always a reason why someone acts unkind. Ask yourself why they might be acting the way they do. Understanding is the key to breaking down resentments.

Step 5: Go to the person who has hurt you. This can be really hard to do! In fact, it seems the opposite of what we naturally do. If someone hurts us, we feel that it's *their* responsibility to come to *us*. But once again, Jesus asks something different of us. Read today's text again. It doesn't mean to go to the person and let them know in no uncertain terms what a sinner they are! But I believe it means to go to them and be honest, yet considerate. Let them know why their words hurt, and do your best to work things out. They may listen, or they may not. But at least you'll know that you were obeying God, and that you tried.

Step 6: Give the same forgiveness Jesus gives you. When we think of the many times He's forgiven us, how can we give any less to others? "Be kind and compassionate to one another, forgiving each other, just as in Christ God forgave you" (Ephesians 4:32, NIV).

Book Full of Answers

There's nothing like the written Word of God for showing you the way to salvation through faith in Christ Jesus. Every part of Scripture is God-breathed and useful one way or another—showing us truth, exposing our rebellion, correcting our mistakes, training us to live God's way. Through the Word we are put together and shaped up for the tasks God has for us. 2 Timothy 3:15-17, Message.

I believe that the Bible holds the answers to life's most important questions. Throughout my years of being a pastor, people have asked me many questions about God. It has always thrilled me that I could open a Bible and show them the answers to their questions. Here are some of those questions with Bible answers. Maybe some are your questions, too.

I've committed a terrible sin. Will Jesus really forgive me? "If we confess our sins, He is faithful and just to forgive us our sins and to cleanse us from all unrighteousness" (1 John 1:9, NKJV).

I used to be a Christian, but I left God a while ago. Will He take me back? "I've wiped the slate of all your wrongdoings. There's nothing left of your sins. Come back to me, come back. I've redeemed you" (Isaiah 44:22, Message).

Someone I loved very much has died. Is there any hope of seeing them again? "For the Lord Himself will descend from heaven with a shout, with the voice of an archangel, and with the trumpet of God. And the dead in Christ will rise first. Then we who are alive and remain shall be caught up together with them in the clouds to meet the Lord in the air" (1 Thessalonians 4:16, 17, NKJV).

Does Jesus care that I'm hurting? "The Lord is close to the brokenhearted; he rescues those whose spirits are crushed" (Psalm 34:18, NLT).

Does God actually listen when I talk to Him? "Before they call I will answer; while they are still speaking I will hear" (Isaiah 65:24, NIV).

Is there hope for a better life than this one? "He will wipe every tear from their eyes. There will be no more death or mourning or crying or pain, for the old order of things has passed away" (Revelation 21:4, NIV).

Have a question? Search your Bible. The answer is in there!

MAY 22

No Moths, Rust, or Thieves Allowed

Don't store up treasures on earth! Moths and rust can destroy them, and thieves can break in and steal them. Instead, store up your treasures in heaven, where moths and rust cannot destroy them, and thieves cannot break in and steal them. Your heart will always be where your treasure is. Matthew 6:19-21, CEV.

My mom recently told me that when she was a teenager, she longed for a particular shirt that all the popular girls were wearing. She wanted one so badly that it was all she could think about. When she finally got her hands on one, she proudly wore it to school—only to have the classmate who sat behind her get sick to his stomach. You can guess what happened. What she thought she absolutely *had* to have ended up in the garbage!

God knew that we would have a hard time being content with what we have. So for the tenth and final commandment, He chose this: "You shall not covet your neighbor's house. You shall not covet your neighbor's wife, or his manservant or maidservant, his ox or donkey, or anything that belongs to your neighbor" (Exodus 20:17, NIV).

What exactly is coveting? Simply put, it is seeing something that belongs to someone else and feeling unhappy and resentful that it's not yours.

This commandment stands out from the other nine in a unique way. While the other commandments are more *behavior*-centered (don't commit adultery, steal, lie, etc.), this commandment focuses on our *motives*—on why we do what we do. It's a commandment directed toward how we think. And how we think shows us the condition of our hearts.

In the tenth commandment God is asking us to control our minds—that secret place where only we ourselves know our thoughts. You can covet something that belongs to someone else, and no one has to know. Yet coveting isn't merely a mind problem—it's a *heart* problem. Your heart has an emptiness that needs to be filled, so you try to fill it with things that you think will make you happy.

But the remedy is to fill your heart with the right things: a friendship with Jesus and the hope of heaven. With Jesus in your life, you'll find it easier to be content with what you have, because you'll know that what really matters in this life is the life to come.

MAY 23

Winning Over Sinning

A man is tempted to do wrong when he lets himself be led by what his bad thoughts tell him to do. When he does what his bad thoughts tell him to do, he sins. When sin completes its work, it brings death. James 1:14, 15, NLT.

Jackson was in jail the first time my husband met him. He'd been addicted to meth for years, and it had cost him his family and his job. But then something good happened to him, because when Keith saw him six months later, Jackson looked completely different. He looked whole and happy and healthy! He had given up meth for good and had a respectable job.

"I walked away from drugs and anyone who had anything to do with them," Jackson told Keith. "I have to be very careful now. If I see someone walking down the road whom I used to do drugs with, I'll cross the street or turn down a different street. In fact, I'll turn around and walk the other way. I cannot afford to go near them."

Different temptations harass different people. What might be a temptation to you might be easy for someone else to resist. One thing is certain: Satan knows your weak areas, and that's where the temptations will hit.

The good news is this: you're not left to face your temptations alone! God has given you the tools to overcome temptation. One important tool is this: "Resist the devil, and he will flee from you. Come near to God and he will come near to you" (James 4:7, 8, NIV). It's a great trade-off! Resist the one who would destroy you, come to the One who will give you life, and He will come near to you! The closer you are to God, the more power you'll have to resist the devil.

Another tool is found in 1 Peter 5:8: "Keep awake! Watch at all times. The devil is working against you. He is walking around like a hungry lion with his mouth open. He is looking for someone to eat" (NLT). It requires alertness to realize that you have an enemy who wants you to give in and blow it. And it takes self-control to turn away from temptation. But each time you resist the temptation, you become stronger.

The reward for resisting temptation is that we become closer to God, become better people, and don't have to carry around a load of guilt. The eternal reward is even greater: "Blessed is the man who endures temptation; for when he has been proved, he will receive the crown of life which the Lord has promised to those who love Him" (James 1:12, NKJV).

MAY 24

Surprised in the Sanctuary

Our Scriptures tell us that if you see your enemy hungry, go buy that person lunch, or if he's thirsty, get him a drink. Your generosity will surprise him with goodness. Don't let evil get the best of you; get the best of evil by doing good. Romans 12:20, 21, Message.

"*Your generosity will surprise him with goodness . . .*" I'll never forget the Sabbath morning when a woman surprised an entire church with her generosity.

My husband was speaking for a Communion service at a small country church. There were two women present who had once been best friends. Now they were bitter enemies. No one really knew who or what had started the problem, but they hadn't spoken in months. One of the women sat with her husband and children in the front of the church; the other sat with hers in the back.

When it was time for the foot-washing part of the service, a miracle happened. Before anyone left their pews to go to the various rooms, the woman in front quickly stood up and walked to the back of the church where her former friend sat. We were all watching. You could have heard a pin drop.

In a forgiving and loving tone, she said, "It's Communion Sabbath. May I wash your feet?" Overwhelmed, her friend quickly accepted. They hugged each other tight, while many of us watched, our eyes filled with tears. I tell you, it was quite the experience to watch love win!

What's beautiful about this gesture isn't merely that a woman wanted to patch up a friendship. It's that she offered to take on the symbolic role of a servant and wash the feet of the very woman who had hurt her. She had chosen to forgive.

We don't always forgive people because they ask for it. Sometimes we forgive because we choose to, even if they didn't say, "I'm sorry." We choose to forgive because we're tired of carrying a load of resentment around. We forgive because we're ready for a fresh start.

If it's ever a struggle for me to forgive someone, I think of Ephesians 4:32: "You must be kind to each other. Think of the other person. Forgive other people just as God forgave you because of Christ's death on the cross" (NLT). Jesus has forgiven me when I didn't deserve it. And when I think of His generosity to me, it's impossible for me to hold a grudge against anyone.

MAY 25

Never Forget!

The Lord blesses each nation that worships only him. He blesses his chosen ones. The Lord looks at the world from his throne in heaven, and he watches us all. The Lord gave us each a mind, and nothing we do can be hidden from him. Psalm 33:12-15, CEV.

I bet you're excited that you've had a three-day weekend from school! Maybe your family went on a camping trip, headed to the river, or just stayed home and chilled. But do you know why you had a three-day weekend? It's because of Memorial Day—a day when Americans remember the soldiers who fought and died for our freedom.

I have an 89-year-old friend, Colonel David Daub, who served our country for 28 years. Memorial Day is full of memories for him—memories of fellow soldiers who were injured, of friends who came home in caskets, and of the day he nearly lost his own life. He shared a bit of his story with me:

"I was serving as a communications officer in Italy. My team was setting up a radio relay when an unsuspected Tiger tank came out of the woods. I remember it firing, but I don't remember anything else. I didn't know that a fragment from a steel shell had hit me in the side. Someone, I never found out who, picked me up and took me to a med station. When I woke up, a sweet-looking nurse was looking down at me, asking, 'Are you OK?' Thankfully, I survived."

When I asked David how he wished Americans would acknowledge Memorial Day, he said, "I would like them to remember those who gave their lives, and to remember the permanently disabled. It would be nice if people visited local veterans or wrote them a thank you for all they've done. I wish they would display a flag outside their homes. I don't see many flags around anymore. Most of all, I wish America's children would be reminded that this holiday is a memorial for those who defended *their* country."

He was quiet for a moment. Then he added, "Can I say one more thing? America must never forget by passing on the memory of our heroes to the younger generations."

So to help Colonel Daub's wish come true, why not do something patriotic today, and something to remember our soldiers? Also, remember that this world, with its wars, is not our home. A better world is coming! Jesus will fight and win the final war and then will take us home.

MAY 26

Hey, Look at Me!

Be especially careful when you are trying to be good so that you don't make a performance out of it. It might be good theater, but the God who made you won't be applauding. Matthew 6:1, Message.

What are some things kids do to stand out—to get noticed? Here are a few:

- He shows off on the basketball court or soccer field.
- She wears excessive makeup.
- She brags about her high grades.
- He bullies kids who look different.
- He tells dirty jokes.
- She wears clothes that show a lot of skin.

All these are negative things that some kids might do to attract attention. Other kids might do positive things, but for the wrong reason—they want to get noticed. For example:

- He makes sure other kids know how much tithe and offering he gives.
- She works hard to become the "teacher's pet."
- He brags about how well he knows his Bible.
- She proudly gives prayer or plays special music for church.
- He "puts other kids in their place" when they do something wrong.
- She goes on mission trips and brags about the hardships she faced.

Why do some kids try so hard to get noticed? The answer is probably different for different kids. Most probably just want to feel important and loved. But even if they're doing something good, if their motives are wrong, then they're seeking the wrong kind of attention.

Do you know that you don't have to do anything for God to notice you? You don't even have to do something "good" to get Him to notice you! He noticed you when you were being formed inside your mom. He noticed you when you prayed every prayer. He noticed you when you succeeded, and He noticed you when you failed. He noticed you when you cried and wondered why life has to be so hard sometimes. He notices you right now.

When you realize that Jesus really values you, then you won't crave other people's attention. You won't want the negative attention, and you'll do good for all the right reasons!

A Good Excuse—Or Is It?

As the deer longs for streams of water,
so I long for you, O God. Psalm 42:1, NLT.

It's test week, Jesus, and you know how busy that can get! There are last-minute papers to write, because I spent too much time playing outdoors in the warm spring weather. There's that outside reading assignment to rush through, because I put it off all quarter. Then there's my science project for extra credit. (You know how much I need that!) And if getting caught up isn't enough, I've got to cram for finals!

"If I've been a little extra cranky at home, I'm sure You understand. It's all this stress! And if I haven't treated my teacher or classmates with respect, it's because every day I come to school is another day I'm reminded of how far behind I am.

"So You see, Jesus, I have a good excuse for not reading my Bible or talking to You these past few days, right? I mean, it's not that I don't love You. It's just that You're always there—and You'll wait for me. But homework can't wait, and tests won't wait.

"What's that again? You say I would actually feel *less* stress if I spent time with You? And that I would get *more* done? Really? You actually miss me when I ignore You in all my busyness? And You've just been waiting for me to realize that You're here?

"Forgive me, Jesus. Forgive me for being a procrastinator. Forgive me for taking You for granted. Just because You've promised to always be there for me doesn't mean that I should save You till last—if I have time—if I can fit You into my schedule. And forgive me for letting my stress affect the way I treat people. I've hurt people, and that's just not right.

"I'm glad that You haven't treated me the way I treat You! I'm glad You're never too busy for me. You have the entire world to look after, but You've never once said to me, 'Come back later; I'm busy now.' Even when You were here on earth, so many people wanted time with You. They crowded around You, begging and pleading for healing, and yet You felt the touch of one woman who barely touched the hem of Your garment. You stopped and talked with her, and You healed her.

"Help me not to spend time with You just when I need something or when I'm in trouble. Help me to *long* for You, as today's text says. Help me to throw out my excuses."

MAY 28

An Extra Five Cents

This is how I want you to conduct yourself in these matters. If you enter your place of worship and, about to make an offering, you suddenly remember a grudge a friend has against you, abandon your offering, leave immediately, go to this friend and make things right. Then and only then, come back and work things out with God. Matthew 5:23, 24, Message.

When my whole family became Christians when I was 10, my brother Dan, then 14, knew he needed to make something right from his past. And he did just that.

There was a little store on the corner that we passed by every day as we went to and from school. After school, and often on weekends, my brothers, my sister, and I would stop in and get some candy. After we became Christians, Dan remembered that years before, he had stolen a roll of Life Savers from that store. Now that he knew better, he wanted to make it right. So he walked down to the store and told the owner, "Years ago I stole a roll of Life Savers from your store. I'm a Christian now, and I want to make it right. Here's five cents."

The store owner looked at Dan and said flatly, "Son, Life Savers cost 10 cents now." So Dan paid the difference.

Now that you're nearing the end of your school year, I'm wondering if there's anything you want to make right. Then, when you walk out the doors one last time, you can walk out with a clear conscience, knowing that you did your best.

Maybe you were tough on your teacher this year. Perhaps you acted up in class and gave her a daily headache. Or maybe you clashed with him and talked back disrespectfully. Regardless, this would be a good time to make things right and leave the school year feeling great! You could talk to your teacher face-to-face and tell them that you're sorry, or, if you're more comfortable writing, you could leave a note on their desk. In addition to an apology, why don't you and your classmates plan a surprise party for your teacher? Get help from parents and throw your teacher a "thank you" party.

Maybe you need to say you're sorry to another kid. Perhaps you bullied someone this year out on the playground. Maybe you had a fight with a friend and you're still not talking. Maybe you gossiped about someone and it harmed their reputation. Whether in person or in writing, let them know you're sorry. Make things right. Then go and enjoy summer vacation!

A God Who Cares

Jesus went on to all the towns and cities. He taught in their places of worship. He preached the Good News of the holy nation of God. He healed every sickness and disease the people had. As He saw many people, He had loving-pity on them. They were troubled and were walking around everywhere. They were like sheep without a shepherd. Matthew 9:35, 36, NLV.

Does Jesus really care? When you're sad, hurting, lonely, and bummed out, and you feel like caving in, does He care? With the whole world to take care of, does He even notice you—one person out of billions? With all the voices rising up to heaven in prayer, does He hear yours?

The best way to answer the question "Does Jesus really care?" is to read how He treated hurting people when He was here on earth. Here are three examples from the Bible.

When Jesus was visiting a village in Galilee, a man with leprosy came to Him. Falling on his knees, he begged Jesus to heal him. But Jesus went a step beyond healing this man. He showed love and compassion by reaching out His hand and *touching* the man—something unheard of in Jesus' time because leprosy was considered a contagious, deadly disease.

Another time, as Jesus was walking into a town, He met a funeral procession for a young man who had died. The mother was weeping because now she was all alone. Her husband had already died, and this was her only son, so her grief was doubled. When Jesus saw her, "his heart went out to her and he said, 'Don't cry' " (Luke 7:13, NIV). He raised the young man to life and gave him back to his mom!

When Jesus visited His friends Mary and Martha after the death of their brother, Lazarus, "His heart was very sad and He was troubled" when he saw Mary and the others crying (John 11:33, NLV). *In fact, Jesus Himself cried.* Even though He knew He would raise Lazarus, He cried with them.

These are just a few of the many stories that show Jesus as a compassionate, caring, and kind God. You may not understand all that happens in your life, but you can be assured that nothing escapes His attention.

He sees your struggles and pain. That's why He's preparing heaven for you. He reassures you, "And if I go and prepare a place for you, I will come back and take you to be with me that you also may be where I am" (John 14:3, NIV). *That's* how much He cares.

MAY 30

Where Was God?

And be sure of this: I am with you always, even to the end of the age. Matthew 28:20, NLT.

I have a friend who was severely injured in a skiing accident. Although he has endured multiple surgeries and months of physical therapy, he will always be handicapped.

Talking to him on the phone one evening, I asked him, "Where do you think God was the day you had your accident?"

"I don't believe God was with me that day," he answered. "God isn't that personally involved in our lives."

I couldn't disagree with him more! I believe that if you're God's child, nothing can happen in your life unless your Father—in His love and wisdom—*allows* it to happen.

Why do we think that the One who loved us enough to die for us—the One who loves us enough to prepare heaven for us—isn't involved in our lives? I believe He *is* involved. I believe He has a master plan for each life. *For your life.*

He loves you too much just to let things happen. You can read all through the Bible that He loves each individual and that He does care.

I learned that lesson on my first backpacking trip. As you read earlier, I used to *really* fear bears. That first night when we were seven miles away from civilization, I couldn't forget about a scary bear movie I'd seen as a kid, and I had a miserable, nearly sleepless night.

The next morning my husband said to me, "Honey, these whole mountains could be full of grizzly bears, but they would have to pass through God first before they got to you!"

That really helped me, and it has helped me many times since. Sometimes God shields people from car accidents, from cancer, from disasters, and from death. But there are times when God allows bad things to happen to us or people we love. But why? Why do some people get sick? Why do some people get hurt? Why do some people die?

I'll be honest and say that I don't know the answer. And I'll be honest and say that in order to be a Christian, I have to have faith. I have to believe that God is loving and is in control. I also have to trust—trust Him the way little kids trust their dads. Trust that He sees a bigger picture that I can't see. And trust that someday, when I get to heaven, I can ask Him *any* question I want, and He will have an answer that makes sense. Until then, I choose to trust Him.

God's Volunteer, Friend to All

Then the ones who pleased the Lord will ask,
"When did we give you something to eat or drink?
When did we welcome you as a stranger or give you
clothes to wear or visit you while you were sick or in jail?"
The king will answer, "Whenever you did it for any of my people, no matter
how unimportant they seemed, you did it for me." Matthew 25:37-40, CEV.

If you died and friends and family tried to describe you, what do you think they'd say? Better yet, how do people describe you now, while you're alive?

In March I shared with you the story of my friend Shannon, who was murdered. Those of us who knew her had plenty to say at her funeral, because she had always lived her life for other people. This is what it says on her grave marker:

God's Volunteer
Shannon Marie Bigger
June 11, 1971 – June 16, 1996
Friend to All

LIVE FOR SOMETHING. DO GOOD, AND LEAVE BEHIND YOU
A MONUMENT OF VIRTUE THAT THE STORMS OF TIME CAN NEVER DESTROY.
WRITE YOUR NAME IN KINDNESS, LOVE, AND MERCY ON THE HEARTS
OF THOSE YOU COME IN CONTACT WITH YEAR AFTER YEAR
AND YOU WILL NEVER BE FORGOTTEN. YOUR NAME
AND YOUR GOOD DEED WILL SHINE AS THE STARS OF HEAVEN.
—THOMAS CHALMERS

Shannon was described as "God's Volunteer" and "Friend to All." Could people say that about you now? Do you volunteer for God? Or would they say that you live just for yourself? Could people say that you're a friend to all? Or would they say that you're part of a clique?

You have the chance to write the script for your life. It's up to you how others perceive you. The closer you are to Jesus, the more you will act like Him. He served, and He was a friend to all. It's a great way to live! And it's a great way to be remembered.

JUNE 1

Sick From Guilt

O God, look at the trouble I'm in! My stomach in knots, my heart wrecked by a life of rebellion. Lamentations 1:20, Message.

You've probably had a parent or grandparent tell you, "Don't eat too much sugar or you'll get sick!" or "You'd better get to bed. You don't want to get sick!" Well, I have another one to add to the list. A very important one: "Make sure you confess your sins to Jesus and receive His forgiveness. If you don't, it could make you sick."

It's true. Guilt *can* make you sick. It happened to King David. He had a lot to feel guilty about. And even though he was king, he couldn't escape the feeling of guilt. It ate away at him day after day and made him physically sick. This is what he wrote about his guilty feelings in Psalm 32:3, 4: "Before I confessed my sins, my bones felt limp, and I groaned all day long. Night and day your hand weighed heavily on me, and my strength was gone as in the summer heat" (CEV). The guilt affected his entire body. He couldn't sleep. Guilt wore him out.

But notice that David said this was *before* he confessed his sins. In time, he finally did confess to God. He admitted that he had sinned and asked for forgiveness. He had to face the consequences of his sin, but he also felt the relief that forgiveness brings. This is what he said in Psalm 32:5: "So I confessed my sins and told them all to you. I said, 'I'll tell the Lord each one of my sins.' Then you forgave me and took away my guilt."

As long as David kept dwelling on his sins, he felt physically and emotionally sick. But when he was honest with God and confessed that he'd done wrong, the guilt was lifted. In fact, David said it was taken away! It's amazing, isn't it?

It's normal to initially have feelings of guilt when you've done something wrong. But God doesn't want to punish you by having you feel guilty for the rest of your life. The very reason Jesus died was to forgive you and set you free from guilt. It happens the moment you repent and ask. It's not something you have to earn or even wait for. It's instant!

If you have guilt that's making you sick, go to God and confess. Do whatever you can to make the wrong right with God and other people involved. If the guilt tries to come back, arm yourself with Bible texts that promise forgiveness. And stay close to the Forgiver. He can keep you from making the same mistake again, and remind you that you *are* forgiven.

JUNE 2

You Belong

Christ brought us together through his death on the cross. . . . Through him we both share the same Spirit and have equal access to the Father. That's plain enough, isn't it? You're no longer wandering exiles. This kingdom of faith is now your home country. You're no longer strangers or outsiders. You belong here, with as much right to the name Christian as anyone. Ephesians 2:16-19, Message.

When I went outside to water our yard today, I discovered a yellow pansy blooming—in our front lawn! I have no idea how the seed got there. I had planted some pansies last year, but they were out back, behind our house.

"Please don't mow down the pansy in the front lawn!" I requested of my husband. "I want it to live!"

It seems that every summer I have what are called "volunteer" flowers—flowers whose seed travels with the wind and lands wherever. I have a soft spot for these "volunteer" flowers. I never pull them up. I figure that if they worked hard enough to make it through the previous winter and find a new place, they deserve to live. I'm sure that a professional landscaper would tell me that I should remove them because they just don't belong where they are, but I can't.

Yesterday, when I was watering my yellow pansy in the middle of all the grass, I thought of the kids I've known who feel like they don't belong:

The girl who doesn't get invited to parties because she's not a part of the "cool" group.

The boy who gets picked last every time teams are chosen in PE class.

The boy who's embarrassed because he learns at a slower pace than his classmates.

The girl who struggles with her weight and is self-conscious during lunchtime.

And I thought: *Why do we ever allow people to make us feel this way? Who made them the judge of who "belongs" and who doesn't?*

Thankfully, in the eyes of the One who created us, we *all* belong. And we're all equal. So if you feel like a pansy surrounded by grass, don't allow anyone to make you feel that you don't fit in. Hold your head high, look people in the eye, talk, laugh, and share your opinion.

You are unique. You are special. And you belong.

JUNE 3

Busted-up Saddle

We were weak and could not help ourselves.
Then Christ came at the right time and gave His life for all sinners.
No one is willing to die for another person, but for a good man
someone might be willing to die. But God showed His love to us.
While we were still sinners, Christ died for us. Romans 5:6-8, NLT.

I loved listening to my dad's cowboy stories when I was growing up. He worked on a ranch during his teen years, so he had lots of stories. Little did he know that years later one of his favorite stories would cause him to think of Jesus and His amazing grace.

In the small town where Dad lived there was a weekly event that all the cowboys looked forward to. They would ride into the hills and bring down a wild mustang. It would be placed in a corral at the edge of town, and all the cowboys would gather to see who could ride it without getting bucked off. Hopefully the mustang could be tamed and used on a ranch.

One Sunday they brought in a particularly feisty pony, but no one had a bucking saddle to put on him. Dad mentioned that his neighbor, Joe, had a brand-new saddle, and he walked to Joe's house to see if he might borrow it. Joe nodded and placed the saddle at Dad's feet.

While the pony was still in the chute, Dad put the shiny new saddle on him, and things got crazy. That wild mustang didn't want anything on his back! He began to thrash around in the chute, banging and scraping the saddle against the wooden poles. Finally one of the cowboys removed the saddle and dropped it in front of Dad. It was now just a bunch of scraped-up pieces of leather, damaged beyond repair.

Dad dragged the saddle down the road to Joe's house, embarrassed and ashamed. When Joe looked at his saddle, Dad said, "I'm sorry, Joe . . ." Joe pulled the saddle into his house, but before he shut the door, he said in a calm and gentle voice, "That's OK, Dave. It's all right."

Dad told me that years later, when he took his broken life to Jesus, all he could offer God was an "I'm sorry . . ." And the incredible thing was that Jesus said, "That's OK. I can repair broken things."

"That's why God's grace is so amazing," Dad told me. "I knocked on Jesus' door. I dropped my messed-up life at His feet, and He made it new. That's what Calvary is all about. It fixes things. It fixes you and me."

Looking Like Jesus

Do as God does. After all, you are his dear children. Let love be your guide. Ephesians 5:1, 2, CEV.

"I'm small."
"My teeth are crooked."
"I don't like my nose."
"I think I'm too fat."
"My eyes are too squinty."
"I think I look weird."

I was hanging out with a group of fifth and sixth graders, and I asked them to write something down on a piece of paper.

"Write down the one thing that messes with your self-worth," I suggested.

Those were some of their answers. And I realized that they all had to do with looks. These kids were letting the way they look affect how they feel about themselves. I wanted to get the group back together and ask the boy who thought he was too small, "Who told you that? You're too small compared to whom?" And I wanted to ask the girl who said she didn't like her nose, "Whose nose are you comparing yours to? Why is theirs any better than yours?"

Then a Bible text came to my mind. It's Isaiah 53:2, where the prophet described Jesus and what He would look like: "He had no beauty or majesty to attract us to him, nothing in his appearance that we should desire him" (NIV). Don't misunderstand this text. It's not saying that Jesus was unsightly or ugly. What it is saying is that He didn't come to this earth as a man decked out in designer clothes fit for a king. He didn't captivate people because of His looks.

Yet everywhere He went, people were drawn to Jesus. Maybe it was the way He looked at them with love and acceptance. Maybe it was the sound of His kind voice. Maybe it was the gentleness of His touch. Regardless, when Jesus passed through a town, people were changed.

Today's text encourages us to imitate Jesus. "Do as God does." What does He do? The answer is in the text "Let love be your guide." Jesus loved people. That's what He was known for. That's *still* what He is known for. And that's what you can be known for, too—regardless of the things you don't like about your looks. Love in your heart is what really matters.

JUNE 5

The Love Outfit

So, chosen by God for this new life of love, dress in the wardrobe God picked out for you: compassion, kindness, humility, quiet strength, discipline. Be even-tempered, content with second place, quick to forgive an offense. Forgive as quickly and completely as the Master forgave you. And regardless of what else you put on, wear love. It's your basic, all-purpose garment. Never be without it. Colossians 3:12-14, Message.

What if there were a store that sold clothes that would make you become a better person? Would you shop there?

What if there were a pair of jeans so powerful that, when you wore them, you'd automatically become a kinder person? Then, when you were tempted to be disrespectful to your parents or to pick on another kid at school or to be impatient with an elderly person, you could put on those jeans and all of a sudden be kind to them!

What if there were a pair of shoes you could put on that made you a humble person? So if you wore them to school and made the winning point of the volleyball game, had the top score on the final exam, or had the highest number of friends on your social media site, you wouldn't see yourself as any better than anyone else.

What if they sold a T-shirt that would give you courage? Courage to stand up for what you believe in. Courage to say no. Courage to walk away.

And what if they sold a jacket that made you disciplined? Whenever you wore it, your room would be clean, and your homework would get done on time. You wouldn't put junk in your body but would eat healthfully. You wouldn't stay up late watching TV but would get the right amount of sleep. You'd feel great every day!

Wouldn't that kind of store be cool? Just buy clothes, put them on, and watch your character change! Unfortunately, there isn't a store like that. But *fortunately*, Jesus can do that for you! Not by what you wear on the outside, but by what you chose to wear on the inside.

The more time you spend with Him—reading in the Bible about His example of how to live—and talking to Him, the more you'll become like Him. He can change you from the inside out so that you wear love. And that's something no store can do.

The Voice That Saved

If you go the wrong way—to the right or to the left—
you will hear a voice behind you saying, "This is the right way.
You should go this way." Isaiah 30:21, NCV.

When Daniel was in the seventh grade, he and his family loved spending Sabbath afternoons at a place they named "Indian Rocks." It had trails, caves, and rocks with preserved Native American paintings on them. Looking for snakes along the trail made the adventure extra exciting!

One day they were hiking at a spot where Daniel had never been. Behind one very large rock was a short cave that went about 40 feet back into the hillside. But before Daniel followed his family inside, he decided to head out onto the point of a huge, flat rock that stuck way out of the hillside.

As he was jogging along, nowhere near the edge yet, he heard his dad shout in a very commanding voice, "STOP!" Daniel had always done his best to obey and not question his parents, so he immediately came to a halt. When he looked down, he saw that just one step in front of him was a large crack in the rock—a gap about four feet wide and 50 feet deep. Just one more step and he would have fallen in!

When Daniel turned around, his dad was nowhere to be seen. *No one was there!* He rushed back, went into the cave, and found his dad.

"Did you just shout something to me?" Daniel asked.

"No," his dad said, shaking his head. "I didn't say anything to you. I've been here in the cave with the rest of the family."

Daniel grew up to become an academy Bible teacher. He recently told me, "I believe that whoever stood on that rock with me and commanded me to stop was a messenger from God. I am glad that I obeyed! And I will continue to obey the voice of God—whether I can hear it out loud or not—because I know He loves me."

If you stop and listen with your heart, you will sometimes hear God's voice. You may not hear it out loud, but you will "hear" it in the Bible, in the words of a song, in something that another Christian tells you, or in a special thought that comes to you. When you do, I hope you will listen. God's voice is a voice of love and protection. It's the voice of your Best Friend.

JUNE 7

The Gospel Girls

Don't get tired of helping others. You will be rewarded when the time is right, if you don't give up. Galatians 6:9, CEV.

So what are you going to do with yourself all summer? Maybe you're looking forward to sleeping in, watching TV, playing video games, swimming, or hanging out at the mall. But if you want to do something life-changing, here's an idea from The Gospel Girls.

The summer between their fifth- and sixth-grade year, Jessica, Kelsie, Liesl, and Melissa decided they needed some adventure in their lives. And they wanted to look outside themselves for it. They wanted to do good for someone else. During the school year they had looked at an ADRA (Adventist Development and Relief Agency) catalog and had seen some of the needs of people in poor countries. They felt especially sorry for the people who were hungry.

"Wouldn't it be cool to raise money and send it to help people?" Liesl suggested. "We could form a club . . . and call ourselves . . . The Gospel Girls!"

Melissa explained to me how it all came together: "We started out by asking some elderly people if they had yard work for us to do. If they gave us a donation for our work, we'd save it for ADRA. I decided to make flyers, and we distributed them in my neighborhood. They said, 'THE GOSPEL GIRLS. If you need any yard work done, we'll do it for donations to a worthy cause.' "

That summer the girls raised $530! They looked through the ADRA catalog and chose four different places to send their money. In one place their money bought chickens for a family who could then have eggs to eat and sell.

They had so much fun that the next summer The Gospel Girls were at it again! This time they added a few more friends to the group. In addition to working for donations, they started playing Ding Dong Ditch—taking baked goods or notes to a front porch, ringing the doorbell, and running away before they could be seen!

You have an entire summer ahead of you. And there's plenty of time to do all the fun things you want to do, plus have an adventure as missionaries in your neighborhood. The possibilities are endless! Get your friends together and start your own club. I bet that at the end of the summer you'll feel great about how you spent it!

JUNE 8

Stargazing

I often think of the heavens your hands have made,
and of the moon and stars you put in place. Then I ask,
"Why do you care about us humans? Why are you concerned for us
weaklings?" You made us a little lower than you yourself,
and you have crowned us with glory and honor. Psalm 8:3-5, CEV.

The night is calm as I lie on the soft grass of our front lawn. For a moment I almost forget where I am, because when I look straight up, I don't see the nearby houses and trees. The rest of the world fades away as I gaze at the stars. There are thousands of them! And they are so beautiful!

There are big stars and little ones. Stars with well-known names that are often talked about, and others that only an astronomer would know. Stars that attract gazers with their brilliance, and others that hide in the corners of the sky, seen only by those who take the time to search.

Yet God has placed each star there, and He knows each one by name. Psalm 147:4 says, "He decided how many stars there would be in the sky and gave each one a name" (CEV). Each star is a part of His sky, no matter how big or small—no matter how bright or dim.

It's the same with people, isn't it? Some people have big names and are often talked about. Even when a room is full of people, they're the center of attention. Everyone knows their name. They get the laughs and the looks.

Then there are those who are considered small in this world. Maybe they don't have a big name or a personality that shines brightly. Maybe they aren't talked about much and hide in the dark corners, seen only by a few who take the time to seek them out.

But God knows each person in this world, just as He knows each star in the sky. He cares equally for each one, no matter how big or how small by the world's standards. He knows them by name. He knows *you* by name. He says in Isaiah 49:16, "See, I have written your name on the palms of my hands" (NLT).

And even though heaven is way up there above the stars, He is not far away. In fact, He's no farther than a prayer away. You are precious to Him. Did you know that? And someday soon we'll be up in heaven with Him, looking at the stars from a different point of view.

JUNE 9

But I Can't Witness!

"Don't say you're too young," the Lord answered. "If I tell you to go and speak to someone, then go! And when I tell you what to say, don't leave out a word! I promise to be with you and keep you safe, so don't be afraid." Jeremiah 1:7, 8, CEV.

What comes to your mind when you hear the word "witnessing"? Do you think of an evangelist on a stage in front of a lot of people? Do you think of a missionary serving in a foreign country? Do you think of a pastor visiting door-to-door?

I'd like to suggest something else. When you hear the word "witnessing," I'd like you to think of a kid. Yes, a kid! A kid like you!

You don't have to be an "in-your-face Christian" to be a witness. In fact, no one likes being around that kind of person. I think that the best text that shows us *how* to witness is found in John 13:35. Jesus says, "By this all men will know that you are my disciples, if you love one another" (NIV).

If we want people to know that we're Christians, if we want to show them what God is like, we need to *love* them. That actually makes witnessing easy! It's easy to love, and sometimes you can do it without saying a word. Here are just a few examples of how you can witness—even as a kid!

Help a neighbor. Mow a lawn, weed a garden, bake cookies, or share from your garden.

Open your home. Ask your parents if you can volunteer to your pastor to open your home for a Bible study group for kids. Or open your home for social get-togethers.

Care for sick people. Visit neighbors or church members who are in the hospital, in nursing homes, or housebound. Send a card, take flowers, or make and take a pot of soup.

Adopt a grandparent. Visit them and include them in some of your family activities.

Show kindness to those in charge. Send an anonymous thank-you note to your principal or teacher or to your local police, firefighters, or mayor.

These ideas are just a start. There are endless opportunities for you to witness in your everyday life. Don't let anyone tell you that you're too young to witness. Jesus needs you! There are a lot of people out there who need to know what a kind and loving God He is. And your kind and loving acts will show them.

I Almost Forgot

On a good day, enjoy yourself; on a bad day, examine your conscience. God arranges for both kinds of days so that we won't take anything for granted. Ecclesiastes 7:14, Message.

Earlier this year I shared with you something from the private journal I kept when I was a kid. Well, I'm going to hold my breath and do it again! When I was 16 years old, an X-ray showed a large tumor in the femur bone of my right leg. This is a bit of what I wrote in my journal from my hospital bed, the night before surgery.

As I lie here and daydream, my thoughts carry me back to when I was little. I remember how excited I was to jump out of bed each morning and make good use of my legs for the day. I would walk, run, jump, skip, and hop all day long. I loved to climb trees, play hopscotch, and jump rope. I loved to make a pile of autumn leaves and jump into them. I loved to wade knee-deep through the snow. And I loved to be chased by the ocean waves, feeling the warm sand between my toes.

But my daydreaming is rudely interrupted by my present condition. I've taken my legs for granted all my life—until now. Now I'm told I may lose my right leg. Funny how all of a sudden I realize how much I love that leg, and how much I would miss it if it were taken away from me.

The last of the visitors have left, and there's nothing to do now but wait. Wait till surgery in the morning, and then wait for the biopsy report to come back. I lie in this hospital bed and stare at the ceiling. Darkness fills the room and tries to fill my soul. All of a sudden I get the urge to jump out of this hospital bed and run for miles and miles and miles, for fear I'll never be able to run again! I want to do what I once took for granted. I want to walk up a flight of stairs, kick a ball, chase a butterfly, and ride a bike.

A single tear rolls down my face.

In the middle of all my worry, I almost forget that Someone has been in my room all night long. And I am in awe of His faithfulness! While much of life outside my hospital room sleeps, He stays awake. I wish I'd reached out to Him sooner, because just the thought that I'm not alone makes me feel better.

The sun is rising, and it's a new day. The day I feared. But now I know I'm not facing it alone. He has given me strength, and I'm prepared to face whatever is in store for me.

JUNE 11

Gotta Praise Him!

It is wonderful to be grateful and to sing your praises, Lord Most High! It is wonderful each morning to tell about your love and at night to announce how faithful you are. Psalm 92:1, 2, CEV.

Yesterday you read my journal entry that I wrote the night before I had surgery on my leg. Here's what I wrote one week later, after the test results came back.

The sun is shining down on me as I rest outdoors on our patio. I'm still living in the joy of this morning. My doctor called with the results of the biopsy done on my tumor. It wasn't malignant! There is no cancer! No fear of losing my leg! I feel like running, jumping, shouting, laughing, and crying all at once.

It seems as though everything out here knows of my joy and is praising God with me! I imagine that the leaves dancing in the wind are applauding Him and that the birds are singing to Him. I wish like everything that I could fly above the clouds and make a quick trip to heaven, because I would love to hug Jesus and thank Him. And I would love to see His smile, because I know that my happiness makes Him happy, too.

I've learned such an important lesson through all of this. We take so many things for granted—even life itself, sometimes. We need to love life and count its blessings as if today were the last day to do so. It could be that someday the things we never realized were so important might threaten to go away. And then we try to grab them, but it's too late.

I took my leg for granted because it never occurred to me that I might lose it. But it's pretty much impossible for me to take it for granted now. I have a scar on the back of my leg to remind me. A scar that I'm not going to let bother me, because God and I know the story behind it. The story about a young girl who had everything going for her. A young girl who took her life and health for granted. Until one day. A girl who was scared and who turned to Jesus in the middle of the night in a hospital room and found Him there, waiting.

Looking back, I realize something very important: Jesus had my back! He was with me all night in that hospital room, through the operation, through weeks of physical therapy, through getting caught up on homework, and through feeling that I was missing out on life.

He's got your back, too. Whatever you might be going through, you are never alone.

JUNE 12

Looking for a Hero?

Faith makes us sure of what we hope for and gives us proof of what we cannot see. It was their faith that made our ancestors pleasing to God. Hebrews 11:1, 2, CEV.

Who is your hero? When my siblings and I were kids, we had heroes. Dan's hero was Superman. Debi's hero was Cinderella. Davey's hero was Batman. And my hero? Zorro, of course! He had a horse!

Whether your hero is a fictitious TV character or a real-life actor, musician, or athlete, if they mess up and make a public mistake, it can be disheartening. It can also be dangerous to have the wrong kind of hero, as my brother Davey found out.

Dad and Mom had bought Davey a Batman costume, and he wore it nonstop for weeks. He even wore it to bed! He was cute in it, but it got annoying having him "fly" around the house all the time. Plus it was dangerous for him to climb up and jump off anything taller than he was. One day he went too far. With his Batman outfit on, he jumped off the retaining wall at my school, thinking that nothing could harm him. But when he landed, he fell on his arm and broke it in two places. Surgery and a cast grounded Batman for a while.

Looking for a real hero? A hero who actually did something great? Hebrews 11 is full of them. And what made them heroes? *It was their faith.* They believed without seeing, and that takes a lot of faith. It takes bravery, too.

Enoch had such a strong faith in God that he escaped death. Genesis 5:24 simply says that "Enoch walked faithfully with God; then he was no more, because God took him away" (NIV). Noah was a hero because he had the faith to build a boat when most everyone laughed at him and thought he was crazy. But his faith saved him and his family. Even though Sarah was old enough to be a grandma, she had faith that God would keep His promise and that she'd have a baby. It was because of his faith that Moses was willing to give up his wealthy, exciting life as a prince to become like a slave, and then lead God's people to the Promised Land. And because of her faith, even though she'd been living wrong, Rahab's life was spared.

Talk about adventure! Talk about heroes! These are just a few of the ones mentioned in Hebrews 11. And they are good role models for us. They're not some fantasy person on TV, but real people who took the risk to believe in a God they couldn't see.

JUNE 13

How Hard Is It, Anyway?

Saving is all his idea, and all his work. All we do is trust him enough to let him do it. It's God's gift from start to finish! We don't play the major role. If we did, we'd probably go around bragging that we'd done the whole thing! No, we neither make nor save ourselves. God does both the making and saving. He creates each of us by Christ Jesus to join him in the work he does, the good work he has gotten ready for us to do, work we had better be doing. Ephesians 2:8-10, Message.

I wanted to know how a group of fifth and sixth graders felt about their own salvation, so I asked them, "If Jesus were to come today, would you go to heaven? Would you be saved? Why or why not?" Here are some of their answers:

Teresa: "Yes, because He gave His life for me."

Peyton: "Yes, because He promised He'd come back for us."

Nicole: "Yes, because He loves me."

Kyla: "I don't know because I'm not sure I've done everything God has told me to do."

Drew: "I don't know because sometimes I get mad."

Erick: "I *may* get to go . . . Sometimes I'm not the best person."

Danny: "I don't know because I'm a sinner."

Brian: "I don't know because my sister and I don't get along very well."

Isaac: "No, because I play video games where I have to kill people."

As you can see, some kids were confident, some weren't sure, and one was sure he wouldn't be saved. But the good news for these kids—and for you—is that heaven isn't for those who are good enough! Because none of us is good enough! That's why Jesus came to die. He died so you wouldn't have to die eternally.

Obeying God's rules just right won't get you into heaven. God doesn't save by the merit system. *Salvation is a gift.* Romans 6:23 says, "For the wages of sin is death, but the gift of God is eternal life through Christ Jesus our Lord" (NIV). The reason we obey Jesus is that we know what He asks us to do is always the best for us. So why would we want to do something that isn't good for us? That just gets us into trouble and separates us from God.

Don't live in fear of not being saved. *Accept the gift.* And then live for the Giver, Jesus.

JUNE 14

I'm So Mad!

He who is slow to anger is better than the powerful, And he who rules his spirit is better than he who takes a city. Proverbs 16:32, NLT.

Davin had spent hours building his imaginary city. Everything was looking great until his big brother, Dylan, ruined things. He came into the family room pretending to be Godzilla, a monster feared by all. He walked right through the city, knocking down buildings and stepping on people. Davin was so angry that his faced turned red and he started yelling at the top of his lungs, "Get out of here! You ruined everything!"

It really would be something to be powerful enough to take down a city. But according to today's text, being slow to get angry is better than being powerful!

What makes you angry? Some answers a group of kids gave me may sound familiar:

"I get mad and argue when I play games."

"I get angry when people forget about me and just walk away."

"I get mad when this one kid picks on me."

"I get mad when teased about the way I look. Sometimes it keeps me awake at night."

"I get angry when kids make fun of me."

We all get angry at times. What matters most is what we do with our anger. You can yell, shove, hit, cry, say a bad word, or storm out of the room. Or you can learn how to control your angry feelings. The next time you feel like you're about to explode, try these tips:

1. Leave the situation until you can calm down. This will keep you from saying or doing something that you might regret.
2. Don't say anything to the person you're angry with until you've chilled.
3. Don't stuff your anger. Find someone to talk with about it.
4. Go do something physical—run, walk, swim, or shoot some hoops.
5. When the time is right, go to that person. Try to help them understand how their words or actions made you feel. If they won't listen, at least you'll know you tried.
6. Go to God and leave it with Him. Ask Him to help you control yourself and move on.

And remember: "He who rules his spirit is better than he who takes a city." Don't let anger rule you. Choose to rule over it instead.

JUNE 15

It's All His Fault!

No test or temptation that comes your way is beyond the course of what others have had to face. All you need to remember is that God will never let you down; he'll never let you be pushed past your limit; he'll always be there to help you come through it. 1 Corinthians 10:13, Message.

It made me feel sad when I read it. They were talking about Someone I love very much and blaming Him for all that's wrong in the world. They were talking about Jesus.

I was reading a thread on a social media site, and the kids were dissing God. It began when one boy said that He didn't believe in God anymore because the world is such a mess. Then someone else suggested that there was a God, but He must be mean to let us suffer like this. They blamed Him for setting up the whole world when He knew that we would sin.

Their talk reminded me of a woman in the Bible, Job's wife. Job had lost everything. His sons and daughters were killed when their house collapsed in a windstorm. His livestock was either stolen or killed, as were his servants. As if that wasn't bad enough, he got painful sores all over his body. And his wife blamed God.

"His wife said to him, 'Are you still trying to maintain your integrity? Curse God and die' " (Job 2:9, NLT). Why not blame God? He could have stopped all those bad things from happening. So it was God's fault that the bad happened, right? Why believe in a God like that?

But Job knew better. He knew that to turn away from God in tough times would be the biggest mistake of his life.

"But Job replied, 'You talk like a foolish woman. Should we accept only good things from the hand of God and never anything bad?' So in all this, Job said nothing wrong" (verse 10).

Wow, that's really a great example for us! If Job could still trust God after losing his family, his possessions, and his health, so can we.

We also know some things that Job may not have fully understood. We know that there's a great battle going on between God and Satan. We know that the enemy is really the one to blame when something bad happens. We understand the bigger picture. And we have the promise in today's text: we won't be tested beyond what we can handle. Although sometimes we may question God's judgment on that, we must believe it. God will always help us through.

No Busy Signal

Evening and morning and at noon I will pray, and cry aloud, and He shall hear my voice. Psalm 55:17, NKJV.

I was curious about what kids your age do with prayer. So I asked a group the other day, "How much time do you spend praying each day, and what do you pray about? Here are some of their answers:

Benjamin: "I should probably start praying more . . ."

Damian: "About one minute. I pray about sport injuries."

Ian: "I pray like 10 minutes a day for family and people who are in need."

Piper: "At least 10 minutes a day. Often for people who need healing."

Tami: "No set time. I pray before I eat, when I have a problem, and at bedtime."

Jenna: "About five minutes. I pray for my family and that we'll get to go on trips."

Dale: "Five minutes total. For Him to bless my food."

Nat: "About 10 minutes. Family, problems, friends."

Braden: "About one minute. About how I'm feeling."

Kim: "I pray a lot! In the morning, before I eat, before I go to bed about different things."

Savannah: "Not enough time . . ."

When I heard their responses, I thought, *Wow, most of these kids are missing out! Jesus is there for them all day long and all night long, but they're not talking with Him much.*

Think of it this way. Think of your best friend. How did they get to be your best friend? You spent a lot of time together, that's how. You talked face to face, maybe texted or e-mailed or talked through some kind of social media. And you didn't just ask them for favors all the time, did you? If you had, they wouldn't care much about being friends with you.

Well, if you want to get to know Jesus—and I hope you do!—you'll need to spend time talking to Him. It doesn't have to be formal, kneeling with your eyes closed. You can talk to Him on the way to school. You can talk to Him while you're doing your chores. You can talk to Him as you're drifting off to sleep at night. You can say a quick "Help!" when you need Him. You can talk to Him about *anything*. And He will always listen. You'll never get a busy signal with God!

JUNE 17

Don't Touch That!

When Jesus came down from the mountainside, large crowds followed him. A man with leprosy came and knelt before him and said, "Lord, if you are willing, you can make me clean." Jesus reached out his hand and touched the man. "I am willing," he said. "Be clean!" Immediately he was cleansed of his leprosy. Matthew 8:1-3, NIV.

I have AIDS," she told me. "I haven't lived the best life . . ."

My first reaction, without thinking, would have been to move away from her. But she had come to me for help. How should I treat her? What should I do? And then I remembered the story from today's text. The story of how Jesus showed compassion to a man who had leprosy. It's probably my favorite miracle story in the Bible, because it really tells what Jesus is like.

There were two kinds of leprosy during the time of Jesus, and both were terrible. One type formed bad-smelling sores on the skin, and death could take up to nine years. The other type affected the nerves and muscles, and the person's limbs would fall off at the joint. It was a long death that could take 20 to 30 years. People were terrified of leprosy. Many believed that the disease was caused by the person's sin, which made them even more of an outcast.

According to the Old Testament laws, touching certain things would contaminate a person. In Jesus' culture touching someone with leprosy was considered worse than touching a corpse. Yet it was a leper that Jesus touched! He could have kept His distance and healed this man by just speaking, but He chose to touch him.

It's interesting that this man approached Jesus. Any leper who approached a rabbi would be chased away with stones. He must have sensed that Jesus was approachable. He must have seen compassion in Jesus' eyes and heard it in His voice.

Love overlooked the leprosy. And that's what we must do. No matter what a kid at your school looks like, smells like, talks like, or acts like; no matter what clothes they wear or how they wear their hair; no matter if they're a social outcast or handicapped in some way, if you want to be like Jesus, you'll want to reach out to them somehow.

What did I do for the young woman with AIDS? I reached out and touched her. I told her that Jesus loves her. I told her that Jesus forgives her for what she did to bring on the disease. And I told her that He accepts her just the way she is. And that accepting Him would make her whole.

JUNE 18

The Best Friend Ever

I no longer call you servants, because a servant does not know his master's business. Instead, I have called you friends, for everything that I learned from my Father I have made known to you. John 15:15, NIV.

Do you ever wish that you had the perfect friend? It would be great if you could pick all the traits of an ideal friend, mix them together, feed them into a machine, and out would pop your perfect friend!

Wouldn't it be great to have a friend who was always available for you to talk to? You could call or text any time, day or night, and they'd be there for you.

Wouldn't it be great to have a friend who understood you completely? Then you'd never get that lonely feeling that no one "gets" you, because your friend would understand you perfectly.

Wouldn't it be great to have a friend who never got mad at you and said, "We're through!"? Instead, they'd always be willing to work out any problem because your friendship was so important to them.

Wouldn't it be great to have a friend who would never be in a bad mood? When you saw them every morning at school, they'd be smiling.

Wouldn't it be great to have a friend who would always forgive you?

Wouldn't it be great to have a friend you could just be yourself around? You wouldn't have to get all fixed up when you two were going to hang out together.

Wouldn't it be great to have a friend who would always have your back, no matter what?

Wouldn't it be great to have a friend who would never make you feel bad about yourself when you mess up?

Wouldn't it be great to have a friend who would always give you a fresh start?

Wouldn't it be great to have a friend who would take you on an amazing trip that was out of this world?

Wouldn't it be great to have a friend who would forget about your mistakes and not remind you of them over and over?

You do! His name is *Jesus*. He will always have your back.

JUNE 19

No Robots Allowed

This is what happened: Sin came into the world by one man, Adam. Sin brought death with it. Death spread to all men because all have sinned.
Romans 5:12, NLT.

"And just as each person is destined to die once and after that comes judgment, so also Christ died once for all time as a sacrifice to take away the sins of many people. He will come again, not to deal with our sins, but to bring salvation to all who are eagerly waiting for him" (Hebrews 9:27, 28, NLT).

These two texts summarize what the gospel is all about. Sin came to the world by one man, Adam. The consequence of sin was death for all. But Jesus loved you too much to let that happen! So He volunteered to die once for everyone's sins. And *that* is incredible!

I was thinking today about Adam and Eve. They had it all, didn't they? God created them and then placed them in a beautiful garden. I'm sure the prettiest places we've seen in pictures can't begin to compare to their outdoor home. Not only that, they could play with all the animals anytime they wanted to. Ride an elephant? Race a cheetah? Swim with an orca whale? Sure!

But even more than these, they had the chance—the privilege—to take daily walks with Jesus! They had the perfect life. God had only one simple rule for them to follow: "You must not eat fruit from the tree that is in the middle of the garden, and you must not touch it, or you will die" (Genesis 3:3, NIV). It seems simple enough, doesn't it? He told them that the whole rest of the garden was theirs, but they couldn't eat from just one tree. *One tree.*

I wonder what it was that caused first Eve, then Adam, to be dissatisfied? With all they had been given, why did they want the one thing they mustn't have? They had even been warned that if they ate from that tree, they would die!

Some kids have asked why God let Adam and Eve do it. He knew that everything would become a big mess if they ate the fruit. He could have stopped them. But He didn't, because He's not that kind of God. He doesn't force us to obey. We're not robots, but daughters and sons. And He wants our love and obedience only if we choose to give it.

I hope that the thought of this kind of love makes God irresistible to you! Don't be like Adam and Eve and think that Jesus isn't enough to satisfy. He is and always will be.

JUNE 20

Planning Your Trip

So do not throw away your confidence; it will be richly rewarded. You need to persevere so that when you have done the will of God, you will receive what he has promised. Hebrews 10:35, 36, NIV.

Tomorrow is the official first day of summer! Is your family planning a trip? If you are, I bet you're planning ahead. Maybe even making a list of all you need to take. When my family goes camping, we take our tent, cooler, camp stove, and sleeping bags. But what if we didn't plan ahead? What if we forgot our stove? We'd be drinking raw pancake batter and eating cold beans out of a can!

Planning ahead in life is even more important than planning for a trip. It's important to plan ahead of time what you will say and do when someone asks you to do something that you know is wrong. Here are some situations that you may come across. What do you think is the best way to handle them?

At lunchtime you go behind the gym and catch two kids smoking. They offer you a cigarette. If you've planned ahead you can:

1. Say that you're into sports and want to take care of your body.
2. Tell them that you don't want to start a habit that can cause lung cancer.
3. Say no, and go talk with your school counselor or an adult you trust.

You're at a park with some friends when two other kids you know show up. They got some beer somehow, and they offer you a can. If you've planned ahead you can:

1. Say, "Hey, we have sodas. Let's have those instead. They're better for us anyway."
2. Say no and leave. When you get home, tell your parents what happened.
3. Say no and stay to make sure the others don't drink. Tell them that even one beer can lead to becoming a teenage alcoholic.

There are many scenarios you can plan ahead for. What to do when someone . . . asks you to cheat; starts bullying another kid; wants you to watch an R-rated movie; encourages you to steal; asks you to lie for them; starts a rumor. If you plan ahead, you won't be taken by surprise. You'll have the confidence to think, *I can handle this! I know what to do.* And when you walk away, you'll feel strong knowing that you had a plan and followed it!

JUNE 21

Be a Copycat

Do as God would do. Much-loved children want to do as their fathers do. Live with love as Christ loved you. He gave Himself for us, a gift on the altar to God which was as a sweet smell to God. Ephesians 5:1, 2, NLV.

Since today is Father's Day, I'm thinking about my dad. When I was growing up, people often told me, "You look just like your dad." It happened when we were visiting relatives; it happened when people looked through our family photo album; and it even happened when Dad and I sang duets at church. After one service, a woman came up to us and said, "I can tell you're father and daughter—your chins look exactly alike!"

Much of who I am today is because of my dad. He is someone I look up to and love. I smile when I look back to when I was little and wanted to be a cowgirl because he had been a cowboy. I would try to imitate him as I rode my stick horse around our yard.

Do you ever try to imitate someone? Maybe a musician, an actor, an athlete, or a model? I got to thinking today: *Why do we try to imitate other people when we really should be imitating Jesus?*

How do we become imitators of Jesus? Well, professional imitators spend a lot of time studying the person they hope to imitate. They spend hours practicing the person's mannerisms, voice, and facial expressions. In the same way we become imitators of Jesus by studying Him. We do that by reading about Him in the Bible. Then we do our best to copy His lifestyle of compassion, acceptance, and servanthood.

Jesus had compassion on everyone He met: "And when Jesus went out He saw a great multitude; and He was moved with compassion for them, and healed their sick" (Matthew 14:14, NKJV).

He showed acceptance to those the world had tagged as unacceptable: "Soon a Samaritan woman came to draw water, and Jesus said to her, 'Please give me a drink' " (John 4:7, NLT).

And His whole life was about serving others: "He put aside everything that belonged to Him and made Himself the same as a servant who is owned by someone. He became human by being born as a man" (Philippians 2:7, NLT).

If we will ask ourselves, "What would Jesus do?" then we can imitate Him.

But It's Not Fair!

He personally carried our sins in his body on the cross so that we can be dead to sin and live for what is right. By his wounds you are healed. 1 Peter 2:24, NLT.

It happened when Kurt was in the sixth grade, sitting in chapel. A special guest had come, and all 10 grades of his school filled the auditorium.

Sitting behind Kurt was Troy, the guy he liked least in the whole school, because Troy was such a bully. In front of Kurt sat a girl named Sophie.

In the middle of the speaker's talk, Troy-the-bully reached his arm past Kurt and jabbed an open safety pin right into Sophie's bottom. She jumped up out of her seat, whirled around, and screamed out, "Kurt Kramer, that hurt!" Now the whole school was looking at Kurt.

"I didn't do it!" Kurt protested.

But the principal up on the platform wasn't buying it. He said, "Kurt, I want to see you in my office immediately after chapel!"

Once in the office, he asked, "Kurt, did you do that? Are you the one who poked Sophie with a pin?"

"Absolutely not!" he answered. "I would never hurt someone like that."

"Then who did?"

"I can't tell you. I don't squeal on other kids."

"Then you'll have to do free labor for not telling me."

Kurt still got punished. He was sent out to pick up garbage around the school for an hour.

Now that Kurt is an adult, he would tell you never to cover for a bully as he did. "Kids who hurt other kids need to be stopped!" he told me.

When I heard Kurt's story, I couldn't help thinking of something else. This earth is like that auditorium. And we are the Troys. We're the bullies. We make wrong choices and hurt people more than we'd like to admit. And though Kurt didn't take Troy's punishment out of love, Jesus took our punishment because He loved us very much. He even *died* in our place.

You might say, "But Troy-the-bully didn't deserve to have someone else take his punishment!" Well . . . neither do we. That's why Jesus' grace is so amazing. It's *amazing grace.*

JUNE 23

Finding a Reason

Rejoice always, pray continually, give thanks in all circumstances; for this is God's will for you in Christ Jesus. 1 Thessalonians 5:16-18, NIV.

I received a newsletter today from an organization that provides summer camps for kids in various locations across the U.S. and Canada. Looking at pictures of campers, I guessed they were having a blast! One photo shows a group of campers singing and clapping with big smiles on their faces. On the next page a boy is plowing through the water on a wakeboard. Across that page is a photo of another guy in archery class with his bow drawn back. Still another photo shows a girl building a trinket box in craft class.

Typical camp photos? No. These kids are blind. They've all attended National Camps for Blind Children, affiliated with Christian Record Services for the Blind. But how can they smile? you may wonder. How can they have fun when they can't see what they're doing? How can they enjoy life? In spite of being blind, they've found things to be grateful for. In spite of being blind, they've chosen to live life and live it to the fullest!

If you talked to your friends and classmates heart to heart, I think you'd discover that at times everyone struggles with something. No one has it all together. Maybe he struggles with depression. Maybe she lives alone with only her mom. Maybe he struggles every day in school just to keep up. Maybe she deals with anxiety.

I've never been one who says we should proclaim, "Praise the Lord anyhow!" when we're going through tough times. And that makes today's text seem a little impossible, doesn't it? How can we "rejoice always"? That's not doable! How can we "give thanks in all circumstances"? No one can manage that!

I think the answer is found in another text from Paul. It's Philippians 4:4: "Rejoice in the Lord always. I will say it again: Rejoice!" (NIV). Paul isn't saying, "Rejoice that your parents are divorced," or "Rejoice that you get picked on at school," or "Rejoice that your grandparent died." He's saying "Rejoice in the Lord always." Don't rejoice in the problem; rejoice in the Solution—Jesus! Rejoice that He's got your back when you're going through a tough time. Rejoice that you have Him to talk to when you're sad. Rejoice that He's working on your problem, even though you can't see Him. And rejoice that He's preparing a better place for you.

JUNE 24

Hold Me Close

He will feed his flock like a shepherd. He will carry the lambs in his arms, holding them close to his heart. Isaiah 40:11, NLT.

"Why did Jesus let my parents get divorced?"

"Why did Jesus let my dog die?"

"Why did Jesus let us move away from my friends?"

"Why did Jesus let my dad lose his job?"

"Why did Jesus let me fail that test?"

Jesus gets blamed for a lot, doesn't He? When things go wrong, we tend to ask, "Why did Jesus . . . ?" as if it's *His* fault. Maybe it's because we feel so helpless and need to blame someone. Maybe it's because we know that He could have stopped the bad thing from happening.

When my brother was diagnosed with cancer, I did what I'd always done when I had a problem—I took it to God. I took it with a mountain of faith, knowing that He could heal Dan. As our family stood helplessly by him, we knew that God was our last and only hope. But when the chemotherapy stopped working and it appeared that God's answer was, "No, not now," I was kind of worried. In my emotional exhaustion I was afraid I might become one of "those people" I'd heard about. People who become angry and blame God when He doesn't say yes to an important prayer. People who remain bitter the rest of their lives.

In fear of pushing Jesus away in the middle of my grief, I prayed, "Hold me close, Jesus. Don't let me blame or be angry with You. Don't let me leave You when I need You the most." In the end, I didn't need to worry. When my brother died, I ran *to* Jesus—not away from Him. I needed Him then more than ever.

If you give up on God when your prayers aren't answered the way you'd hoped, then the enemy wins. Cancer may have taken my brother's life, but I chose not to let it take away my trust in Jesus. When all is said and done, God will win the final battle for all of us. God is your strength to make it through today—He will hold you close. And He's your hope for tomorrow—He's promised that someday He will come to take you to a place where you won't have to ask for prayers to be answered, because everything will be perfect!

JUNE 25

You're No Good!

You, Lord, will always treat me with kindness. Your love never fails. You have made us what we are. Don't give up on us now! Psalm 138:8, CEV.

"You'll never amount to anything good!"

How many times had Dawson heard that line? It began to be his life's slogan. The older he got, the more he believed it. He would *never* amount to anything good.

When he was in the eighth grade, his mom sent him to live with another family and attend a different school. She hoped that a change would be good for him. At his former school he was flunking out and constantly getting in trouble. He had no motivation, mainly because he didn't have anyone to motivate him. No one ever encouraged him, so there was no reason for him to excel.

But a teacher at the new school saw something in Dawson that no one else had bothered to look for. She saw potential. She saw intelligence.

One day she approached him and said with confidence, "Dawson, I believe that you could pass the state test at the end of the school year with the highest grade in this class—if you would try."

"I stood there in amazement," Dawson told me years later. "I couldn't understand why she'd say that. But somehow I believed it. She put in my heart that I could do it! It gave me confidence. And it turned my life around."

When it came time for the state test at the end of the school year, Dawson passed it! And guess what? He passed at the top of his class! He continued his education and later became a great evangelist for God, leading thousands of people to know Jesus and give their lives to Him.

All of us need an encouraging word at times, don't we? We need to be told that we're worthwhile and that we can make it.

This is where I think Jesus has your back. He's there behind you to encourage you. He sees possibilities in you because you are one of His creations! And He knows that you can do something great with your life—if you will try. So don't believe anybody who tells you that you won't amount to much. Only believe what God has told you. And He has told you that you have potential!

JUNE 26

Just Trust Me!

It is better to trust in the Lord
than to put confidence in man. Psalm 118:8, NKJV.

Milwaukie was playing St. Helens, and it was a close game. The teams seemed to be evenly matched. When one team would make a touchdown, the other team would follow with one as soon as they got the ball. The lead went back and forth all night long.

In the fourth quarter Milwaukie was down by two points. All they needed was a field goal or touchdown to win. Now they had the ball and were driving down the field.

With 20 seconds left to play, they were about 35 yards away from a field goal. The coach called a time out. They couldn't afford a mistake, so they got in a huddle to look at options.

Griffin, the team's kicker, kept looking at the coach—and the coach knew exactly what he was thinking. But a field goal for the win was pretty far-fetched. If Griffin succeeded, it would be the longest field goal any team member had ever made.

"Just trust me!" Griffin pleaded. But none of the players wanted to trust him.

"Don't trust him! He can't kick that far!" some of the adult advisors argued.

But the coach said, "No, he can do it!"

Milwaukie ran the clock till there were just five seconds left in the game. Then they called another time out. When the players came back on the field, the entire stadium fell silent. Everyone was worried. Could Griffin do it? He knew that everything depended on him now. He focused. He ran. He kicked the ball with all his might. It flew high into the air . . . and sailed right between the goal posts!

The team went crazy! People in the stands went crazy! Everyone was jumping up and down and hugging each other. The coach had taken a chance by trusting Griffin, and it paid off.

I'm sure glad that when we trust Jesus with something, it's never taking a chance. It's not iffy whether or not He'll come through. He'll always do what He's promised.

When He says He hears your prayers, you can trust Him.

When He says you're forgiven when you're sorry, you can trust Him.

When He says He will always be with you, you can trust Him.

When He says He is preparing a place and will come back to get you, you can trust Him.

You'll never find a truer, more trustworthy friend than Jesus.

JUNE 27

Without a Doubt

There are many rooms in my Father's house. I wouldn't tell you this, unless it was true. I am going there to prepare a place for each of you. After I have done this, I will come back and take you with me. Then we will be together. John 14:2, 3, CEV.

There are some things that I'm sure about. *Very sure.* There are some things that I believe—without a doubt.

I believe without a doubt that Jesus loves you. He doesn't play favorites. He doesn't pick and choose whom He loves. He doesn't love only those who obey Him. He doesn't even love only those who love Him back. He loves everyone. And He loves you.

I believe without a doubt that Jesus forgives you when you ask Him. Although some sins hurt more people and may have bigger consequences than others, His forgiveness isn't based on the size of the sin. He doesn't say, "I'll forgive this and this, but not that!" And He doesn't say, "Sorry, you've messed up too many times. There's no forgiveness left here." He forgives. Always.

I believe without a doubt that God knows who you are. The Bible says He even knew you when you were being formed inside your mom! He knows your name, He knows your address, and He knows where you go to school. He knows what makes you laugh and what makes you cry.

I believe without a doubt that He fights for you. Although the devil wants you on his side, Jesus reminds him that He died for you. Jesus claims you as His own and tells the devil to leave, because "this one is taken. This one has been purchased."

I believe without a doubt that Jesus listens to every word of every prayer you pray. He's never too busy. He's never too tired. He always answers. And when His answer isn't the one you wanted, it's because He sees the bigger picture.

I believe without a doubt that Jesus cheers you on. When you say no to a temptation, I bet He and the angels celebrate! And when you do well in a sport or on a test, He's proud just like any big brother would be.

And I believe without a doubt what today's verse says. He's preparing a place for you. He's coming back for you. Because He loves you. Without a doubt.

JUNE 28

Saying Goodbye to a Dream

The nights of crying your eyes out give way to days of laughter. Psalm 30:5, Message.

Chrissie had prepared for this day for an entire year. When she discovered that her new school had an elite choir, she just knew that she was meant to be in it. Besides loving the way the choir sounded, she knew the girls in the group got to wear beautiful floor-length gowns, and the choir went on tour during the school year.

So she worked hard her first year. She paid attention to all the musical instructions the choir teacher gave. She often practiced the music at home, and she even took voice lessons to prepare for the audition.

"The night of the audition, I felt that it was the most important night of my life," Chrissie told me. "We had to sing a capella, which meant no piano accompaniment. Our voices had to prove themselves. I stood in front of the teacher and more than 100 students, in the spotlight, in a darkened auditorium.

"As soon as I finished my song and sat down, I felt terrible! Compared to most of the other singers, I knew I hadn't done well. They'd taken lessons for years and been in musicals."

The week of waiting for the list to be published was a tough one for Chrissie. When it was finally posted, she anxiously scanned it—but her name wasn't there. She read it more carefully, but it *still* wasn't there. After all that work, her dream wouldn't come true.

"I felt I wasn't good enough," she told me. "Most of my best friends were on the list, so I knew that it would be a tough year having to watch them perform and hear what I was missing."

"I'm never going to sing again!" she announced to her parents that night. But that lasted only about a week. She soon realized that she loved music far too much to quit. And she realized that her teacher knew what he was doing. She sang in the regular choir and gave it her very best effort. "It was a great year musically!" she told me. "My best one ever!"

It's tough to have a dream not come true. But what really matters most is what we do with ourselves after the dream is gone. Do we give up? Or do we look for other dreams? When your dreams don't come true, don't let it mess with your self-worth. Remember who you are—a child of the King! Do your best at whatever you find to do, and know that your value isn't in lost dreams, but in picking yourself up and moving on, holding your head high.

JUNE 29

Come Join the Team!

If the foot should say, "I am not a part of the body because I am not a hand," that would not stop it from being a part of the body. If the ear should say, "I am not a part of the body because I am not an eye," that would not stop it from being a part of the body. If the whole body were an eye, how would it hear? If the whole body were an ear, how would it smell? But God has put all the parts into the body just as He wants to have them. 1 Corinthians 12:15-18, NLT.

My nephew Carl plays slow-pitch softball year-round. As the captain of two teams, one of his jobs is to place players in the best position for the sake of the team. And because he has to make these decisions, he's discovered that there are two types of players.

"I've had many different players on my teams throughout the years," Carl told me. "But there is one particular player that stands out in my mind. He wanted to choose which position to play. Before one particular game, I asked him to be the catcher. It isn't a very popular position in men's softball, because you don't get to do much. He was pretty unhappy with my assignment because he wanted to play the infield.

"After the first game, he announced to me, 'I'm not going to be catcher anymore.' So I had to move him, and I played catcher after that. It was an attitude of, 'I'm not going to do that,' even if it's the best thing for the team.

"Then there's this other guy I have on a team who is the complete opposite. He's good enough to play any position, but he'll go wherever I need him and is always ready to play wherever. When I have a good team, it's made up of people who are like this second player.

"I've discovered beyond softball, in life in general, there are people who are willing to do what will help, and others who will do only what makes them look good, what's easiest, or what gives them the most recognition."

According to today's text, we're all needed. We all make up different parts of a family, a classroom, and a church. And if one of us is missing, we feel it, because our group isn't complete. Why do we think that the ones who are seen the most or heard the most are the most important? You're needed whether you're the finger in your family, or the arm; whether you're the eye of the classroom, or the head; whether you're the little toe of the church, or the whole foot. Don't miss out! Don't think your opinion and work don't matter. They do! *You* are needed!

Wanted: True Friends

God blesses those people who refuse evil advice
and won't follow sinners or join in sneering at God. Psalm 1:1, CEV.

My problems started when I was in junior high," Nikki told me. "There were the athletic kids who were into sports and the preppy kids who were into fashion. Then there were the other kids—the cool kids, who really didn't care about school. My family didn't have money to put me in the sports programs, and we didn't have money for nice clothes, so I thought my only option was the cool kids.

"I wanted friends so badly, and I wanted to be cool. I didn't want to be the kid who was all alone, so I did whatever it took to get friends. I let kids talk me into doing things I knew were wrong. They told me, 'If you'll do this, we'll be cool with you.'

"One day I was in the girl's bathroom with two of the cool girls, and they talked me into writing a bomb threat on the bathroom wall. When we went back to class, an alarm rang, and all the students and faculty were evacuated and sent home. We were really excited that we'd pulled off the prank and gotten the day off from school. But the next day the principal somehow found out we had done it. And because I had done the writing, I was expelled from school."

Nikki, who is now 19, recently told me, "I decided that it was time to grow up and do something with my life. I'm going back to school to get my high school degree. I've joined a youth group and started going to counseling. I had no idea that what I was doing in junior high would affect my future like it has. I thought those girls were my friends, but now that I've turned my life around, I can see they really weren't friends.

"If I could go back to my junior high years, I would change three things: First, I would find someone at school to talk to, and ask for help. Second, I wouldn't choose the kids who pulled me down. And third, I would never leave God. When I came back to Him, I remembered how wonderful life could be with Him, and I asked myself, 'Why did you ever let this go?'

"I thought I'd done too many bad things to have God forgive me. But someone told me that God erases my sins, and He throws them to the bottom of the sea. I loved hearing that! And I'll *never* leave Him again."

JULY 1

The Replacement Principle

When a demon is gone out of a man, it goes through dry places to find rest. It finds none. Then it says, "I will go back into my house from which I came." When it goes back, it sees that it is empty. But it sees that the house has been cleaned and looks good. Then it goes out and comes back bringing with it seven demons more sinful than itself. They go in and live there. In the end that man is worse than at first. Matthew 12:43-45, NLV.

When you do some major cleaning in your bedroom, you don't move all your stuff out, clean it, and then just leave it empty. You throw away the clutter and put what's worth keeping in the empty spaces.

It's the same with your life, and that's why Jesus gave this illustration. When you give your life to Him and do some cleanup, you can't just leave your life empty. You need to replace the bad you got rid of with a whole lot of good! My husband calls it "The Replacement Principle."

The first step in cleaning up your life is to confess your sins to Jesus and repent. To confess is to admit to Him that you've done wrong. To repent is to feel truly sorry for what you did and to walk away from that sin—and keep on walking!

The second step is to do your best to remove whatever temptations you can. Don't give yourself easy access to the things that tempt you. If you own movies or video games that aren't good for you to watch, don't leave them lying around where they can tempt you—get rid of them. If you have magazines and books that aren't good for you to read, toss them out.

The third step is to put something better in their place, and that's where The Replacement Principle comes in. Replace the bad movies and video games with positive ones. Replace those books and magazines with reading that will make you a better person. When you get rid of sin in your life, you're in a vulnerable place. You can be easily tempted. But if you've used The Replacement Principle, the bad has been replaced with good, and it's a lot easier to walk away from temptation, saying, "No! I've got something better."

The final step is to stay close to Jesus. Romans 13:14 says, "Let the Lord Jesus Christ be as near to you as the clothes you wear. Then you won't try to satisfy your selfish desires" (CEV). With Him that close, you're not fighting temptation alone.

Hiding in His Shadow

Show me loving-kindness, O God, show me loving-kindness. For my soul goes to You to be safe. And I will be safe in the shadow of Your wings until the trouble has passed. Psalm 57:1, NLV.

When you imagine a bully, you probably picture a big boy on the playground who pushes smaller kids around. But girls can be bullies, too—most often by using cruel words.

Trissa found that out when she was in second grade. And even though she's now a sixth grader, she still remembers the pain of being bullied by a girl at school. At the time she wasn't bold enough to stand up to the bully or even to report her to a teacher or parent. So she wanted me to share her story with you to help you take a stand if you're ever bullied:

"I used to be friends with her," Trissa whispered to herself, drying her wet eyes. At first Samantha had seemed sweet, but she turned out to be the meanest girl in the whole school! Trissa will never forget the day Samantha walked up with a group of girls behind her.

"Well, well, well," she said in a snide tone. "If it isn't Trissa, the idiot who still wears diapers!" Her friends laughed. "Why aren't you with your mommy, little girl?" They laughed again as Trissa just walked out of the room, feeling sick with embarrassment.

After school that day she told her big brother everything. He said he was going to tell their mom, but Trissa begged him not to. "I asked him to keep it as our secret, which turned out to be a *big* mistake!"

The bullying went on for months, and she never told anyone but her brother. She often went straight to her room after school to cry on her bed. Finally her brother couldn't take it any longer and told their mom. With Mom's help, and the school's, the bullying finally stopped.

Trissa has this message for you: "If you're being bullied, tell someone. It *can* stop. I promise. Don't hide in the shadows like I did."

I agree with Trissa: "Don't hide in the shadows." *Unless* it's in the shadow of God's wings, as today's text suggests. That's a good place to be when you feel you're being picked on. How do you hide there? By going to His Word, the Bible, and reading about how much He values you. By talking to Him about your feelings. By praying for strength to face the bully. When it comes to being bullied, He's got your back.

JULY 3

More Than Berries

And regarding the question, friends, that has come up about what happens to those already dead and buried, we don't want you in the dark any longer. First off, you must not carry on over them like people who have nothing to look forward to, as if the grave were the last word. Since Jesus died and broke loose from the grave, God will most certainly bring back to life those who died in Jesus. 1 Thessalonians 4:14, Message.

My family thought it would be a fun way to kick off the Fourth of July. We got up at the crack of dawn, drove out into the country, and picked blueberries. In spite of the overpopulation of earwigs, we had a lot of fun!

We were some of the first people to arrive at the field, and the owner gave us a section to ourselves. After we'd been picking for a while, I heard a voice from the other side of the blueberry bush ask, "How's your brother doing? We prayed for him at church."

Her question made my heart ache because I had to tell her, "He died three months ago."

The woman, whom I recognized from a neighboring church, went on to tell me that she understood my pain because her grandson had died in a car accident the year before. She talked about the wonderful person he was and how much she missed him.

"You know," I told her, "it would have been quite the miracle if God would have healed your grandson's broken neck and my brother's terminal cancer. But the greater miracle is coming! At the Second Coming your grandson and my brother will be raised from the dead. Injury- and illness-free! To live forever!"

As I got up from my stool to move to a different row, I noticed that many pickers had arrived since our conversation began. All up and down my row and hers were people listening to our every word. Maybe they'd lost someone, too. And maybe something we'd said had given them hope.

When it was time to leave, an elderly woman walked up to me and said, "I couldn't help overhearing your conversation. My husband died from cancer recently. He was a Christian, too."

I touched her arm and said, "Someday you'll see your husband, and I'll see my brother in heaven. We can even introduce them to each other!"

As I left the field that day, I left with more than blueberries. I left with renewed hope.

JULY 4

Happy "Dependence" Day!

Jesus replied, "Very truly I tell you, everyone who sins is a slave to sin. Now a slave has no permanent place in the family, but a son belongs to it forever. So if the Son sets you free, you will be free indeed." John 8:34-36, NIV.

Happy Fourth of July! I love this holiday! It's a day when family and friends go to the river to swim and ski, have picnics in the park, attend a town parade, enjoy a barbecue—and, of course, watch a fireworks show. All this to celebrate America gaining its independence in 1776.

But did you notice today's title? It's not a mistake. I titled it *Dependence* Day for a reason. Because although we celebrate America's *independence* once a year, we can celebrate our *dependence* on Jesus every day.

According to today's text, when we sin, we become slaves to sin. It rules over us. It controls us. And then it leaves us feeling ashamed and guilty.

But when we give our lives to Jesus and get close to Him, sin can no longer rule over us! Sure, we still get tempted, and sometimes we give in to a temptation and sin, but that doesn't mean we're done for! It means we made a mistake that Jesus will forgive when we ask Him.

The cool thing is this: when we give our lives to Jesus, we become *independent* of the devil and slavery to sin, and *dependent* on Jesus. But it's a wonderful dependence! Depending on Him actually gives you independence (and you all want that!) because you're free from being a slave to sin. You're also free from guilt, hurting yourself, hurting others, and eternal death.

So what else can you depend on when your dependence is on Jesus?

You depend on Jesus to forgive you from your sins every single time you ask.

You depend on Jesus to hear you every time you pray.

You depend on Jesus to plan just the right future for you and to show you the way.

You depend on Jesus to give you a reason for living.

You depend on Jesus to resurrect the people you love who have died.

You depend on Jesus to prepare a place for you in heaven.

You depend on Jesus to come back and take you there.

And you depend on Jesus to win the final battle with Satan and destroy sin forever.

Sounds pretty great to be dependent, doesn't it? I'll take that kind of dependence any day!

JULY 5

Prisoner for Christ

Count it a blessing when you suffer for being a Christian.
This shows that God's glorious Spirit is with you. . . .
Don't be ashamed to suffer for being a Christian.
Praise God that you belong to him. 1 Peter 4:14-16, CEV.

Would you be willing to go to prison for God? Dr. Samuel Sih was. He was arrested twice during China's Cultural Revolution. "I openly professed my faith, so the Communists hated me," he told me. "There was no religion in that society. Churches and Bibles were not allowed. If a Bible was found, it was destroyed." Yet Dr. Sih never hid his faith.

When he was a young man, a group of Red Guards came and ransacked his home. They asked him, "Do you believed in Jesus Christ?"

Without shame he answered, "I believe." So they beat him.

The Guards destroyed a portrait of Jesus hanging on the wall in his house, along with many other belongings. Then they left.

Two years later Dr. Sih was wrongly accused of a crime and was taken off to prison. He was the only prisoner who openly confessed his faith in Jesus Christ. The other prisoners often laughed at him and insulted him.

"I had no hope of ever being released," he told me. "No hope at all. There was darkness all around. I was questioned and forced to stand before the prisoners and told to denounce my faith, *but I would not!* One prisoner said to me, 'If I were the judge, I would have you sentenced to death!' Daily I would silently pray and ask to be released and to see my mother again. I had read through the Bible several times and quoted memorized Scripture in my head."

After 19 months in prison, Dr. Sih was declared innocent and released. But two years later he was arrested again. After more than a year in prison, he was asked if even now he still believed in Jesus. And again he answered, "I do."

Those in charge realized he would not deny his faith, so they decided to release him. "During my combined stay in prison of more than three years, I learned to trust in God," Dr. Sih said. "I learned that if I would be my own best, God would help me and bless me."

If Dr. Sih was willing to go to prison because he was not ashamed of his beliefs, surely we can show our faith in Jesus in our everyday life at school, at home, and wherever we go.

JULY 6

Miracle in Joppa

As for the rest of you, dear brothers and sisters,
never get tired of doing good. 2 Thessalonians 3:13, NLT.

There's a woman in the Bible we don't talk about much, but her story is an amazing one. This is how she's introduced in Acts 9:36: "At Joppa there was a certain disciple named Tabitha, which is translated Dorcas" (NKJV). Wait. There were women disciples in New Testament times? Yes, there were! After Jesus was resurrected, women became His followers and helped to spread the good news, and Tabitha was one of them.

This is how verse 37 describes her: "She did many good things and many acts of kindness" (NLV). That's quite a way to be described, isn't it? The text didn't say:

"She was stunningly beautiful."

"She was very wealthy."

"She was the most talented woman in the town."

It says that "she did many good things and many acts of kindness."

One day Tabitha got very sick, and she died. Her friends washed her body and placed her in an upstairs room to wait for the funeral. It seemed that her acts of kindness were over.

The disciple Peter was in a nearby town when this happened, and two men raced to him and begged him to come to Joppa. He went back with them, and when he got to the room where Tabitha was, many widows were there, standing around and crying. They showed him some of the clothes that Tabitha had made for people and talked about her kindness. Peter was touched.

Then a miracle happened! Peter sent them all out of the room. He got down on his knees and prayed. Then he said, "Tabitha, get up." She opened her eyes and sat up! Peter then helped her to her feet and called in all the people who had come there to mourn her. Now, instead of mourning, they began rejoicing! This miracle became known all over Joppa, and many people believed in Jesus because of it.

Tabitha's life teaches an important lesson. It's easy to get caught up in doing things to get praise and recognition from people—going after awards and trophies, getting our name in the paper or on a plaque on the wall. But Tabitha's example shows us that what matters most when all is said and done is how we served. What matters most is how well we loved.

JULY 7

You Are More

What marvelous love the Father has extended to us! Just look at it—we're called children of God! That's who we really are. 1 John 3:1, Message.

A few years ago I had the opportunity to meet and interview the Christian music band Tenth Avenue North. I especially wanted to talk to them about their hit song "You Are More."

"What inspired you to write that song?" I asked lead singer Mike Donehey.

"It was a result of an irritant from Christian songs, movies, and books that kept saying: 'It's the choices you make that make you who you are.' I know what they're getting at," he told me. "They're trying to say, 'Hey, your choices have consequences.' But to say your choices make you *who* you are—period—is in direct opposition to the Christian message. The Christian message is this: *In spite of the wrong choices you make—in spite of the mistakes—you are awarded righteousness that you didn't do anything to earn.* So I wanted to get it across: you are much more than the sum of your choices and mistakes.

"That song spoke directly to kids with addictions—in particular, to girls who were addicted to self-harm. Several girls came up to us at summer festivals and said, 'This song is what helped me stop cutting. I have surrendered my life to God and am now free!' "

When I told the band that I was writing this devotional book, I asked if they had a personal message for you. This is what Mike said: "You can't be cool enough to save yourself. No matter how many people may like you, the feeling that you can't save yourself will never go away. You have to turn to Jesus. When you're done with school, all those people that you worried so much about what they thought of you—you're not going to care anymore. And you'll ask yourself, 'Why did I care so much about what they thought?' "

Jason Jamison, the band's drummer, added: "Even if you fall, God is there to catch you and help you back up. We can believe the gospel. Salvation isn't based on our performance or how well we do. It's based on Jesus and how well He lived and died for us."

So the next time you're being too hard on yourself, remember: If you add up all the bad choices and mistakes you've made, *you are more.* They don't define you. What defines you is today's text. You are a child of God! You are someone worth loving, dying for, and saving.

Tear the Roof Off!

Stoop down and reach out to those who are oppressed. Share their burdens, and so complete Christ's law. If you think you are too good for that, you are badly deceived. Galatians 6:2, 3, Message.

He couldn't have asked for better friends. They believed that Jesus had the power to heal their paralyzed friend. So when they heard that Jesus was teaching in a house in town, they put their friend on a mat and carried him there. But the house was packed full of people, and they couldn't even get through the door. So what did they do? They went up on the roof, tore off some of the tiles, and lowered their friend down in front of Jesus! And their friend was healed.

Wouldn't it be great to have friends like that? People who would be there for you when you need help, making sure that you get it? People willing to tear the roof off for you?

Destiny was that kind of friend. There was a small group of sixth-grade bullies who went to her school. She told me, "They looked mean, and everyone was afraid of them. They were so big for sixth graders that it was frightening!"

They never picked on Destiny, but they did bully a friend of hers. Her friend was different from the other boys in many ways, so kids often talked behind his back, accusing him of being gay. The bullies especially liked to pick on him—that is, until Destiny put a stop to it!

She was walking home from school one day and saw the bullies chasing her friend down the street. The three closed in on him and started pushing him around, calling him names. Even though Destiny was a petite girl, she felt she had to stand up for her friend.

She marched up to those bullies and with her hands on her hips demanded, "Hey, you guys! Just leave my friend alone!"

They started laughing at her and said to the boy, "Well, at least you've got your little friend to take care of you!"

But Destiny persisted until they finally quit and walked away.

"Thanks for helping me," her friend said, a bit embarrassed.

Think about the different kids at your school. Is there someone who needs your help? Is there someone who needs you to "tear the roof off" for them?

JULY 9

Show 'Em Who's Boss

We often suffer, but we are never crushed.
Even when we don't know what to do, we never give up.
In times of trouble, God is with us, and when we are knocked down,
we get up again. 2 Corinthians 4:8, 9, CEV.

One of the greatest things God has ever done for me was being with me in a time of danger," Fisher told me. "I love motorcycles, and riding them is one of my favorite pastimes. But one day I tried riding something new, and it could have killed me.

"It was a Sunday afternoon, and we invited some friends over to go riding. They brought a four-wheeler—something I had never driven before—so I was pretty stoked! I rode it for just a little while but decided that my motorcycle was easier to handle, so I headed back to the house. On the way home I lost control and ran into a fence. My dad helped me get the four-wheeler backed up and turned around.

"There was a bridge about 10 feet above a creek that I had to cross in order to get home. Dad pointed the four-wheeler in the right direction and I took off, but something went wrong. I lost control again and drove straight off the side of the bridge!

"I remember everything going black, and when I woke up, I was lying in the creek. Dad said it was a miracle that I didn't die by having the four-wheeler land on me or by hitting my head on the rocks. He said that by falling 10 feet, I should have at least broken a bone or two. I think God was with me and kept me safe.

"In a couple of days I was out riding on my motorcycle again. I haven't ridden a four-wheeler since. But I can't wait to ride one someday and show it who's boss!"

Fisher's desire to get back on a four-wheeler to "show it who's boss," instead of giving up, goes along with today's text. It's basically saying that in this life you will have tough times. But nothing is ever hopeless. For every tough thing you face, God is there.

You may experience loss in your life. But you're never crushed.

You may not know what to do at times. But you don't have to give up.

Troubles may be all around you. But there is still room for God to be with you.

You may get knocked down again and again. But you can choose to get up.

You're not alone in this life. He's got your back.

JULY 10

Barricade the House!

Set your minds on things above, not on earthly things. For you died, and your life is now hidden with Christ in God. When Christ, who is your life, appears, then you also will appear with him in glory. Colossians 3:2-4, NIV.

Oh, how she wished she hadn't watched that scary movie!

Irene was home alone one evening and decided to see what was on TV. She chose a movie that caught her up in its drama. It was about two criminals who were after a woman, but she kept outsmarting them.

"I knew I should have turned it off, but I just had to keep watching so I could see how it ended!" she later told me.

The worst part was that it was dark outside, and Irene was home alone. She finally decided to turn off the movie because the criminals were closing in on the woman, and now she was way too scared to see how it might end.

She went to her bedroom, put on her pajamas, and played some Christian music. *Surely that will help make up for what I did wrong tonight,* she thought.

But she kept hearing noises throughout the house. And she kept thinking about that movie. The only way she would feel safe, she decided, was to barricade herself inside the house.

First she leaned the ironing board against the back door. If an intruder came in, he'd knock it over and she'd hear the bang. Next she piled cans of food in front of the front door. If someone managed to pick the lock and get in, surely the crashing cans would alert her!

But that wasn't enough. In case someone did break in and she didn't hear them, she wanted it to look like there were other people home. So she rolled up blankets and put them under the covers of each bed in the house! She also left the lights on in the hallway.

Feeling somewhat safe now, she took a blanket and sat on the couch. All of a sudden she heard someone outside the front door, playing with the lock and doorknob. *It's criminals! Just like in the movie!* she thought. The front door opened and the cans spilled everywhere. Irene was shaking! And then her family walked in, looking very confused. Was she ever glad to see them!

Irene learned her lesson that watching scary movies can mess with your mind. After that night she started making better choices.

July 11

Your Invitation Has Arrived

Then Jesus said, "Come to me, all of you who are weary and carry heavy burdens, and I will give you rest." Matthew 11:28, NLT.

It was a warm summer evening, and my cousins had come for a weekend visit. We were playing in our front yard, doing cartwheels. Actually, my cartwheels looked more like somersaults! To this day I cannot do a graceful cartwheel. So if you can, I think that's cool!

My dad and uncle were sitting on the front porch visiting when I overheard my uncle tell Dad, "I just wish that my girls would come to me when they're hurt or feeling sick. They always run straight to their mom. It makes me feel kind of sad. I'd like to comfort them, too."

I remember feeling sorry for my uncle. There was sadness in his voice. Not more than a few minutes had gone by when I tried doing a cartwheel and landed on my knees in the grass. I felt an instant pain in my left knee, and when I stood up, I saw that a sharp, thick piece of glass had gone deep into my knee!

In a bit of a panic, I started to run to Mom, who was in the house. But before I reached the front porch, I remembered what my uncle had said to Dad. And I thought, *If I run right past Dad to get to Mom, he might feel sad like my uncle does.*

So I ran up the steps and showed Dad the glass in my knee. He lovingly scooped me up in his arms and carried me inside to the kitchen counter. Then he got a pair of tweezers and skillfully took out the glass. Maybe it was all in my imagination, but even though Dad and I had always been close, I felt that we became even closer that day.

If our earthly dads and moms want us to come to them when we're hurting, how much more does God, our heavenly Parent, want us to come to Him? But so many times we don't. Sometimes we blame Him. Sometimes we don't go to Him because we can't see or hear Him. But He's there, waiting on the front porch, hoping we won't pass Him by on our way to get help from someone else.

The invitation from Jesus to you is, "Come." If you're hurting, go to Him. He's always available. He may use another person, or words you read in the Bible or hear in a song, to comfort you. Sometimes He'll simply send a feeling of comfort and peace. Regardless, after you go to Him, you'll somehow feel that the two of you have become even closer.

JULY 12

Alone on a Dark Highway

Be strong and have strength of heart. Do not be afraid or shake with fear because of them. For the Lord your God is the One Who goes with you. He will be faithful to you. He will not leave you alone. Deuteronomy 31:6, NLV.

"I had been driving for only about two months," Greg told me, "and I wasn't familiar with freeway driving at night. I was cruising around 60 to 70 miles per hour when from out of nowhere I saw a full-grown elk—with antlers—standing in my lane. There was no time to even think. As my windshield shattered, glass and dust flew into my mouth as I gasped for air.

"The next thing I remember was realizing that my car was off the road on its side, with the driver's-side window facing the ground. I tried to crawl out, but my seatbelt stopped me. I managed to unbuckle myself and crawl through another window onto the ground. In shock I cried out loud to God.

"I walked onto the road, where shattered glass was spread everywhere. I realized that I needed to get help, so I went back to my car to find my cell phone. It was nowhere, so I went back to the road. I found myself helpless, stranded, and alone in the darkness, out in the middle of nowhere. I was powerless. I looked at my SUV lying off the road. It was totaled.

"Finally in the far distance I saw headlights coming toward me. Earlier in the trip I had removed my shoes because they were uncomfortable, but I started running barefoot toward the oncoming car, jumping and frantically waving my arms. That's when I saw the elk, lying dead on the opposite side of the road.

"At first the car passed me, but then the driver realized what had happened and stopped. I ran to the car, and the driver called 9-1-1, then checked my injuries. It was a miracle that only my wrist felt sore, and my arm was scraped up and bleeding."

A few months after the accident, I asked Greg if he learned a lesson from that night. He told me, "After the accident, when I was standing there in the road, I was completely alone. There was no sign of people, cars, houses, or stores for as far as I could see. I felt completely and utterly helpless. When I felt that feeling of aloneness, I called out to God. I called out to Him because there was no one else. My accident made me realize that I am *never* alone, despite helpless feelings. God is there—always there—whether I can see Him or not."

JULY 13

Not a Nightmare

There will be no more night. They will not need the light of a lamp or the light of the sun, for the Lord God will give them light. And they will reign for ever and ever. Revelation 22:5, NIV.

If you read yesterday's devotion, you read about Greg's accident and the important lesson he learned: You are never completely alone. Even if you feel lost and alone, God is always there.

Remembering that night, Greg realized another lesson. He recently told me, "I wanted someone—anyone—to be there. In that isolation I felt powerless. I wanted to help myself so badly, but there was nothing I could do. I was angry. Looking back, I just wanted someone to be there. I felt as though everyone had deserted me, and no one was there when I needed them most.

"I was so tired because it had been a long day, and I just wanted to wake up from this disaster of a dream that I was having. But I never woke up. In my shock and confusion, I was scared that I would be stuck there—alone forever."

Maybe you've had something tragic happen in your life, and you wished that it were just a bad dream. Then you could wake up and it would all be over. When your parents divorce . . . when you lose a friendship . . . when you move to a new town . . . when someone you love is diagnosed with a terminal illness . . . when someone you love dies . . . you wish you could wake up, shake your head, and say, "Wow, that was a bad nightmare!"

So what do you do when it's not a nightmare? What if your nightmare is a reality that you will never wake up from?

First, you decide to fight. You decide that this circumstance will not be the end of you, but that you will fight to live through it.

Second, you decide to get the help and support you need—help and support that will give you ways to cope and heal.

Third, you hold on to Jesus. You hold on to Him through reading His Word, through praying, through listening to encouraging Christian music, and through hanging around Christian friends.

And finally, you believe. You believe that someday the sting won't be so sharp and you'll laugh again. And you believe that someday you will go to a place with no more nightmares. A place where reality is better than you could have ever dreamed!

JULY 14

Right Where He Belongs

But when he was still a long way off, his father saw him and felt sorry for him. He ran to his son and hugged and kissed him. Luke 15:20, CEV.

As he walked down the center aisle of the church, I watched a few eyes dart his way and a few heads turn to follow him. I wondered what people were thinking. Some, including me, knew about his addiction—how it had torn his family apart and robbed him of years of peace and happiness. I silently wondered if some were thinking thoughts like these:

"Why is *he* here?"

"The nerve of someone like *him* coming to church after all he's done!"

"He needs to stay home and get his act together and then come to church."

I had mixed emotions when I first saw him, because his addiction had deeply hurt one of my good friends. But as I watched him walk humbly down the aisle, I thought, *He's right where he belongs.* And I felt respect for him because he was brave enough to come.

As he walked by my pew, our eyes met, and I motioned for him to come and sit with my family. He looked relieved and gladly joined us.

Guess what the sermon was about that day? *The prodigal son!* It's the story of a son who took his inheritance and left home. Before long he'd partied away all his money and had absolutely nothing. He was even eating food with pigs! So he decided to go back home and ask his dad to forgive him. Even being one of his dad's servants would be a better life than this.

Here's what happened: "When he was still a long way off, his father saw him. His heart pounding, he ran out, embraced him, and kissed him. The son started his speech: 'Father, I've sinned against God, I've sinned before you; I don't deserve to be called your son ever again.' But the father wasn't listening. He was calling to the servants, 'Quick. Bring a clean set of clothes and dress him. Put the family ring on his finger and sandals on his feet. Then get a grain-fed heifer and roast it. We're going to feast! We're going to have a wonderful time! My son is here—given up for dead and now alive! Given up for lost and now found!' And they began to have a wonderful time" (Luke 15:20-24, Message).

Jesus told this story so you would know that if you ever choose to leave Him, and then decide that life is empty without Him, He'll welcome you back with open arms.

JULY 15

The Last Shot

Be good friends who love deeply;
practice playing second fiddle. Romans 12:10, Message.

My nephew Davey had been friends with Dillon since they were little kids. Now it was their senior year of high school. Dillon had played baseball through the years, but this year he had signed up for basketball tryouts. Davey was cocaptain of the team, so the coach asked for his advice.

"Should we put Dillon on the team?" he asked Davey.

"Yeah, let's give him a chance," Davey said.

Dillon wasn't that great during tryouts, but the coach put him on the team and used him mainly for practices. During a game the coach would let him play the last few minutes if it looked like they were going to win or lose by a wide margin anyway.

Then came senior night. The final game night, when players were brought onto the court with their parents and recognized for their achievements. It was a big night.

Toward the end of the game Davey's team was way ahead of the rival team. All at once the students in the stands began chanting, "Dillon! Dillon! Dillon!" They wanted him to play one last time. He hadn't scored a point all year long. If he was going to, this was his last chance.

Someone passed the ball to Dillon when he was wide open for a layup—but he missed the basket! Now there were only 30 seconds left in the game. Davey was driving in for a layup when he saw Dillon out of the corner of his eye. He had to make a split-second decision. Would he end his own high school basketball career by making the final point of the final game? Or would he pass the ball to Dillon, giving him one last chance?

Davey passed the ball to Dillon. Dillon positioned himself for the shot. *SWOOSH!* It dropped through the net! The crowd went crazy! All the players gathered around Dillon, slapping him on the back and congratulating him. He had made his first basket and the team's last points.

Davey told me that looking back on that night, he'd do it all over again. What were just two more points on his record compared to the look of triumph on Dillon's face?

As today's text says, to be a good friend we have to love deeply and practice playing second fiddle. I know we're not used to aiming for second fiddle. But when we learn to play that part well, we discover that it makes us feel first-rate.

Feeling Forsaken?

About three in the afternoon Jesus cried out in a loud voice, *"Eli, Eli, lema sabachthani?"* (which means "My God, my God, why have you forsaken me?"). Matthew 27:46, NIV.

"My God, my God, why have you deserted me?" (CEV).

"My God, my God, why have you abandoned me?" (Message).

"My God, My God, why have You left Me alone?" (NLV).

No matter what paraphrase or version you read, Jesus' words as He was dying on the cross are painful to read. It's heartbreaking to think that Jesus actually felt that God, His Father, had forsaken Him. He believed that He was left to die alone. Think how terrifying that must have been for Him!

"But didn't Jesus know better?" you might ask. He did, but at that moment on the cross, while He was dying for our sins, He actually felt the separation—the deep hole—that sin puts between God and us.

In all of His 33 years of life on this earth, Jesus had never sinned. He resisted *every single temptation* that came His way. But now, on the cross, He took your sins and mine on Himself. The sins of the whole world—past, present, and future. And that feeling was one of darkness—of being forsaken.

I've talked to a lot of kids your age who have felt forsaken. They have their own question that they cry out to God:

"Why did you let my pet die?"

"Why did you let my family move?"

"Why did I have to be born with a learning disability?"

"Why did you let my grandma get cancer?"

"Why did you let my dad kill himself?"

"Why do you let terrorism happen?"

When you feel forsaken, remember that you are no more forsaken than Jesus was. God was with Him, and God is with you. Take a look at God's track record all throughout the Bible. *He doesn't forsake His children.* He rescues! Jesus had to wait to be rescued, and you may have to wait, too. But it will happen. If not in this life, then for sure in the life to come.

JULY 17

The Good Samaritan Mishap

The man said, "You must love the Lord your God with all your heart. You must love Him with all your soul. You must love Him with all your strength. You must love Him with all your mind. You must love your neighbor as you love yourself." Luke 10:27, NLV.

How many actual neighbors do you have? If I were to count the people living in the houses around us, we'd have eight neighbors. But according to Jesus' story about the good Samaritan, everyone is my neighbor. So I want to do my best to help people whenever I see a need. But I'll never forget the one time that trying to be a good Samaritan backfired on me!

It was a hot July day, and I had our van full of kids. It was our daughter's birthday, and some of her cousins had come from out of town to celebrate. The highlight of the day was a trip to the water park. On the way there, we stopped by a grocery store to get the kids a snack.

Standing in front of the store was a woman holding a cardboard sign that read: "Hungry. Need money for food." I was so excited to see her sign! Not only was I excited to help someone in need, but also our daughter and her cousins could see firsthand how rewarding it is to serve.

I wasn't going to give her money because I couldn't be sure that she'd use it for food. But I did want to help her. We hurried to the little snack shop in the store and read the menu, then went back outside to where the woman was standing. I told her what the snack shop had to offer and asked what she'd like. She said she'd like a hot dog, fries, and a soda.

We went back inside, bought the meal, and then took it to her. We sure weren't expecting what happened next!

In one dramatic scoop she snatched the bag of food out of my hand. She raised the hot dog over her head and yelled, "I don't like hot dogs!" Then she threw it into a nearby trash can. She did the same with the fries and then the soda. But it wasn't over. She was so angry that she came chasing after me with a shopping cart! My daughter and her cousins watched in horror! She caused such a ruckus that the store manager came out and asked her to leave.

Being a good Samaritan isn't always easy. Sometimes it's hard, and it always takes some kind of sacrifice: sacrifice of time, money, or possessions. Most of the time the receiver will be grateful to you for what you've done. But even if they're not, giving will somehow change you for the better. Because when you give of yourself, you find that you also receive.

JULY 18

The Bottomless Lake

In every way I showed you that by working hard like this we can help those who are weak. We must remember what the Lord Jesus said, "We are more happy when we give than when we receive." Romans 20:35, NLV.

"Hey, guys! Let's swim to the other side of the lake!"

Fourteen-year-old Darlene felt a knot in her stomach when she heard those words. She had taken swimming lessons, but she was happy just floating on inner tubes near the dock. Besides, the lake where she and her friends swam was known as "The Bottomless Lake," and that just sounded creepy. If she did decide to swim across, what would be beneath her when she reached the middle of the lake? Was it really bottomless? She imagined a big, dark hole that went down . . . and down . . . and down . . .

By now the other kids were in the water, and she didn't want to be left alone on the dock. Peer pressure got the best of her, so she jumped in and started swimming.

But about halfway to the other side, Darlene knew that she was in trouble. She wasn't going to make it! She'd go under and sink forever into the bottomless lake!

What am I going to do? What am I going to do? she thought frantically. *I can't tell them that I'm not strong enough to make it. That would be so embarrassing.*

She cried out a silent prayer: *God, help me! I'm not going to make it!*

One of the boys turned around, saw that Darlene was struggling, and called out, "Are you having trouble?"

"Yes! I'm having trouble!" she finally admitted.

There was a log floating nearby. The boy swam over and pushed the log toward Darlene so she could throw her arms over it and paddle to the other side.

When it was time to swim back to the dock, Darlene didn't know what she was going to do. Then one of the kids suggested, "Darlene, get on the log and we'll push you back!" So that's what she did. And this time she wasn't embarrassed.

Isn't this something we should all do? When someone is weak, shouldn't those who are strong give them a hand? That's what Jesus does for us every day.

He's got your back. So why not let someone know that you've got theirs?

JULY 19

Guard Your Heart

Guard your heart above all else,
for it determines the course of your life. Proverbs 4:23, NLT.

By the time you graduate from high school, you'll have a collection of yearbooks. I hope that you keep yours, because years from now it will be fun to look back and remember.

I hadn't seen mine for a long time until I came across them in storage a while back. As I looked at the pictures of some of my former classmates from junior high and on, I felt sad. Some have left the church or have left God completely. I wondered to myself, *What could they have done differently? How could they have made better choices and stayed friends with God?* I think I found the answer in today's text: they didn't guard their hearts.

I'm sure you "guard" the things that mean a lot to you. If you own a bike, you probably lock it when you park it at school. If you get allowance, you may guard it by putting your money in a piggy bank or hiding it somewhere in your room. If you're a snowboarder, you likely guard your belongings by keeping them locked in a locker while you're up on the slopes.

In today's text King Solomon is talking about the most important possession of all to guard: your heart. Why is it most important? Like the text says, *it determines the course of your life*. And your own life's course is right in front of you, waiting to be lived.

How do you "guard your heart above all else"? You shield it from anyone or anything that might separate you from God. Proverbs 4 gives us some ideas on how to do this:

"Never tell lies or be deceitful in what you say" (verse 24, CEV). Whether you fib to your parents to keep out of trouble or you gossip about another kid, lying can do a lot of harm.

"Let your eyes look straight ahead; fix your gaze directly before you" (verse 25, NIV). Don't look at what everyone else is doing. Make your own choices. Keep your eyes on Jesus.

"Know where you are headed, and you will stay on solid ground" (verse 26, CEV). Where are you headed? If it's heaven, then stay on that course, regardless of what everyone else does.

"Don't make a mistake by turning to the right or the left" (verse 27, CEV). If one of your friends turns away from God, don't follow him or her. Follow only Jesus. He knows the right way for you to live.

You have years of life ahead that hold a lot of choices for you. Choosing now to guard your heart will determine the course of your life. It's a choice you'll never regret!

Forgetting Jena

The Lord is your protector, and he won't go to sleep or let you stumble. The protector of Israel doesn't doze or ever get drowsy. Psalm 121:3, 4, CEV.

Have you ever pulled an all-nighter? My best friend and I once did. We thought it would be so cool to see what it was like not to sleep for a whole night, so we got permission from Mom. We made it till 6:00 a.m.—and then slept till noon! So we had breakfast for lunch that day. We were *so* tired all day. It really wasn't as fun as we thought it would be. It was hard to stay awake!

But staying awake all night isn't hard for God. He's always awake. Always watching over the world. *Always watching over you.* No matter what time zone you live in, He's awake. If you can't sleep at night because you're sick or worried about something, He's wide awake to keep you company. You're never completely alone at night, even if no one else is around.

Jena will never forget the camping trip her family took when she realized that she wasn't alone—even though it sure felt like it. She and her brother were left behind!

Because they had so much gear to take, her parents had to drive two cars. After several fun days of camping, it came time to pack up and head home. Because Jena and her brother hated to leave, they got permission to take one last walk around the campgrounds.

"We walked around for about 20 minutes, and when we got back to the campsite my parents were gone!" Jena told me. "We both started crying, and then I decided to pray. I prayed that my parents would come back for us. I believe Jesus helped me that day, because as soon as I opened my eyes, I saw a friendly-looking woman walking toward us. My parents had called the campgrounds and asked her to take care of us. She gave us a snack and something to drink.

"When Dad finally came back, I was so happy! Their cars had been so full of gear and our other siblings that Dad thought we were in Mom's car, and Mom thought we were in Dad's car! An hour later, we were all back home and together again."

Even though Jena's parents didn't know exactly where she and her brother were, God knew exactly where they were. I don't know about you, but I find it comforting to know that God constantly watches over me. According to today's text, He never sleeps! He stays awake and keeps His eye on us.

He's like a bodyguard, a big brother, a heavenly Parent who always has your back!

JULY 21

Camp Meeting Crisis

Anyone who steals must stop it! He must work with his hands so he will have what he needs and can give to those who need help. Ephesians 4:28, NLV.

Better to be poor and honest
than a rich person no one can trust. Proverbs 19:1, Message.

Katie never imagined that she would have to stand up for what she believed at camp meeting, of all places. She thought that kids who attended knew the difference between right and wrong. Well, as Katie and her friend found out, at least one girl didn't seem to know.

When Katie and Desiree weren't attending meetings in the junior tent, they loved going to the Adventist Book Center. It was full of so many interesting things! Their favorite section was a shelf full of plastic horses. On their second day visiting the store, another girl joined them at the horse display.

"Hey," she said quietly to them. "Could you like help me switch some of these price tags? Let's put some of the cheaper tags on the more expensive horses." She wanted to be able to get better horses for less money.

"No!" Katie answered. "That's illegal! We're not going to help you with that." Then Katie and her friend left to go to their meeting.

Afterward, they came back with money to buy some horses. But when Katie added up her money, she realized that she had enough to buy only two horses—one for herself and one for Desiree. And she had wanted more for herself.

"Satan tried to tempt me," she said. "I thought about that girl's idea of switching the tags. But then I decided that wasn't a good idea. So I bought just the two horses."

The next day Katie and Desiree reported what had happened to the store clerk so she could watch out for the other girl. "Thank you very much!" she told them. "I'm very proud of you for not switching the tags. God will reward you for your honesty someday."

I asked Katie, "Why did you choose not to switch the tags?"

"It just didn't feel right," she told me. "It would have been a type of stealing—and dishonest. And I didn't want to make Jesus sad."

Two horses purchased honestly are better than a whole herd purchased dishonestly!

JULY 22

The Big Questions

My God, I cry out by day, but you do not answer, by night, but I find no rest. Psalm 22:2, NIV.

Do you ever feel like David in today's text? Have you tried to get answers from God, but all you heard was silence? There are some answers that won't come until heaven, while others may not come until years down the road. But there are some answers that we can find right away in the Bible.

When I recently visited a few junior high Bible classes, I asked the students: "If you could ask God just one question, what would it be?" Since you might be able to relate to their questions, I'll be sharing several "Kids' Questions for God" during the coming week.

Question 1 was the most asked by far: *"Will I be saved?"*

The answer to that is a simple one: If you choose to be, yes! *But it's up to you.* Here's why. Jesus has done His part to save you. Romans 5:8 says, "But God demonstrates his own love for us in this: While we were still sinners, Christ died for us" (NIV). If this were the only text in the Bible that shows how much Jesus wants you to be saved, it would be enough. He died for you not when you deserved it most, but when you deserved it *least.*

And the most awesome part? Salvation isn't something you can earn. *It's a gift.* Romans 6:23 says, "Sin pays off with death. But God's gift is eternal life given by Jesus Christ our Lord" (CEV). And Romans 3:24 says, "Out of sheer generosity he put us in right standing with himself. A pure gift. He got us out of the mess we're in and restored us to where he always wanted us to be. And he did it by means of Jesus Christ" (Message).

So, you *will* be saved. If you choose to be. If you accept the gift.

Think about it. If a poisonous snake bit you and someone said, "Here's the antivenin that will save your life!" wouldn't you grab it from them?

If you were drowning and someone in a boat yelled, "I'm throwing you a lifesaver!" wouldn't you lunge toward it and hold on for dear life?

If you fell while rock climbing and someone on the cliff above hollered, "Here comes a rope! Clip in and I'll pull you up!" wouldn't you clip in and hold on as tight as you could?

If you are born into a sinful world and Jesus says, "Come to Me. I died to save you from eternal death!" wouldn't you go to Him?

JULY 23

Peter's Big Fail

What is the price of two sparrows—one copper coin? But not a single sparrow can fall to the ground without your Father knowing it. And the very hairs on your head are all numbered. So don't be afraid; you are more valuable to God than a whole flock of sparrows. Matthew 10:29-31, NLT.

Here's "Kids' Questions for God" 2, one that several students asked: *Am I a failure?*

No, no, no! Shall I say it again? No! You are *not* a failure. God, your Creator, definitely doesn't think that you're a failure. And neither do I. Even if you feel like you're a failure. Even if someone has told you that you're a failure. Even if you've messed up. *God values you.* And He'll give you a new start—another chance—each morning before your feet hit the floor.

Jesus' disciple Peter certainly felt like a failure. Do you remember what he did? He blew it—not once, but three times in a row! The night that Jesus was arrested, Peter three times denied that he even knew Jesus. Talk about feeling like a failure! He felt so ashamed that he went outside where he could be alone and wept. Yet Jesus forgave him, and here's the proof.

After Jesus rose, an angel appeared to two women who went to the tomb on Sunday morning. He told them, "Now go and tell his disciples, and especially Peter, that he will go ahead of you to Galilee. You will see him there, just as he told you" (Mark 16:7, CEV). How thrilled Peter must have been when the women gave him his own personal message from Jesus! A message that let him know he was forgiven. A message that let him know he had another chance. A message that let him know he was still valued by God.

Did you repeat that sin even though you promised you wouldn't? *You're not a failure.*

Did you miss the winning basket at the basketball game? *You're not a failure.*

Did you not get invited to the popular girl's birthday party? *You're not a failure.*

Did you flunk your math test? *You're not a failure.*

Did you lose the class election? *You're not a failure.*

Did you get into trouble with your parents and get grounded? *You're not a failure.*

Reread today's verse. If God values a sparrow to the point of knowing when one falls, how valuable you must be! He didn't forget Peter, and He won't forget you.

JULY 24

He Loves You Just as Much

Peter fairly exploded with his good news: "It's God's own truth, nothing could be plainer: God plays no favorites! It makes no difference who you are or where you're from—if you want God and are ready to do as he says, the door is open." Acts 10:34, 35, Message.

Kids' Questions for God" 3: *Do You love me as much as You love everyone else?*

Jill felt that her parents loved her younger sister, Bethie, more than they loved her. She would compare what her parents wrote in each of their birthday cards. She would keep track of the time their dad spent with each of them. She would compare their presents on Christmas morning. She thought that she had all the proof needed to show that her parents played favorites.

But it wasn't true. It was all in her imagination. Jill's parents loved her just as much as they loved Bethie. They had enough love in their hearts for both girls, and they valued both equally.

Sometimes we fall into the trap of thinking that God must love other people more than He loves us. We look at what a good Christian someone is and think, *God must love him more than He does me.* Or we look at how many prayers another has had answered and think, *God certainly loves her more than He does me.*

But that's not possible with God! He doesn't play favorites. He loves you as much as He loves the evangelist who has brought thousands of people to Jesus. He loves you as much as that kid in your class who gets A's in Bible. He loves you as much as the missionary who's serving on a remote island. He loves you as much as the kid who offers prayer up front at church.

Did you know that Jesus was criticized for having friends who weren't religious? He once went to dinner at a house full of people who were obviously sinners. According to the religious laws of that time, Jesus shouldn't have been visiting with the likes of them.

Shocked, the Pharisees questioned why He was hanging out with these low-life people. Jesus overheard them and asked, "Who needs a doctor: the healthy or the sick? I'm here inviting the sin-sick, not the spiritually-fit" (Mark 2:17, Message).

So there's some proof for you. Yes, He does love you as much as He loves everyone else. He didn't come to die for a few. He came to die for all. He's not coming back for His favorites. He's coming back for all who will follow Him. We're all His favorites! *You* are His favorite.

JULY 25

You Can Do Great Things!

Each of you has been blessed with one of God's many wonderful gifts to be used in the service of others. So use your gift well. 1 Peter 4:10, CEV.

"Kids' Questions for God" 4: *How can I do great things for You?* I'm sure God loves a question like this one! He does want to do great things through you! There are many stories in the Bible that prove that God uses kids to witness, to lead, and to help others. Here are some examples:

An unnamed slave girl encouraged Naaman to visit the prophet Elisha because she believed God could heal him of leprosy.

Samuel was such an obedient boy that God chose him to serve as His spokesman.

Josiah became king over Jerusalem when he was just 8 years old.

Mary was chosen as a teenager to be the mother of Jesus.

The boy who shared his sack lunch watched Jesus turn it into enough food to feed more than 5,000 people.

God did great things through boys and girls alike, and He can do great things through you. But don't get caught up in what the world might see as "great."

Preaching a sermon would definitely be doing something great for God—but being kind to the kid at school who gets picked on is doing something great too.

Some things we do for God are public, while others may be private. But both are great. In fact, I don't think there's anything you can do for Him that wouldn't be considered great, no matter how small you think it is.

First Corinthians 12:4-6 says, "There are different kinds of gifts. But it is the same Holy Spirit Who gives them. There are different kinds of work to be done for Him. But the work is for the same Lord. There are different ways of doing His work. But it is the same God who uses all these ways in all people" (NLV).

How can God use you? Well, what are your interests? What's your talent? Maybe it's witnessing or performing music. Maybe it's using your hands to make things. Maybe it's being helpful at school and at home. Maybe it's being a student Sabbath school leader. Maybe it's cooking. Whatever your gift, if you're using it for Him, it's great!

How Much Longer?

When the good news about the kingdom has been preached all over the world and told to all nations, the end will come. Matthew 24:14, NIV.

"Kids' Questions for God" 5: *When are You coming to take us to heaven?*

When my parents come from out of state to visit, we keep in touch through our cell phones. "When are you going to get here?" is the question we excitedly ask. It usually seems like a long wait, but in time they always arrive.

Sometimes it feels like a long wait for Jesus to come, too. And for various reasons, many people wish they knew exactly when He is coming to take us home.

According to the Bible, not even the angels or Jesus Himself know. He said in Matthew 24:36, "But about that day or hour no one knows, not even the angels in heaven, nor the Son, but only the Father" (NIV). The apostle Paul warns, "You surely know that the Lord's return will be as a thief coming at night" (1 Thessalonians 5:2, CEV).

Although we don't know the exact day when Jesus will return, the Bible does give us some signs to look for—signs to show us that the end is getting closer. Second Timothy 3:1-5 says: "You can be certain that in the last days there will be some very hard times. People will love only themselves and money. They will be proud, stuck-up, rude, and disobedient to their parents. They will also be ungrateful, godless, heartless, and hateful. Their words will be cruel, and they will have no self-control or pity. These people will hate everything that is good. They will be sneaky, reckless, and puffed up with pride. Instead of loving God, they will love pleasure. Even though they will make a show of being religious, their religion won't be real. Don't have anything to do with such people" (CEV).

Kind of sounds like people today, doesn't it? In Matthew 24 Jesus said that we'll hear about wars, earthquakes, starvation, and floods. That also sounds like today. And then there's today's text. It says that God is waiting so that everyone in the entire world can hear about Him and have a chance at eternal life.

So be patient! Don't give up, even if you get tired of waiting. Instead, remember Jesus' advice in Matthew 24:13: "Staying with it—that's what God requires. Stay with it to the end. You won't be sorry, and you'll be saved" (Message).

JULY 27

Jesus to the Rescue!

God rescued us from the dark power of Satan and brought us into the kingdom of his dear Son, who forgives our sins and sets us free. Colossians 1:13, 14, CEV.

Kids' Questions for God" 6: *Do You really forgive my sins?* I'm going to love answering this question! Not only is the answer a big YES, but there are many Bible texts that prove God really does forgive your sins. And that's good news that I love to pass on!

I loved passing it on to the boy who once asked me, "Can a person who's spent time in jail go to heaven?" What would you have told him? I told him that if the person has asked for God's forgiveness and has given their life to Him, then yes, they would certainly be able to go to heaven. I reminded him of the thief who was dying on the cross next to Jesus. His life had been so messed up that the government was giving him a criminal's death. Yet in his dying moments, when he asked Jesus to save him, Jesus assured him that he would go to heaven.

God wanted us to be absolutely certain of His forgiveness, so He gave us a lot of reassurances in the Bible. Texts like these:

"If we tell Him our sins, He is faithful and we can depend on Him to forgive us of our sins. He will make our lives clean from all sin" (1 John 1:9, NLV).

"How far has the Lord taken our sins from us? Farther than the distance from east to west!" (Psalm 103:12, CEV).

"Where is the god who can compare with you—wiping the slate clean of guilt, turning a blind eye, a deaf ear, to the past sins of your purged and precious people? You don't nurse your anger and don't stay angry long, for mercy is your specialty. That's what you love most. And compassion is on its way to us. You'll stamp out our wrongdoing. You'll sink our sins to the bottom of the ocean" (Micah 7:18, 19, Message).

Stop and think about it. Jesus came to this earth to die in our place. Why would He go through all that pain and suffering if His death didn't really do what it was supposed to do—give us the gift of forgiveness? His death happened nearly 2,000 years ago. And that's when forgiveness was offered to everyone—past, present, and future!

So don't hold on to your guilt for a single day longer. Jesus is waiting to forgive you.

JULY 28

Answering the "Why?" Question

Some people trust the power of chariots or horses, but we trust you, Lord God. Psalm 20:7, CEV.

Today is the last day we'll look at "Kids' Questions for God." Here's a question that was asked in different ways by several students. **Question 7 is *Why?***

"Why do bad things happen to us?"
"Why did You let my parents get divorced?"
"Why did my mom have to get cancer?"
"Why did You let my dad die?"

We know *why* all these bad things happen. It's because we live in a world full of sin. But these kids wanted to know why God *allowed* them to happen. And that's a tough question to answer. In fact, my answer is: I don't know. I don't know why God allows certain things to happen. I don't know why He sometimes steps in and other times He steps back. But even though I don't know the answer to these whys, there are some things that I do know for sure.

Bad things happen in this world not because of God, but because of Satan. So be sure to put the blame where it belongs. When Satan successfully tempted Eve and Adam in the Garden, they started to die that very day. God had created them with free choice, and they chose to sin. They had to live with the consequences—and unfortunately so do we. The consequences of living in a world full of sin are death, sickness, terrorism, crime, and all the other ugly things.

But that's not the end of the story! Out of love for you, Jesus came to die. And then He went back to heaven to prepare a place for you. A place like He meant the Garden of Eden to be—*perfect.* A place where no one can ever touch you, your family, or your friends with sadness or pain again.

Do you feel ripped off because you were placed in this broken world? After all, you didn't have a say in the matter! It's true, you weren't given the choice to live anywhere else. But you *do* have the choice to live in the perfect world to come! And if you choose that, it will be the best choice you'll ever make! Once you're there, God will answer all of your whys.

With the new world will come understanding. First Corinthians 13:12 says, "Now all we can see of God is like a cloudy picture in a mirror. Later we will see him face to face. We don't know everything, but then we will, just as God completely understands us" (CEV).

JULY 29

Herbie the Rainmaker

Encourage those who are timid. Take tender care of those who are weak. Be patient with everyone. 1 Thessalonians 5:14, NLT.

His name was Herbie. He was short and small. When my husband, Keith, worked as a counselor at Camp MiVoden, Herbie was assigned to his cabin. The other boys definitely saw Herbie as a misfit. On the first day they gave each other cool nicknames, but Herbie was left out.

One night Keith's cabin camped out at the Space Station—a one-of-a-kind tree house that looked like a yellow rocket built around a tall pine tree near the top of a hill. It had four decks of round plywood going up the tree and vertical strands of yellow ski rope running up the sides to hold everyone safely inside.

The boys scrambled up the rungs in the moonlight to claim where each would sleep. Except for Herbie. Turns out he was deathly afraid of heights, so Keith climbed up with him.

Once all the boys were settled down for the night, they heard crashing and roaring sounds coming from the woods. They didn't know it, but some of the staff were out there pretending to be bears. They wanted to give the boys an adventure to remember!

When the fun was all over, Herbie was missing. Guess where Keith found him? Forty feet up on the highest level with his arms and legs wrapped around the tree, holding on for dear life!

When they all finally got to bed, one of the boys hollered, "My sleeping bag's all wet!"

Herbie timidly said, "Um . . . guys . . . I got so scared that, uh, I wet my pants."

Oh, no! Keith thought. *Now they're really going to make fun of Herbie!*

But one boy, who was the leader of the group—a popular, athletic boy—said, "It's OK, Herbie! I was so scared that I almost wet my pants, too!"

"Me too!" another chimed in.

Then the leader said, "Hey, Herbie, I just thought of a nickname for you, and no one but our cabin will know what it means. We'll call you Herbie the Rainmaker!

Herbie and the gang loved the idea! They thought it sounded like an Indian brave. No one ever told the other cabins about Herbie's accident or how they came up with his nickname. His secret was safe with them. And he wore his title, "Herbie the Rainmaker," with great pride!

JULY 30

Family Feuds

Put up with each other, and forgive anyone who does you wrong, just as Christ has forgiven you. Colossians 3:13, CEV.

I was bound and determined not to leave the greenhouse until I found a particular shade of pink flower that my mother-in-law wanted.

There was a woman standing on the far side of a wide table full of flowers, and I asked her, "Could you please look at the tag on that flower in front of you and tell me the color?"

"It's hot pink," she replied.

"Bummer," I said. "My mother-in-law wants two magentas, and I can only find one."

"Well, get her this color and tell her to deal with it!" the woman said roughly.

"Really?" I asked surprised. "You want me to tell my 89-year-old mother-in-law to 'deal with it'?"

"Well," she backed down, "maybe you like your mother-in-law. I can't stand mine. I haven't talked to her in five years. She hates me." And with that she walked away.

Several minutes later, outside the greenhouse, that same woman raced up to me holding a magenta flower. "I found one for you!" she said as she happily presented it to me.

I was touched. "You're such a nice person!" I told her. "Why would your mother-in-law hate you?"

"Because I married her son."

Now the woman's husband was standing beside her. "Mom hasn't talked to *me* in five years, either," he told me.

"I hope that one day you can all work this out," I told them. "Life is short, and she won't live forever." They both told me that they'd tried, but she wouldn't respond to them in any way. I told them I'd pray that she someday would.

Family conflicts aren't limited to adults. When you have a problem with a parent, sibling, or other family member, God wants you to work it out and to forgive each other. Sometimes it might take professional help to work through an issue, and that's OK. But family feuds that never get settled can lead to a lot of regrets down the road. Life is too short. Give each other a break. Work it out. Forgive. And heal.

JULY 31

Happy Birthday!

You made all the delicate, inner parts of my body and knit me together in my mother's womb. Thank you for making me so wonderfully complex! Your workmanship is marvelous— how well I know it. You watched me as I was being formed in utter seclusion, as I was woven together in the dark of the womb. You saw me before I was born. Every day of my life was recorded in your book. Every moment was laid out before a single day had passed. Psalm 139:13-16, NLT.

The very first time I saw our daughter, Christina, I thought of this text. I actually saw her for the first time seven months before she was born! I was only two months pregnant when my doctor performed an ultrasound. It's kind of like an X-ray in which doctors can see what's going on inside the mother's womb.

There she was, no bigger than a peanut! Her small heart was beating strong. She had little arms and little legs, and she seemed to be doing a cha-cha dance! I was *amazed* at the miracle of life. Today is her birthday, and I can't believe how much she's grown since that first time I saw her. She's taller than I am now!

I don't know when your birthday is, but whenever it is, happy birthday! Whether you have a big party or no party; whether you get tons of gifts or maybe none; whether you enjoy a cake with candles or something else, I hope that on your birthday you will celebrate *you* and the gift that you are to this world. You were wonderfully made! An amazing creation of God. *You are a miracle.*

My friend Allison is a physician. She told me recently that the miracle of life always amazes her. "I've had the privilege to be at the birth of many babies," she said, "and every time I witness that, it's a miracle. It's a miracle that a dad and mom can form a tiny being. It's a wonder to realize that during the first three months inside the mother's womb, all of the baby's organs are formed. And in the following six months, the organs are growing and maturing. For nine months the baby depends on its mother. But a series of additional miracles happens at birth that allows the baby to begin living on its own. It all makes me appreciate the Creator."

From the moment you were conceived, you were a miracle. And you still are. Every morning that you wake up, every breath that you take, every day that you live is a wonder. So try not to take life for granted. It took a lot of miracles to get you here.

Are You Tough Enough?

Anyone who belongs to Christ Jesus
and wants to live right will have trouble from others.
But evil people who pretend to be what they are not will become worse than ever, as they fool others and are fooled themselves. Keep on being faithful to what you were taught and to what you believed. After all, you know who taught you these things. 2 Timothy 3:12-14, CEV.

I was walking through the parking lot at a Christian musical festival when I saw these words painted on a van window: "Are You Tough Enough?" Next to the question was a cross.

No doubt about it, sometimes it's tough to be a Christian. Especially when you need to stand up for what you believe in front of your peers.

Allie and Charles told me that they recently chose to take a stand. And they discovered that with God's help, they *could* be tough enough.

It was the first friends' party of the summer, and they were excited to see all their classmates from school. At first they had fun just sitting around and talking, playing volleyball, swimming, and eating snacks. But then some of the kids started making some pretty poor choices. When Allie and Charles realized what was going on, they chose to leave.

What do you do when you're with a group of friends and they start making poor choices? You're at a party and someone puts in a horror movie that you don't feel right watching. You're with a group of guys who decide to play a violent video game, and you don't want to shoot and kill someone—even though it's pretend. You're at a sleepover with a group of girls and they start gossiping—or worse yet, cyber bullying—and you don't want to be a part of it. What do you do? Do you go along with the crowd because it would be too embarrassing to get up and leave, or to say, "I don't think that's right to do—let's do something different"?

Are *you* tough enough? Yes, I believe you are! With God's help you can stand up for what you know is right. Philippians 4:13 says, "I can do all things through Christ who strengthens me" (NKJV). You're not tough enough on your own, but you are tough enough through Christ. The reason Allie and Charles were able to walk away from the party was that they had a close friendship with Jesus. He was the One who helped them be tough. And He'll help you, too. The key is to spend time with Him. Because when you're close to Jesus, you can easily tell when something is wrong or right. And you'll be tough enough to choose what's right.

AUGUST 2

When the Dust Settles

For now, we can only see a dim and blurry picture of things, as when we stare into polished metal. I realize that everything I know is only part of the big picture. But one day, when Jesus arrives, we will see clearly, face-to-face. In that day, I will fully know just as I have been wholly known by God. 1 Corinthians 13:12, Voice.

You've probably been in a rainstorm. Maybe even a snowstorm or hailstorm, depending on where you live. But have you ever been in a dust storm? In the Walla Walla Valley of Washington State, where we live, dust storms are common in the summer. When the asparagus, Walla Walla sweet onions, and wheat fields have been harvested, the topsoil gets dry from the heat. One good wind can stir up the dirt and carry it away. It's not unusual for winds to reach 30 to 40 miles per hour.

During a bad dust storm, you want to stay inside. Believe me. Our family was out walking one day when a dust storm kicked up fast. By the time we got home, we had to clean dust out of our eyes, our teeth, our noses, and even our ears! Sometimes the dust clouds get so thick that it's not safe to drive because you can't even see down the road. You just have to stay indoors until the dust settles and you can see again.

About four months after my brother died, my husband and I were driving home from a hike when a dust storm hit. My heart was still aching from Dan's death, and the dust made life seem extra dreary. By the time we reached home, the wind had settled and a few sprinkles of rain were falling. I got out of the car, looked up, and saw it. A beautiful rainbow in the sky!

I'll always think that God sent the rainbow that day. Seeing its brilliant colors cheered me. And it reminded me of today's text. Sometimes I don't understand God's ways. Sometimes I can't see His will clearly—just as I can't see clearly during a dust storm. I don't know why Dan had to die. I couldn't see any possible reason why our prayers for healing weren't answered. And I don't know why you have your own "dust storms" that you can't see through.

But today's text promises that someday we'll see the big picture. Someday we'll understand. Someday we'll see Jesus face to face and get answers to all the questions we have.

Until then—until the dust settles—there will be rainbows to remind us that He's here. He hasn't forgotten about us. And we will understand. Someday.

Answers to Everyday Prayers

We are sure that if we ask anything that He wants us to have, He will hear us. 1 John 5:14, NLV.

We've talked some this year about prayer, and about how God may not always answer with a "yes," but that He *does* answer. I've also told you that I believe in prayer and that I believe in miracles. For the next couple days I'm going to share with you some stories by kids your age. They wanted me to share their answers to prayer—just for you! Because they want to encourage you to keep praying, and to remind you that our God is an awesome God!

Jon: "I hurt my shoulder real bad while playing quarterback for my school's football team. The doctor said that I'd have to sit out for three weeks. Before my next game, I asked my grandpa if he would pray for my shoulder. He said he would, and added, 'Give every pass to God, Jon.' So before each pass I said out loud—right there on the field—'*Jesus, this one's for You.*' I passed a total of 200 yards in that game, and my shoulder wasn't reinjured."

Kristy: "My biggest answer to prayer happened when my family went to the mountains for a picnic. My dog ran off and was gone for a long time. I thought I might never see him again. But I didn't give up. I prayed, and we waited. After three hours, he came back!"

Trissa: "One time my mom got very sick. She was in the hospital for more than a week! She kept getting worse, and we all thought she was going to die. We prayed that she would get better, and God answered our prayers! It's been three years now, and she is fine."

Christian: "Something happened when my mom was pregnant with me, and I was born too soon. Parts of my body weren't fully developed, including my lungs, and I had to be on a respirator. My parents prayed that I would live, and God answered their prayers. I'm thankful that my parents prayed!"

Jeffery: "It was a Saturday night when I realized I'd lost my cell phone. I prayed for almost a week that I'd find it. I started losing hope. The next Saturday night I went to my friend's house to play games. We finished one game and went to grab another one. There was my phone on the top shelf! I quickly prayed and thanked God for helping me find my phone!"

These are just a few answers to prayer from everyday kids like you. Kids who had a need and took it to their heavenly Father. Kids who don't think that anything is too small—or too big—for God. In the next two days, I'll share more stories of answers to prayer.

AUGUST 4

Even More Answers to Prayer

I call to God; God will help me.
At dusk, dawn, and noon I sigh deep sighs
—he hears, he rescues. Psalm 55:16, 17, Message.

Yesterday I shared with you some answers to prayer that kids your age wrote just for you. Today I have a few more. You can't spend too much time talking about God's goodness!

Jennifer: "The day my grandma died was very hard. I was kind of mad at myself because I hadn't visited her much at the assisted living home. I asked the Lord to forgive me and to help me feel better. And in time I did feel better."

Matthew: "I was scared. My friend and I were skiing and somehow got lost. We decided to pray, and after a few minutes we found my parents!"

Lydia: "My best answer to prayer happened after my great-grandpa had a heart attack. I prayed for a really long time. Awhile later I got the news that he was going to be all right. That was the biggest thanks I've ever had!"

Joe: "Our youth group prayed for protection as we headed home from an outing. As we turned the corner on a city street, the front wheel came off and just rolled away! Pranksters had removed the lug nuts. If we had been on the highway already, we all could have been killed."

Natalie: "When my sister had to have her feet operated on, I was so scared. I prayed that God would keep her safe and that the doctors would be careful with her feet. She was kept safe, and now she can walk without pain."

Lindsay: "Before I left on a mission trip to Mexico, I prayed that I would make a difference there. A local 12-year-old boy named Javier started hanging around our worksite. In the evenings he'd come back to study the Bible with us. Then the next day he would gather the local kids around him and give *them* a Bible study! It was cool to see the ripple effect."

These kids believe that God *did* hear and answer their prayers—and so do I! I believe that He hears and answers your prayers, too. The Bible is full of proof that God loves His kids and listens when they talk to Him.

That doesn't mean He'll always answer your prayers in the way you want. When the answer doesn't go your way, believe that the same God who loved you enough to listen—and who can see the end from the beginning—knows what's best for you in the long run.

The Day God Sent a Cat

Blessed are those who mourn, for they will be comforted. Matthew 5:4, NIV.

Matthew's answer to prayer was painful for him to share, but he wanted you to know that God was there for him when he prayed. And for all you cat lovers out there, his prayer was actually answered with the help of a cat. Yes, a cat! Matthew wrote me this note:

"One morning at about 4:00, Mom woke me up with horrible news: Dad had suddenly died! It was like a nightmare. I felt like I was falling into nothing. First my parents had gotten a divorce—and now this? The only thing that brought me comfort was cuddling with our new cat, Jackson.

"Several days later, a limo drove up our driveway. It was the coolest car to ride in on the worst day of my life. When we got to the funeral, I just couldn't listen to the service, so I played with my mom's phone. At the cemetery I watched as they slowly lowered my dad's casket into the ground. My vision blurred as I watched them shovel dirt into the hole.

"When I got home, I ran to my room and stayed there. I asked for a sign from God—anything to show me that He was with me. I heard a sound, and when I looked up, I saw Jackson staring right at me. It had made me feel so much better to cuddle with him on the night my dad died, and now he had come back to comfort me again. I didn't feel so alone, and I felt that my prayer had been answered."

Matthew's story reminds me of the time when the prophet Elijah needed to be comforted, and God sent animals to him. Elijah had delivered a message from God that made King Ahab angry, so God told Elijah to hide in the desert. He said, "You will drink from the brook, and I have directed the ravens to supply you with food there" (1 Kings 17:4, NIV). And it happened just the way God promised! The birds faithfully brought breakfast every morning and dinner every evening. Since Elijah was all alone, imagine how happy he must have been to see those birds twice a day.

God makes a promise to you, too. He promises in today's text that if you're sad about something, you'll be comforted. He may comfort you through something you read in the Bible, through the words of a song, through something a friend says, even through a cat. God is great at comforting. He won't leave you all alone. He's got your back.

AUGUST 6

All You Have to Do Is Call

Call on Me in the day of trouble. I will take you out of trouble, and you will honor Me. Psalm 50:15, NLV.

We were all sitting around on my parents' deck last summer, enjoying a warm summer evening. Dad was in a storytelling mood, and his grandkids were excited. So was I! I love hearing Dad tell stories of his life—especially if they're cowboy stories. When he was 14 years old, Dad longed for adventure, so he spent the summer working as a ranch hand. This particular story was about his close encounter with a Durham Red bull.

"After a long, hard day's work, I'd spent the evening in town with some friends," Dad began his story. "The moon was behind the clouds, and it was a dark, dark night. Once I entered the gate to the ranch, it was about a two-mile walk to the ranch house.

"As I walked through the open pasture, I heard a bull bellow in the distance. It was a low, deep, loud sound, unlike the moo of a cow. But since it sounded far away, I didn't worry about it. Then I remembered that just that day, my boss had purchased a big red bull that weighed well over 2,000 pounds. The moon was now out from behind the clouds, and I realized that I was wearing a white shirt.

"I heard the bull bellow again, but this time it sounded very close—and that scared the living daylights out of me! I knew of nothing to do but run! I ran so fast that I could have qualified for the Olympics! As I was jumping over sagebrush and rocks, all I could hear was the bull's thundering hooves behind me. I didn't know what he'd do to me if he caught up with me.

"Finally I came to a fence, jumped over it, and hid behind a rock. I knew that the bull could go through the fence if his 2,000-plus pounds wanted to, so I stayed behind the rock for a long time.

"I had about a half mile to go before I reached the ranch house, and that's when I remembered old Shep, the ranch collie dog. I thought, *If I could just get that dog up here, I'd be OK.* So I called out, 'Shep! Shep!' And from out of the darkness Shep came running up to me. As soon as he was there, I wasn't afraid anymore. I wasn't alone. I felt secure.

"When I became a Christian, I realized that the same secure feeling comes when I call on God. At some point you may need to call out, 'Lord! Lord!' and He'll come to you, too."

AUGUST 7

How Healthy Is Your Tongue?

Words kill, words give life; they're either poison or fruit—you choose. Proverbs 18:21, Message.

Think of all the figures of speech we use concerning the tongue:

"I can almost remember . . . it's on the tip of my tongue!"

"When I got up to give my speech, I was tongue-tied."

"That poem we have to learn for English class is a real tongue-twister!"

"Why aren't you talking? Cat got your tongue?"

The tongue is a much-needed organ in your mouth. Without it you couldn't taste food. Without it you couldn't form words to speak. And with it you can do a lot of good—or you can do a lot of bad.

Moses' sister, Miriam, chose to use her tongue in a hurtful way. She and their brother, Aaron, were Moses' helpers. One day Miriam used her tongue to criticize Moses. She and Aaron had become jealous of him. " 'Has the Lord spoken only through Moses?' they asked. 'Hasn't he also spoken through us?' " (Numbers 12:2, NIV). God heard this and spoke to them about it. And when Aaron turned to look at his sister, she was white with leprosy!

Moses pleaded with God to heal her, and after she was made to sit outside the camp for seven days, she was healed.

What do you think she did during those seven days? Probably a lot of soul-searching. Probably asking herself such questions as "Why did I say such an awful thing? Why didn't I keep better control of my tongue?" And probably asking for God's forgiveness.

If you had seven days—alone—to sit outside your home or your school because of something critical you'd said, what would you do during those days? Would you do some soul-searching? Would you ask God to forgive you?

The sad thing about using our tongues to speak critical words is that we can never take the words back. We can't pretend they never happened. And even though God will forgive us—and hopefully the people we hurt will, too—the fact is that those words still hang in the air.

So wouldn't it be better never to say them at all? A critical tongue is like leprosy. It eats away at us and at the people we hurt. But according to today's text, you can choose what your words will do: they can bring death to a relationship, or they can bring life. You choose.

AUGUST 8

Enough Love to Go Around

If God gives such attention to the appearance of wildflowers—most of which are never even seen—don't you think he'll attend to you, take pride in you, do his best for you? What I'm trying to do here is to get you to relax, to not be so preoccupied with *getting,* so you can respond to God's *giving.* People who don't know God and the way he works fuss over these things, but you know both God and how he works. Steep your life in God-reality, God-initiative, God-provisions. Don't worry about missing out. You'll find all your everyday human concerns will be met. Matthew 6:31-33, Message.

If a girl in your class lived in a mansion, had all the expensive clothes she wanted, and even had servants who rushed to her side when she clapped her hands, you'd think she had it made. But what would you think if you found out that she wasn't satisfied and wanted more?

Such was the case with Potiphar's wife. She had all these things and then some, yet she wanted even more. She wanted handsome Joseph, even though she already had a husband.

Do you ever find yourself wanting more?

A dirt bike like his?

Designer clothes like hers?

A snowboard like his?

A horse like hers?

And do your wants ever consume your thoughts, as with Potiphar's wife?

We all see things that we think would be cool to have, and that's normal. As I'm writing this on my couch, I wish I had a new one. So many kids sat on this couch through the years that it became worn, and we had to buy a cover for it. It's OK to want a new couch—as long as I don't envy my friends who have newer couches, and as long as wanting a new one doesn't consume me. If it does, I'm living in an "if only" dream world and missing out on reality.

You may not always get everything you want, but God will always take care of you. He's promised to take care of all our needs. You may feel that you're missing out on some of the newer, cooler stuff, but no one has to miss out on the eternal life Jesus has to offer! When it comes to His giving out love, we're all equal. As today's text says, "Don't worry about missing out. You'll find all your everyday human concerns will be met."

AUGUST 9

How Gross!

Dogs return to eat their vomit,
just as fools repeat their foolishness. Proverbs 26:11, CEV.

I didn't believe it until I saw it for myself. I had always heard that a dog would return to its vomit and eat it. I couldn't imagine my dog doing such a gross thing! But one day it happened. Needless to say, I didn't allow him to lick my hand or cheek for a very long time!

I called a veterinarian's office today and talked to a vet assistant. I asked her, "Is there any logical reason why a dog returns to its vomit and eats it?" She said that it's a mystery. There's just no medical reason why a dog would do this. It doesn't make sense.

Let's say you're the dog in this verse from Proverbs, and the vomit is sin—a bad habit you can't shake. Maybe that habit makes you sick. Maybe it gets you grounded. Maybe it gets you school detention. Maybe it gets you in trouble with the law. Or maybe only you know about this sin. You know it's wrong before you do it; you know it's wrong while you're doing it; and you feel guilty after you've done it. But you return to it like a dog returns to its vomit. Why?

Here are some reasons kids have given me: "It feels good." "I like the rush." "I like feeling a part of the group." "I'm lonely." "I know God will forgive me later." These reasons sound like what the vet assistant told me, don't they? There's no good reason to return to the sins that make us spiritually, emotionally, or sometimes even physically sick.

One of the fruits of the Spirit mentioned in Galatians 5:22, 23 is "self-control." Notice that the text doesn't talk about being God-controlled, but *self*-controlled. We need to learn to control ourselves. Not even God will do that for us. Why? Because He created us with the freedom to make our own choices—both good and bad ones.

You gain self-control over temptation much the way you gain control over other things in your life—whether it's a sport or your schoolwork. You do it by practicing, by trying again if you fail, and by keeping your eye on the goal.

Is there something gross in your life that you keep returning to like a dog returns to its vomit? You *can* take control. It starts by wanting to change, then by getting as far away from the temptation as possible; by planning ahead what you'll do when you're tempted; by not giving up if you fall; by getting help if you need it; by spending time with Jesus every day. You can win this! Because He's got your back.

August 10

One Thing in Common

All of us have sinned and fallen short of God's glory. But God treats us much better than we deserve, and because of Christ Jesus, he freely accepts us and sets us free from our sins. Romans 3:23, 24, CEV.

When I was speaking to a group of junior high kids last year, I wanted to know who they idolized—who they most wanted to be like in the entertainment world.

My first question was "Who's your favorite actor or actress?" Some of the most popular answers: Taylor Lautner, Robert Downey Jr., Johnny Depp, Brad Pitt, Jim Carrey, Sandra Bullock, Adam Sandler, and Angelina Jolie.

Then I asked, "Who's your favorite musician?" They answered: Adele, Black Eyed Peas, Carrie Underwood, The Band Perry, Selena Gomez, Taylor Swift, Skillet, and Coldplay.

I've often wondered why we idolize people. For actors and musicians, I think it's because we like the whole fame thing, and we think that they're gorgeous, handsome, talented, and wealthy.

But it doesn't stop with the rich and famous. Think about it. Do you idolize kids in your school, wishing you could be like them? The girl with the flawless complexion, the boy who gets straight A's, the boy who's always chosen first for sports teams, the girl who wears only designer clothes, the girl who's good in sports, the boy who wins every election.

If you're ever tempted to think that these people are better than you—that they're somebody and you're nobody—I have something to tell you. When it comes to being sinners in need of a Savior, we're all equal. Take another look at today's text. It says that *all* of us have sinned. It says that *all* of us have fallen short.

On judgment day, when you stand with the whole world before God, fame won't save you. Looks won't save you. Money won't save you. Your talent won't save you. It's Jesus who will save you. *Only Jesus.* So when you look at it that way, we're all equal. No one can save himself or herself—we all need Jesus. And that's something we all have in common.

Jesus doesn't care what you look like, how popular you are, whether you struggle in math, or if you wear hand-me-downs. He's got your back. He gives salvation freely to all. And guess what? In heaven, we won't idolize anyone. We'll all be perfect!

AUGUST 11

Trade It for a Crown

God blesses those who patiently endure testing and temptation. Afterward they will receive the crown of life that God has promised to those who love him. James 1:12, NLT.

Have you ever felt really bummed because you tried hard to win something that was important to you, but in the end you lost?

You tried for the top grade in your class but lost to the kid in the front row.

You tried to score the most points in the volleyball game but lost to an opponent.

You ran for class president but lost by just a few votes.

You put a quarter in the gumball machine to get a prize, but only gum came out.

You trained hard to win first place at the track meet, but you came in third.

You studied to win the spelling bee but lost on supercalifragilisticexpialidocious.

Why do we want to win so badly? Is it the recognition from peers? Is it the trophy to put on a shelf? Is it the blue ribbon to hang on a wall? Is it the certificate to frame?

Everybody loses sometimes. But I'm so glad that there is one event that everyone can win. Everyone who wants to, that is. When we get to heaven, we will *all* receive the prize: the crown of life!

And the great thing is this: it's not a competition. The prize doesn't go to the fastest or the smartest. According to today's text, it goes to the ones who *endure*. The ones who hang in there when the going gets tough. The ones who don't give up on God when prayers aren't answered the way they'd hoped. The ones who come to God after they've sinned and ask for forgiveness. The ones who are willing to go against the crowd when needed.

I've won several awards in my life, and you know what? They're put safely away in a souvenir box in our garage. I don't even look at them anymore. Sure, when I first received them I hung them on the wall or placed them on a shelf. But as the years went by, they ended up in a box. They're nice memories, but they don't define who I was or who I am today. When Jesus comes again, I'm certainly not going to say, "Wait a minute, please!" and run back to my house to get my box of awards.

I'll gladly trade those in for a crown any day!

AUGUST 12

Physically Short, Spiritually Tall

Don't be hateful and insult people just because they are hateful and insult you. Instead, treat everyone with kindness. You are God's chosen ones, and he will bless you. 1 Peter 3:9, CEV.

Have you ever been made fun of because other kids thought you were somehow different? If so, Nate knows how you feel. And he asked me to share his story with you:

"I'm now in the sixth grade and doing well, but two years ago my life was tough. Because I was short, it seemed that everyone made fun of me. They called me cruel names like 'Midget' and 'Preschooler.'

"When I told my parents, they said, 'Be nice to those kids, and they might be nice to you.'

"I took their advice, but when I went to school the next day and said hi to the kids who had been mean, they just got meaner. I tried again later in the day, and they turned even meaner!

"When I got home from school that day, my parents asked, 'Were they nice to you?' I lied and told them yes. I would have told them the truth, but they'd threatened to call the mean kids' parents and even the principal if they didn't stop bullying me. I should have told the truth, because things actually got even worse, and I was more miserable than before.

"When I'd finally had enough of the name-calling and mean treatment, I told my parents. But I should have told them earlier. In the end, it all got worked out and the bullying stopped.

"If you're being bullied, I know what you're going through. Don't keep it a secret. Don't be too embarrassed to tell someone. Because if you don't tell, it could get worse."

So what did Nate do wrong? He lied to his parents. That's never a good thing to do.

But what did he do right? He followed God's instruction in today's text. He wasn't mean to the bullies when they were mean to him. That was good advice from God and his parents, and many times it works—even though it didn't in this case. The other thing he did right was that he was finally honest with his parents. Only then did the bullying stop.

It doesn't make you a weak person to report bullying. It's actually saying, "I'm taking charge of this situation so the bullying will stop." And it doesn't make you a weak person to follow today's text and not return hate for hate. These things actually make you more mature than the bully. And more like Jesus.

AUGUST 13

When Death Dies

"He will wipe every tear from their eyes,
and there will be no more death
or sorrow or crying or pain.
All these things are gone forever." Revelation 21:4, NLT.

To have one person or pet you love die is enough. But to lose two, as Abbey did, is pretty tough. She wrote about her losses on a piece of paper and handed it to me:

"One of the most difficult times I've ever been through was when my grandma died. I cried for almost three days. I prayed day and night for God to help me to feel better, and He did. Even though it's been four and a half years since she died, I sometimes still cry. But I know God is with me.

"Another hard time for me was when my cat died. He was my best friend. Every morning before I left for school he would lie on my lap or my back and purr. One day when my mom called him, he didn't come. She found him sick and took him to the vet. The vet said he had to be put down. Once again I was sad. But once again God helped me. If you're sad because someone you love has died, God can help you too, just like He helped me. So talk to Him and read His promises in the Bible."

Probably most kids reading this book have lost a person or pet they loved. Looking back on my own life, a lot of pets and people I loved have died. I've had fish (too many to count!), a turtle, a parakeet, a bunny, a guinea pig, a cat, and a dog die. All four of my grandparents, some aunts and uncles, a cousin, several dear friends, my father-in-law, and my big brother have died.

Read today's text again. It's almost too good to be true, isn't it? But just imagine: someday you won't cry or feel sad anymore, because there will be no more death! It even makes me sad to see a dead bird or opossum lying on the road. And of course, it makes me terribly sad to see people I love lying in a casket. So I'm really looking forward to this promise coming true!

I've had people ask me, "How can you be sure that God will someday end death?" I tell them, "*Because He promised.* Because He has too much invested in this world not to keep His word. He created us. He died for us. Why would He not someday save us from death, forever?"

Someday even death will die. And you'll never again lose anyone or anything that you love. He's promised.

AUGUST 14

Don't Wait to Appreciate

Don't look out only for your own interests,
but take an interest in others, too. Philippians 2:4, NLT.

"I'll never forget the day when my dad had a heart attack," Calin told me. "Since my dad's a paramedic, he knew what was happening. I was scared! I thought, *This is the end.* I think that Dad thought it was the end, too, because he told me, 'I love you more than anything.'

"Once he got to the hospital, the doctors did some procedure that helped him breathe normally again. When I was able to see Dad, he told me that he felt like he was coming out from underwater where he'd been holding his breath. I'll never forget that day."

Sometimes it takes a scary situation like Calin's to help us realize just how much we love the people in our lives—and just how much we'd miss them if one day they were gone. It's called taking people for granted.

Who do you take for granted in your life? Your parents? Your siblings? Your grandparents? Your friends? It's easy to do. We get caught up in our own lives, with our own busyness and stresses, and forget to appreciate the people around us. But after they're gone, it will be too late to let them know how much you do appreciate them.

Think what life would be like without your dad or mom. Who would make sure you get up in the morning and drive you to school? Who would make you dinner and help with your homework? Who would teach you how to cook, change a tire, sew on a button, or build a model airplane? Who would take care of you when you're sick or comfort you when you're afraid?

Think about what life would be like without your friends. Who would you share your secrets with? Who would you invite over to hang out? Who would play soccer with you at recess? Who would braid your hair? Who would understand what you're going through because they've been there themselves?

We shouldn't wait till someone is gone to show them that we appreciate them. I say we do it now! Think of all the things you appreciate about your parents. Why not write those down and give them the list? Then think of all the things you appreciate about your friends. Why not write each friend a note and leave it in their locker or on their desk? Then those you love will know—before it's too late.

AUGUST 15

The Fake Messiah

Jesus answered: "Don't let anyone fool you.
Many will come and claim to be me. They will say that they are the Messiah,
and they will fool many people. You will soon hear about wars
and threats of wars, but don't be afraid. These things will have to happen
first, but that isn't the end. Nations and kingdoms will go to war against each
other. People will starve to death, and in some places there will be earthquakes. But this is just the beginning of troubles. Matthew 24:4-8, CEV.

About a year after my family became Christians, we had a strange visitor knock on our door. When Dad opened it, he was surprised to see a man dressed in only blue jeans—no shirt or shoes. He had long hair and a beard and was carrying a bow and arrows and a hunting knife.

"I am the Messiah!" he declared to Dad. "I have come here to set up my kingdom in the hills above this city, and I want *you* to be my commander."

Dad remained calm. "I have a problem with that," he said. "I've read my Bible and know that when Jesus does come, He will come in the clouds, and every eye will see Him."

When the man couldn't convince Dad, he finally gave up and walked away. However, some people in town were convinced. We saw the man several days later jaywalking across a busy street. He was wearing a long robe and had a few followers trailing behind him. I was very glad that my family had studied the Bible so we could recognize this man as an imposter!

The Bible tells us clearly what we can expect at the Second Coming: "For the Lord Himself will descend from heaven with a shout, with the voice of an archangel, and with the trumpet of God. And the dead in Christ will rise first. Then we who are alive and remain shall be caught up together with them in the clouds to meet the Lord in the air. And thus we shall always be with the Lord" (1 Thessalonians 4:16, 17, NKJV). " 'Look, he is coming with the clouds,' and 'every eye will see him' " (Revelation 1:7, NIV).

Dad's experience was an unusual one, but it goes to show you how important it is to know your Bible. It's important so you'll understand what to expect before Jesus comes. It's also important to know your Bible in case someone asks you such questions as "What happens to a person when they die?" or "Is hell a real place?" or "Why do you go to church on Saturday?"

You're old enough to become a student of the Bible. Find a translation you like and begin to realize the treasure that you're holding in your hands!

AUGUST 16

School Is Cool

Get all the advice and instruction you can,
so you will be wise the rest of your life. Proverbs 19:20, NLT.

Within the next few weeks most of you will probably be heading back to school. As much as I loved summer as a kid, there was always something exciting about the first day of school—even if I didn't want to admit it! There was the new notebook with crisp sheets of white paper, the new pink eraser without a dent in it, the new sharpened pencils, and often a new outfit.

I didn't think much about the whole year to come on the first day of school. I was mostly excited to see friends. But I'm thinking that you can do better than that. I'd like you to plan ahead before your first day of school. It can't help but improve your year!

Just what do I mean by planning ahead?

Decide what kind of *student* you will be. Set some goals for yourself. You could even write them down and keep them in your notebook. Set such goals as: I'll really listen in class rather than daydream, doodle, or pass notes. I'll turn in every assignment on time. I'll study for a test before I play. I'll never cheat. I'll ask for help if I don't understand a concept. I'll always treat my teacher with respect. I'll take an active part in class and not be the kid with an attitude.

Decide what kind of *sports player* you will be. Set such goals as: I won't be a sore loser. I won't be cocky if I win. I'll be helpful and use my abilities to help other kids learn. I won't lose my temper on the court or on the field.

Decide what kind of *friend* you'll be. Set such goals as: I'll talk to the new kid on the first day and welcome him or her to our school. I won't be a part of a group or clique but will make lots of friends. I'll make sure that I have other friends outside my circle of close friends. I'll sit by a kid who's sitting alone at lunch and play with a kid who's all alone at recess.

Finally, decide what kind of *son or daughter* you'll be. And by that I mean what kind of son or daughter of *God*. Set such goals as: I'll practice WWJD (What Would Jesus Do?) when I'm not sure how to handle a situation. I'll say no when someone asks me to do something I think is wrong. I will make my heavenly Father proud of me!

You get to decide how you'll live this school year. By planning ahead, you can keep from having regrets on the last day. So set some goals—and have a great school year!

AUGUST 17

Campfire Invitation

Those who are wise will shine as bright as the sky, and those who lead many to righteousness will shine like the stars forever. Daniel 12:3, NLT.

As I write this, my family and I are camping at beautiful Wallowa Lake in Oregon. If you were here, you'd love it! A big three-point buck came wandering through our campsite late last night, and a squirrel and blue jay joined us for breakfast.

As I was walking from our campsite to the lake this afternoon, I remembered when I was 12 and my family went camping. We had been Christians for only a few years and were very "on fire" for God. We were so excited about what we'd learned about Jesus that we couldn't quit thinking and talking about it—even on vacation!

So the first evening we were at our campsite, my brother, sister, and I went around to neighboring campsites and invited other campers over. "Come to our campfire this evening," we told them. "We're going to play guitars and sing."

We weren't sure whether anyone would come, but several people did. We began to sing songs about Jesus. Happy songs about His love and His goodness. Then we each gave a short talk about what Jesus meant to us. And do you know what? They all stayed! And they listened!

I had to smile today when I remembered that camping trip. And I reminded myself that I need to always keep that same enthusiasm for God that I had at first. I should never become too timid to witness, worry about what others might think, or worry that I'll be rejected.

I'll always remember a Sabbath when I was visiting a church and the pastor asked if anyone wanted to come up front and give their testimony of what God had done in their lives. There was an awkward silence as the congregation sat very still, nervously looking around to see if anyone would actually go forward.

Then from the back of the church I heard a woman's voice. "If Jesus could walk the road to Calvary for me," she said, "surely I can walk down this aisle for Him." And she did.

That's what being a witness is about. Simply telling your story of the good things Jesus is doing in your life and why He means so much to you. It's not in-their-face preaching. It's talking—and just as important, it's living. Living in a way that your life is a witness, without even speaking a single word.

AUGUST 18

The Lost Watch

Or suppose a woman has ten silver coins and loses one. Won't she light a lamp and sweep the entire house and search carefully until she finds it? And when she finds it, she will call in her friends and neighbors and say, 'Rejoice with me because I have found my lost coin.' In the same way, there is joy in the presence of God's angels when even one sinner repents." Luke 15:8-10, NLT.

When my mom graduated from the eighth grade, her dad gave her a beautiful watch. She used to let me hold it when I was little. It had a dainty square face with a real diamond, almost too tiny to see, on each side. The band was a unique braided band rather than the traditional leather or metal band.

I had no idea that someday it would be mine, but when I graduated from eighth grade, Mom gave it to me! It was my most treasured possession. I rarely wore it for fear of losing it. I wore it only on special occasions. And I did keep it safe—until my senior year at college.

I wanted to wear it one day, so I looked in the box where I kept it . . . but it was gone! I began to tear apart my dorm room. Clothes went flying out of the drawers; I emptied my closet; and I even cleaned out under my bed. But my watch was nowhere to be found.

What will I say to Mom? I thought.

I was so upset that I felt sick. I quickly took out several sheets of blank paper and wrote with a fat marker in bold letters: LOST WATCH—IF YOU FIND IT, PLEASE CALL NANCY. $25 REWARD!

I had no idea how I was going to get $25, but I'd sell anything I owned just to get that treasured watch back. But by bedtime no one had contacted me.

The next day I felt down between my bed and the wall. My fingers touched something. It was the watch! It had been safely in my room the whole time. I was so excited! I ran down the dorm hallway telling all my girlfriends that my lost watch had been found.

Today's text tells us that all of heaven gets excited, too, when we repent. Why? Because repenting means that we've been found. It means that the Holy Spirit got to us!

You are much more valuable than a coin or a watch. *You are God's child.* So if you feel that He's looking for you, I hope you'll let Him find you.

AUGUST 19

Today's Top 10

You know that the Lord your God is the only true God. So love him and obey his commands, and he will faithfully keep his agreement with you and your descendants for a thousand generations. Deuteronomy 7:9, CEV.

Scholars say that the Ten Commandments were given to Moses in 1446 B.C. That was a long time ago! Since they were given so many years ago and are a part of the Old Testament, some people think that they just aren't important anymore—that they're old-fashioned and unnecessary. But believe me, we need them more now than ever before!

Take a look at the commandments in Exodus 20. Each of the 10 was given for one of two reasons: either to bring us closer to God or to keep us from hurting each other. The first four have to do with how we treat God, while the remaining six have to do with how we treat others.

Recently I thought about how the last six have affected my life. When people didn't obey God's commandments, either I got hurt or people I love got hurt. For example:

If a teenage friend of mine had obeyed "Honor your father and your mother," she wouldn't have broken her parents' hearts.

If a criminal had obeyed "You shall not murder," my dear friend Shannon would still be alive.

If another friend had obeyed "You shall not commit adultery," her kids would still have a dad and mom living at home together.

If a burglar had obeyed "You shall not steal," my husband and I would still have our backpacking and snorkeling gear.

If a church member had obeyed "You shall not give false testimony against your neighbor," one of my family members would have been spared a lot of hurt.

If still another friend had obeyed "You shall not covet," she would have been happy to see the presents I got and not made jealous remarks that hurt our friendship.

When we ignore God's law, someone always gets hurt. And that's why He gave it. God's law isn't our enemy! It's our protection and our freedom from very painful consequences. He didn't give His law to make life less fun. He gave it to make our lives more safe, peaceful, and happy. He gave it because He loves us and wants what's best for us.

AUGUST 20

What a Mighty God!

O Lord, You have great power, shining-greatness and strength.
Yes, everything in heaven and on earth belongs to You.
You are the King, O Lord. And You are honored as head over all.
Both riches and honor come from You. You rule over all.
Power and strength are in Your hand. The power is in Your hand to make
great and to give strength to all. 1 Chronicles 29:11, 12, NLV.

What a mighty, powerful God we serve!

- He spoke the entire universe into existence through His words.
- He wrote the Ten Commandments in stone with His finger.
- He changed Aaron's rod into a serpent.
- He caused bread to fall like rain six days a week to feed the Israelites.
- He parted the Red Sea so the Israelites could safely cross.
- He caused the walls of Jericho to fall down.
- He gave David the strength to conquer the giant Goliath.
- He kept Shadrach, Meshach, and Abednego alive in the fiery furnace.
- He shut the mouths of the lions when Daniel was thrown into their den.
- He became a tiny baby inside of Mary.
- He cast out demons.
- He gave sight to blind men.
- He made a paraplegic walk again.
- He fed more than 5,000 people with just five loaves of bread and two fish.
- He raised Lazarus from the dead.
- He died on the cross in our place so that we could live.
- He conquered death and burst from the dark tomb!

What kind of power do you have? Are you the captain of a team? Are you the class president? Are you the leader of a club? What do you do with that power?

In spite of all His power, Jesus was gentle with children. He stopped and talked to the poor, the social outcasts, and the unimportant. He helped people in need.

Guess we'd better quit thinking that we're really something and use whatever little power we might have to do some good. Just as Jesus did.

A New Best Friend

Here is a simple rule of thumb for behavior:
Ask yourself what you want people to do for you;
then grab the initiative and do it for *them*! Luke 6:31, Message.

Do you remember what it was like when you started kindergarten? Did you have butterflies in your stomach? Did you feel alone and wonder if you'd make friends?

Joey is now in fifth grade, but when he started kindergarten, he had a tough time. On the first day of school everyone was friendly. But after about a week, Joey and the one friend he had were feeling left out. Groups of kids had formed their cliques for the year, but the two of them weren't included. Not only were they left out, but some of the kids started being mean to them.

"I felt so bad," Joey told me. "No one was letting us be a part of their group."

What did Joey do about it? He could have started being mean back. He could have crawled into his own little shell and just given up on friends for the year. But he had a better idea. He prayed!

"I prayed and asked God to help me and my friend to be included. I waited and waited and waited, but kids were still mean to us. Then one day a boy named Hector started to let my friend and me hang out with him at recess. After he started being nice to us, all the other kids started being nice, too. It felt so good!

"The next school year Hector became my best friend. We did everything together. Now we're both in the fifth grade and are still best friends. From kindergarten through fourth grade we were always in the same class. This year we're in different classrooms, but we're still best friends. I believe God answered my prayer, and He still is."

What if you could be the answer to someone's prayer for friendship? Wouldn't that be great? Think about it: God using *you* to answer another kid's prayer!

With a new school year about to begin, you're probably excited to see all your old friends from last year. And it will feel good to have the security of knowing that you have friends to hang out with at recess and to sit with at lunch.

But what about the Joeys in your class? Are you willing to be a Hector and invite someone who seems lonely to hang out with you and your friends? If you do, then you'll be acting like Jesus. He always welcomed anyone who was lonely and needed a friend.

August 22

New Day, Fresh Start

Because of the Lord's great love we are not consumed, for his compassions never fail. They are new every morning; great is your faithfulness. Lamentations 3:22, 23, NIV.

My friend Cody was a student teacher in a fifth- and sixth-grade classroom last spring. Although his students were a great group of kids, it *was* springtime—and they were getting restless! In order to keep them on task, he came up with a really neat idea: a "Be Respectful, Be Appropriate" chart.

The chart hung in the front of the room. Each student had a slot with their name on it that contained five blank cards. Every time a student was disrespectful to the teacher or to another student or otherwise acted inappropriately, they were calmly asked to go pull a card. Here's what the consequences were for each card pulled:

First card: a warning. This gave the students one chance to realize that they were on the wrong path for the day.

Second card: one missed recess to sit in the room and reflect on what had happened.

Third card: a second recess missed—this time reflecting with the teacher.

Fourth card: problem solving began. It could involve writing a "management contract" or writing the teacher a note telling how they planned to better control themselves.

Fifth card: a student-parent-teacher conference (possibly including the principal).

The system worked well, and it was fair. The students knew exactly what the rules were, along with the consequences. Whether or not they pulled a card was up to them.

But here's the best thing about the chart: when the students walked into the classroom each morning, the chart started all over again! Regardless of whether they pulled one card or five cards the day before, each slot had a full five cards. Students had a fresh start and a chance to exercise self-control and to display good behavior with no past judgments hanging over them from the day before.

This is what God does for you. No matter what you did yesterday, each day is a fresh start. I like how today's text reads in the Good News Translation: "The Lord's unfailing love and mercy still continue, fresh as the morning, as sure as the sunrise." What a great gift!

So learn from yesterday, get a fresh start, and change today.

AUGUST 23

Put Up Your Dukes!

Abraham's faith never became weak, not even when he was nearly a hundred years old. He knew that he was almost dead and that his wife Sarah could not have children. But Abraham never doubted or questioned God's promise. His faith made him strong, and he gave all the credit to God. Abraham was certain that God could do what he had promised. Romans 4:19-21, CEV.

God asked Abraham to go outside and count the stars—if he could indeed count that many! And then He said, "Your children and your children's children will be as many as the stars" (Genesis 15:5, NLV). In spite of the odds against him (he was nearly 100 years old!), Abraham didn't give up believing that God would keep His word. And God *did* keep His promise.

Abraham's story reminds me of other people in the Bible who chose to trust God and not give up:

Noah didn't give up building the ark, even though people laughed at him because there wasn't a cloud in sight—and when the Flood did come, he and his family were saved.

Esther didn't give up when she was taken from her home to be the wife of King Ahasuerus—and God used her to save her people.

Joseph didn't give up when his brothers sold him into slavery or when he was wrongly put in prison—and in time he was promoted to second-in-command over all Egypt.

Moses didn't give up when Pharaoh repeatedly denied his request to free the Israelites—and God finally set them free.

Hannah didn't give up when she couldn't have a child—and Samuel was born, later to become a prophet and leader of God's people.

David didn't give up when he saw how huge Goliath was—and he won the battle.

Shadrach, Meshach, and Abednego didn't give up when they were thrown into the fiery furnace—and they came out with not a hair singed!

The woman who had been sick for 12 years didn't give up when the doctors couldn't help her—and Jesus healed her when she simply touched His robe.

With all these Bible heroes as our examples, we shouldn't give up, either. When life gets tough, don't throw in the towel. Put up your dukes with your Bible and prayer, and fight!

AUGUST 24

Hitting the Window

He gives strength to the weary and increases the power of the weak. Isaiah 40:29, NIV.

I was in the kitchen fixing lunch today when I happened to look out our glass sliding door. *WHACK!* A little goldfinch hit the glass hard, her feathers flying everywhere. I rushed over to the door and saw her lying on the patio. She was in a spread-eagle position with her head tucked under her chest. Hoping she was only stunned and not dead, I decided to leave her alone.

When I checked on her a few minutes later, she was still lying in the same sad position. But the next time I checked, her head was up. A few minutes later one wing was back in place, and the next time I checked, the other wing was in place. The final time I looked, she was gone! She'd flown off so quickly that I'd missed it.

I was impressed that she survived such a hard, feathers-flying hit. And I told myself, *I want to be like that little bird when I hit hard experiences head-on.* I may be stunned. I may need to stop for a bit to catch my breath. But then I want to get up and keep going.

King David did just that when he hit a crisis. His newborn baby was sick, and for seven days he pleaded with God to heal his child. He was so upset that he couldn't eat and spent his nights lying on the ground.

After a week, his baby died. You'd think that David would have remained there on the ground. But the Bible says that he did just the opposite: "Then David got up from the ground. After he had washed, put on lotions and changed his clothes, he went into the house of the Lord and worshiped" (2 Samuel 12:20, NIV).

He got up! Like the stunned bird, he got up. And he went to worship the One who could comfort him and give him a reason to keep on living. It was a choice he made, and a choice that you and I will need to make at times.

What "window" have you hit? Is it a broken family? losing a friendship? being bullied? having someone you love die? Whatever it is, when you get knocked down, don't stay there. Pick yourself up by surrounding yourself with positive people; by getting help from a pastor or counselor; by taking care of your health—getting enough sleep, eating right, and exercising. But most important, spend time with Jesus, the one who can give you both comfort and a reason to keep on living.

August 25

Friend or Foe?

The godly give good advice to their friends; the wicked lead them astray. Proverbs 12:26, NLT.

Sometimes you think that you have a great, trusted friend, but then they turn into a foe—someone who's against you rather than for you. But friends Anita and Paola are true BFFs. They've been through thick and thin together. And since they seem to know the true meaning of friendship, I asked them to share some friendship tips that they've written:

- Want to know how to avoid fake friends? *Stop being fake.* Be *you.* Your true friends will love you for who you are.
- Do what makes *you* happy and love whatever it is that *you* wish to love. Don't let others define who you are.
- If a friend believes a rumor about you, they were never truly your friend. As hard as it is to accept, move on and keep your head up! Learning who your true friends are is part of life.
- Be friends with those who seem "uncool." Shy kids may not even be shy, but maybe they're going through a hard time. Loud kids may not really be that annoying, but maybe they're trying to distract themselves from a reality that is painful. Unfashionable kids may not be unfashionable, but maybe they don't have the money to spend on the clothes they would like to have. Kids with "unattractive" appearances may be the nicest and best kids you will ever meet. Don't judge the book by its cover. Give it a chance and read it!
- God is the "bestest" friend you will ever have. He is your bodyguard at all times—even when you don't invite Him. He listens to your cries and cries with you—even if you don't share with Him what's going on. He doesn't stop calling you after you've ignored Him a bunch of times. He loves you even when you hardly ever tell Him that you love Him. He forgives you no matter how badly you've hurt Him. And He died for you so that you could live. Stop pushing your one-and-only true Best Friend away!

I especially like their last tip. God *is* the best friend that you'll ever have! He'll never gossip about you. He's never too busy for you. He always thinks the best of you. He'll always forgive you. He's a constant on good days as well as bad days. And He's got your back.

AUGUST 26

Squeaky Clean

And I will give you a new heart—I will give you new and right desires—and put a new spirit within you. I will take out your stony hearts of sin and give you new hearts of love. Ezekiel 26:36, TLB.

She stinks!" That's what all the kids in Lindsay's sixth-grade class said about Amy. It was obvious that she didn't shower often, that she never wore deodorant, that she seldom washed her clothes, and that she rarely shampooed her long, oily, tangled hair. But it really wasn't her fault. She lived with her grandma, who had never taught her about personal hygiene.

Lindsay told me, "Amy's self-esteem was pretty low, so she was quiet and just stayed to herself. To make matters worse, all the other girls in class talked behind her back. And the boys? They bullied her by making her their main target during dodgeball."

But Lindsay and her three girlfriends, who had formed a best friends' club, decided to reach out to Amy. They started by sticking up for her when the other girls said mean things about her. And they started going out of their way to be nice and talk to Amy. But the best thing they did was to plan a special "girls' night" sleepover just so they could invite her. She acted totally shocked when the "popular" girls invited her over, and she couldn't wait to go.

When Amy arrived, the girls gave her a gift basket. They'd gone shopping and filled it with things a girl would want: perfumed body wash and mist, some new tops, shampoo, lip gloss, razors, and even laundry soap. It was like Christmas to Amy! That night the girls talked to her like a big sister would about personal hygiene and gave her a squeaky-clean makeover.

When Amy looked in the mirror, her mouth dropped open! So did her classmates' mouths when she walked into school the next morning. Instead of slouching in, Amy walked in with a bounce! Even the teacher noticed. He pulled the girls aside and said, "Good job."

Lindsay and her friends treated Amy the way Jesus would. Every person with low self-esteem who met Jesus was changed after He looked into their eyes, spoke to them, and reached out and touched them. That's something we can all do. Is there an "Amy" at your school? Whether they're a girl or a boy, you can give their self-worth a makeover. You obviously wouldn't give a boy a basket full of beauty supplies! But you can help him improve in some sport or be his study partner. You can be like Jesus. And it starts by simply being a friend.

AUGUST 27

Just Passing Through

By an act of faith, Abraham said yes to God's call to travel to an unknown place that would become his home. When he left he had no idea where he was going. By an act of faith he lived in the country promised him, lived as a stranger camping in tents. Isaac and Jacob did the same, living under the same promise. Abraham did it by keeping his eye on an unseen city with real, eternal foundations—the City designed and built by God. Hebrews 11:8-10, Message.

Do you ever have the feeling that something just isn't right in your life? It's an unsettled feeling that you can't put your finger on. Something's missing. Something isn't complete.

Before my dad became a Christian, he had that unsettled feeling quite often. He knew that there was something more out there. He recently told me, "After I became a Christian, life was wonderful! But there was sometimes a sense that something was still missing—that something wasn't completely right."

One morning when he was reading in his Bible about heaven, it struck him: *No wonder I sometimes feel the way I do! I don't belong here! I'm not home. Heaven is my real home.* For Dad it was almost like a feeling of homesickness.

Maybe you've had that feeling when you've been away at camp or have taken a long vacation. You're having fun with family and friends, and it's exciting and adventuresome—but you also miss being home.

Like Abraham in today's text, we're all on a journey. You may love your home and the people in it, just as I do. And yet we will never feel like we're truly home until we get to our permanent home in heaven.

Growing up can be a lot of fun! When you look ahead to the years to come, it may seem that your life can only get better. There's a lot to look forward to: graduation, college, a career, marriage, and a family. And it's good to look forward to these things with excitement. Jesus wants you to live a full life here on earth.

But in the middle of it all, if those days come when you feel like something is missing, I hope you'll remember that maybe what you're missing is heaven. Maybe what you're missing is a world in which all the pain will be replaced by joy! Maybe what you're missing is Jesus.

AUGUST 28

Heartache and Hope

A thief comes only to rob, kill, and destroy. I came so that everyone would have life, and have it in its fullest. John 10:10, CEV.

It's been a while since I've shared from the journal I began when I was a teenager, so here's another entry:

The other night I had a conversation with a friend who told me that he feels life is meaningless. He admitted that at times he has no desire to live. He even admitted that there have been nights when he has gone to bed and prayed that he would die in his sleep. Then he wouldn't have to wake up and face another day.

Life has been very tough for him, and he's had enough. He was ready to say goodbye to new days, new opportunities, and new hope.

When I went to bed that night, I lay awake, thinking. Some of the things he said were true. Life can be tough. Life can seem incredibly unfair. And sometimes we expect life on this old earth to be more like heaven—we expect to escape heartaches and heartbreaks.

But that is only one side of life! There's another side that so many don't see. There are times when we can get a taste of heaven on earth. Because I believe—I really, really believe—that with every heartache comes hope. For example:

God doesn't promise you no pain—but He does promise to help you survive.

God doesn't promise you no lonely days—but He does promise never to leave you.

God doesn't promise you fame—but He does promise that you're important to Him.

God doesn't promise you no death—but He does promise you eternal life.

God doesn't promise you good looks—but He does promise inward beauty.

God doesn't promise that you'll never sin—but He does promise always to forgive.

God doesn't promise that every prayer will be answered in the way you wish—but He does promise to hear every prayer—and that His answer is what's best for you.

God doesn't promise no tears—but He does promise that someday you'll live in a place where tear ducts won't be needed for crying.

So you see, if you look for it, there is good in this life. God does provide a way to make this life not only bearable, but also even enjoyable! Along with every heartache there is *hope*.

August 29

Rock-solid in a Crumbling World

Truly he is my rock and my salvation; he is my fortress, I will not be shaken. Psalm 62:6, NIV.

Of all the growing-up stages, I think that the preteen and earliteen years are some of the hardest. Would you agree?

Being a little kid is so easy. Dad and Mom make all the decisions for you. They dress you, feed you, bathe you, protect you—you don't have to worry about a thing. When you're old enough to start kindergarten, much of school consists of coloring, story time, and crafts. The biggest ordeal of the day would be to fall and scrape your knee.

Once you're an adult, you've made it through school and have had all those preparation years to learn about life. You're more settled and secure in who you are.

But those in-between years can be tough. You're too old to simply color apples, but not mature enough to make all of your own decisions. You have to start convincing Mom and Dad that you're older now and should be allowed more privileges. School becomes harder because your brain can now handle more.

During these in-between years, there are a lot of self-worth obstacles that can get in your way. Here's what kids your age have told me:

You boys are worried about your height and whether or not you'll grow taller. You're also worried about your muscles—where are they? You're worried about whether or not you're popular, if you're good enough in sports, and if your acne will ever clear up.

And you girls? You're concerned about your hair—does it look good? Will it grow longer? You're also concerned about your weight and wonder if skipping meals would help you look thin. You want to be popular, even sometimes at the cost of being mean to another girl. Competition is happening left and right.

So with all these insecurities, how does a kid make it through in one piece? Psalm 62:6, 7 says, "He alone is my rock and the One Who saves me. He is my strong place. I will not be shaken. My being safe and my honor rest with God. My safe place is in God, the rock of my strength" (NLV).

God is your solid Rock. How do I know? I've been your age. I've been there, done that. And God helped me through. He's there to help you through, too.

August 30

The Eagle and the Snake

With all my heart I praise the Lord! I will never forget how kind he has been. The Lord forgives our sins, heals us when we are sick, and protects us from death. His kindness and love are a crown on our heads. Each day that we live, he provides for our needs and gives us the strength of a young eagle. Psalm 103:2-5, CEV.

When Jack was a young boy, he and his family moved to a faraway country in Africa, where his dad served as a missionary doctor.

Sometimes Jack felt the forces of good and evil fighting over him—pulling on his feelings and influencing his decisions. In his young, imaginative mind, these forces were a snake and an eagle. He told me, "Whenever I had a decision to make—whenever I had to choose—it was a battle between the selfish, sneaky, lowdown snake and the brave, kind, high-up eagle."

He imagined that the eagle would say to him, "Come on, Jackie; let's get up high and fly with the eagles." But the snake would say, "Oh, Jackie, you're a clever boy. Now just do what you want to do and stay down here in the dust with me."

One day Jack went to play with Tukiko, an African boy who lived in a hut. When he realized that his new friend didn't have any shoes, the eagle and the snake came to visit. The eagle said, "Oh, that's too bad—why don't you give him your other pair?" But just then the snake came to pay a call: "Well, he's Black and poor, and you're White and have two pairs of shoes. I guess you're better than him, aren't you?"

When Jack's birthday came, the snake said, "Jackie, be sure to invite just the other White missionaries so you can get lots of gifts!" But then in his imagination the eagle flew in from the heavens, grabbed the snake by its neck, and shook it as if to kill it. "You slimy creature!" it said. "Do you really want Jackie to spend the rest of his life crawling around in selfishness with you?" Then it said to Jack, "What a wonderful day a birthday is to be thankful for life and to share. Why not invite Tukiko and give him a present since he can't afford to buy one for you?"

So he did. On the porch they had a party, and on a chair sat Tukiko with a big smile on his face. Jack gave him one of his Matchbox cars, and the eagle inside was very happy. Jack was happy, too, because he'd celebrated his birthday not just by getting, but also by giving.

Cornfield Scare

There is nothing deceitful in God, nothing two-faced, nothing fickle. He brought us to life using the true Word, showing us off as the crown of all his creatures. James 1:17, 18, Message.

This story is almost too embarrassing to tell, but here goes. When my husband and I first moved to our rural town, we lived in a four-bedroom split-level home on the edge of town. The first time he had to be gone for meetings overnight, I thought, *No big deal. This is a safe place, and we have good locks on our doors and windows.*

I busied myself all that evening, and then at dusk I went around to shut the blinds and close the drapes on all the windows. When I started to close the drapes on the sliding glass door on the upper level, I saw something that made me feel just a little bit uncomfortable.

Behind our backyard was an empty field, and behind that a cornfield. There was a semi-truck parked to the right, and out in the middle of the cornfield stood a man in blue jeans and a white T-shirt. And he was staring straight at our house! I told myself that he was probably the trucker stretching his legs, and I went back to some cleaning I was doing.

But curiosity got the best of me, and after awhile I pulled back the drapes just a little to see if he was still there. It was getting darker, but I could see that the man hadn't moved at all! Now I was starting to get nervous! Why was he out there staring at our house? Right before complete darkness came, I peered out one last time. I could still see his white T-shirt! I finally went to bed, knowing that all the doors and windows were locked, and drifted off to sleep.

When morning came, the very first thing I thought about was that man out in the cornfield. I opened the drapes—and there he was! But in the morning light he had changed from a trucker into . . . a scarecrow!

So he wasn't what I thought he was. Have you ever thought of God like that—afraid that He means you harm when He's actually there to help you? Some kids get the wrong view of God and think He's out to get them. Well, let me assure you that you don't need to be afraid of Him.

He's someone you want by your side as you grow up. He is in the night who He is in the day. He isn't fickle. He isn't two-faced. He'll never turn His back on you. He isn't judgmental. He's the same today as He was yesterday and will be tomorrow. You can count on Him. Always. *He's real.* And He's the best friend you will ever have.

SEPTEMBER 1

Want Some Proof?

I am lonely and troubled. Show that you care and have pity on me. Psalm 25:16, CEV.

I don't remember her name. I can't even picture her face. But years ago she handed me a poem that she'd written. "This is how I'm feeling right now," she said.

Does God remember that I'm here?
Does He know my aching heart?
Does He listen with attentive ear?
Does He know every little part?

What answers would you give to her questions? A simple, "Yes, God does," wouldn't be enough. She needed proof. One of the best things about exploring your Bible is that you'll find answers to life's questions. For example, there is a Bible text for each one of this girl's questions in her poem. Check these out:

Does God remember that I'm here? Yes, He does: "Can a woman forget her own baby and not love the child she bore? Even if a mother should forget her child, I will never forget you" (Isaiah 49:15, TEV).

Does He know my aching heart? Yes, He does: "If your heart is broken, you'll find God right there; if you're kicked in the gut, he'll help you catch your breath" (Psalm 34:18, Message).

Does He listen with attentive ear? Yes, He does: "Is anyone crying for help? God is listening, ready to rescue you" (Psalm 34:17, Message).

Does He know every little part? Yes, He does: "You have looked deep into my heart, Lord, and you know all about me. You know when I am resting or when I am working, and from heaven you discover my thoughts. You notice everything I do and everywhere I go. Before I even speak a word, you know what I will say, and with your powerful arm you protect me from every side. I can't understand all of this! Such wonderful knowledge is far above me" (Psalm 139:1-6, CEV).

Maybe you've had days when you've felt like this girl—alone, invisible, aching. When you have those days, don't go by your feelings. Instead, go by what you know for sure—by what the Bible tells you. Jesus knows you're hurting, and it hurts Him, too. Through His words in the Bible, He wants you to know that He's there. He wants you to know that He's got your back.

Late-Night Discovery

Here's what I want you to do: Find a quiet, secluded place so you won't be tempted to role-play before God. Just be there as simply and honestly as you can manage. The focus will shift from you to God, and you will begin to sense his grace. Matthew 6:6, Message.

I've heard this saying many times: "Prayer changes things." And I believe it does! It changes individuals, and it changes families. After we became Christians when I was 10, prayer changed my family and me. Here's another journal entry from when I was a kid—one I wrote about prayer:

It was late at night when I finished the last of my homework. I got up from the dining room table, switched off the light, and tiptoed down the darkened hallway. As I turned to enter my bedroom, I noticed a soft light coming through my parents' door, which was ajar.

"H'mm . . . I thought they went to sleep 30 minutes ago," I said to myself.

Wanting to say goodnight again, I put my hand in the crack to open the door a little wider. But I didn't speak. I only looked. There in the dim light of a bedside lamp were Dad and Mom, kneeling across the bed from each other—heads bowed in silence, hands folded in prayer.

Seeing them praying made me think back to when they didn't know God—to when none of us did. Little did we know that for years something was missing. Actually, Someone was missing. Now we all know Jesus. He's a part of our family!

Not wanting to interrupt my parents, I quietly swung the door closed, smiled to myself, and went into my room. I put on my pajamas, pulled back the covers, knelt by my own bed—and prayed.

I still kneel down by my bed at night and pray. That's when I talk with God about the day. But that's not the only time I talk with Him. You wouldn't want to talk with your best friend only once a day, would you? It's the same with God. He's interested in what you have to say all day long! King David knew this, and that's why he wrote: "Morning, noon, and night my complaints and groans go up to him, and he will hear my voice" (Psalm 55:17, TEV).

But I don't just talk with Him when I have a need. My favorite prayers are when I'm thanking Him! Paul said, "Tell God what you need, and thank him for all he has done" (Philippians 4:6, NLT). He certainly deserves it!

SEPTEMBER 3

Never Too Young

Now the Word of the Lord came to me saying, "Before I started to put you together in your mother, I knew you. Before you were born, I set you apart as holy. I chose you to speak to the nations for Me." Then I said, "O, Lord God! I do not know how to speak. I am only a boy." But the Lord said to me, "Do not say, 'I am only a boy.' You must go everywhere I send you. And you must say whatever I tell you. Do not be afraid of them. For I am with you to take you out of trouble," says the Lord. Then the Lord put out His hand and touched my mouth, and said to me, "See, I have put My words in your mouth." Jeremiah 1:4-9, NLV.

Do you ever grow tired of people telling you that you're too young to do certain things?

You're too young to drive. You're too young to stay at home alone. You're too young to have a big motorcycle. You're too young to go out on a date. You're too young to use a dangerous power tool. You're too young to stay up late on a school night.

Usually it's the adults in your life telling you, "You're too young." But in today's text it's the boy, Jeremiah, who's telling God, "But I'm too young!"

God had asked Jeremiah to be a witness for Him to the nations, and Jeremiah felt way too inadequate. But God assured him that even before he was born, He had planned out how to use him. He assured Jeremiah that He would put just the right words in his mouth.

Here's one thing that no one should ever tell you you're too young to do: you're never too young to witness! Anyone at any age can witness for God, whether it be through their words or through their actions.

When Jesus was just 12 years old—the age of a sixth or seventh grader—He witnessed to grownups! He had traveled to Jerusalem with His parents to celebrate the festival of the Passover. When it was over, Jesus' parents headed home, thinking that He was traveling in their group of relatives and friends. Imagine their panic when they realized He was missing!

It took three days of frantic searching to find Him. They finally found Jesus in the synagogue, talking with the teachers. Everyone who heard Him was amazed at His knowledge and understanding of the Scriptures. He blew them away with His words!

Once again Jesus was setting us an example of how to live. And you're not too young to follow it! You're not too young to become like Him.

Waterproof Yourself

Watch what God does, and then you do it,
like children who learn proper behavior from their parents.
Mostly what God does is love you. Keep company with him and learn a life of love. Observe how Christ loved us. His love was not cautious but extravagant. He didn't love in order to get something from us but to give everything of himself to us. Love like that. Ephesians 5:1, 2, Message.

It was a busy day, and my daughter and I had three different grocery stores to go to. While we waited in the checkout line at the first store, a woman cut right in front of us. I mean right in front! There was a small space between my cart and the man ahead of me, and she just worked her way in.

How rude! I thought, wondering if I should say something like, "Um, excuse me, but I was next in line."

A few shoppers looked at me to see what my reaction would be. So did my daughter.

"Let it go, Mom," she quietly told me. "Just let it roll off your back. It's not that big a deal."

I looked at her with surprise because this is what I'd taught her since she was little. I'd say, "Give people a break. You never know what they might be going through. If someone is rude or unkind, just let it go. Let it roll off your back."

That saying comes from observing ducks. Have you ever seen a wet duck? Nope! Even if they duck under the water (now you know how they got their name!), when they pop up, the water just rolls off their feathers. The oil in their feathers makes them waterproof.

When you're at school or hanging out with friends, you're being watched, just as I was that day at the store. When someone bumps into you in the hallway and your books go flying, kids look at you to see how you'll react. When someone calls you a name on the playground, all heads turn your way to see what you'll say. If you spill your lunch in your lap and a kid at your table points and laughs, the whole table waits to see how you'll react.

I say, be like a duck! Be waterproof. Let it roll off your back. But you'll have to be prepared in order to do this. You prepare by doing what today's text suggests: spending time with Jesus. "Keep company with him and learn a life of love."

SEPTEMBER 5

Plum Jelly Lava

How far has the Lord taken our sins from us?
Farther than the distance from east to west! Psalm 103:12, CEV.

"When I was growing up, I spent as much time with my grandmother as I could," Jeff told me. "I referred to her as 'Memo.' Because life at home was pretty rough, I'd go over to her house every chance I got. She was a strong Christian woman who had a heart of gold. My grandparents were what you would call 'dirt poor.' They didn't own much, and nothing was ever wasted. The best way to describe Memo is to tell you this story.

"One summer day I went to Memo's house to help her make plum jelly. Together we went to an orchard and spent hours picking fresh plums from the trees. After we'd filled several grocery bags, we went back to her house to start the process. They had to be rinsed, cooked down, skinned, and strained, and then we added the sugar. The entire process took most of a day.

"Memo cooked the plums in a huge pot on her stove, and I helped her stir. While the jelly was cooking, we got out the canning jars and set them on the table.

"When the jelly was cool enough, I announced that I would carry the big pot to the table. Memo told me that I couldn't. It was too heavy. But just as soon as she turned her back, I picked it up off the stove. I took two steps. I could do this! But then the weight of the pot threw me off balance, and I tripped. The pot fell to the floor, and plum jelly spread everywhere like hot lava from a volcano. A whole day's work now splattered across the floor.

"Immediately I feared what my punishment would be. Grandma turned around and looked at me. She saw the fear in my face. She immediately ran over to me, knelt on the floor in the plum jelly, and wrapped her arms around me. She said, 'You're not in trouble. It's going to be all right. I'm not mad at you. But I do want you to learn from this—and to help me clean up.'

"So together we cleaned it up. Then Memo suggested we make another batch. And that time I did things right."

That is what God is like! Like Jeff, we know what's right and wrong. But sometimes we choose the wrong. We think we can handle it, but then we make a mess of things. Just like Memo, Jesus quickly forgives. Just like Memo, He wants us to learn a lesson so we don't make the same mistake again. And then, just like Memo, He gives us another chance.

SEPTEMBER 6

What Changed the Team?

How wonderful it is, how pleasant,
for God's people to live together in harmony! Psalm 133:1, TEV.

How would you feel if you were on a baseball team that went from twenty-sixth place to first place in just one year? Sounds almost impossible, doesn't it?

My nephew Carl has been a part of a Labor Day weekend tournament for five years, playing for WM Construction. A few years ago his team wasn't playing well at all. Because they were doing so poorly, the players started focusing inward rather than encouraging each other. When the tournament ended, they finished in twenty-sixth place out of the thirty-some teams that participated. That was a pretty low blow, ranking almost at the bottom. The whole team went home disappointed.

But by the next Labor Day weekend, Carl told me, they had a completely different team. Sure, there were a few new faces. But that wasn't the real difference. The *real* difference was the attitude of the players.

"There was a visible difference," Carl said. "Whenever the team came in from playing the field, those on the bench would come out to meet them, and we would all high-five each other. When it was someone's turn to bat, the team would shout out encouraging words. There was no negative talk in the dugout. If someone struck out, they would hear words like, 'Hey, that's all right.' There was a camaraderie, an attitude of, 'Let's do this as a team!' "

So the big difference that year was the *attitude* of the players. It was positive and not negative, and they worked together as a team. And it paid off—they won first place!

Imagine what your home would be like if everyone in your family worked together as a team. Rather than being buried in your computer or a video game, with the rest of the family doing their own thing, you would come together and work on a family project. You should suggest that to your parents!

Imagine what your class would be like if there was no negative talk in your classroom. When someone made a mistake, others in the class would say, "Hey, that's all right."

We're always happier when we work as a team, because we really do need each other. This is how Jesus wants us to live. So treat others the way He treats you. He's got your back.

SEPTEMBER 7

Ride the Bull Like a Pro

God's Spirit doesn't make cowards out of us.
The Spirit gives us power, love, and self-control. 2 Timothy 1:7, CEV.

It's a family tradition. Every Labor Day weekend my dad and mom fill their SUV full of grandkids and come to our little town for the county fair.

I remember the first time Dad saw the mechanical bull ride. He stopped and watched it for a long time as cowboys and wannabe cowboys were thrown off, chose to bail, or made it through the three-minute ride.

I'd grown up listening to Dad tell stories of his cowboy days, so I encouraged him, "Dad, you should ride it! After all, you're an ole cowboy!" But he didn't. He just stood and watched.

Fairs came and went through the years, but Dad never faced the bull. He'd only stand and watch. That is, until recently. That's when he announced, "This year I'm going to ride the bull!"

Dad put on the leather glove and mounted the bull like a pro. I bragged to the man operating the ride that my dad had once been a *real* cowboy.

Holding on with one hand and raising his other arm to the sky, Dad nodded that he was ready. As the bull gained speed, Dad got into the groove. The two were moving in rhythm.

The operator shouted to me, "He's still got it! He's still got it!" And even though I'm a grownup, I felt that same pride I'd felt when I was a little girl. My dad was still a cowboy.

Our family stood there whooping and hollering and cheering him on. He didn't fall off, but rode until the time was up. We clapped for him when he came back to us. Mom and I played the part of rodeo queens and kissed him on each cheek.

Do you ever feel that your life is like riding a mechanical bull? Sometimes life can whip us around like that bull did its riders. There are highs and lows. Jerks and stops. Twists and turns.

Dad stayed on the bull because he knew how to hold on. And so can we. We hold on through the tough times by holding on to Jesus. How do you do that? By talking to Him—being completely honest about how you feel. By reading Bible texts that remind you that He loves you, that you're never alone, and that heaven is coming. And by confiding in Christian friends.

Don't choose to bail! Don't let the bull throw you! You can do this. You can make it. Hold on. Hold on to Jesus.

SEPTEMBER 8

Get Away From Me!

All whom My Father has given to Me will come to Me.
I will never turn away anyone who comes to Me. John 6:37, NLV.

When we were kids, my brother Dan woke up one morning looking like a chipmunk. His cheeks were all swollen. Mom immediately took him to the doctor. When they came home they shared the diagnosis: mumps! It's a contagious disease that can be spread when the sick person coughs, sneezes, or even talks.

My sister and I weren't going to take any chances. We ran into our bedroom and slammed the door! When we knew that Dan was resting in his room, we covered our faces and shoved a rolled-up towel under his door. We even put a sign on his door that warned, "STAY OUT!" But later on we felt bad and made him a get-well card—which we slid under his door.

The way we treated Dan reminds me of the Bible story of a man who had leprosy. Back then if you had leprosy you were as good as dead. It was a contagious, incurable disease. If you wonder what it looks like, get permission from your parents or teacher to Google it.

If the priest declared that you had leprosy, you had to immediately leave town. You were sent to live in a place with other lepers, and on the way there you had to shout, "Unclean! Unclean!" to warn people that you were coming. Usually they would run away from you in fear.

Matthew 8 tells the story of a man with leprosy who went to Jesus for help. He must have heard some wonderful things about Jesus, because he was bold enough to leave his leper colony and find Jesus. He shouldn't have even been in the crowd that was following Jesus, but he was.

When he asked Jesus to heal him, Jesus could have said, "Go away! You're unclean! Don't even think about coming any closer!" But what did He do? "Jesus reached out his hand and touched the man" (Matthew 8:3, NIV). He touched the untouchable. The gross. The ugly. The contagious. And He healed him. Jesus could have healed the leper without touching him, but He chose to touch a man who had been rejected by everyone else.

If Jesus was so loving to a leper who was physically unclean, then surely He's that loving to you and me when we're spiritually unclean. When you go to Him and ask to be cleansed, He doesn't send you away in disgust. He puts His hand on you and forgives you.

SEPTEMBER 9

That's So Embarrassing!

But the Lord said to Samuel, "Do not look at the way he looks on the outside or how tall he is, because I have not chosen him. For the Lord does not look at the things man looks at. A man looks at the outside of a person, but the Lord looks at the heart." 1 Samuel 16:7, NLV.

What's your most embarrassing moment? A group of kids your age were brave enough to share theirs with me—and you!

"During a band concert my saxophone reed chipped. Every time I tried to hit a high note, it squeaked!"—Rose

"I had an important part in a school play. I forgot my lines not once, not twice, but three times!"—Chase

"I was playing goalie in a soccer game when I slipped in the mud, and the other team scored a goal."—Connor

"I was walking on the icy sidewalk to school when I slipped and fell right in front of a bunch of kids. I hid in the bathroom until I calmed down."—Lynnie

"I was asked to sing for special music at church. I walked up in front of all those people, opened my mouth to sing, and forgot *all* the words to the song. I was mortified!"—Josie

"When I was younger, we had a bunch of people over. I went to hug my dad but soon realized that I was hugging someone else's dad. I was so embarrassed that I locked myself in the bathroom. Then I became even more embarrassed because I couldn't get out!"—Breanna

"I was playing in a basketball game and got excited when someone passed me the ball. But I started dribbling toward the wrong basket!"—Henry

Do you think Zacchaeus was embarrassed that he had to climb a tree to catch a view of Jesus? Everyone else was on the ground, but he was too short! Imagine how the crowd reacted when they saw a grown man climbing a tree so he could see.

And what did Jesus do? (Are you singing the song in your head yet?) He told Zacchaeus to come down, and He went to his house for a visit. Jesus didn't care that he was short. He accepted him just the way he was. Jesus also knew that Zacchaeus was a dishonest man. But He saw the good in him. And He sees the good in you, too—no matter how awkward or clumsy you may feel at times! If Jesus were here today, I think He'd like going to your house, too.

Not So Perfect

And you know that Jesus came to take away our sins, and there is no sin in him. 1 John 3:5, NLT.

It happens every year on the day before my birthday. Mom calls and relives the day I was born.

She tells me, "When you were born I couldn't believe how tiny you were! You were just like a little baby doll. I held you in my arms and looked at your little hands and feet. Your eyes were bright and fixed on my face." And then Mom says those words: "You were *perfect*."

Well, the "perfection" didn't last long. In fact, I recently asked Mom what her earliest memory is of when I did something wrong.

She started laughing. "When you were just a toddler, I heard giggling coming from the kitchen. When I walked in, there you sat, stirring raw eggs that you had cracked open on the floor. Your older brother and sister, who knew that you were doing something you shouldn't, stood by giggling. I asked you, 'Nancy, did you make this mess?'

"You looked up at me, shook your head, and answered, 'Nah.' "

So I wasn't born perfect after all, and neither were you. Unfortunately, we didn't have a choice. We were born into a world that was already in a battle between good and evil. And as perfect as we may have looked to our moms when we were born, sometime later we all committed that first sin . . . and the second . . . and the third . . .

The good news is that God knows we aren't perfect! He knows we can't fix our sin problem on our own. So He gave His Son—who *is* perfect—to die in our place. Romans 3:23 says, "But God treats us much better than we deserve, and because of Christ Jesus, he freely accepts us and sets us free from our sins" (CEV).

Jesus also came to show us how to live. If you read the book of John, you'll see His example. He talked to a Samaritan woman, whom the religious law said He shouldn't associate with. He fed more than 5,000 people who were hungry. He calmed His disciples' fears during a storm. He comforted Mary and Martha when they were grieving because their brother had died. He acted like a servant and washed His disciples' dirty, dusty feet. What a great example He is! Even though we won't be perfect until heaven, we can still do our best to be like Him every day.

SEPTEMBER 11

The Day the World Changed

For God has not given us a spirit of fear and timidity, but of power, love, and self-discipline. 2 Timothy 1:7, NLT.

I'll never forget September 11, 2001. Not because it was my birthday and my family had planned a fun party for me, but because that's the day our world changed forever—the day terrorists flew planes into the World Trade Center. My friend Rosa was living in New York and witnessed it firsthand. Here's what she told me:

"It was a beautiful September day. As I commuted to work on the subway, I had no idea what was happening above ground. We stopped at the station right under the World Trade Center, but the doors stayed shut. Passengers waiting to board were crying and screaming. They started pounding on the doors and windows of our train. Some even tried to pull the doors open, begging to be let in. It was a horrifying sight to watch.

"Finally, as many as possible were allowed on, and we exited at another station. As I made my way up the staircase, I could see people just standing and looking in the same direction. When I got to the street and looked up, I could see billowing black smoke and flames coming from the North Tower. It seemed as if the world just stood still. All I could hear were sirens, because not a soul was speaking.

"At my office I grabbed large bottles of water and a stack of paper towels. I wet the towels and placed them over my nose and mouth as I tried to make my way home. I was soon covered in whatever was in the air. My eyes burned and my lungs ached. I finally got home at 10:00 p.m. I had to stand outside, undress, and hose myself down before entering my house.

"A few weeks later I walked near the site where the Twin Towers had been and stood in a crowd of people about a block long. We all stared in horrified silence. Then I heard what sounded like singing. Like a ripple, it got louder as it traveled from the front to the back, where I was standing. I soon realized that people were singing "God Bless America," and I joined in.

"Every day I tell my family how much I love them. I don't know if it's for the last time."

Rosa said that 14 years later it's still emotional for her to remember that day. I know that I will never forget the emotions of 9/11. I'll also never forget God's promise that in the new earth "nothing will hurt or destroy in all my holy mountain" (Isaiah 11:9, NLT).

SEPTEMBER 12

Sweetened With Whipping Cream

He asked him, "What is the most important commandment?" Jesus answered . . . " 'You must love him with all your heart, soul, mind, and strength.' The second most important commandment says: 'Love others as much as you love yourself.' No other commandment is more important than these." Mark 12:28-31, CEV.

I was so young that I barely remember the time I took revenge on my sister, so Mom recently filled me in on the details. Evidently I was mad at my big sister, Debi. We shared a room, but she didn't share my love for stuffed animals. And I had a lot of them! I treated them as if they were real. I talked to them, tucked them in at night, and probably would have fed them if Mom had let me! Debi didn't like it if any of my animals ended up on her side of the room. So when she found my Rudolph reindeer on her bed, she threw it on the floor.

Right before bedtime that night, I sneaked into the kitchen and got a spray can of whipping cream out of the fridge. With delight I sprayed it on Debi's pillow and sheet. Needless to say, after the lights were turned out and she crawled into bed, she was traumatized!

"Nancy Joy! Why did you do such a thing?" Mom asked when Debi told on me.

"Because she needs to be more sweet," I answered. "And whipping cream is sweet!"

Whipping cream may be sweet, but there's a better way to sweeten up someone who's been unkind to you. And you can find it in today's text: "Love others as much as you love yourself." The Message Bible says, "Love others as well as you love yourself."

In other words, give people the same treatment that you yourself want to get. If you're unkind to someone, it's usually because something negative is going on inside of you. Something is hurting. Maybe you're having a hard day. Maybe there's arguing at home. Maybe there's stress at school. Maybe you're reacting to someone else's unkindness to you.

So the last thing you need is for that person you've hurt to take revenge. Instead, you need them to be kind. You need them to love you as well as they love themselves—to treat you the way they want to be treated. How do we all want to be treated? With respect. With kindness. With patience. We want to be treated the way Jesus treated people.

So save your whipping cream and try being extra kind to that unkind person. It will make a big difference—for both of you.

SEPTEMBER 13

Grandparents Are Great!

Gray hair is a glorious crown worn
by those who have lived right. Proverbs 16:31, CEV.

"They're too old to understand."
"They're old-fashioned."
"They've forgotten what it's like to be a kid."
"They're boring to be around."

Maybe you've had these thoughts about your grandparents. It's true that there's a huge age gap between you and them. But that doesn't mean that grandparents aren't important, aren't wise, and aren't full of love for you. They are a gift from God.

A few days ago my husband met a college student from Africa, and they got to talking about the importance of the older generation. The young man said, "I've noticed that here in America older people aren't valued by younger people. In my country, when an older person speaks, you'd better listen! Because they always have important things to say."

I think we should start doing that here in America! Wouldn't your grandparents be shocked if you stopped, looked them in the eye, and listened closely when they spoke?

Your grandparents have lived many years longer than you have. And with those years have come some valuable insights. They're a lot smarter than you might think! They may not know much about iPads, iPhones, and texting, but I bet they do know some great stories and would probably love to tell you a few if you'd ask.

Today is Grandparents Day. Why not let yours know how much they mean to you? Give them a call, write them a letter, or send them a card. Better yet, if they live nearby, go talk to them face to face and give them a hug.

If none of your grandparents are living, there are plenty of senior citizens who are lonely. So adopt one! Ask your parents to find a church member or neighbor whom you can treat like a grandparent.

By the time I was in my late 20s, all my grandparents had died. Since then there have been many times that I've wished they were here to share life with me. Your grandparents are aging, too, and won't always be around. Take time to learn from them. Take time to listen to their stories. And take time to let them know that you love them, and you're glad they're here.

SEPTEMBER 14

It Really Does Get Better! (Letter 1)

I thank God for you whenever I think of you.
I always have joy as I pray for all of you. It is because you have told others
the Good News from the first day you heard it until now. I am sure that God
Who began the good work in you will keep on working in you
until the day Jesus Christ comes again. Philippians 1:3-6, NLV.

You could probably give some good advice to a first or second grader, don't you think? I mean, you've been their age and lived through it! And with that living came some lessons.

Well, I know some "older kids" who are friends of mine. It hasn't been all that long since they were your age—and they survived. I asked a few of them to share some thoughts with you from the lessons they learned. So over the next few days you'll be reading letters from people who have experienced what you might be going through now. And they were written just for you.

Dear Kid Who Feels Unpopular,

When I was your age, the negative experience I can remember the most is that I was insanely "uncool." I didn't have pretty hair, either my teeth were crooked or I was in braces, I had no curves, and I was too tall to find jeans that fit me right! I worried a lot about my looks.

It took me until I graduated from high school to realize that if the other kids at school had been honest, they would have admitted that they were having the same crises. Everyone was trying to fit in and be cool. And in the process, some kids were mean.

I guess my best advice would be to accept the fact that you might be going through a tough time at home or at school—but know that it gets better! You will change physically, emotionally, and spiritually, and so will everyone around you.

So stay confident in yourself and keep looking forward to what lies ahead. It's probably way better than you think!

Love, Brittany

Now that her early teen years are over, Brittany is a lovely, confident, strong Christian girl who has found her niche. She no longer compares herself to other girls and doesn't let others' opinions of her drag her down. She has let God bring out the best in her.

SEPTEMBER 15

Finding Forever Friends (Letter 2)

Friends come and friends go, but a true friend sticks by you like family. Proverbs 18:24, Message.

Dear Kid Who Thinks You're the Weird Kid,

Ever since I can remember, I have been the "weird kid." And by weird, I mean the unusual—not the norm—"nerdy" kind of a kid. As the weird kid, I didn't exactly fit in with the cool or popular group of kids. Even though I enjoyed being different, I really did want to fit in. In fact, I actually tried hard to fit in with the popular and cool kids. I mean, everyone wanted to fit into that group. It had power!

Well, that didn't work out. And the more I got to know the cool kids, the more I realized that they were not fun for me to be with. But the small group of kids—the kids like me—were fun!

What I'm saying here is that you may feel unpopular or uncool, but there are always other kids that feel the same way, too. And those kids are the ones that know what it's like to be the odd one out. When I was your age, my friends consisted entirely of kids whom the popular kids considered outcasts. And do you know what? I still hang out with these kids. For more than six years they have been my best friends. They have been true friends.

Your friend, Gabers

I love Gabe's story! I love it because it shows the importance of finding true friends, just as today's verse says. Friends who will stick by you like family—through thick and thin.

Take a look at the friends Jesus chose. He could have chosen from the rich and powerful, but He didn't. He chose common, everyday people. He didn't choose friends by their looks, by their popularity, by the clothes they wore, or by the things they owned. He chose His friends by looking into their hearts.

If you're like Gabe once was, and are wishing to fit into the "popular" group of kids, maybe ask yourself why. Do you really like them? Do you like how they treat other kids? Do you want to be like them? Do you think they would be true, lifelong friends?

I'm always surprised when a seemingly popular kid tells me that she or he is lonely. They want true friends, too. So what might you be able to do in your classroom to get rid of the titles "popular" and "weird" and just have one title: "friend"?

When Death Dies (Letter 3)

For what is mortal must be changed into what is immortal; what will die must be changed into what cannot die. So when this takes place, and the mortal has been changed into the immortal, then the scripture will come true: "Death is destroyed; victory is complete!" 1 Corinthians 15:53, 54, TEV.

Dear Kid Who's Lost a Loved One,

About halfway through my eighth grade year, my grandpa had a massive stroke and died. I hardly knew how to deal with the grief. That was the first time I had ever experienced the death of a family member, and Grandpa and I had been close.

Although it was really tough to say goodbye, I found comfort in what the Bible says in 1 Thessalonians 4:13, 14: "And regarding the question, friends, that has come up about what happens to those already dead and buried, we don't want you in the dark any longer. First off, you must not carry on over them like people who have nothing to look forward to, as if the grave were the last word. Since Jesus died and broke loose from the grave, God will most certainly bring back to life those who died in Jesus" (Message).

Through prayer, reading my Bible, and the support and love of my family, I was able to get a handle on my loss. Death hurts. You can't get around that. But I know that the day is coming when Jesus will return and death will be no more.

With hope, Katie

One of the things I hate most about death is that it's beyond our control. You can control what grades you get by studying. You can control whether or not you get grounded by obeying your parents' rules. But you can't control death. Only God can. And one day He will wipe it out!

Until then, we have the hope of Jesus' coming. Titus 2:13 calls it "the blessed hope" (NIV). Without this hope, when the funeral is over and we leave the graveside of someone we love, we would think that this is the absolute end and we'll never see them again.

But there *is* God's promise. A promise too bright for the darkness of this world to dim. As my husband told me after my brother's funeral, "It's a dark tunnel. But if you look closely, there's light at the end of the tunnel. It's the Second Coming." *It's hope.*

SEPTEMBER 17

Going for the Frontside Air (Letter 4)

We can rejoice, too, when we run into problems and trials, for we know that they help us develop endurance. And endurance develops strength of character, and character strengthens our confident hope of salvation. And this hope will not lead to disappointment. For we know how dearly God loves us, because he has given us the Holy Spirit to fill our hearts with his love. Romans 5:3-5, NLT.

Dear Kid Who Wants to Give Up,

I'm a skateboarder. It has been a great experience, but it has also been tough. You need to learn how to have lots of self-confidence in this sport because there are split-second decisions to be made and new tricks to try. Let me tell you a quick little story about a rough time I had.

It all started in an amazing town called Salt Lake City where my uncle lives. He's been a huge positive influence in my life! There was a beautiful summer sunset when we arrived at the skate park. I was ready to shred it up, so my uncle and I threw on our pads and helmets (always wear protective gear—it's cool to do!) and started skating.

After we'd skated hard for about an hour, I was pretty tired and had taken some pretty good falls. I looked over and saw my uncle doing a huge frontside air, which is a vertical air move above the coping (the metal bar on top of the ramp). I wanted to try that! When I went in for my first try, I dropped in at full speed. But when I popped out of the coping in midair, I realized that my board wasn't even with me! So I bailed and slid down on my kneepads. Rather than giving up, I climbed out of the bowl and asked myself what I could do better.

I threw my board down on the coping ready to drop in again for the second try. I started to push down on my front foot, and away I went, headed for the 12-foot wall. This time I hit the wall too fast and went way higher than expected, so I bailed again. But I bailed way too high. I fell right on the corner of the coping, landing on my ribs and hip. It knocked the wind right out of me, but I got up and walked out of the bowl. I was hurt, but I could walk!

Skateboarding has taught me to not give up in life. When things get tough and you get knocked down, you have to choose to pick yourself back up and get back on the board. God will always be there to help you, but you have to want to try again. Don't give up! Try again.

Stay cool and be safe, Chandler

SEPTEMBER 18

Dying to Fit In (Letter 5)

With all your heart you must trust the Lord and not your own judgment. Always let him lead you, and he will clear the road for you to follow. Proverbs 3:5, 6, CEV.

Dear Kid Who Wants to Fit In,

When I was in the seventh grade, all I wanted was to fit in. I wanted to be a part of a group, but not just any group. My best friend, whom I'd known for years, started hanging out with the "in crowd." That's the group I wanted to fit into. But they didn't want to include me.

I told my mom that I would do anything to fit in. Luckily, I didn't. But I did get so discouraged that I stopped doing my homework and had totally given up on God. It took me almost failing the seventh grade to get my act together. It took the help of my parents, teachers, and the school principal, but I finally started to change my priorities.

After I got my act together, life started improving. I told my parents that I wanted to try a Christian school. That decision was a great one! At my new school I made new friends with a group of kids who would be true friends. I even ended up getting awards for good grades!

I got through all of this because of God. He knew right where I needed to be and was waiting for me to come back to Him during this time. If you ever feel left out, like I did, talk to God about it. Make the changes you need to make, like I did. Don't let the "in crowd" take control of your feelings and your self-worth. Take control of your own life, and be ready for some great changes!

Stay brave, Staci

I noticed several sad things about Staci's story. The first is that she thought she had to be a part of the popular group in order to be happy. The second is that she was willing to do anything to be accepted. And the third is that she basically gave up on God and life for a while. What a waste of time it would have been to fail seventh grade just because she wasn't accepted into the group!

But there are several happy things about Staci's story, too. She allowed her parents and school to help her. She chose on her own to change her priorities. And when she realized that she needed to find some Christian friends, she asked to change schools. But the best decision of all? She let God back in.

SEPTEMBER 19

My Basketball Blessing (Letter 6)

God is good, a hiding place in tough times.
He recognizes and welcomes anyone looking for help,
no matter how desperate the trouble. Nahum 1:7, Message.

Have you ever had that feeling of so much rage building up inside of you that you don't know how to deal with it? Well, the biggest reason for so many of my frustrations throughout life has been my parents' divorce.

Because I was so young when my parents separated, I don't remember them ever living together. I almost think it was better for me that I was too young to remember the details of their separation. The earliest memory I have of them being together is this: I was at my dad's house, ready to go outside and shoot hoops in the driveway. I overheard my parents outside, arguing about my siblings and me—who was going to have the majority custody over us. In my mind I thought, Does it really matter? Can we please just get along?

But my wishes later turned to rage. It's hard to admit, but I didn't always process and show that rage in the best ways. However, over the years I've developed a few positive ways to handle this frustration of mine.

The one that has been most important to me is the game of basketball. Every time I wanted to avoid conflict in my home, I went outside to shoot hoops. The game of basketball quickly became something I always focused on when something bad happened.

On top of everything else, one of my parents got cancer. Even though they assured me that it was treatable, I felt really lost and depressed. I found myself wanting to quit playing ball.

I really cannot tell you—it must have been a miracle—because I don't know how I came out of that whole experience with a decent heart. Instead of playing the "poor me" card, I once again found myself being rejuvenated by that wonderful game.

I truly consider it a miracle from God that He has put me on the right path. Maybe you too can find something good that will become your distraction from pain in life—maybe music, sports, art, photography, or caring for animals. Whatever it may be, I strongly encourage you to grasp that and make it your own. And let God perform a miracle in your life, too.

Love ya, Charlotte

On the Court With My Enemy (Letter 7)

Here's another old saying that deserves a second look: "Eye for eye, tooth for tooth." Is that going to get us anywhere? Here's what I propose: "Don't hit back at all." Matthew 5:38, 39, Message.

Dear Kid Who Gets Bullied,

When I was in sixth grade, a kid that I didn't like very much shoved me. I shoved him back and ended up in the principal's office. When I got home, Dad gave me a lecture a mile long! He said that I shouldn't have shoved back. He told me that the Bible says we're supposed to love our enemies, and that two wrongs never make a right. Of course, being the 12-year-old that I was, I tried to forget about his mini-sermon. That is, until I played a game of basketball against Jesse and his gang of four. Jesse was my archenemy!

I got together with my team and hoped like everything that we could show Jesse how to play "real" basketball and that we could win the game. His team was a lot bigger and stronger than mine, but we had speed and agility.

My moment to shine arrived. I had the ball when there was no one between the basket and me—except Jesse. I dribbled the ball up to Jesse, faked left, and hung him out to dry as I zoomed by him to the right! Just as I was about to make the shot, Jesse ran up behind me in a rage and shoved me so hard to the ground that my upper lip turned into hamburger on the rough asphalt court. As I slowly got up and saw blood dripping off my face, I knew that he had gone too far this time and needed to be taught a lesson!

My first instinct was to grab Jesse and pound on him until his face matched mine. But then I remembered what Dad said: "Two wrongs don't make a right." So I decided to try something new. I went to the principal's office, got help with the situation, and got my face cleaned up. Jesse got expelled because of his long history of troublemaking, and I was treated like the school hero. All the girls were concerned about me, and the guys looked up to me after that day. I finally realized what Jesus meant when He said, "Blessed are the meek, for they shall inherit the earth" (Matthew 5:5, NKJV).

Take care of each other, Jake

SEPTEMBER 21

Letter to Girls (Letter 8)

Be friendly with everyone. Don't be proud and feel that you are smarter than others. Make friends with ordinary people. Don't mistreat someone who has mistreated you. But try to earn the respect of others, and do your best to live at peace with everyone. Romans 12:16-18, CEV.

Dear Girls,

When I switched from public school to a private Christian school in the seventh grade, I thought that the girls would be more kind. I thought they wouldn't care so much about how they looked or what clothes brands they wore. Why care about those things when Christians should be different from the rest of the world? I asked myself.

As the school year went on, I started noticing how insecure I was feeling. I wanted to be the pretty girl and the girl with the brand-name clothes. But I managed to stay grounded and to find myself. I tried to not worry about what others thought about me by using laughter and humor in tough situations.

Because kids are getting on the Internet at a younger age now, it opens us up to a whole new world out there. I think that's where we girls start falling into our insecurities, wanting to look like someone else. Seeing my little sister at the age of 9 being insecure is not healthy. When she starts complaining about her looks, I tell her, "God created us uniquely and beautifully, and you shouldn't try to be someone else."

I hate how we girls sometimes treat each other. We hold grudges. We talk about each other. And we bring each other down. We forget that we are ladies! It's embarrassing and disgusting for us to tear each other apart and bring one another down with negative words—words that can only hurt. We should be having each other's backs and not hoping for the worse for each other. You know, I've met some pretty rude and immature girls. And sometimes it's hard to hold back the anger and not have a bitter heart that wants revenge. I'm trying so hard, and I'm glad I've held back the negative.

Girls who bully girls are insecure and get their false worth by bringing others down. If you're being bullied, talk to someone about it. And remember that you are never alone as long as you have God by your side.

Love, Kendra

Letter to Boys (Letter 9)

How can a young man keep his way pure? By living by Your Word. I have looked for You with all my heart. Do not let me turn from Your Law. Your Word have I hid in my heart, that I may not sin against You. Psalm 119:9-11, NLV.

Dear Boys,

Making your way through middle school is a very tough time for us guys. We have emotions we've never felt before, and we're changing physically. We used to avoid girls, but now we find them kind of interesting. We don't want to ever do anything that makes us look stupid.

When I was in the sixth grade, I was pushing my little sister on a swing, trying to show off to some girls who were watching. The swing set was on the top of a hill, and I decided it would be cool to grab onto the swing, swing out over the edge, and let go. That would impress them for sure! Well, maybe it would have, if I hadn't done a backflip and broken both arms.

I got my casts off before I started seventh grade. Because I hadn't been able to work out, I was very skinny and kind of embarrassed about how weak I looked compared to a lot of the other guys. I felt intimated by all the boys who, compared to me, were physically fit—especially the two who were into martial arts.

Dealing with bullies is another difficult thing for guys. It seems like in junior high the tough guys get tougher and the not-so-tough guys get more intimidated. I was friends with a lot of the guys who got bullied. And the hard thing is, who are you going to go to as a guy? You don't want people to think that you're weak, so you hide the hurt when you really should tell someone. I think that bullying is a ridiculous show of power. And if you're a bully, someday you're going to wake up and realize that it's degrading. You'll realize how much it hurts others.

Being a friend to everyone is really a good thing. I found my self-worth in how I treated people—how I made others feel about themselves. Even to this day, I don't feel that I'm the most muscular or attractive guy out there. That's just the way I was made. But if I can make somebody else feel good, then I'm treating them the way Jesus would. He was loving, compassionate, and stood up for the underdog. If you're kind to people, then they will respect you for reasons that really matter.

Your friend, Cody

SEPTEMBER 23

The Unchangeable One

Jesus Christ never changes! He is the same yesterday, today, and forever. Hebrews 13:8, CEV.

Happy first day of autumn! I think this is my favorite season of all. Tree leaves turning yellow, orange, and red; brisk morning air; hot chocolate; popcorn; baking pumpkin cookies; squirrels out back gathering and burying nuts—it's a special time of year!

But it also speaks of change—and change is something that happens a lot at your age.

Your body is changing. You're growing out of your clothes and shoes. And you're also heading through puberty.

Your complexion is changing. All of a sudden you find bumps on your cheeks and forehead—acne!

Your teeth are changing. You've probably lost most of your baby teeth and might already be in braces.

Your schoolwork is changing. You have more homework and harder concepts to learn.

Your Sabbath school class is changing. You get placed in a new room with older kids.

Your friends are changing. Some may begin to pull away from you and branch out to make new friends. Some may be starting to experiment and make wrong choices.

Your parents are changing. They probably expect more from you now that you're older, and they probably have also given you more responsibilities and privileges.

Your tween and earliteen years are full of change. That can make you feel excited and maybe even a little anxious. And that's OK.

You will go through more changes in your life—many more. Some will be easy, and some will be hard. Some will be welcomed, and some will be heart-wrenching. But here's some great news for you: *Jesus never changes*! No matter what changes you go through while you're growing up, He will remain the same. He's the same God you trusted with every prayer when you were little. He's the same God to whom you shouted songs of praise in Sabbath school class.

Wherever life takes you from this day on—whatever changes come in your body, your family, your school, your friends—you have one Friend who will always be the same. He doesn't have grumpy days. He doesn't have days when He's too tired to listen. He doesn't have a single day when He doesn't want your company. He's always there for you. He's got your back!

SEPTEMBER 24

You're Not Finished Yet!

God is the one who began this good work in you,
and I am certain that he won't stop before it is complete
on the day that Christ Jesus returns. Philippians 1:6, CEV.

My friend Trevor is now a competent, secure young adult. But he didn't feel that way about himself when he was in junior high. Here's his story, along with some great suggestions:

"When I was in the seventh grade, I grew like a foot in one year. I was six feet three inches and rail-thin. One of the biggest things kids face is that they do *not* want to stick out—but I was so awkward! I was very aware that I was too tall for my class and was always stumbling over my feet. Even though I was tall, I wasn't good in sports—not even basketball. Then when my voice started cracking, it was horrible! People laughed when it happened because it sounded funny.

"Every boy goes through adolescence at a different time, and that's difficult for guys. For instance, if you have a high voice and don't get your lower voice when all your friends do, if you're clumsy, or if you're short and waiting for your growth spurt, it can be hard because all these other guys have started maturing.

"A lot of people think that guys don't have body issues, but we do—and it's becoming more and more common. It used to be that girls were the ones with body issues, but now it's starting to swing more evenly.

"But the thing to remember is this: you're not finished yet! You're still growing, changing, into the adult you will someday be. It's hard to be patient because in our society everything is immediate gratification. Do you want a quick dinner? There's the microwave. Do you want to watch a movie right now? There's Netflix. Our fast-paced society says, 'I want it now! I don't want to wait.'

"Adolescence is something everyone has to go through in order to be an adult. If you're struggling with the changes that are—or aren't—happening, it's important that you talk to someone. If you don't talk about it, then no one can help you. Also focus on what you are good at—even if it's something that isn't considered 'cool.'

"Think of it this way: the Bible says that we are all made in God's image. When you look around, we are all so different. And that's OK! We were created in His image on the outside, and we can choose to be His image on the inside. No matter how short or tall!"

SEPTEMBER 25

From "Giant" to "Shorty"

God loves you and has chosen you as his own special people. So be gentle, kind, humble, meek, and patient. Put up with each other, and forgive anyone who does you wrong, just as Christ has forgiven you. Love is more important than anything else. It is what ties everything completely together. Colossians 3:12-14, CEV.

Trevor's story yesterday reminds me of my own growing-up worries. The first day of fourth grade, I realized that not only was I the tallest girl in my class, but I was even taller than all of the boys! And it didn't help that one of them nicknamed me "Giant."

"Why do I have to be so tall?" I would complain to Mom.

"Just be patient," she would tell me. "You'll stop growing someday, and other kids will catch up."

She was right. In fact, at five feet three inches I ended up on the shorter side! And I remember how good it felt when a tall college friend called me "Shorty."

Maybe you'll stay short. Maybe you'll be tall. Maybe you won't have the hair you long for or the muscles you want. Maybe your parents won't be able to afford braces. Maybe some of your clothes will have to be hand-me-downs. Regardless of how it turns out, there are some things you can do between now and then to make life easier for yourself.

Change what you can change physically. You may not look like the singer you admire, the actress you think is cool, or another kid in your class. But you can look the best for you! You can keep your clothes and hair clean and put a smile on your face.

Accept the things you can't change. Everyone has flaws. No one is perfect. So accept those unchangeable things about yourself. When I was in college, I had to have part of my left kidney removed. The surgery left me with a 12-inch scar around my side. It took me a few years to realize that the scar didn't change who I was. It didn't change my mind or my heart.

Don't compare yourself to other guys or girls. Honestly, that gets you nowhere. Start liking *you*! You are your own unique person. One of a kind! You can always find someone you might wish you were like. But remember, you have your own strengths and abilities.

Realize your worth in God's eyes. How does He value you? You're worth dying for! In fact, you're worth so much to Him that someday He's going to give you a new, perfect body.

SEPTEMBER 26

The Trouble With Mrs. Odell

Do not judge, and you will not be judged. Do not condemn, and you will not be condemned. Forgive, and you will be forgiven. Luke 6:37, NIV.

Years ago I used to get my hair cut at a small salon called Mr. Odell's Hair World. A married couple, Mr. and Mrs. Odell, owned and ran it.

Mr. Odell was a kind older gentleman. We always enjoyed chatting during my appointments. He was relaxed and treated his clients well. But then there was Mrs. Odell.

The trouble with Mrs. Odell was—well—she didn't show very good customer service. Whenever I came for an appointment with her husband, she ignored me unless I said hi first.

The trouble with Mrs. Odell was—well—she wasn't very friendly. If I did try talking to her, she would reply with very short answers.

The trouble with Mrs. Odell was—well—she never smiled. She had a permanent cranky expression on her face. I tried hard to find something I liked about her, but I never could.

One day when I went in for an appointment with Mr. Odell, Mrs. Odell said, "Sit down. I'll be cutting your hair today." She proceeded to roughly wash my hair and yank a comb through it, all in silence—while I judged her behavior in silence.

What a cranky woman! I thought to myself. *I'll be glad when this cut is over.*

After about 15 minutes I said, "Where is Mr. Odell today?"

There was silence. Then she answered quietly, "He died. Died from a stroke about two weeks ago. I miss him terribly and am left to run this business all alone."

The trouble with Mrs. Odell was—nothing. The trouble with *me* was that I judged her.

Matthew 7:1-5 says: "Don't pick on people, jump on their failures, criticize their faults—unless, of course, you want the same treatment. That critical spirit has a way of boomeranging. It's easy to see a smudge on your neighbor's face and be oblivious to the ugly sneer on your own. Do you have the nerve to say, 'Let me wash your face for you,' when your own face is distorted by contempt? It's this whole traveling road-show mentality all over again, playing a holier-than-thou part instead of just living your part. Wipe that ugly sneer off your own face, and you might be fit to offer a washcloth to your neighbor" (Message).

SEPTEMBER 27

Picture or It Didn't Happen

My friends, don't say cruel things about others! If you do, or if you condemn others, you are condemning God's Law. And if you condemn the Law, you put yourself above the Law and refuse to obey either it or God who gave it. God is our judge, and he can save or destroy us. What right do you have to condemn anyone? James 4:11, 12, CEV.

Maybe you've heard the phrase that is today's title. If someone's bragging about something they did that seems unbelievable, their friends might say, "Picture or it didn't happen." In other words, show us proof—through a picture—or we won't believe you.

I was thinking what a great concept that is, and how we could use it in a different way in our lives. Through the many years I've worked with kids, I've tried to teach them this principle: Unless you saw the person do it, or they told you that they did it, you shouldn't believe it.

So if someone comes to me and says, "Ashton was cheating on the science test," I'll ask, "How do you know? Did you see him cheating? Did he tell you that he cheated?"

"Well, no," they say. "But Kira said she heard it from Jessie."

And my response will be, "Unless Ashton told you that he cheated, or you're sure that you saw him cheat, you can't believe what you hear."

Think about it. You wouldn't want people spreading rumors about you, would you? So why do that to someone else? It's always important to check the facts. Here are some examples that show just how easy it is to start a rumor when you don't have all the facts.

Event: Chris comes to the Saturday night school party acting dopey and out-of-it.

Assumption: Chris must be "on something."

Fact: He had a tooth pulled after school on Friday and is on pain meds.

Event: Larissa didn't show up for her best friend's birthday party.

Assumption: Larissa must not be a very good friend.

Fact: Her parents' car broke down on the way and she didn't have a phone to call.

It's best to get all the facts instead of spreading rumors. We get the facts by asking and listening to the people who were directly involved. As James 1:19 advises, we "should be quick to listen, slow to speak" (NIV), rather than being quick to speak and slow to listen.

SEPTEMBER 28

If Love Could Heal

The Lord your God is with you, a Powerful One Who wins the battle. He will have much joy over you. With His love He will give you new life. He will have joy over you with loud singing. Zephaniah 3:17, NLV.

While my brother battled cancer for five months, I made the eight-hour round trip every weekend to be with him. One weekend early in his illness, I was cooking in the kitchen with our mom. The truth that his condition was incurable was almost too much for her to bear.

"He's not that old!" she told me. "We have access to modern medicine. Maybe we should take him to another hospital. Maybe we should get another opinion."

I cannot describe for you the helpless feeling that comes from knowing that someone you love is leaving you, and you can't do a thing about it. We'd already done all we could. We'd prayed. We'd researched. We'd gotten second and third opinions from doctors. And he'd tried chemotherapy.

Mom then looked at me and said a sentence I will never forget: "If love could heal, he'd be better by now."

Maybe you feel that way about the heartache in your life:

If love could heal, your parents would get back together.

If love could heal, you and your best friend would make up.

If love could heal, your grandparent wouldn't die.

If so, I'd like to remind you of what came to my mind a few days after my conversation with Mom. Dan's story isn't over. It's on hold right now, as if God has pushed the "pause" button. And if you're going through a tough time, your story isn't over, either.

The day will come when love *will* heal, and all that is wrong in this world will be made right. I grew up hearing my dad say, "There won't be any disappointments in heaven." We won't arrive there, look around, and feel bummed out. It will be exactly the opposite. We'll arrive there, look around and say, "It's perfect! Is better than I ever dreamed it could be."

"The people the Lord has rescued will come back singing as they enter Zion. Happiness will be a crown they will always wear. They will celebrate and shout because all sorrows and worries will be gone far away" (Isaiah 35:10, CEV).

SEPTEMBER 29

Your Heavenly Team

But we know that there is only one God, the Father,
who created everything, and we live for him. And there is only one Lord,
Jesus Christ, through whom God made everything and through
whom we have been given life. 1 Corinthians 8:6, NLT.

"But the Holy Spirit will come and help you, because the Father will send the Spirit to take my place. The Spirit will teach you everything and will remind you of what I said while I was with you" (John 14:26, CEV).

Have you ever thought it would be cool to have an entourage to follow you around as the rich and famous do? There would be someone to style your hair, choose your clothes, run your errands, cook your meals, and act as a bodyguard.

Well, you *do* have an entourage! You have a heavenly Team of three: God the Father, Jesus the Son, and the Holy Spirit. It might be hard for our human minds to understand, but according to the Bible they are three separate beings—yet together they are *the* one God. For example, Jesus Himself spoke of three separate individuals when He told His disciples, "Therefore, go and make disciples of all the nations, baptizing them in the name of the Father and the Son and the Holy Spirit" (Matthew 28:19, NLT). Yet Moses said, "The Lord our God, the Lord is one" (Deuteronomy 6:4, NIV). Together they are called the "Trinity" (consisting of three). Think of it this way: three strands, braided into one, can form one strong rope.

The Bible describes God the Father as a God of love: "Think how much the Father loves us. He loves us so much that he lets us be called his children, as we truly are" (1 John 3:1, CEV).

The Bible describes Jesus as our Savior: "When we were utterly helpless, Christ came at just the right time and died for us sinners" (Romans 5:6, NLT).

The Bible describes the Holy Spirit as our Comforter: "And I will pray the Father, and he shall give you another Comforter, that he may abide with you for ever" (John 14:16, KJV).

What an awesome thought: you are never alone! You have three mighty Beings with all the power of heaven at their command—to help you! You have a God who is your loving Father. You have a God who is your Savior. And you have a God who is your Comforter. They are one in their mission: to help you out in this life and to see you into heaven. They've got your back.

SEPTEMBER 30

Hope—It's in There!

God cannot tell lies! And so his promises and vows are two things that can never be changed. We have run to God for safety. Now his promises should greatly encourage us to take hold of the hope that is right in front of us. This hope is like a firm and steady anchor for our souls. Hebrews 6:18, 19, CEV.

When you stop and think about it, we use the word "hope" a lot.

"I hope I get what I want for Christmas."

"I hope you can come to my party."

"I hope I get to go to camp this summer."

Hope is what keeps us going, because it's looking into the future for something wonderful to take place. But some people lose hope along the way. They get discouraged after so many disappointments and just give up. They walk around sad, negative, and dark. They've lost hope.

If you ever find yourself living life without hope, I know where you can get a good dose of it—in your Bible! The word "hope" is mentioned in the Bible 133 times (in the King James Version). That's a lot of hope! You can go online or grab a concordance to look up some texts on hope. And you'll walk away feeing very hopeful!

In Matthew 24:13 Jesus says what I think are some of the most reassuring words in the entire Bible: "But he who endures to the end shall be saved" (NKJV). That's *the* hope! If you stay faithful to God; if you don't give up on Him when peer pressure hits, when things don't go your way, or when the world makes you think it can offer you more, you will be saved.

If you were in a race that you really wanted to win, you would do your best and stick with it till the finish line. You wouldn't stop racing and sit down if you got tired. You wouldn't look ahead to the finish line, think it was too far away, and walk off the track. No! You would stay in the race with the hope of finishing strong.

It's the same in the race of life. The finish line is the Second Coming. All we have to do is endure—stay strong—not give up. I like how the Message Bible talks about hope in Hebrews 6:18: "We who have run for our very lives to God have every reason to grab the promised hope with both hands and never let go."

OCTOBER 1

Make the First Move

Do not repay evil with evil or insult with insult. On the contrary, repay evil with blessing, because to this you were called so that you may inherit a blessing. 1 Peter 3:9, NIV.

James was playing flag football with some friends in the gym one day when an accident happened that changed the course of a friendship.

"Last year I was the new kid in fifth grade," James told me. "It took a while, but I started making what I thought were good friends.

"One of those friends accidentally hit me in the face with the football. It smacked me so hard that my eyes started to water. Another boy, who I thought was turning out to be a good friend, started to call me a baby because it looked like I was crying.

"He kept on calling me that, and the more he did, the more my anger level went up. Finally I couldn't stand it any longer, and I did something that I wish I hadn't done. I kicked him.

"I'm afraid that I've lost a friend," James told me. "It's been more than a year, and I hope that someday he will be my friend again. If he reads this, I want to say to him, 'I'm sorry.' "

A wasted year in this friendship could have been prevented if only James had read these words of Jesus and acted on them: "If a fellow believer hurts you, go and tell him—work it out between the two of you. If he listens, you've made a friend" (Matthew 18:15, Message). Instead James did what today's text said *not* to do. He repaid evil for evil and insult for insult.

We're all guilty of doing this. Sometimes it happens just by reacting before we think. Someone at recess calls you a name, and you call them a name back. Someone shoves you during PE class, and you shove them back. Someone in class tells you to shut up, and you tell them to shut up back.

But God asks you to do something better than just react. He actually asks you to make the first move—to go to the person who has hurt you and work it out. James has been waiting for the boy he kicked to come to him. But the last time I saw James, I encouraged him, "Don't wait for him to come to you. Go to him." I don't know whether he did or not.

Should the boy who called James a baby have apologized to him? Sure, he should have. But by following God's way, does James still have the chance to try to repair that friendship? Yes, he does!

October 2

While We Wait

"Look, I am coming soon! My reward is with me, and I will give to each person according to what they have done." Revelation 22:12, NIV.

Jesus really is coming again! He's promised that He would, and I believe that He will—without a doubt.

Some kids have wondered, "What am I supposed to do while I'm waiting for Jesus to come? Should I read my Bible and pray all day? Should I plan my future? Should I quit school?"

After the Resurrection, before Jesus went back to heaven, He gave His disciples one last command: "Go to the people of all nations and make them my disciples. Baptize them in the name of the Father, the Son, and the Holy Spirit, and teach them to do everything I have told you" (Matthew 28:19, 20, CEV).

Jesus knew that He wasn't going to be here on earth any longer, but He still wanted the whole world to know about Him and the gift of salvation. He wanted everyone to get ready for His return. So He asked His disciples to go out and tell the world.

That's what we're supposed to do while we wait. Since the disciples aren't here any longer, Jesus needs you and me! He needs us to spread the good news. Think of it this way: when I was in school, and a teacher had to leave the room for a while, they would choose a student to be in charge. I always loved hearing, "Nancy, you're in charge." Not because I wanted to boss around the other kids, but because it made me feel important that the teacher trusted me and that I had a job to do.

Well, Jesus trusts you! And you have a job to do. That job is to tell others about Him. How? In whatever way you can. In whatever way suits your personality and the abilities God has given you.

Is it a bit intimidating at times? Yes, it is! But the reward of telling someone about Jesus is well worth it. And besides, you won't be doing it alone. When Jesus asked His disciples to go tell the world about Him, He also promised, "I will be with you always, even until the end of the world" (Matthew 28:20, CEV).

Another important thing you can do while you wait is to spend time reading your Bible and talking to Him every day. The more time you spend with Him, the more you'll act like Him.

OCTOBER 3

Healing Rain

You are kind, God! Please have pity on me. You are always merciful! Please wipe away my sins. Wash me clean from all of my sin and guilt.
Psalm 51:1, 2, CEV.

Our daughter, Christina, just returned from a Christian music festival and couldn't wait to tell us what happened on closing night. A pastor was speaking about the time when Jesus disrupted a funeral. Sounds highly unusual, doesn't it? Funerals are usually solemn occasions.

Here's how Luke 7:12-15 tells the story: "As he approached the town gate, a dead person was being carried out—the only son of his mother, and she was a widow. And a large crowd from the town was with her. When the Lord saw her, his heart went out to her and he said, 'Don't cry.' Then he went up and touched the bier they were carrying him on, and the bearers stood still. He said, 'Young man, I say to you, get up!' The dead man sat up and began to talk, and Jesus gave him back to his mother" (NIV).

Quite an awesome story, isn't it? The festival speaker went on to tell the crowd that God was there, wanting to disrupt their funeral, too. In other words, if anyone in the audience felt that their life had ended because of sins they'd committed, Jesus wanted to "resurrect" them into a new life.

The speaker then asked the 15,000 people in the outdoor arena to close their eyes while he prayed. His prayer focused on anyone in the audience who felt that their life was over because they had gone too far and too long without God.

Christina told us, "As the pastor was praying, a few sprinkles of rain began to fall. The more powerful his prayer became, the harder it rained, until it was a downpour. And no one cared! No one was putting up umbrellas or covering their heads. We just let the rain pour down over us. It was like God was saying, 'I'll wash you clean from your sin and guilt.' "

It's an amazing thought to me that when we are truly sorry for our sins, we can be washed clean on the inside. Psalm 51:17 says, "The way to please you is to feel sorrow deep in our hearts. This is the kind of sacrifice you won't refuse" (CEV). God knows your heart better than anyone. He can read you like a book. And when you're sorry for your sins, today's text promises that not only will He wash away your sins the way rain washes the earth, but He will also wash away your guilt. And then your new life can begin.

OCTOBER 4

A Promise That Can't Be Broken

"Look, I am coming soon! My reward is with me, and I will give to each person according to what they have done." . . . He who testifies to these things says, "Yes, I am coming soon." Revelation 22:12-20, NIV.

It was about a month before our October wedding when my soon-to-be-husband and I found our first rental house. After we'd decided to rent the house, Keith took me back to my parents' place about an hour away. Then he went back to the new town we would soon live in. While I worked on the wedding details we'd planned, he worked on getting our new home ready.

It never occurred to me that Keith might not come back to get me. I knew that he loved me, and besides, he'd promised to show up for the wedding weekend!

Because it's been nearly 2,000 years since Jesus promised to return, some wonder if the Second Coming will really happen. I believe without a doubt that it will! Why would Jesus come to earth to die for us and return to heaven to prepare a place for us if He weren't planning to come back?

In John 14:1-3 Jesus speaks these reassuring words to His disciples—and to us: "Do not let your hearts be troubled. You believe in God; believe also in me. My Father's house has many rooms; if that were not so, would I have told you that I am going there to prepare a place for you? And if I go and prepare a place for you, I will come back and take you to be with me that you also may be where I am" (NIV).

When the disciples heard this, they must have been thrilled! They understood Jesus' promise because of a marriage custom in their culture. After a man proposed to a woman, he would leave her and return to his father's house. He would build a home for the two of them on his father's land and then come back for his bride. After the wedding ceremony, the two would return to their new home. There was no doubt in the bride's mind that her groom would return. His purpose in leaving was to prepare a home for her—for them.

There doesn't need to be any doubt in our minds, either, that Jesus will return for us. His whole purpose in leaving was to go to heaven and prepare a home just for us!

I really like how the Message Bible paraphrases Jesus very last words in the Bible: "I'm on my way! I'll be there soon!" (Revelation 22:20).

OCTOBER 5

My Teen Guidebook

Your word is a lamp for my steps;
it lights the path before me. Psalm 119:105, Voice.

"I know it's in here somewhere!" I told my husband.

When we had to downsize into a smaller house, a lot of our books had to go into a storage unit. I had kept out my favorite reading Bible and the Bible my parents gave me when I was 10 on my baptism day. But now I was bound and determined to find the Bible my parents gave me when I was in the seventh grade. It was called *Reach Out* and was the Living New Testament paraphrase. That Bible held so many memories for me. It had been an anchor.

"Found it!" I exclaimed after looking through several boxes. I carried it out of the storage unit close to my heart. I couldn't wait to get into the car to open it. But I didn't need to open it to remember how often I'd used it during my preteen and teen years. The cover was worn and the corners of the pages curled. That Book had truly been a light that guided me through those years.

All over the inside front and back cover I'd written my favorite texts with colorful pens. Texts like these:

"Put on all God's armor so that you will be able to stand safe against all the strategies and tricks of Satan" (Ephesians 6:11, TLB).

"Jesus Christ is the same yesterday, today, and forever" (Hebrews 13:8, TLB).

"Then when you realize your worthlessness before the Lord, He will lift you up, encourage and help you" (James 4:10, TLB).

"Never be lazy in your work but serve the Lord enthusiastically" (Romans 12:11, TLB).

"For God has said, 'I will never, *never* fail you nor forsake you" (Hebrews 13:5, TLB).

I even found a blank page where I'd written my own personal concordance. I wanted to be ready with answers if someone ever asked me questions about God. So I wrote out topics and then searched my Bible for texts to write next to them.

Do you have a Bible that you treasure? If not, you're missing out! Ask your parents to buy you one—they'll like that request. Go together and choose whatever version you like best.

Then as you're growing up you can read it often, and it will be a lamp for your feet. It will light your path when you go through dark days. And it will remind you that God's got your back.

OCTOBER 6

Ten-Story Fall

Every test that you have experienced is the kind that normally comes to people. But God keeps his promise, and he will not allow you to be tested beyond your power to remain firm; at the time you are put to the test, he will give you the strength to endure it, and so provide you with a way out. 1 Corinthians 10:13, TEV.

If anyone should have a reason to give up on God, it would probably be my friend Frank. I first met him when I was the guest speaker at a church one Sabbath morning. I remember seeing a man sitting alone in the last pew on the left-hand side. It was Frank. He came up to me after church and said, "I've been away from God for 17 years. When I woke up this morning, something told me to go to church, and this was the closest one. Your sermon reached me, and I've given my life back to God."

That was Sabbath morning. By Monday afternoon Frank was a quadriplegic. Along with his job as a local fireman, Frank also owned a tree service business. That Monday morning he was 100 feet up a tree—the height of a 10-story building. He was sawing off the top of the tree, and just as it started to fall, he realized his safety line was hooked to it! So he fell with it to the ground. The impact of his 100-foot fall was so great that his left hipbone was driven out through his pants. Still awake, Frank felt and heard his lungs gurgling and fizzing, filling up with blood. He could barely breathe, and his sight and hearing were gone.

With what he thought was his last breath, he cried out to God, "Don't let me die!" *Instantly* he could see and hear, and he could breathe! In the emergency room he overheard one doctor say, "I can't believe this guy's alive. Both lungs are totally collapsed, but he's breathing normally."

Frank was told in the ER that he was paralyzed. "For the first three months, all I could move were my eyeballs," he told me. "At times I wondered if this was what the rest of my life would be like—lying in bed, only able to move my eyeballs. I had to hold on to hope. I had nothing else but hope that I might improve. I was almost constantly praying, 'God, please don't let this turn out as bad as it looks.' "

Frank could have said, "If you give your life to God on a Saturday and two days later you're a quadriplegic, forget it!" But he didn't. God was at work. Tomorrow I'll tell you how.

OCTOBER 7

Hope Kept Me Alive

Do not forget to rejoice, for hope is always just around the corner. Hold up through the hard times that are coming, and devote yourselves to prayer. Romans 12:12, Voice.

Yesterday I told you about my friend Frank and his 10-story fall from a tree. He told me recently, "When I was in the hospital, people would ask me, 'Are you mad at God?' I'd tell them, 'No, I'm not mad.' "

"How can that be?" I asked him. "Many people would have blamed God."

Frank said, "Because God answered my prayer! I cried out to Him that morning I fell and asked Him to not let me die. He immediately answered my prayer! *And from that moment on, I've trusted Him.*"

But things were still tough for Frank. "The pain was incredible," he told me. "At times I thought it would have been easier to die. The fall broke 13 vertebrae, badly damaged my spinal cord, broke every bone in my upper back, broke 11 ribs (five of which went through my lungs), tore a mitral-valve heart muscle, damaged one of my kidneys, injured my head, and broke my left hip."

But Frank didn't give up. Through eight months in the hospital and another five in rehab, he fought and he hoped. And it paid off.

Frank is a quadriplegic, which means that he's paralyzed from the shoulders down. But he learned how to drive a special van, feed himself, and take care of his personal needs. He's made a living out of doing design work on his computer—using a pencil between his teeth to type. He designed and patented two machines. He also writes songs and has made two CDs.

Today I asked Frank if he would send you readers a message. This is what he said: "If you're depressed, the best thing you can do is to think about the hope that you have in God. The second thing is to get out! Get out and go find someone who's worse off than you are and encourage them. When I feel depressed, I go to the hospital and visit other quadriplegics. I talk to them and tell them, 'It's not going to be as bad as you think it is right now. In the future you can have fun! You can work, you can be productive, you can marry, you can even have kids. You may be confined to a wheelchair, but it's not the end of your life.' "

Frank's final words sum it all up: "Never give up hope, kids!"

Dreaming of Heaven

And when he comes, he will open the eyes of the blind and unplug the ears of the deaf. The lame will leap like a deer, and those who cannot speak will sing for joy! Isaiah 35:5, 6, NLT.

For the last two days I've shared with you the story of my friend Frank. He fell 100 feet from a tree and is now a quadriplegic. The accident was bad enough, but in the months afterward he lost everything he owned—"what I held dear," as he described it. But even then he didn't blame God, and he didn't give up. He held on for dear life to hope. Hope that God would help him cope with his disability, and hope that someday he would regain the use of his arms and legs in heaven. Forever!

I once asked Frank, "Do you ever dream about heaven?"

He started laughing. "Oh, Nancy!" he said. "Yes, I've had many dreams about heaven. When I'm dreaming that I'm in heaven, I'm out of my wheelchair and walking! I'm walking through a stream or in a forest. Here's one dream I had that is my favorite:

"I was in heaven, but I hadn't seen Jesus yet. Then I saw Him off in the distance with a crowd of people. Jesus turned around, and His eyes connected with mine. We held the gaze for a moment. Then He started running toward me—and I *ran* toward Him! When we met we locked arms and danced around and around like a couple of little kids!"

By the time Frank finished telling me about his dream, we were both crying. Wouldn't it be great if we could all have a dream of what heaven will be like? Even though we can't make ourselves dream about heaven at night, we can sure daydream about it during the day.

You can picture in your mind's eye how beautiful it will be. You can imagine what kind of animals you will be able to play with. (My daughter, Christina, can't wait to swim with orcas!) You can imagine what it will be like to have your emotional or physical pain gone. And you can imagine what it will be like to actually *see* Jesus.

What can we learn from Frank's story? Hope is there if we want it. It's something we *choose* to have. Without it this life would look pretty dark at times. But with it we see the light at the end of the tunnel. Things *will* get better someday. So don't give up hope!

"This hope is a strong and trustworthy anchor for our souls" (Hebrews 6:19, NLT).

"And this hope will not lead to disappointment" (Romans 5:5, NLT).

OCTOBER 9

Terror in the Dark

But the Lord our God is merciful and forgiving,
even though we have rebelled against him. Daniel 9:9, NLT.

Anita was terrified to go to bed at night. She knew that once the lights were turned off, she would start to fear again. And her fear would turn into feelings of sheer terror.

She had recently heard a sermon about sin. The speaker said that if someone should die before they confessed every single sin, they would not be saved. So she lay awake each night trying to remember every sin she'd ever committed. She was afraid to close her eyes because she might fall asleep. And then if for some reason she died in her sleep and had forgotten to ask forgiveness for just one sin, she would be lost!

Poor Anita! When I heard her story, my heart ached for her. The first thought that came to my mind was, "God is not that way!" There is no Bible verse that even suggests that God wants us to have this type of fear about our own salvation.

Our salvation isn't based on being paranoid that we might have forgotten to ask forgiveness for a sin. Rather, it's based on a gift—the gift of Jesus' death on the cross. And it's based on our acceptance of that gift.

God is a God of love. He is a Father who wants to reassure and comfort His kids. So He has given us many reassuring Bible verses about our salvation. Verses like these:

"You were saved by faith in God, who treats us much better than we deserve. This is God's gift to you, and not anything you have done on your own. It isn't something you have earned, so there is nothing you can brag about" (Ephesians 2:8, 9, CEV).

"I am writing all of this to you who have entrusted your lives to the Son of God—so you will realize eternal life already is yours" (1 John 5:13, Voice).

"If you belong to Christ Jesus, you won't be punished. The Holy Spirit will give you life that comes from Christ Jesus and will set you free from sin and death" (Romans 8:1, 2, CEV).

So tonight when you go to bed, think about your day. If you know that you've sinned, ask for God's forgiveness. Not because you don't want to be "lost" but because you want to have a friendship with Him—because you want to be like Him—and sin gets in the way of that. And then close your eyes and go to sleep peacefully. Tomorrow is coming!

OCTOBER 10

Termites in Your House

That means you must not give sin a vote in the way you conduct your lives. Don't give it the time of day. Don't even run little errands that are connected with that old way of life. Throw yourselves wholeheartedly and full-time—remember, you've been raised from the dead! —into God's way of doing things. Romans 6:12, 13, Message.

I was talking to a group of eighth graders just two days before their graduation. "What is your class motto?" I asked them.

Jimmy, one of the class officers, answered, "Pay attention to little things, because little hinges open big doors."

"That's cool," I said. "What does that mean to you?" Some of their answers were:

"Pay attention to detail. Like doing all your problems on your math assignment."

"Show responsibility in your job, and your employer will give you a good recommendation someday."

"Bake something following the recipe. Make sure the oven temperature is set right, or you might burn something you spent a lot of time making."

"Be careful how you talk. People will remember what you say."

And of course Jarin, the class clown, had to add, "Termites eating your house!"

"Termites eating your house?" I asked, surprised.

"Yes!" he answered. "Termites are little. If they're eating on your house and you don't pay attention to them, in a few days your house will be gone!"

The entire class and I had a good laugh about that. But later I got to thinking how true Jarin's statement is when it comes to sin in our lives. Usually people don't separate from God in an instant. It happens over time. Like termites eating a house, sin can take over our lives little by little until we're infested—and separated from God.

We compromise by telling ourselves such things as "I'll do it just this once" or "I'll experiment only a little with this." And pretty soon the wrong choices in movies, music, video games, Internet sites, magazines, books, or friendships can lead to trouble.

I like what today's text says. Don't give sin a vote. Don't even let one termite in for a taste. Keep your house strong!

OCTOBER 11

Removing the Red Jacket

So encourage each other and build each other up, just as you are already doing. 1 Thessalonians 5:11, NLT.

Peter's mom was desperate! When he was in the sixth grade, she felt that she was somehow losing him. His personality was fading away, he was depressed, he had no desire to go to school, and he had no friends. After Peter had gone through various medical tests, the doctors gave his mom the diagnosis: her son had high-functioning autism.

His mom had requested that he be accepted into a nearby Adventist school. Although the principal wasn't sure that Peter's needs could be met, she agreed to give it a try.

On his first day at the new school, Peter was extremely anxious. He had been beat up and teased at his old school and was afraid of the same treatment. If anyone tried talking to him, he thought they were going to make fun of him, so he would back away. If a person made any physical movement toward him, he saw it as a threat. He would step back in fear and then lash out—even to the point of hitting other kids.

Peter found security in his classroom chair and his red jacket. He wouldn't leave his chair all day long—not for PE class, recess, or even lunch. And he would leave his red jacket on, with the hood over his head, the entire day—regardless of the warm weather. It seemed as if he wanted to just withdraw inside it and be protected from the world.

The principal and Peter's mom met with Peter's classmates and tried to explain what was going on. "Kids misbehave because some of their needs aren't being met," the principal told them. His mom then explained about autism.

What did Peter's classmates do with this information? They took it on as their mission to break through the barriers Peter had built and to love him into their group. They coaxed him out of his chair by saving him a special seat at the lunch table. And they got him out to recess by giving him a chance to shoot baskets. They praised him for positive behavior and ignored the negative. Before spring came that year, Peter was completely connected with his class!

Peter grew up to be a polite, respectful, confident young man who works as a computer technologist. Because one sixth-grade class chose to accept and love Peter, he didn't need his red jacket anymore.

OCTOBER 12

Forty Years Later

Let me give you a new command: Love one another. In the same way I loved you, you love one another. John 13:34, Message.

I recently asked a group of girls, "What subjects do you want me to cover in my book?"

Almost in unison they answered, "Girl bullying!"

So whether you're a guy or a girl, here's a story that I hope will change your mind if you're ever tempted to bully.

It happened 40 years ago, but Becky still remembers the pain of being bullied by a group of older girls when she was in seventh grade.

She was the new kid at a school where grades K-10 shared the same space. It became obvious to Becky right away who the "cool" kids were and who were the "losers." She immediately got pegged as a loser.

First, the group of girls called her names like "curly" and "frizzy" and made fun of everything she wore from her hat down to her shoes. But that was just the start of it. When the group of girls saw Becky in the hallway, they either shoved her against the wall or wouldn't allow her to pass. They even threw things at her, including snowballs and ice balls, while she waited at the bus stop. That was painful both physically and emotionally.

The girls would watch down the hall to see when Becky went into the restroom. Once she was in a stall, they would turn out all the lights, leaving her to finish and find her way out in total darkness.

Becky went home crying most days. She *hated* going to school. She did tell her mom about the bullying, and her mom talked to one of the parents. But looking back, Becky wishes that she'd told her teacher and the principal, too. She changed schools four months later.

Becky told me recently that the bullying made her feel "less than" and not as good as the other girls. She felt unwanted, alone, isolated, afraid, ugly, awkward, and stupid. But the saddest thing is that she started to hate herself. Even today, her eyes fill with tears when she talks about those four months of rejection and ridicule.

Guys and girls, *be kind to each other*. You don't want to affect someone's life in a way that they get teary-eyed when they remember how badly you treated them—40 years later.

OCTOBER 13

Starving to Be Thin

Don't you know that your body is the temple of the Holy Spirit who comes from God and dwells inside of you? You do not own yourself. You have been purchased at a great price, so use your body to bring glory to God! 1 Corinthians 6:19, 20, Voice.

When Madelyn looked at her friends, she thought, *They're so pretty and thin,* and she wanted to look like them. As a seventh grader she felt that she was too heavy. But rather than getting healthy through nutritious food and exercise, she became obsessed with getting thin.

She ate a light breakfast and then wouldn't eat again until family dinnertime. Madelyn told me that she was "consumed" with what she ate. She counted every calorie that went into her mouth and then planned what her next meal would be. Every day she would jog, do an hour of aerobics, and then do 500 sit-ups.

When she started to look too thin and unhealthy, people started asking her, "Are you OK?"

"I'm fine," she would answer. And she really thought she was fine. But she wasn't.

When it became obvious that there was a problem, those who loved Madelyn took her to see a doctor, where she received both physical and emotional help.

Eating disorders such as anorexia, bulimia, and binge eating are on the rise. A former school counselor recently told me that boys are now beginning to have almost as many concerns about their body image as girls do.

I have a friend who is currently a school counselor. She says that when someone has an eating disorder of any kind, it can progress rapidly. They find themselves in too deep and can't stop, even though they're doing damage to their body organs—sometimes irreversible damage. Very few kids can face an eating disorder alone and come out of it. They need professional help.

If you ever feel that you're struggling with your image, please tell somebody who can help you. If you're already harming your body, for certain tell someone. And if you have a friend you're concerned about, you must help them, because they probably don't see a need for it. This isn't a time to keep secrets. You're *helping* them by telling a trusted adult.

Take a look at today's text. God purchased *you* at a great price! Jesus gave His body on the cross to free you. So take care of yourself—and your friends. *You are most valuable to Him.*

OCTOBER 14

Ted's Most Precious Piece of Paper

But encourage one another daily, as long as it is called "Today," so that none of you may be hardened by sin's deceitfulness. Hebrews 3:13, NIV.

I once asked a group of fifth and sixth graders to write down their thoughts about how other kids treat them. Quite a few responses were sad ones, like these:

"I feel left out."

"Sometimes kids ignore me, and I feel like I get forgotten. I feel like I'm not loved or important. And I feel sad."

"I feel small."

"A certain kid treats me like I'm a joke and picks on me."

"I feel lower than everyone else."

"I get picked on because I'm bigger than the other kids. It bothers me so bad that sometimes I can't sleep at nights."

"Some kids make fun of me."

When I got home and read their papers, I thought, *This just doesn't have to be! There's a whole classroom full of potential friends and supporters in that room. No one needs to feel left out or unimportant. Some kind words would go a long way.*

The power of words is such an amazing thing. Here's an example.

My friend Ted is now a confident young adult. But when he was in seventh grade he felt like a misfit in many ways. At the end of the school year, someone wrote him a note telling him of his good qualities and what they appreciated about him. Ted told me that he kept that note through the years and would read it whenever his old insecurities started coming back. Now in his mid-30s, he still carries that piece of paper, folded in his wallet!

Are there some kind words that you can say to kids at your school so they feel loved and accepted? It's quite easy! Words like these: "Your art project is awesome!" "Nice shot in basketball today." "Congratulations on acing that spelling test!" "You're good on the violin."

Proverbs 18:21 says, "Words kill, words give life; they're either poison or fruit—you choose" (Message). You can kill a classmate's self-worth by saying mean words, or you can give life to their self-worth. Which will you choose?

OCTOBER 15

Crushed by a Crush

Then I called on the name of the Lord:
"O Lord, I beg You, save my life!" Psalm 116:4, NLV.

I was hardcore in love with this girl," Daniel told me. He chuckles about it now that he's in his late teens. At the time he was 6 years old . . . and she was 12! Regardless, she was his first crush. He looked forward to church every Sabbath because he knew he would see her—Roxanna. It didn't matter that to her he was just a little 6-year-old boy. Obviously she didn't like him back. But that didn't stop his puppy-love feelings for her.

One day their church had a pool party at one of the members' houses, and Daniel and Roxanna both attended. "Something that I loved even more than Roxanna was water," Daniel told me. "I loved pools and swimming." Roxanna, on the other hand, didn't know how to swim. She had been playing in the shallow end of the pool, but before she knew it, she was in over her head. In a panic she began splashing and yelling for help.

"She was drowning!" Daniel told me. "And I wanted to be her hero and impress her. So I jumped in the water and swam toward her. When I got to her, she was so freaked out that she started to drown me! I was giving my life to save her, and she was drowning me!" Daniel's dad saw what was happening and jumped into the water to save them both.

Looking back on that day, Daniel told me that the story reminds him of how Jesus came to save the world. Like Roxanna, we can find ourselves drowning in sin. Rather than staying in the shallow end where we're safe and protected, we're attracted to the deep end because it seems that almost everyone else is there. We may think it's a lot of fun for a while, but then we realize we're going under. We're drowning! Parents, friends, and teachers may talk to us. They may say, "Hey, are you OK?" or "We're worried about you." But just as Daniel couldn't save Roxanna, they can't save us. They can encourage and help us, but only One can save.

That's where Jesus comes in—a strong, fearless, and most capable lifeguard! He will firmly grab you by the hand and pull you up to safety. How do you actually get rescued? Like the writer of today's text, you cry out to God. "O Lord, I beg You, save my life!" he prayed. In other words, "Help! I'm drowning!" So you make that first step. That first cry for help to God. And then you go and tell someone else about it, too. Someone you respect who is a strong Christian. Someone who can help you as you make your way out of the deep end and back to safety.

Avoid the Dark Side

God rescued us from the dark power of Satan and brought us into the kingdom of his dear Son, who forgives our sins and sets us free. Colossians 1:13, 14, CEV.

After my family and I became Christians, we drastically changed our viewpoint on Halloween. We used to decorate with "cute" witches, ghosts, and skeletons. But then we learned that those were a part of a very dark holiday. A darkness that my family wanted no part of.

Just walk down the Halloween aisle at the store and you'll see for yourself. It's all about death, horror, and scary creatures. In my opinion, dressing and decorating with this theme can gradually condition us to become numb to evil. Tragically, there are real people who commit real acts of violence that look like some Halloween costumes and scenes.

But there's a bigger issue for me, and that is the origin of Halloween. Its roots are in the occult—which is satanic. I don't want to celebrate that kind of holiday. When I discovered the history of Halloween, I asked myself, "Since you've chosen to be on God's side, why would you want to celebrate a holiday from the devil's side?"

But that doesn't mean that as Christians you and I can't have any harvest fun. Not at all! There are many things that you, your family, and your friends can do.

I know kids who go door-to-door on Halloween night and collect canned food (and candy the people offer!) and give it to their local food bank.

Rick and Tony's parents planned a kids' harvest party complete with games, caramel apples, pumpkin pie, and a sing-along hayride.

Lizzie and her siblings dress up like Bible characters and give out candy at their home. When the trick-or-treaters ask who they're dressed as, they get to tell them.

But I think the idea I like most is what my friends Loree and Lonna do with their kids. They do a "reverse trick-or-treat." They make homemade cookies and breads and take them around to people they know who need some cheering up.

Whether it's deciding what your family will do on Halloween this year or deciding what movies you'll watch, what video games you'll play, or what music you'll listen to, I hope your family will take a stand for God and say what Joshua said: "But as for me and my family, we will serve the Lord" (Joshua 24:15, NLT).

OCTOBER 17

Keep Your Hair!

Stay alert; be in prayer so you don't wander into temptation without even knowing you're in danger. Matthew 26:41, Message.

When I first became a Christian and started reading Bible stories, I was so disappointed in Samson's story. I thought he was going to be a Bible hero like Noah, Moses, and Esther.

Samson's life started out great. An angel appeared to his mom and told her that she was going to have a special child. After his birth the Bible says that "he grew and the Lord blessed him" (Judges 13:24, NIV).

But then Samson started making poor choices. He got involved with a woman, Delilah, who didn't believe in God. But the biggest mistake he made was giving in when she begged him to tell her the secret of his strength. She wanted to know because if she told the Philistines (the enemies of Samson's people), she would get a lot of money.

Judges 16:16, 17 says, "Delilah started nagging and pestering him day after day, until he couldn't stand it any longer. Finally, Samson told her the truth. 'I have belonged to God ever since I was born, so my hair has never been cut. If it were ever cut off, my strength would leave me, and I would be as weak as anyone else' " (CEV). So she told his enemies. They cut off his hair, and he lost his strength. Then they dug out his eyes and made him work in prison like an ox.

Do you have a "Delilah" in your life? A friend who keeps nagging and pestering you to watch a movie that you know you shouldn't watch; to go online to that site you know you shouldn't look at; to listen to that song that has bad language; or to experiment with something you know is wrong? And like Samson, have you finally given in to their pressure?

I remember how excited I was when I found out that Samson's story ended in victory! He was sorry for what he had done, and God gave him back his strength. And not only that, Samson is listed as a Bible hero in Hebrews 11!

Samson's story wasn't over—and neither is yours. You can ask God for forgiveness and regain the spiritual strength you had before. And you can learn from the experience so that the next time someone pressures you to do wrong, you won't let them cut your hair! You won't let them take your strength. You'll say no and walk away—even from the friendship if that's what it takes.

OCTOBER 18

Nothing Can Separate

Look! Listen! God's arm is not amputated—he can still save.
God's ears are not stopped up—he can still hear.
There's nothing wrong with God; the wrong is in *you*. Your wrongheaded
lives caused the split between you and God. Isaiah 59:1, 2, Message.

Do you want to know how strong and how mighty our God is? No, I'm not going to ask you to sing the song! But I do want to share with you one of my favorite texts that shows me just how much power He has: "For I am convinced that neither death nor life, neither angels nor demons, neither the present nor the future, nor any powers, neither height nor depth, nor anything else in all creation, will be able to separate us from the love of God that is in Christ Jesus our Lord" (Romans 8:38, 39, NIV).

Pretty amazing, isn't it? *Nothing* can separate us! Nothing, that is—except *us*. If separation ever comes between God and us, it is by *our* choice.

God created you with the freedom to move toward Jesus or to move away from Him. Jesus has done His part. He left heaven to live in this world for 33 years to set an example for you to follow. Then He died so you could live forever. What more could He do? He gave His all. The gift of salvation is there, waiting. The next move is yours—to move closer to Him or to stay separated from Him.

So what can get in the way to separate you from God? Going through a tough time can do that. I've known people who have completely given up on God when tragedy struck. Choosing the wrong kind of friends can do that. If they aren't friends with Jesus, hanging out with them certainly won't bring you any closer to Him. What you choose to do in your free time can separate you: what movies you choose to watch, what Internet sites you choose to visit, what kind of music you choose to listen to, what kind of video games you choose to play, and what kind of books and magazines you choose to read.

There were two guys in my youth group who felt that their music choice was separating them from God. So what did they do? They drove up a mountain and threw 20 music albums off the edge like Frisbees! I think they set a pretty good example for all of us.

If there's something separating you from God, don't be afraid to throw it away. It's not worth holding on to, really. Holding on to God is better by far.

OCTOBER 19

WWJD?

But those who obey God's word truly show how completely they love him. That is how we know we are living in him. Those who say they live in God should live their lives as Jesus did. 1 John 2:5, 6, NLT.

As I looked out at the classroom of energetic kids that I was going to substitute teach for a week, I knew that I needed a game plan. An idea came to mind, and it worked!

When the bell rang, I went to the whiteboard and announced, "There is going to be only one rule for the week."

The kids got so excited! Only *one* rule? All of a sudden my "cool factor" went way up. I turned around and wrote in bold, black letters: WWJD.

The kids were silent for a moment, until one blurted out, "What Would Jesus Do!"

"That's right!" I said. "The one rule this week is to ask yourself, 'What Would Jesus Do?' For instance, what would Jesus do if He had a substitute teacher? How would He treat them?"

"With respect!" one boy called out.

"And how would Jesus treat a classmate who said something rude to Him?" I asked.

"He would be kind back," another student answered.

We imagined several different scenarios of what might happen during a typical school day and what Jesus would do if He were here. It worked great for the entire week! In fact, the kids really caught on. If something happened that typically would have caused a problem, someone would call out, "WWJD!" And those involved would stop, think, and make a decision on how they should act.

The teacher told me that when she returned to the classroom the next week, a boy walked by a girl's desk and accidently bumped her basket, sending pencils, pens, and markers flying across the floor. The class started laughing until one student called out, "WWJD!" Then some kids got up and began picking up the girl's things, placing them back in her basket.

Why not give the WWJD rule a try at school and at home? Whenever you're tempted to get angry, disrespectful, jealous, or boastful, ask yourself "WWJD?" And then be like Him.

Sticky Situation Solution

In your relationships with one another,
have the same mindset as Christ Jesus. Philippians 2:5, NIV.

Yesterday I talked about how kids in a classroom practiced the acronym WWJD: What Would Jesus Do? If you asked yourself this question every day, would it make a big difference?

You're watching your favorite TV show when your dad calls from the garage, "Would you please come out here and help me for a minute?" Inside you might feel like hollering, "Not now! I'm busy!" But instead you ask yourself, *What would Jesus do?* And you know that the right response is, "Coming, Dad!"

You're tired from a busy week, and your room shows it. Your mom asks, "Please clean your room before dinner." Inside you might feel like saying, "I don't have to! It's my room and I don't care if it's messy." But instead you ask yourself, *What would Jesus do?* And you know that the right response is, "OK, Mom."

A kid in the school gym deliberately smacks into you during a game of basketball. Inside you might feel like shoving him and yelling, "Back off!" But instead you ask yourself, *What would Jesus do?* And you know that the right response is "Hey, let's cool down and show some sportsmanship here."

A girl in your class has been spreading gossip about you. Inside you might feel like gossiping about her to get the attention off you and to get revenge. But instead you ask yourself, *What would Jesus do?* And you know that the right response is to approach her and say, "Please quit spreading rumors about me. Gossip is just going to cause our classroom to fight."

A kid at school tells you of a great plan to cheat on a test and asks you to join. Inside you might feel tempted because you know that it's going to be a tough test, and you didn't study. But instead you ask yourself, *What would Jesus do?* And you know that the right response is, "No. I'm not going to cheat, even if I get a bad grade."

Who knew that four letters could help you solve so many sticky situations? I hope that you'll always remember WWJD and ask yourself that question. Because then you'll be acting like Jesus. And there's no one better to imitate!

OCTOBER 21

Taking the Hit

My God is my protection, and with him I am safe. He protects me like a shield; he defends me and keeps me safe. He is my savior; he protects me and saves me from violence. I call to the Lord, and he saves me from my enemies. Praise the Lord! 2 Samuel 22:3, 4, TEV.

There I stood, ready to be embarrassed again. I was in a line with other fifth graders who were being chosen for dodgeball teams. I knew what would happen. It would get down to the last three or four kids, and then I would be left there standing alone. I hoped that just this once I wouldn't be the last one standing. But I was. And the captain who got me just rolled his eyes.

Why? Because I was *terrified* of dodgeball! I didn't mind playing against a girls' team. But it was a different story when guys and girls were mixed. The boys could throw hard!

There was one boy, a bully, who knew my fears. And he would deliberately seek me out. He would toss the ball up and down in his hands while eyeing me. There was no escape, since we played with a wall behind us. And rather than trying to outsmart him by dodging from left to right—or even trying to catch the ball—I would pretty much just freeze. (Even though the name of the game *is* "dodge" ball.) He would throw the ball with all his might, and when it hit me it would sting.

I remember one particular PE class when I was once again on the opposite team from the bully, and once again I feared him. But this time was different. A boy on my team did something so kind that I will never forget it. He knew I was afraid. So he came up to me and said, "Whenever that guy throws the ball at you, I'll move in front of you and take the hit."

I was so relieved! I didn't have to be afraid anymore! And sure enough, when the bully threw the ball with all the strength he could muster, that boy was my shield and took the hit.

There's something even stronger than a dodgeball being thrown at you and me. Ephesians 6:16 says, "Let your faith be like a shield, and you will be able to stop all the flaming arrows of the evil one" (CEV). The devil tries to attack us and get us to sin. But we can stop his arrows with a shield, and that shield is our faith. The only way to have strong faith is to spend time with Jesus. The more you read about Him, the more you talk to Him, the stronger your faith becomes.

He has given you what you need for a shield—your Bible and prayer. And you're not alone in the battle. He's always there, and He's got your back.

OCTOBER 22

You Won't Be Disappointed

And this hope will not lead to disappointment. For we know how dearly God loves us, because he has given us the Holy Spirit to fill our hearts with his love. Romans 5:5, NLT.

Imagine your excitement if you really loved Jesus and thought that you knew the exact date of His return. Then imagine how you would feel if that day came—and went—but Jesus didn't come. Would you feel betrayed? heartbroken? Would you give up believing in Him?

This actually happened to a group of people called Millerites on this day in 1844. Their leader and teacher, William Miller, misunderstood a prophecy in the book of Daniel and taught that Jesus would come on that actual day. Some of those who believed gathered at his farm and stood waiting on a rock that is now known as Ascension Rock—because they fully believed that they would ascend from there to heaven. The group waited—hour after hour until after midnight. But Jesus didn't come. That day is known as the Great Disappointment, and you can see why.

I've actually stood on that rock myself with a group of friends. We stood there in silence, looking up at the sky. We each imagined what it must have been like to stand there waiting for Jesus to return. I don't think I would have wanted to even blink! And then we imagined what it must have felt like to be so bitterly disappointed.

We don't know when Jesus will return. He said in the Bible, "But about that day or hour no one knows, not even the angels in heaven, nor the Son, but only the Father" (Matthew 24:36, NIV). So He tells us, "Therefore keep watch, because you do not know on what day your Lord will come. But understand this: If the owner of the house had known at what time of night the thief was coming, he would have kept watch and would not have let his house be broken into. So you also must be ready, because the Son of Man will come at an hour when you do not expect him" (verses 42-44, NIV).

So how do you "keep watch"? Not by living in fear because you don't know when it's going to happen, but by keeping your friendship with Jesus the top priority in your life. By living like someone who is getting ready to go home with Jesus! Sure, there are other great things in life, like family and friends, school and sports, but Jesus needs to be number one.

He *will* come again! We have His promise and the hope it brings us. And as today's text says, "This hope will not lead to disappointment."

OCTOBER 23

Give Because You Want To

Just then he looked up and saw the rich people dropping offerings in the collection plate. Then he saw a poor widow put in two pennies. He said, "The plain truth is that this widow has given by far the largest offering today. All these others made offerings that they'll never miss; she gave extravagantly what she couldn't afford—she gave her all!" Luke 21:1-4, Message.

Who would have thought that such a simple act would be talked about 2,000 years later? Jesus drew attention to this woman's gift—and Luke wrote about it—not because of the size of her gift, but rather the size of her heart. It was easy for the rich people to give. They had a lot of money! But this woman—she couldn't afford to give. Yet she gave her all.

When I was your age, there was a time that my family couldn't really afford to give. We were fairly new Christians, and my parents had to rework the family budget to include tithe and offerings. Dad was paid weekly, and I remember one week when money was tight.

Dad called a family meeting and said, "If we give tithe and offering this week, there may not be much money for food. What do you kids think we should do?"

We took a vote. It was unanimous—we would give to God first. Then some amazing things happened. Each day for the next week, God provided food! One morning we woke up to find that someone had left several loaves of fresh bread on our front porch. On another day we were invited out to dinner. On yet another day, friends brought us produce from their garden. These "coincidences" happened all week long until Friday, when a church member brought over a casserole for our Sabbath lunch. And we hadn't told a soul about our lack of money for food.

The lesson for my family was this: when we give to God, He always gives back. Sometimes it's through gifts like the ones my family was given. Other times what we get back is the satisfaction of knowing that we've given to God. Even that itself is enough.

It's hard to give money, isn't it? Especially when you're a kid. God doesn't force you to give. As with everything else, He gives you the choice. Second Corinthians 9:7 says, "Each of you must make up your own mind about how much to give. But don't feel sorry that you must give and don't feel that you are forced to give. God loves people who love to give" (CEV).

Here's how I look at it: Jesus gave His life! And one of the ways to thank Him is to give. But don't stop with giving Him just money. The best thing you could give Him is your heart.

OCTOBER 24

Warm Fuzzies or Cold Pricklies?

Do not use harmful words, but only helpful words, the kind that build up and provide what is needed, so that what you say will do good to those who hear you. Ephesians 4:29, TEV.

I know of a school that had a board in the hallway called the "Warm Fuzzy Board." The purpose of the board was for kids to leave anonymous notes to classmates—notes that would make someone else feel all warm and fuzzy inside.

It was the kids' idea. They asked their teacher, "Can we have a Warm Fuzzy Board?"

"Sure!" she answered. "As long as you keep it positive. As long as the warm fuzzies never turn into cold pricklies, I'm all for it."

The teacher later told me, "It was so much fun to watch! Kids would get a note with their name on it and read it. They would kind of shyly look around, wondering who pinned it there. Then they would get a big smile on their face, stand a little taller, and walk on down to their next class. What was remarkable to me was how their body language changed when they read something positive about themselves from a peer."

Some warm fuzzies were superficial things: "I like your hair today" or "That's a nice shirt that you're wearing." But others had deeper meaning: "Thanks for talking with me last night" or "Thanks for being my friend."

The board was the first thing the kids looked at in the morning, and when class was over, it was the first place they went. They were eager to read something nice about themselves.

After about three months, the teacher started noticing a change in some of the kids' body language as they read their notes. "It was watching their reactions that gave me a hint that some cold pricklies were being written," she told me. "Instead of a smile and a head held high, I noticed that some kids just drooped. And some seemed just devastated by what they read."

Some of the cold pricklies were words like "I hate the way you walk" or "That was sure a stupid question you asked in class." Sadly, the teacher had to take the board down.

There are many times during the day when you have the chance to give someone a warm fuzzy or a cold prickly—whether you do it in writing or in person. Do you want to help someone to stand a little taller, or to droop? Today's text says we should use the kind of words that build each other up. And I think that's pretty good advice.

OCTOBER 25

Here Comes the Bride

Since you have been raised to new life with Christ, set your sights on the realities of heaven, where Christ sits in the place of honor at God's right hand. Think about the things of heaven, not the things of earth. For you died to this life, and your real life is hidden with Christ in God. And when Christ, who is your life, is revealed to the whole world, you will share in all his glory. Colossians 3:1-4, NLT.

Some girls grow up daydreaming about what kind of wedding they want to have. I was not one of those. I was too busy with my horses, my friends, my youth group, and my family to sit and daydream much. When I did daydream, it was about winning a blue ribbon in a horse show or having the voice to sing a solo in front of hundreds of people.

So when my future husband proposed to me, I had a lot of daydreaming to do—fast! I prepared for the big day for almost four months. Then, dressed in white, I stood with my dad in the church foyer. As the organ struck its first chord, the doors leading into the sanctuary swung open. And there he stood at the end of a long aisle—my bridegroom. I'd worked all summer to buy the perfect-yet-affordable wedding dress and veil. I wanted Keith to think I was beautiful.

That day reminds me of the way John describes the New Jerusalem approaching the earth made new someday: "Then I saw New Jerusalem, that holy city, coming down from God in heaven. It was like a bride dressed in her wedding gown and ready to meet her husband" (Revelation 21:2, CEV).

If you've ever been to a wedding, you know what a beautiful sight it is to see a bride walk down the aisle toward her groom. What makes it so special is the love between the two. And the love between Jesus and us is what will make His second coming such a beautiful sight.

Although we can daydream about what the new earth will be like, the Bible says that we can't even come close to picturing how incredibly awesome it will be! But we can try to imagine—to dream. And we should. Living on this earth can get discouraging at times. But dreaming of our new one brings us hope!

Picture your favorite place here on earth. It can't even compare to how beautiful heaven will be. First Corinthians 2:9 says that "no eye has seen, no ear has heard, and no mind has imagined what God has prepared for those who love him" (NLT).

OCTOBER 26

How to Save a Life

If you see some brother or sister in need and have the means to do something about it but turn a cold shoulder and do nothing, what happens to God's love? It disappears. And you made it disappear. 1 John 3:17, Message.

The bullying started the first week of school. When my nephew Michael was in the sixth grade, there was one kid in his PE class who was always getting picked on. He was different—a bit odd, you might say. While the other boys wore T-shirts, basketball shorts, and athletic socks and shoes to PE, he wore a collared shirt, cargo shorts, long wool socks, and outdoor shoes.

Some of the boys called him "Little Girl" and other mean names. They would make fun of him at every possible opportunity. They especially picked on him during PE because he wasn't good at any sport, and he wouldn't change his clothes in front of the other boys. He always undressed in a stall, and they would try to pull pranks on him while he was in there.

Whenever Michael and his friends witnessed the bullying, they always put a stop to it. Michael told me about one day when he was especially glad that he was there to step in.

"Toward the end of the school year, the bullies cornered this kid in the locker room," Michael said. "When he was trapped, they told him that they were finally going to beat him up.

"Another guy and I walked up to the group of boys, even though we were outnumbered. 'Stop it!' I told them. 'What you're doing isn't funny. Stop picking on him and get out of here! The teacher is going to hear about this.'

"They walked away, leaving the boy curled up on the floor, crying. He wouldn't talk to us. He wouldn't get up. He looked like he was done. Lunch was coming up, and we told him that we'd save him a place at our table. But he never showed up. In fact, he missed afternoon classes.

"But he did come back the next day. He walked up to me and said, 'I had planned to commit suicide yesterday. But then you showed me that I have two friends, so I chose not to.' "

I looked at my nephew and said, "Michael! God used you to save a life!"

Could God use you to save a life? Yes! He could! How do you save a life? By looking out for someone who's always alone. By being kind. By being a friend. By defending him or her.

There are kids you see every day that may not need their lives saved, but they're sad and lonely, and you could save their day. And I say that would make a pretty awesome day!

OCTOBER 27

God's Lost-and-Found Department

"We must celebrate with a feast,
for this son of mine was dead and has now returned to life.
He was lost, but now he is found." So the party began. Luke 15:23, 24, NLT.

Have you ever lost something that was valuable to you? Maybe a wallet, an iPod, a cell phone, or a major homework assignment? If you found it, do you remember how excited you were?

Luke 15 tells three stories of things that were lost: a sheep, a coin, and a son. They represent people who have left God—who are lost spiritually. What I love about these stories is that they show that while God actively searches for us, He never forces us. The first two stories teach that He seeks us. The last story teaches that He also waits for us.

Who knows why the lost sheep wandered off? Maybe it thought it could find greener grass, so it left the protection of the shepherd. Or maybe it decided to explore—just a little—and then became lost. Whatever the case, the shepherd missed it, left his herd of 99, and searched for the one lost sheep until he found it.

Have you ever lost a pet? If so, you probably searched the whole neighborhood for it. Maybe you put up signs or placed an ad in the newspaper. And if you found that pet, do you remember how happy you were? Well then, you've had just a taste of how happy God is when He has searched for people who are spiritually lost and finds them.

The story of the lost son adds this: that while God searches for us, He never forces us to come to Him. He waits. In this story the son deliberately chooses to be "lost." He leaves home, thinking that the grass really is greener somewhere else. But he soon finds out that life away from his father is miserable, so he decides to go home and ask his dad to forgive him.

His dad could have yelled, "Get off my property! You chose to leave. Now go live with the consequences!" But he didn't. He had been waiting, searching the horizon for his son to come home. And when he saw him a long way off, he ran out to welcome him home with a hug.

I hope that you never choose to wander from God. But if you do, and if you sense that He's looking for you, I hope you'll turn to Him. If you're tired of being away from God because you realize that life without Him is miserable, you can go home to Him. The God who seeks and waits is always ready to start the welcome-home party for you!

OCTOBER 28

He Knows Your Name

Do not be afraid. For I have bought you and made you free. I have called you by name. You are Mine! Isaiah 43:1, NLV.

Have you ever wondered if God even knows that you exist? If so, do I have a story for you! It's found in Mark 5:25-34.

Jesus had a crowd of people following Him one day. In the crowd was a very sick woman. For 12 years she had suffered from some sort of internal bleeding. She had seen many doctors—so many that now she was broke. But none of them could help her get well. In fact, she was getting worse.

But she'd heard about Jesus, and something made her seek Him out for healing. She told herself, "If I just touch his clothes, I will be healed" (Mark 5:28, NIV). So she reached her arm through the crowd and touched Jesus' clothes. Instantly the bleeding stopped! She felt healthy and strong again.

Although Jesus was in a crowd of people, He somehow knew that someone had touched Him—even though she had touched only the edge of His cloak. He felt the healing power go out of Him and asked, "Who touched my clothes?" (verse 30). The disciples reminded Him that He was surrounded by people. How could even He ask such a seemingly ridiculous question?

Jesus searched the crowd, looking for the person who had touched Him. Finally the woman came forward and fell at Jesus' feet, shaking with fear. Impressed by her faith, He told her, "Daughter, your faith has healed you" (verse 34).

If Jesus knew it when someone merely touched His clothes in faith, then surely He knows that you exist! The Bible says that He knew you while you were being formed inside your mom. He was there when you took your first breath. He was there when you took your first step. He was there when you spoke your first word. He was there on the first day of school. He was there when you were sick. He was there when you woke up terrified from a nightmare. He was there when you got grounded. He was there when your friend let you down. He was there that night you cried yourself to sleep.

In all your life you've never had a more constant friend than Jesus. Hold on to Him. He's a friend worth keeping. The best friend you'll ever have.

OCTOBER 29

The Trouble With Guys and Girls

Don't hit back; discover beauty in everyone. If you've got it in you, get along with everybody. Don't insist on getting even; that's not for you to do. "I'll do the judging," says God. "I'll take care of it." Romans 12:18, Message.

Most of the time you kids are pretty great! You make us grownups proud. We admire you. But the trouble is, sometimes you can be mean to each other.

I was talking with a group of fifth and sixth graders, and I asked the girls, "What's tough about being a girl at your age?" Here are some of their answers:

"Girls can be vicious when they get in fights with each other."

"Some girls choose who they like and exclude everyone else."

"Girls can really be mean to each other with the words they speak."

"Guys fight physically—girls fight with words."

I then asked, "How can girls be kinder to each other?" They said:

"Compliment other girls. Say nice things to them and about them."

"Don't lie to each other."

"If you have a party, include everyone."

"Don't talk behind another girl's back. It will always get back to them, and it hurts."

Next I asked the boys, "Why do you think boys bully each other?" They said:

"Some guys think that they're better than everyone else."

"They don't have any friends."

"They think it will make them feel better about themselves."

I then asked, "So give me some ideas. How should you react to bullies?" They said:

"Ignore it because the bully wants you to shrink and be scared."

"Don't give the bully an audience. If you ignore him and walk away, no one will watch."

"Don't get mad. It will draw attention to the bully."

"Report him to your parents or the teacher."

These kids' answers to my questions proved two things: kids hurt other kids, and there are ways to stop the hurt. I like what today's text suggests: "Discover beauty in everyone." After all, that's what Jesus does. He's discovered it in you. Now go and discover it in someone else.

OCTOBER 30

Logan's Weekly Appointment

For a day in Your house is better than a thousand outside.
I would rather be the one who opens the door of the house of my God,
than to live in the tents of the sinful. Psalm 84:10, NLV.

Going to church every week is a major time commitment. How major? Well, if you go to church every week until you're 70 years old, you will have been at church the equivalent of *every* morning for 10 years straight!

After Logan and his family became Christians and were baptized when he was 12, he didn't want to miss a single week at church. Even when his parents couldn't go, Logan would somehow find a ride. It was too far to walk, so he'd call different church members until he found someone who was able to pick him up.

What was his reason for going? To worship God and to serve. Even at age 12, Logan was actively involved in his church. He didn't go just to hang out with friends, to catch a good nap during the sermon, or to play on his phone. He went to give—to give to God and to others.

So why do *you* go to church? Have you discovered the benefits from attending regularly? Are there good reasons to attend church? I think so!

I go to church because it's God's house on this earth. And even though I can meet with Him anytime, anywhere, His sanctuary is a special place to me. There I can sing praises to Him, pray to Him, and learn more about Him. I also go to church because I want to be like Jesus, and He set the example by regularly going when He was here. And if God Himself went to church, then why shouldn't I? Another reason I go to church is to be with other Christians. Unlike any other public event, church is a place where people come together because they believe in God.

You may sit in church and feel that the sermon is boring or that the music isn't your style, but I've discovered that when I go to church with a plan to worship God, I always get something out of it. And if I get involved, it's even better because I'm not just a spectator.

Right now you may go to church because your family goes. But someday you will make your own decision. And I hope that you always choose to go. God invites you to His house to praise Him, talk with Him, read about Him, learn more about Him, and be with other people who love Him too. When you stop and think about all the other places you go during the week, even one morning a week doesn't seem enough to give the One who has given you so much.

OCTOBER 31

Bread, Fish, and Popcorn

Remember that the person who plants few seeds will have a small crop; the one who plants many seeds will have a large crop. You should each give, then, as you have decided, not with regret or out of a sense of duty; for God loves the one who gives gladly. 2 Corinthians 9:6, 7, TEV.

If you looked through our family photo album, you'd see a picture of our daughter when she was 3, holding a glass jar of plastic food. I'm looking at the picture now and can see a plastic hot dog, a plastic banana, a plastic muffin, and a plastic chocolate cookie.

"I'm the boy who shared his lunch with Jesus!" she had announced.

Christina was fascinated with that story. She thought it was pretty cool that a kid could share just two fish and five loaves of bread with Jesus and have Him turn it into a meal that fed more than 5,000 people! We often talked about sharing in our home.

Your parents probably talked to you about sharing, too, and told you that *true* sharing isn't being forced to share but sharing willingly. I wasn't sure if Christina really understood that.

Then came our church's old-fashioned harvest party. The most exciting event for Christina was buying popcorn in a bag (at home we just ate it out of bowls). She held her bag close to her chest, eating one kernel at a time.

Then two women and three young children whom none of us knew showed up at the party. By the way they were dressed, it was obvious that they didn't have much money. The littlest girl, about Christina's age, was wearing a thin, stained dress. And she wasn't wearing a jacket, even though it was a chilly autumn evening. Her face was dirty, and her blond, curly hair was tangled. She stayed close by her mom, clutching onto her leg, looking anxious.

As I was welcoming her mom, I glanced down and saw Christina holding one of her prized pieces of popcorn to the little girl's closed mouth. The girl looked up at me with wide eyes, as if she thought she'd get in trouble if she accepted it.

Christina looked up at me and said, "She's hungry, Mommy." And so together we went to buy the girl her own special bag.

What do you have that you might be able to share? A closetful of clothes you never wear? A spare skateboard? A book you've already read, or extra CDs? Why not share them with someone? It's actually fun! And when you give to others, you're giving to God, too.

NOVEMBER 1

Surprise Visitors

Then these righteous ones will reply, "Lord, when did we ever see you hungry and feed you? Or thirsty and give you something to drink? Or a stranger and show you hospitality? Or naked and give you clothing? When did we ever see you sick or in prison and visit you?" And the King will say, "I tell you the truth, when you did it to one of the least of these my brothers and sisters, you were doing it to me!" Matthew 25:37-40, NLT.

It was November 1, and the weather seemed to know it. The ground was frozen from the night before, and I was thankful for our little warm house on such a cold morning.

Right after breakfast there was a knock on our front door. *Too early for any company we would know,* I thought.

When my husband opened the door, we saw a young man standing there. Puffs of warm air hit the cold as he talked. "My car's engine started smoking," he said. "I parked it down the road and started knocking on doors until someone would answer. No one did till you."

He asked to use our phone to call his dad for help. When his dad didn't answer, he mentioned that his wife and baby were waiting in the car with no heat. Immediately my husband and I said to bring them in. So in from the cold and into our warm living room came the man, his wife, and their baby boy.

After several tries, the couple found a friend available who lived about a mile away. Before long they were thanking us and walking out the door. The whole incident lasted only about 10 minutes.

After they left I asked myself, "What if?" What if we hadn't opened our door because it was so early? What if we'd slammed it shut when the man asked to borrow a phone? What if we'd let his wife and baby wait in the cold car until help came?

The world has changed so much that we're often afraid to help strangers nowadays. But rather than not help others because we're afraid, maybe we should weigh each situation. If it's a true need and it would be safe to help, just go for it! On the other hand, if you feel it's unsafe, you could still help by telling an adult or calling the proper authorities.

It was such a simple thing to help that family. But it felt *so* good! Afterward I thought of today's text. In a way, we brought Jesus in from the cold. And that's an awesome thought.

NOVEMBER 2

Cucumbers and Sand

But what about the ocean so big and wide?
It is alive with creatures, large and small. Psalm 104:25, CEV.

Have you ever had the chance to see any creatures of the sea for yourself? The first time I went snorkeling was when I was on a mission trip with my youth group. We'd gone to a little island off Honduras called Utila. On our day off we went out into the Caribbean Sea.

I couldn't believe all the creatures that I got to see on my first venture: a nurse shark, a moray eel, a barracuda, a stingray, an octopus, and my favorite: a parrotfish! I can't say that I was all that excited when we saw the shark, but all of the other creatures were amazing! There's a whole remarkable world full of God's creation under the sea. And His creation can always teach us lessons.

For instance, my friend Liesl is an avid scuba diver and has done research on sea cucumbers. If you don't know what they look like, Google it. Some actually look like the vegetable you eat. They live on the bottom of the ocean, and if you saw them eating, you'd think they were just eating sand. But they're smarter than that. They do eat the sand, but they're after nutrients that lie on the ocean floor. Their body knows what's good for them and what's not. So it draws out the nutrients, and when they go to the bathroom, out comes the sand.

When she told me that, I thought, *If we could just be like a sea cucumber! If we could simply sort out what's good for us—what will spiritually feed us and help us grow closer to Jesus—and throw the rest away, we'd be better people.*

Another lesson I learned came as I was walking on the beach one day. I picked up a handful of sand and spread it out on my palm. Each grain was so tiny! I thought of the verse where David said: "How precious are your thoughts about me, O God. They cannot be numbered! I can't even count them; they outnumber the grains of sand! And when I wake up, you are still with me!" (Psalm 139:17, 18, NLT).

I looked down the long beach stretched out in front of me and thought, *God's thoughts about me outnumber the grains of sand?* Yes, they do! And His thoughts of you do, too. If you tried to count how many times He thinks of you, the numbers wouldn't go high enough. You are always on His mind. And that makes me wonder: how often is He on *my* mind, and yours?

When the Unexpected Happens

Why am I discouraged? Why is my heart so sad? I will put my hope in God! I will praise him again—my Savior and my God! Psalm 42:11, NLT.

Rose had a blast at the fifth- and sixth-grade Christmas party! All three classrooms had gone ice skating, and now she had two and a half weeks of vacation to look forward to. She thought it was a bit odd that her grandpa was waiting outside to pick her up after school. Usually one of her parents was there. *Oh, well,* Rose said to herself. *My parents must be busy this afternoon.*

When they got to her grandparents' house, Rose recognized her aunt's and uncle's cars in the driveway. Everyone was quiet and sad when she walked into the house. She soon found out that there had been a horrible accident. Her grandma had traveled to another state to pick up her great-grandparents and bring them back for Christmas. On the way home, she hit black ice and rolled their truck three times. Rose's great-grandpa was thrown from the truck and died instantly. Her grandma was able to climb out, but her great-grandma was left hanging upside down for almost an hour until help arrived. Two men who were working on the road came by and called 911. Rose's great-grandma was airlifted to a large hospital and recovered. But things just wouldn't be the same without her great-grandpa. What had started out as a great day turned into a day of shock and sadness for Rose and her whole family.

I hate it when the unexpected happens. When I'm having a great day and then, *BAM!* A phone call, a visit, or an e-mail can change everything in a heartbeat. You never know what a day might bring: the death of a family member; a call from the doctor's office with bad news; an announcement that you're moving; finding out that a friend doesn't like you anymore; the vet saying you need to put your dog down; or your parents telling you that they're divorcing.

So what do you do when the unexpected happens? You have no choice but to go through it. But you don't need to go through it alone. Surround yourself with people who care. Talk about it as much as you need to. Talk to God about it and search your Bible to hear His voice. Even though it's hard to imagine now, believe that someday you'll begin to feel better again—just as today's text says. Your unexpected news is no surprise to God. He knew it was coming. And He's got your back.

NOVEMBER 4

Going the Extra Mile

You know that you have been taught, "An eye for an eye and a tooth for a tooth." But I tell you not to try to get even with a person who has done something to you. When someone slaps your right cheek, turn and let that person slap your other cheek. If someone sues you for your shirt, give up your coat as well. If a soldier forces you to carry his pack one mile, carry it two miles. When people ask you for something, give it to them. When they want to borrow money, lend it to them. Matthew 5:38-42, CEV.

"He hit me first! I had every right to hit him back!"

"I only shoved her because she shoved me first!"

"But he started yelling and name-calling first! I was just giving him what he deserves."

"I only gave her a dirty look after she gave me one first."

"He started playing rough on the court first. I just gave him some of his own medicine."

"She gossiped about me first. I only gossiped about her to show her how it feels."

Do these sound familiar? For some reason we think that just because someone hurt us first, we're justified in hurting them back. Retaliate! Pay back! Give 'em what they deserve!

But Jesus is asking us to do something different. He's asking us to go the extra mile and do what's hard. He's asking us not to return evil for evil. He's asking us to be kind instead.

Don't mistake what today's text is teaching. Jesus isn't asking you to be a doormat and let people walk all over you. It actually takes a much braver and more mature person to choose not to fight back verbally or physically.

So what are some alternatives? What do you do when someone hits you? You walk away. You report it. What do you do when someone shoves you? You tell them that was unkind, and you walk away. What do you do when someone yells at you and calls you names? You answer calmly, and you don't stoop to name-calling back. What do you do when someone gives you a dirty look? You smile back at them! What do you do when someone is playing rough on the court? You show true Christian sportsmanship. And what do you do when someone gossips about you? You keep quiet and refuse to say anything bad about them.

I believe that with Jesus' help you can go the extra mile! You can use self-control. You can choose to be like Him. He treated everyone with respect and kindness.

NOVEMBER 5

At the Foot of the Cross

When he had received the drink, Jesus said, "It is finished." With that, he bowed his head and gave up his spirit. John 19:30, NIV.

I was helping with a spiritual retreat that involved students from several different schools. After a long day, all the kids were supposed to be in their cabins, and I was getting ready for bed. Then came a knock on my door. It was Angie, one of the girls I'd gotten to know.

"Can you please come down to the chapel?" she pleaded. "My friend Wylie is there, and he's having a really tough time."

I grabbed my coat, and we walked through the darkness to the chapel. When I opened the door, in the dim light I saw a boy sitting on the stage, slumped over.

Angie and I sat down on the floor next to him. I reached out my hand and placed it on his shoulder. "Hey, are you OK? Can I help you?" I asked quietly.

Through tears he told me the story of how he'd started choosing the wrong kinds of friends. Before he knew it, he was doing things that he thought he'd never do. Now he felt trapped—trapped in the friendships, trapped in the habits, and trapped in the guilt.

The longer he talked the more he cried, until he was sobbing. Now Angie and I were crying, too. I told him that Jesus forgave him. I told him that Jesus loved him. But nothing I said eased his pain and guilt.

In desperation I looked up. I looked up and saw that we were sitting at the foot of a large wooden cross. I'd seen it earlier that evening but hadn't noticed it again till now.

"Wylie!" I exclaimed. "Look up! *Look where you're sitting!* You're sitting at the foot of the cross! Don't you see? This is your answer! Jesus died on the cross so your sins could be forgiven. Jesus died in your place so you could be saved."

Wylie looked up at the cross, and his crying stopped. It finally sank in. He finally got it. We sat there in silence for a long time, thinking about the cross and all that it means. The cross means that Someone loved you enough to actually die in your place. The cross means that when Jesus said, "It is finished," He had won the war against evil. The cross means that you're forgiven. The cross means that you don't need to carry around guilt. The cross means that you are saved. And the cross means that you are deeply loved.

NOVEMBER 6

Go Ahead, Be Proud!

The disciples, seeing the Master with their own eyes, were exuberant. Jesus repeated his greeting: "Peace to you. Just as the Father sent me, I send you." John 20:21, Message.

You know by now that my family and I became Christians when I was 10. Dad read his way through the Bible and became a Christian before he ever belonged to any church. When he felt that he knew enough of what God's Word was teaching, he went searching for a church that taught what the Bible teaches. And that's how we became Seventh-day Adventists.

I was proud to be a Seventh-day Adventist Christian, but as I got older I was a little more reluctant to tell people what church I belonged to. It wasn't that I didn't fully believe in what our church teaches, but I was afraid that some people might have a misunderstanding about what an Adventist is. I thought maybe people judged us as being weird or having strange beliefs.

But then the thought came to me one day: *Why not show them that their impressions are wrong! Show them that Adventists are happy, fun, kind, loving people who follow God's Word, the Bible.* And that's what I've done ever since. I'm not embarrassed to say that I belong to the Adventist Church, and I enjoy showing people that I'm "normal" as I show them God's love.

There are several things that make our church unique. One is our name: Seventh-day Adventist. It means that we believe Saturday is the Sabbath, and we observe that day. This is the day that God made holy and rested on after creation (Genesis 2:2, 3). It's the day God reminded us to keep holy when He wrote the Ten Commandments (Exodus 20:8-11). It's also the day when Jesus went to church (Luke 4:16).

The second half of our name, Adventist, comes from the word "advent," which means "coming"—the second coming of Jesus. Even our church's name is based in the Bible.

When I worked as a youth pastor, I prepared many kids for baptism. Since their baptism meant that they were voted into church membership, I wanted to make sure that they knew what Adventists believe. There are 28 core beliefs, and I was always so excited and proud to be able to show the kids that everything we believe can be found in the Bible! There are multiple texts for each belief. If you'd like to know what those beliefs and texts are, ask a pastor.

If you are a Seventh-day Adventist Christian, you have nothing to be embarrassed about. You belong to a church whose beliefs are based on the Bible, and you can take pride in that.

NOVEMBER 7

Know What You Believe

All Scripture is inspired by God and is useful to teach us what is true and to make us realize what is wrong in our lives. It corrects us when we are wrong and teaches us to do what is right. God uses it to prepare and equip his people to do every good work. 2 Timothy 3:16-18, NLT.

Do you know what you believe? Better yet, do you know *why* you believe what you believe? And can you prove what you believe in the Bible?

As you were growing up, your parents, teachers, and Sabbath school leaders told you what they believed was truth. But maybe now you're starting to investigate on your own. And that's a good thing! Because now you're old enough to start searching the Bible for yourself. Then you can know—without a doubt—what you believe and why.

It's really important to know the "whys" of your beliefs. Here's a story to prove that.

My husband, Keith, was on a long flight, sitting next to a middle-aged man. They began with small talk and then moved to more personal things.

The man said, "My mother died a few months ago. She was a very loving and giving person. Because I loved her so much, I was concerned about what had happened to her after she died. At her funeral, I asked an acquaintance where my mom was now. As he described to me what he believed, I was horrified! Ever since her funeral, I often wake up in a cold sweat or in tears from nightmares about my mom."

Keith silently prayed, *Lord, help me to show him the truth that will set him free!* Then he gently began explaining what the Bible teaches about what happens when you die. The man listened intently as he discovered that the truth was far kinder than what he had been told.

If you don't know for yourself what the Bible teaches, then you won't know what's true and what's false when people tell you what they believe. But if you study what the Bible teaches, you won't be easily swayed by other people's opinions. You'll know God's Word firsthand.

Psalm 119:11 says, "I have hidden your word in my heart that I might not sin against you" (NIV). I hope you will hide God's Word in your heart. You do that by studying your Bible for yourself. It can protect you from teachings that are false. It can help you help others when they're confused as to what is truth. And you'll feel confident because you've studied and know why you believe what you believe. It's one of the perks of growing up!

NOVEMBER 8

Pride Is for Losers

First pride, then the crash—the bigger the ego, the harder the fall. Proverbs 16:18, Message.

Too much pride can put you to shame. It's wiser to be humble. Proverbs 11:2, CEV.

It's like David up against Goliath when the Knights soccer team plays the Warriors.

"They're really good," Alex, one of the Knights' midfielders, told me. "And they usually beat us—badly—like 12-0. It's humiliating! They have a lot of guys who have been playing soccer their whole lives. They're a very talented team. They've even won the state championship a few times. They're *that* good!"

But then came the game that changed the way the Knights felt about their giant.

"It was a home game for us," Alex said, "and the Warriors came onto our field *very* confident. Their attitude was like, 'We're really good. You're not so good. And we can beat you easily.' But their attitude backfired on them. They weren't playing very well. They weren't playing as a team. They were careless in their passes and seemed to care only about scoring by themselves.

"The Warriors got a goal in the first 10 minutes, but then we scored! I can't remember a time when we even scored against them. They later scored another goal and wound up winning the game. But even our one point felt like a victory because we'd worked as a team.

"We'd learned our lesson the season before, when we were playing a different team. Within the first few minutes of that game, the Knights had scored two goals. We were feeling pretty confident! We were feeling good! And we were all fired up.

"But the other team did something that was very impressive. They gathered themselves together. Some teams would have given up, but with an ounce of team spirit they began to play even harder and smarter. They tied it up. And with two minutes left in the game, they scored! They scored for the win."

When it comes to thinking that we're better than someone else, Philippians 2:5-7 says, "Think as Christ Jesus thought. Jesus has always been as God is. But He did not hold to His rights as God. He put aside everything that belonged to Him and made Himself the same as a servant who is owned by someone. He became human by being born as a man" (NLV).

NOVEMBER 9

Don't Be an Elephant

So each of you needs to be careful. If your brother sins against you, confront him about it, and if he has a change of mind and heart, then forgive him. Even if he wrongs you seven times in a single day, if he turns back to you each time and says he's sorry and will change, you must forgive him. Luke 17:3, 4, Voice.

If you had the choice of being like any mammal, which would you chose? Would you want to be like a kangaroo so you could easily dunk a basketball? Would you want to be like an orca so you could swim underwater for up to 15 minutes without needing air? Or how about a cheetah? Then you could run to school every morning at 70 miles per hour! Then there's the elephant. They say that an elephant never forgets. Wouldn't that be great? You'd have to read something only once in class, and you'd remember it. No more studying for tests!

But not being able to forget could be bad when someone hurts your feelings.

While you can't magically erase the memory of someone hurting you, dwelling on the memory doesn't do you any good. In fact, it harms you. It makes you stressed, angry, and bitter, and it wears you out. I know a boy who refuses to forget how a classmate embarrassed him, and he hasn't spoken to the other kid for a whole year. I know some girls who got in a fight and split up a group of friends because no one was willing to work things out.

When you forgive someone—whether they ask for it or not—you can also choose to let go and not hold a grudge. Jesus wants us to forgive others the way He forgives us. Think about it. When you go to God and say you're sorry, it doesn't take Him a day or two to decide whether He'll forgive you. He doesn't say begrudgingly, "OK, you're forgiven," and then give you the cold shoulder. He forgives instantly and completely. And He choses to forget about it!

My father-in-law, Joe, was a very loving man. My mother-in-law once told me that his way of forgiving *and* forgetting was one of the things she loved most about him.

She said, "If I had a stressful day at work and brought that stress home, I'd always feel bad about it later. So I'd say to Joe, 'I'm sorry about that.' He would look at me with a twinkle in his eye and say, 'Sorry about what?' as though he'd already forgotten."

When it comes to forgiving *and* forgetting, don't be like an elephant. Be like Jesus.

NOVEMBER 10

Sidewalk Chalk Message

So then, faith comes to us by hearing the Good News. And the Good News comes by someone preaching it. Romans 10:17, NLV.

My husband and I took a walk at an athletic track this evening. I wasn't having the best day. As we walked I noticed that someone had been there before us and had left messages on the track. The writing looked like a kid's writing, and the words were written with sidewalk chalk.

The first message said, "Believe." We walked a little farther and found the next message: "You Are Amazing." Later on we spotted another message that said, "You Can Do It!" Then, "Don't Give Up!" And the final message was "You're Almost There!"

Whoever wrote these messages was trying to encourage the people who walk or run at the track. I don't know if the writer was a Christian or not, but as we left I thought, *Those are some of the same messages that God gives us in the Bible!*

God tells us, *Believe*. "I tell you the truth, those who listen to my message and believe in God who sent me have eternal life. They will never be condemned for their sins, but they have already passed from death into life" (John 5:24, NLT).

God tells us, *You Are Amazing*. "For You shaped me, inside and out. You knitted me together in my mother's womb long before I took my first breath. I will offer You my grateful heart, for I am Your unique creation, filled with wonder and awe. You have approached even the smallest details with excellence; Your works are wonderful; I carry this knowledge deep within my soul" (Psalm 139:13, 14, Voice).

God tells us, *You Can Do It!* "Christ gives me the strength to face anything" (Philippians 4:13, CEV).

God tells us, *Don't Give Up!* "But if you keep on being faithful right to the end, you will be saved" (Matthew 24:13, CEV).

And God tells us, *You're Almost There!* "Look, I am coming soon! My reward is with me, and I will give to each person according to what they have done" (Revelation 22:12, NIV).

The next time you're having a not-so-good-day, you don't need to find sidewalk chalk messages to cheer you. Just go to your Bible! The Bible tells you how valuable you are. The Bible tells you that you are unique and special. And the Bible tells you that you are loved.

You Chew Like a Cow!

Here is a simple, rule-of-thumb guide for behavior: Ask yourself what you want people to do for you, then grab the initiative and do it for them. Matthew 7:12, Message.

It's one of my husband's earliest childhood memories. Keith was playing with a group of neighborhood kids when one of the boys called out, "Hey! I've got some gum to share!"

The kids gathered around him in a circle. They were all excited because they didn't get gum very often. The boy began pulling out sticks of gum and handing them to each kid. Until he got to Keith.

"You don't get any!" he said meanly. "You chew crooked like a cow!"

Who knows why the boy said this, because Keith doesn't chew crooked like a cow! But regardless, Keith was devastated. He missed out on a treat *and* was ridiculed. He ran home crying and found a mirror to check and see if he really did look like a cow when he chewed.

Years later, when Keith was a pastor, he told this story at a school for morning worship. He read to the kids the text that says, "The tongue has the power of life and death" (Proverbs 18:21, NIV).

Keith had a reason for sharing his story that day. One of the sixth-grade boys had a large, thick scar on his face. When he was just a toddler, he'd fallen toward a wood stove, and his head had wedged between the handle and the front of the hot stove. His mom had raced to free him, but it was too late. One side of his face was severely burned. Some of the kids at that school had been saying cruel things to him about his scar. So Keith thought this story might help them to think. It probably did. But something else wonderful happened, too.

When Keith finished telling his story and had prayer, the kids ran off to recess. All of them, that is, except for the boy with the scarred face. What happened next was heartwarming. He walked up to Keith and, without saying a word, handed him a stick of gum.

This boy's sensitivity shows the power of turning your own pain into sympathy for someone else who is hurting. Look around your classroom. Is there another kid who's experiencing a hurt that you've gone through? Maybe they've lost a friendship, maybe they've lost a pet, or maybe their parents have divorced. And you, better than anyone else, can help them.

NOVEMBER 12

Two Really Are Better Than One

Two are better than one, because they have a good return for their labor: If either of them falls down, one can help the other up. But pity anyone who falls and has no one to help them up. Ecclesiastes 4:9, 10, NIV.

I'll never forget the day I learned the truth of this verse. The dad of a girl in our class died suddenly of a heart attack. She left school immediately and didn't return for a month. When she did come back, none of us kids knew what to say—so we said nothing. Just a few lame "Glad you're back" and "It's nice to see you again" greetings.

Finally she couldn't take the pain anymore. One afternoon, during a break between classes, she threw her books down in the hallway and cried out, "WOULD SOMEONE PLEASE TALK TO ME ABOUT MY DAD?" So we gathered around her, hugged her, and talked to her about her dad. For weeks we supported her until the pain began to ease a bit.

Like my classmates and me, maybe you struggle with what to do or say when another kid is hurting. You don't know how to help them. If so, here are a few ideas you can try:

- Send a card signed by you and a group of friends.
- Give your phone number or e-mail with a note offering to talk.
- Make sure they're not sitting alone at lunch or in church.
- Give a huggable stuffed animal.
- Share an encouraging worship CD.
- Bake and take a batch of homemade cookies.
- Send a bouquet of flowers from a group of friends.
- Encourage your parents to invite the kid's family over for dinner on the weekend.

A few years ago a junior high student showed me a note she'd written to a friend whose sister had died: *I'm so, so, so, so, so sorry about your sister. I wish I could help you, but I don't have any idea what it's like. I do know how it feels to hurt, though. My parents are divorcing, and I know how much that hurts. I want you to know that I love you. If I had a magic wand, I would wave it and make everything better. But I can't, and I'm sorry. I totally admire your courage, and I want you to know I'm praying for you. You're awesome.*

It's just that easy for two to become better than one.

Where's Your Treasure?

Do not gather together for yourself riches of this earth. They will be eaten by bugs and become rusted. Men can break in and steal them. Gather together riches in heaven where they will not be eaten by bugs or become rusted. Men cannot break in and steal them. For wherever your riches are, your heart will be there also. Matthew 6:19-21, NLV.

You've probably been asked the question: "If your house was on fire and you could grab only one thing, what would it be?" What "treasure" would you not want to turn to ashes? Your video games? Your clothes? Your bike? Your music? When Michelle went on a mission trip to Mexico with her youth group, she realized just how different some kids' treasures can be.

The group went to build a house for a family of nine that didn't have a home. But before they left the U.S., they went to a toy store to buy toys for the children. They bought dolls, soccer balls, jump ropes, and even a Barbie doll that spoke Spanish! They also took a bunch of candy.

While they were building, they got to know the family that would live in the new house and grew to love them. On the last day, they brought the toys to give the kids for goodbye gifts.

Michelle told me, "Of course the kids loved the toys. But what was surprising is that they seemed to cherish the boxes and wrapping that the toys came in as much as they cherished the toys themselves! They didn't rip into the boxes and packaging, but very carefully took everything apart. We told them, 'You can throw away the boxes,' but they didn't want to because they thought the boxes were colorful. I watched as they went into their new bedrooms with their new toys and displayed the *boxes* on their shelves! Even the packaging that the jump ropes came in! Seeing them treasure what we would toss away moved our youth pastor to tears.

"On the way home we stopped at a mall in San Diego to take a break and shop. But we all just wandered around. No one felt like buying anything. We had all grown up with everything at our fingertips. But now our feelings about 'things' had changed."

Why do we put so much value on what we own on this earth—those things that don't last? They get broken, stolen, or lost, or we outgrow them and sell them at a garage sale. But a friendship with Jesus is unbreakable, unstealable, and unlosable, and you'll never outgrow Him!

So the next time you think that you just can't live without a certain "thing," remember that the *only* thing you really can't live without is Jesus.

NOVEMBER 14

Making His Wish Come True

So now I am giving you a new commandment: Love each other. Just as I have loved you, you should love each other. Your love for one another will prove to the world that you are my disciples. John 13:34, 35, NLT.

I've always thought of today's text as Jesus' dying wish. He was eating His last meal with His disciples the night He was arrested. And He shared His wish for them: that they love each other.

How can you make Jesus' dying wish—for us to love each other—come true today? I asked a group of kids your age this question in three ways.

First I asked, "How can you show love in your classroom?" They said:

"If you're in a multigrade room, be nice to the kids in the grade below you."

"Don't let little things separate friendships."

"Forgive each other quickly."

"Invite someone who is alone to sit next to you during lunch."

"If someone hasn't had the ball during a game at recess, then pass it to them."

"Be nice to everyone, even if they aren't a close friend."

"Don't always choose your best friends when choosing teams."

Next I asked, "How can you show love at home?" They said:

"Respect your parents."

"Do your chores and homework without complaining, or even without being asked."

"Listen. Don't talk back."

"Don't make your parents ask you twice to do something."

Finally I asked, "How can you show love in your town?" They said:

"Hold the door open for someone."

"Help someone get an item off the store shelf that they can't reach."

"Go read a story to an elderly neighbor."

"If someone drops something, help them by picking it up."

What acts of love might you add to the lists? Today's text says that if you want the world to know you're a follower of Jesus, love each other. Let's do it! Let's show the world.

NOVEMBER 15

Warm Hearts on a Cold Night

And now these three remain: faith, hope and love. But the greatest of these is love. 1 Corinthians 13:13, NIV.

It was a bitter cold November night as I pulled into a gas station to get my car's antifreeze checked. Being a college student, I hoped that adding some wouldn't cost much.

An attendant helped me and was ready to send me on my way when something caught my eye. A white kitten, not more than 6 weeks old, was leaning against the gas pump.

"Is that your kitten?" I asked the attendant.

"Nope," he said. "But it looks like she's been hit by a car."

Just then she started moving toward me, her back legs pitifully dragging on the cold cement. I asked the man if he had something to wrap her in. He took a rag out of his pocket, picked her up, wrapped it around her, and handed the kitten to me through the window.

All the way back to the dorm she lay still in my lap, her green eyes never leaving my face. The girls on my hall fell in love with her. Everyone pitched in, and soon she had a little bed, a blanket, a heater, and some warm milk. I decided to name her "Plouie" after two of my good friends and classmates, Paul and Louie.

I began looking through the phone book for a veterinary clinic that was still open. I couldn't afford it, but neither could I let her suffer. The only one that was open told me that I'd have to pay at the time of service. Out of options, I called the police station. The dispatcher was touched by my story. And though she'd never met me, she offered the use of her credit card to pay the vet's fee! So I zipped Plouie into my jacket, and Paul and Louie drove us to the clinic.

The vet examined her, took x-rays, and then came out with the results: Plouie's spine had been severed. "There's only one humane thing to do," he said. He let me carry Plouie to a holding cage. I hugged her, told her that I was sorry, and gently placed her in the cage.

When I told the vet why I had the police dispatcher's credit card, he looked at the floor for a moment. "Don't worry about it," he said. "We'll cover the expenses."

On that night a gas station attendant, a group of dorm girls, a police dispatcher, three college friends, and a vet all learned the meaning of Jesus' words: "More blessings come from giving than from receiving" (Acts 20:35, CEV).

NOVEMBER 16

One Body, Many Parts

The body of Christ has many different parts, just as any other body does. 1 Corinthians 12:12, CEV.

When my husband, Keith, spent a year in Bangladesh as a student missionary, he never knew what surprises a day might bring.

One Sabbath a grandmother came hurrying up the walk toward the church. She was carrying her 8-year-old granddaughter, whose foot was wrapped in a rag. The mission doctor, who was preaching, stopped and went out to see what was wrong. When he unwrapped the girl's foot, he discovered that her fourth toe was being held in place by cow dung! A cow had stepped on her toe and cut it off.

The doctor and Keith took her immediately to the mission hospital for surgery. Keith's job was to thoroughly scrub the detached toe with a toothbrush and solution. Then he held it in place while the doctor sewed it back on. Each day after that, they checked on the girl's progress. Soon the toe had blood flowing through it and was healing nicely.

If the doctor hadn't reattached her toe, would the girl have missed it? Sure. Toes are needed for balancing and traction. Even something as small as a fourth toe would be missed because each member of our body—no matter how big or small—has a part to play.

The apostle Paul uses the human body to illustrate how much we need each other to be whole. The kids in your class make up a type of "body." Paul said, "God put our bodies together in such a way that even the parts that seem the least important are valuable. He did this to make all parts of the body work together smoothly, with each part caring about the others. If one part of our body hurts, we hurt all over. If one part of our body is honored, the whole body will be happy" (1 Corinthians 12:24-26, CEV).

If we are truly one body, then we should hurt when one of us is hurting—not laugh or ridicule. That will only make the pain worse. And we should celebrate when someone succeeds—not be jealous and throw them a mean look. That will only take away their joy.

You may think that the kids who are the most talented or hold the highest offices are more important than the other kids, but that's just not true. Everyone is needed. So support each other and build each other up. You're all a part of the same body!

Not Guilty!

So now there is no condemnation for those who belong to Christ Jesus. And because you belong to him, the power of the life-giving Spirit has freed you from the power of sin that leads to death. Romans 8:1, 2, NLT.

Cynthia had worked very hard on her report for English class. She read newspapers, books, and magazines for her sources. When she was finished, she proudly showed her dad.

The day after she turned her paper in, the teacher called her out of class. "I'm giving you a zero," he said. "It's obvious that you cheated on this paper."

"But I didn't!" Cynthia protested. "Ask my dad. He saw how hard I worked on it. I'm not guilty of cheating!"

But for some reason the teacher just would not believe her. It's been a few years now, but Cynthia still remembers that awful feeling of being accused when she was really innocent.

What if the opposite happened? What if you *were* guilty of something, and someone else took the punishment for you, making you the innocent one?

Here's a possible scenario. You don't do your chores after school because you'd rather play a video game. When your dad gets home, he tells you that you're grounded for the weekend. You begin to protest because your class is going snow skiing on Sunday and you've looked forward to this trip for weeks.

Just when your life seems doomed, your big brother steps in and says, "I'll take the grounding for him, Dad. I'll stay home all weekend."

You'd think that you had the best big brother in the world! You'd feel like you owe him your life!

Whether you realize it or not, this has actually happened to you. You are guilty of sinning. The punishment for sin is much bigger than being grounded for a weekend. It's eternal death. But Someone has your back! Jesus stepped in and said, "I'll die in her place so she can live forever" and "I'll die in his place so he can live forever."

First Peter 2:24 says, "He personally carried our sins in his body on the cross so that we can be dead to sin and live for what is right. By his wounds you are healed" (NLT).

Do you feel like you owe Him your life? That's because you do! So go and live for Him.

NOVEMBER 18

Beginning Again

Peter said, "Change your life.
Turn to God and be baptized, each of you,
in the name of Jesus Christ,
so your sins are forgiven." Acts 2:38, Message.

Today is the anniversary of my baptism. Now that it's been many years, how do I feel about that decision? *Best decision of my life!* I'll tell you why.

Baptism took away my guilt. Although at the age of 10 I hadn't done anything terribly wrong, I certainly hadn't been perfect. But when I confessed my sins to Jesus and was baptized, He forgave me and cleansed my life from sin.

Baptism gave me a chance to begin again. I had lived without Jesus for the first 10 years of my life. But I had the chance to start over—now as a daughter of God. Not in a physical sense, but very much in a spiritual sense.

Baptism gave me a purpose for living. Before I became a Christian I didn't have the purpose that I do now. Now my life is about helping others to know Jesus, sharing hope with people who are sad, and helping people see how valuable they are in God's eyes.

Baptism gave me a church family. I belonged somewhere. Sure, I had belonged to various clubs, but now I had a second family. A church full of various types of people of different ages who became like second parents, siblings, and adopted grandparents to me.

A few years ago a girl asked me, "Don't you feel like you missed out by being a Christian during your teen years?"

My answer with a smile was, "Are you kidding me? I wouldn't trade my teen years with God for anything! Those were great years! I had fun! And now that I'm an adult looking back on them, they aren't filled with a bunch of regrets and emptiness."

The baptism ceremony is kind of like a marriage ceremony. When I married my husband, I wanted to show Keith and the world that I loved him enough to commit the rest of my life to him. Baptism is telling God and the world that you love Him enough to commit the rest of your life to Him.

I hope that you will make this "best decision ever" for yourself. If you do, I believe that when you're an adult and look back on your baptism day anniversary, you'll be glad you made the decision too.

The Forgotten Thank-You

Thank the Lord! Praise his name! Tell the nations what he has done. Let them know how mighty he is! Isaiah 12:4, NLT.

You're invited to the birthday party of a good friend. You get all excited about shopping for their gift. Using your allowance, you go to the store and look up and down the aisles, searching for just the right gift. Then, score! You find it! So you take it home, wrap it, and tie a bow on top.

At the party your friend begins to open the pile of gifts on the table. When they come to yours they tear off the paper, barely look at it, set it on the pile of opened gifts, and then grab another gift to unwrap. No acknowledgment. No thank-you.

How do you feel? Lousy. Unappreciated. You don't even know if they like it or not. And maybe you even wish that you hadn't spent your money on a gift.

I feel sad for Jesus when I read how He healed 10 men of leprosy, but only one came back to thank Him. The story is found in Luke 17.

Jesus was on His way to Jerusalem when 10 lepers saw Him. They knew they weren't supposed to get near anyone with their contagious, deadly disease, so they cried from a distance, "Jesus, Master, have pity on us!" (verse 13, NIV). Jesus simply told them to go show themselves to the priests. The law stated that a priest had to declare them "clean" and give them permission to return to society. On the way there all 10 were healed!

One of them, when he saw his newly healed skin, was so excited that he ran back to Jesus. Jesus could hear him coming because the man was shouting praises to God! When he reached Jesus, he threw himself at His feet and thanked Him.

The part that always makes me feel sad for Jesus is when He asked this man, "Were not all ten cleansed? Where are the other nine?" (verse 17). It seems so ungrateful, doesn't it? These men were going to die! And Jesus healed them. But nine didn't even return to say thank you.

We ask Jesus for so much. Many of our prayers are for what we want or need. But how many times do we respond with "Thank You"? Thanksgiving is coming up next week. That would be a good time for Jesus to hear these words from you: "Thank You!"

NOVEMBER 20

Put the "Thanks" in Thanksgiving

Don't worry about anything; instead, pray about everything. Tell God what you need, and thank him for all he has done. Philippians 4:6, NLT.

"OK, it's time for prayer requests and praise," I said to the students at the beginning of a Friday Bible class. Some of the requests they made were these:

"I want it to snow so I can go skiing!"

"I want a puppy."

"I want to be stronger. I want muscles!"

"I want a skateboard."

"I want my birthday to hurry up and get here!"

"I want to go to Disneyland!"

Those were a lot of "I wants." But then a boy in the back row raised his hand and turned this prayer time completely around.

"I'm thankful for the sunshine," he said with a smile.

"Whoa!" I said to the class. "Did you hear what he just said? He's *thankful* for something! Shouldn't we spend equal time saying what we're thankful for? We're good at telling God what we want, but too often we forget to tell Him thanks for all that He's done for us."

The next day I tried an experiment. I decided to spend time deliberately looking for things to be thankful for. It's amazing how my eyes were opened to the simplest things to be thankful for when I just looked for them.

At the grocery store I saw a man with oxygen tubes in his nose—and I was thankful for healthy lungs that take me on long hikes. I noticed a woman trying to do her shopping while riding an electric scooter—and I was thankful for legs that work so I can walk. Moments later I heard a dad yelling at his child—and I was thankful for my loving parents. After school my daughter hopped in the car and said her favorite line: "Hi, Mom, where are we going?"—and I was thankful for our daughter and for ears to hear the voices of those I love.

With Thanksgiving just around the corner, why not try what I tried? Take a day to deliberately look for things to be thankful for. I bet you'll find both little and big things. Their size doesn't matter. They're all gifts. And once you do find them, *don't forget to thank the Giver*.

NOVEMBER 21

Put the "Giving" in Thanksgiving

And don't forget to do good and to share with those in need. These are the sacrifices that please God. Hebrews 13:16, NLT.

Mom! Do you want to see something really sick?" my daughter hollered as she came through the door. "Look at this," she said, handing me two brochures that had come in the mail.

One brochure was from a worldwide organization whose mission is feeding starving children around the world. It shared statistics of how many children die every day from a preventable problem: hunger. Below was the picture of a 5-year-old boy. Because he's starving, he suffers from a bloated stomach, pain, stunted growth, and brain damage. The brochure then asked for a small donation—the amount of about two fast-food meals—that would feed two families in that country for a month.

My activist daughter then handed me the other brochure, saying, "Now look at this!" It was from a mail-order company that sells fruit and candy baskets for the holidays. For the price of one box of fancy packaged fruit, *five* families in a distressed country could eat for a month!

I later thought about the boy who shared his meal with Jesus. It didn't seem like much—five loaves of bread and two fish. But Jesus used it to feed more than 5,000 hungry people!

Could Jesus use your family to multiply food this Thanksgiving? You could make a donation to ADRA (Adventist Development and Relief Agency), our church's humanitarian agency that serves more than 120 countries worldwide. Maybe your gift will help to feed a lot of people, or maybe it will feed just one—but that's one less hungry person. (You can go to www.adra.org and choose a project to support.) Locally, you could assist a food bank by organizing a canned food drive or by buying extra food and dropping it off. Your family could also serve a meal at the local mission. Or maybe your family's way of feeding the hungry at Thanksgiving is setting another place at your own table for someone who wouldn't get a dinner.

Thanksgiving is made up of two words—*thanks* and *giving*. In our family we try to experience both to make this holiday what we feel it's supposed to be. So we give thanks for what we have, but we also give. And whether it's giving money, time, or things, we always come away with that good holiday feeling. The feeling that our family can make a difference in the world—no matter how small a difference. Your family can, too.

NOVEMBER 22

Three Thousand Five Hundred Seventy-Three

Your promises have been thoroughly tested; that is why I love them so much. Psalm 119:140, NLT.

I don't feel like celebrating Thanksgiving," the woman told me. "I have no desire."

I could understand why she felt that way. She'd experienced a year full of loss. But I am an eternal optimist! I believe that no matter how bad life gets, there is *always* something to be thankful for.

If you're searching for reasons to be thankful this Thanksgiving, look no further than your own Bible. It contains 3,573 promises that give you a reason to be thankful—regardless of what you and your family might be facing this year. Here are a few of my favorites:

"If your heart is broken, you'll find God right there; if you're kicked in the gut, he'll help you catch your breath" (Psalm 34:18, Message).

"No need to panic over alarms or surprises, or predictions that doomsday's just around the corner, because God will be right there with you; he'll keep you safe and sound" (Proverbs 3:25, 26, Message).

"You can be sure that God will take care of everything you need, his generosity exceeding even yours in the glory that pours from Jesus" (Philippians 4:19, Message).

"But I, yes I, am the one who takes care of your sins—that's what I do. I don't keep a list of your sins" (Isaiah 43:25, Message).

"No test or temptation that comes your way is beyond the course of what others have had to face. All you need to remember is that God will never let you down; he'll never let you be pushed past your limit; he'll always be there to help you come through it" (1 Corinthians 10:13, Message).

"I've been carrying you on my back from the day you were born, and I'll keep on carrying you when you're old. I'll be there, bearing you when you're old and gray. I've done it and will keep on doing it, carrying you on my back, saving you" (Isaiah 46:4, Message).

Do you see what I mean? You *do* have reasons to be thankful. If you or your family has had a tough year, I'm sorry. But I believe that if you will look for the gifts that God has given you—such as His 3,573 promises—you'll find that there are things to be thankful for, after all.

NOVEMBER 23

Reverse Thanksgiving

Every good and perfect gift comes down from the Father who created all the lights in the heavens. He is always the same and never makes dark shadows by changing. James 1:17, CEV.

Think about a Christmas or a birthday when you got something that you really, really wanted. You probably hugged the giver and thanked them over and over. You may have even said, "I love it so much! I don't know how to thank you enough!"

Sometimes I feel that way about God's gifts. I just can't thank Him enough.

I'm thankful for this beautiful earth. I'm thankful that it's full of all different shapes and colors. What if everything in the world was shaped like a square? Can you imagine playing basketball or volleyball with a square ball? Or what if everything in the world was the color purple? Just imagine purple teeth, purple mashed potatoes, or a purple dog.

I'm also thankful for family and friends. They're not perfect (neither am I!), but the world would be a lonely place without them. Imagine being the only person who lived in your house or the only person who showed up at church each Sabbath.

I'm thankful that God always hears my prayers. Imagine if He used a giant phone system. If you needed to talk with Him while someone else was talking, you'd get a busy signal. Or if He chose to go for a walk around heaven, you'd get an answering machine asking you to leave a message. But the Bible says that *before you even speak*, He will answer (Isaiah 65:24).

I'm thankful that Jesus is always the same. He's never moody, and He doesn't have days when He's just too busy for me. I can count on Him. He's got my back, day and night.

I'm thankful that heaven is a real place—and that we get to go there someday!

These are just a few things that I thank God for. But what about God—the One who has given us all these things and more? Does He have something He's thankful for? Is there anything you can give Him in thanks for all He's given you?

Let's do a "reverse Thanksgiving" this year! Let's not do all the thanking ourselves, but let's give God something to be thankful for. What does God need? Nothing. He owns it all already! What does God want? You. *He wants you.* He wants you to give your life to Him so you can live forever with Him in heaven.

So why not give God something *He* can be thankful for this year? Give Him *you.*

NOVEMBER 24

The Unthankful Thanksgiving

Always be joyful. Never stop praying. Be thankful in all circumstances, for this is God's will for you who belong to Christ Jesus. 1 Thessalonians 5:16-18, NLT.

There was one Thanksgiving Day in my life when I didn't feel very thankful. Just three weeks earlier my brother Dan had been diagnosed with terminal cancer. At his request the whole family gathered at his house for the traditional meal. Although the table was full of bright autumn decorations and all the traditional homemade food, it was like playing a game of pretend. We knew it would be Dan's last Thanksgiving with us. Who even felt like eating? But we all tried to do our best to make it a warm family time for him.

Maybe you have similar feelings about this Thanksgiving. Maybe you don't think you have much to be thankful for, either. Maybe your parents have divorced, and this is your first Thanksgiving without your whole family together. Maybe a grandpa or grandma has died, and there's an empty seat at the table. Maybe one of your parents lost their job, and the meal looks like anything but a feast. Regardless, there are some things that you *can* be thankful for this Thanksgiving, if you take the time to look.

I asked some kids your age to list what they're thankful for this Thanksgiving—even though some of them are facing tough situations. Maybe you can relate to some of the things in their list. It's a long list, so are you ready? Here goes!

Family, friends, water, food, books, trees, houses, cats, music, school, clothes, gloves, blankets, leaves, dolphins, stars, ropes, turtles, ladybugs, jump ropes, pies, snow, fingers, laughter, elephants, dogs, Psalm 100, flowers, rain, sunshine, holidays, church, cookies, teachers, prayer, frogs, shoes, beds, gardens, hamsters, basketball, stuffed animals, clocks, instruments, coats, the moon, birds, pictures, volleyball, hair, kiwis, colors, and *KidsView* magazine!

So you see, there *are* things to be thankful for! What could you add to this list?

Today's text says to "give thanks in all circumstances" (NIV). Notice that it's not asking us to give thanks *for* all circumstances, but *in* all circumstances. In other words, when you're going through a tough time, and you're not thankful for what's happening, you can still find things to be thankful for—in spite of what's going on. Being thankful will help take your mind off your problems. It will give you a better outlook on life. Why not give it a try?

NOVEMBER 25

The Best Thanksgiving Ever!

Thank God for this gift, his gift. No language can praise it enough! 2 Corinthians 9:15, Message.

The Thanksgiving dinner when I was 9 years old was like any other Thanksgiving. Mom got up at the crack of dawn to make the whole meal from scratch. My siblings and I sat in front of the TV watching the Thanksgiving Day parade, while Dad did whatever Mom asked. The dinner was delicious, as usual, and we kids washed the dishes afterward.

But then came the next Thanksgiving, when I was 10. It was the best Thanksgiving ever! Why? Because just the week before, my family had all been baptized.

Back in April I told you that my family and I were not always Christians. I told you about a Bible that someone had accidentally left at our house. Looking for some meaning in life, my dad took that Bible down from the bookshelf and read into the night. He also read from that Bible to teach us kids and Mom about God.

On that special Thanksgiving, Dad read from that same Bible at the table, and then he laid it there among the food. It belonged there. It had given us a new life. Before we had prayer, Dad had each of us share something that we were thankful for—a tradition we still carry on today. Then we held hands and prayed. We had so much to be thankful for that year.

Dad still has that Bible, and this Thanksgiving he will once again place it on the table. And once again we will all be thankful that as a family we found God and gave our lives to Him. What a difference Jesus has made in our lives! Without Him, I wouldn't be writing this book for you. Who knows what I'd be doing or how my life would have turned out?

Long before the Pilgrims and Indians shared that first Thanksgiving meal, and long before President Lincoln proclaimed Thanksgiving Day a national holiday in 1863, this was King David's prayer of thanksgiving:

"Let all that I am praise the Lord; with my whole heart, I will praise his holy name. Let all that I am praise the Lord; may I never forget the good things he does for me. He forgives all my sins and heals all my diseases. He redeems me from death and crowns me with love and tender mercies. He fills my life with good things. My youth is renewed like the eagle's!" (Psalm 103:1-5, Message).

NOVEMBER 26

Thanksgiving Poems

Give thanks to the Lord, for he is good;
his love endures forever. Psalm 107:1, NIV.

Happy Thanksgiving! For this special day, sixth graders Jaymi and Rachel wanted to share their poems with you.

A Time to Give Thanks

I am so very thankful
For my family and my pets.
I am thankful that God keeps me healthy
And that He keeps me safe.
I am glad that God gives me the courage to live in Him
Without being embarrassed
Or made fun of.
I am thankful for all the things
My family does for me.
I am thankful for this Thanksgiving Day,
So I can be with all my "familia."

Thankfulness

I am thankful for my parents' love
and the love from God above.
I am thankful for freedom, for liberty
and the right to raise the colors free.
I am thankful for all the foods I eat, bitter or sour, salty or sweet.
I am thankful for the roof above my head
and my nice warm and cozy bed.
I am thankful for my school and the teachers in it that make it cool.
I am thankful for my friends that make life so wonderful.
I am thankful for the rain that makes the flowers grow.
I am thankful for the sun that lightens up the sky.
I am thankful for every little smile that brightens up my day.
My hope and my dream is that people of this earth
will be thankful for what they have.
They say if you wish upon a star your wish will come true—
what more could I wish for?
I am thankful for what I have.

NOVEMBER 27

Christmas All Year Long

Do not let yourselves get tired of doing good. If we do not give up, we will get what is coming to us at the right time. Galatians 6:9, NLV.

What's Thanksgiving dinner without pumpkin pie? That's what my brother Dave and his family thought. Since they'd spent Thanksgiving in the emergency room with one of their kids, they hadn't gotten much of a holiday dinner.

So the next day—the first official day of the Christmas season—Dave thought he'd surprise his family and buy a pumpkin pie. He checked several grocery stores in town, but all the pumpkin pies were sold out. So he drove to a local restaurant known for its homemade pies.

The place was busy with holiday shoppers, and people kept crowding in front of him as he waited his turn at the counter. So he asked a young man who was clearing tables, "Do you have pumpkin pie?"

"Let me go in back and check," he volunteered helpfully.

"Thanks," Dave said. "We didn't really get a Thanksgiving dinner."

Moments later the boy returned with a pumpkin pie. But before he could hand it to Dave, the manager of the restaurant yelled, "You're not supposed to bring that out! That's the last pumpkin pie we have!" The whole restaurant was now listening as the boy explained that Dave's family didn't get to have Thanksgiving dinner.

"Why didn't you?" the manager asked gruffly. After Dave finished telling his story, she left and then came back—holding not just the pie in a box, but also a full can of whipping cream!

"Have a wonderful Thanksgiving," she said warmly. Dave offered to pay, but she wouldn't have it. He offered a tip, but she said, "You don't tip gifts."

"She changed every person in that place," Dave said as he told me the story. He was right. They'd witnessed what it means to celebrate that Christmas feeling all year long.

It means sharing your lunch with a kid who forgot theirs. It means helping a classmate who's stuck on a math problem. It means staying after school to help your teacher. It means doing your part at home without complaining. It means sharing with your brother or sister.

This is what will give us that Christmas feeling we so much long for all year—because giving and sharing is the heart of Christmas.

NOVEMBER 28

James Fights the Game

But remember this—the wrong desires that come into your life aren't anything new and different. Many others have faced exactly the same problems before you. And no temptation is irresistible. You can trust God to keep the temptation from becoming so strong that you can't stand up against it, for he has promised this and will do what he says. He will show you how to escape temptation's power so that you can bear up patiently against it. 1 Corinthians 10:13, TLB.

James had spent all summer feeling that he and God were very close friends. But a few weeks after school began, he couldn't figure out what was going wrong. He felt at a distance from God. When he tried to read his Bible, things just weren't connecting.

James told me, "I kept asking God, *What's going on? What's wrong in my life? Is there something that I'm doing wrong?* In the back of my mind I knew what was wrong, but there was no way I wanted to admit it. I knew what God was asking me to do, but I talked myself into believing that it was *my* voice and not God's."

What had come between James and God? An Internet war game—and he was addicted to it. Getting to a higher and higher level in the game consumed his time. Desperate to get more points, he created an account under a family member's name—without her permission. He told me, "If I was playing the game and someone walked into my room, I quickly shut it off. Anytime you have to hide something from someone, you know it's not right."

James was tempted to compromise and just play the game less often. Then one day he finally admitted to himself: *This game is not who I am. In real life I wouldn't trade weapons and hurt people. I cannot come to God when I'm running from Him.* He fought the temptation, and God helped him overcome the desire to spend his free time playing a fantasy game.

How can you do what James did? How do you give up something that you're hooked on? These two verses tell you how: "So I say, let the Holy Spirit guide your lives. Then you won't be doing what your sinful nature craves" (Galatians 5:16, NLT). "Surrender to God! Resist the devil, and he will run from you" (James 4:7, CEV). You let the Holy Spirit guide your life by first giving your life to God and then listening to what the Holy Spirit tells you when you read your Bible and pray. You resist the devil by walking away. Just physically get up and walk away from the temptation. It's tough, and it takes guts, but God can help you overcome anything!

NOVEMBER 29

Snow Shoveling Samaritans

He has shown you, O mortal, what is good.
And what does the Lord require of you? To act justly and to love mercy
and to walk humbly with your God. Micah 6:8, NIV.

The winter that our daughter, Christina, was in the eighth grade was "the year of the snow" in our valley. It snowed on top of snow. We hadn't seen anything like it in years!

One morning, when we woke up to eight inches of new snow, we had an idea. We bundled up, threw shovels and brooms in our trunk, picked up one of Christina's friends, and ventured out into the snow.

We thought it would be a great idea to drive around town to see if anyone needed help. I, for one, had slid off the road three times that month, and someone had always stopped to help me. Now it was our turn to give back.

When we saw a car stuck, we helped dig it out. We took our brooms and swept off windshields downtown that were covered in snow. We even gave an elderly woman a ride home because she was too afraid to drive. When we finished we were tired, cold, and wet. But it was worth it. Every minute of it.

In Luke 10 a man asked Jesus what he had to do to receive eternal life. Jesus answered, " 'Love the Lord your God with all your heart and with all your soul and with all your strength and with all your mind'; and, 'Love your neighbor as yourself' " (verse 27, NIV). The man asked Jesus who was considered his neighbor, and He told him the story of the good Samaritan.

A man was traveling and was attacked by robbers. They beat him till he was half dead and then took everything—even his clothes. As he was lying there, naked and dying, both a priest and a Levite came along, but they didn't stop to help. In fact, they crossed to the other side of the road. But when a Samaritan man saw him, he felt sorry for him. He bandaged him up, put him on his own donkey, and took him to an inn. He even paid the innkeeper to take care of him!

After the story, Jesus asked the man who he thought acted like a true neighbor.

"The man replied, 'The one who showed him mercy.' Then Jesus said, 'Yes, now go and do the same' " (verse 37, NLT).

And we should go and do the same, too.

NOVEMBER 30

Hold On for Dear Life

Live in me. Make your home in me just as I do in you. In the same way that a branch can't bear grapes by itself but only by being joined to the vine, you can't bear fruit unless you are joined with me. John 15:4, Message.

When Daniel was a young boy, he loved going to visit his grandma. Especially when there was snow on the ground. At the top of her property was a hill, and then the long driveway below that went on and on. It was the best sledding hill around!

One night Daniel was there sledding with his dad on a runner sled. That sled could fly down the hill at lightning speed. Daniel had never sledded at night before, and things look a lot different in the dark. Hopping on his dad's back, they pushed off, and the sled flew down the hill. All too soon they were so far from Grandma's house that Daniel couldn't even see her lights. In front of him all he could see was darkness. It felt like they were traveling into nothingness, and he was terrified!

In his fear Daniel bailed off, and his dad and their sled disappeared into the darkness. Now he was completely alone. He couldn't see anything, but he could hear owls hooting and coyotes howling in the distance. Too afraid to go anywhere, he just sat in the snow and started crying. There was nothing to do but wait for his dad to stop and walk back up the driveway.

Now that Daniel is grown up, he told me, "I learned something from that night. When things get bad, when life gets rough, that is no time to leave the Father—my heavenly Father."

Daniel's story reminds me of a time when the disciple Peter did something similar. The disciples were out in a boat at night during a storm, and Jesus could see from land that they were having trouble. So He walked out on the water to help them.

When Peter saw Jesus, he asked if he could walk to Him on the water. Jesus said yes, so Peter got out of the boat and actually walked on water—for a little way. But he became afraid when he took his eyes off Jesus and saw the waves crashing all around him. Immediately he started to sink, and Jesus reached out His hand to save him.

When you're going through a tough time, that's not the time to leave Jesus. He's the one who knows what He's doing! Hold on to Him. Keep your eyes on Him. He's got your back.

DECEMBER 1

'Tis the Season

This is how much God loved the world: He gave his Son,
his one and only Son. And this is why: so that no one need be destroyed;
by believing in him, anyone can have a whole and lasting life.
God didn't go to all the trouble of sending his Son merely
to point an accusing finger, telling the world how bad it was.
He came to help, to put the world right again. John 3:16, 17, Message.

It's December 1, and you know what that means—twenty-five days till Christmas! Regardless of how your family celebrates Christmas—or if you celebrate it at all—this is the time of year when many Christians pause to remember what Jesus' birth means to us. So for the next several weeks I'll be writing the 25 Days of Christmas, with a Christ-centered Christmas theme each day. I hope these devotionals will help you remember what this season is all about.

I like the way the Message Bible translates John 3:16 in today's verse, but there's nothing like the King James Version that says, "For God so loved the world, that he gave . . ." *He gave.* He gave His one and only Son, Jesus, to you. Jesus' birth was the beginning of that gift—a gift that will someday save your life.

Think of how awesome it is that God had the power to provide this gift! Through a miracle, Jesus was placed inside Mary's womb, where He grew for nine months like any other baby. There was nothing spectacular about the way He was born. It happened in a stable. And if it weren't for the chorus of angels singing to the shepherds, it would have been a silent night. But what started out as a humble beginning would change the course of earth's history!

Thousands of years before His birth, Jesus had created a perfect world for you to live in. In that world He created Adam and Eve with the power to choose. They could choose to obey Him or to listen to the serpent. In one tragic move they chose to disobey God. Sin entered this planet, and with sin came death.

Fortunately for us, Jesus didn't just walk away when Adam and Eve blew it. He loved us too much to do that. Instead, *the Creator chose to become our Savior*! It blows me away as I write this to think that Jesus would choose to leave heaven—where everything was perfect—and be born here on earth in order to die for you and for me.

"For God so loved the world, that he gave . . ." He gave Jesus. To you. You'll never receive a more unselfish, loving gift. The Gift that can give you life. Eternal life.

DECEMBER 2

Passing On the Gift

Religion that God our Father accepts as pure and faultless is this: to look after orphans and widows in their distress and to keep oneself from being polluted by the world. James 1:27, NIV.

I have a lot of great Christmas memories from when our daughter, Christina, was little. But my favorite is from the year when she was only 3 and reminded her busy mom of the true meaning of Christmas.

It was December 23, and I was cleaning in a back room of our house when I realized that for a 3-year-old, Christina was being much too quiet. So I walked into the kitchen and discovered why. She was standing in the pantry closet, and all around her were bags of food.

"Christina, what are you doing?" I asked. Here I was trying to clean house, and she was making a big mess.

"I want to give hungry people food for Christmas!" she declared.

Her excitement and giving spirit touched my heart. It would have been so easy to let that moment pass and say, "Sweetie, I don't have time for this right now" or "I need these things for our own meals." But I knew I couldn't. Now both our hands were in the pantry as I let her choose what to give, making a mental checklist of the items I'd need to replace.

Before bedtime on Christmas Eve my husband drove us through neighborhoods while Christina chose which houses would get the bags of food.

"That house!" she said, pointing to one that looked old and run-down.

"That house! They have kids!" she said about another with toys in the yard.

So we wouldn't get caught, I ran the bags to the porches while Christina watched from the car, giggling as I dashed from car to porch and back.

On the way home we imagined how excited the people would be on Christmas morning when they found food on their doorstep. We went to bed with that warm holiday feeling inside.

A 3-year-old reminded me of what really matters at Christmas. It's not just about decorating, baking, shopping, wrapping, eating, and going to programs. It's about sharing. It's about giving. It's about passing on the gift that Jesus gave to us, so we can give to others.

What can you and your family give to others this Christmas season? Brainstorm together, and pass on the gift!

DECEMBER 3

God With Us

"Behold, the virgin shall be with child, and bear a Son, and they shall call His name Immanuel," which is translated, "God with us." Matthew 1:23, NKJV.

Do you know what your name means? You can probably find out by looking in a book of baby names or by searching online. I've discovered that my name, Nancy, means "grace."

Hundreds of years before Jesus was born, Isaiah prophesied that a miracle would take place. That's what today's verse refers to. The promise was passed on for generations, and people waited, watched, and hoped for the One who would be called "Immanuel."

To some people today, the name Immanuel doesn't have much significance. But to the Hebrew-speaking people in Isaiah's time, it meant everything! They were thrilled when they heard the prophecy! They knew that the name Immanuel means *God with us.*

This is what the universe had been waiting for ever since sin first entered our world. On that day we humans lost daily face-to-face communication with God. The more time passed, the greater our separation became. Almost immediately selfishness, jealousy, hatred, anger, lying, stealing, and the worship of false gods became common—separating us from God.

If we choose not to have God with us, sooner or later we humans feel an emptiness. So we search for other things to fill that space, such as choosing the wrong friends, partying, and making poor choices about what we watch and listen to. But this Christmas you don't have to feel empty. God has given you a Gift. His name is "Immanuel," and He is with *you.*

When we realize that Jesus is Immanuel—God with us—we can no longer say, "No one understands how I feel," because He does. *He really does.* He's been here and experienced life the way we have. Isaiah 53:3 says that "he was despised and rejected by mankind, a man of suffering, and familiar with pain" (NIV).

When Jesus was on earth He experienced being tempted, judged, bullied, laughed at, and gossiped about. People hurt him physically and emotionally. His grief was so great that He wept at the grave of His friend Lazarus. He was lonely in the Garden of Gethsemane when the disciples fell asleep. He understands what life is like for you. He gets it in a way no one else can.

So this Christmas, celebrate the fact that you've been given the greatest gift of all: Immanuel, God with us. Immanuel, God with *you.*

DECEMBER 4

Not Feeling So Jolly?

So we're not giving up. How could we!
Even though on the outside it often looks like things are falling apart on us, on the inside, where God is making new life, not a day goes by without his unfolding grace. 2 Corinthians 4:16, Message.

My family and I wondered how we would make it through Christmas. There would be an empty seat at the table, a face missing from the family photo, and one less present under the tree.

Eight months earlier my brother Dan had died after a brave battle with cancer. Our hearts were still aching. Who felt like celebrating? Christmas had always been such a big event for my family. And my siblings and I still returned home every year, eventually with our own kids.

But we did survive that first Christmas without Dan. How? By remembering. By looking back—with both tears and laughter—at the memories of happy times. But more important, we did it by looking *forward*—by believing in the hope that one day we will see him again!

Sitting around the Christmas tree at my parents' house that night, we realized that all our hopes of being a complete family again depend on a Baby born more than 2,000 years ago. Here's how the Bible describes the One who brought hope to our world: "For to us a child is born, to us a son is given, and the government will be on his shoulders. And he will be called Wonderful Counselor, Mighty God, Everlasting Father, Prince of Peace" (Isaiah 9:6, NIV).

Maybe you don't feel all that jolly this Christmas season. Maybe it's been a tough year for your family financially. Maybe you feel that you don't have any friends at school. Maybe your parents argue a lot. Maybe a family member who has always been there has died.

Regardless of the reason, Christmas is not about what *isn't*. Rather, it's about what *is*! Jesus' birth rescued the world! And now you can look forward to that day when He will return, take you to heaven, and fix everything. *Forever.*

Every Christmas Eve when Dan and I were little, our family traveled an hour to Grandma's house for the evening. Driving home late at night, we kids would always look up at the sky, hoping to see Santa Claus. Once I thought I saw Rudolph's shiny red nose! However, it turned out to be the light on an airplane wing. But then we became Christians. Now I look up at the sky in anticipation for a whole different reason. I look up and imagine what it will be like to see Jesus come the second time. And *that's* a thought that makes me not just jolly, but joyful!

Open Every Gift!

And this is the promise that
He has promised us—eternal life. 1 John 2:25, NKJV.

Through all the Christmases in my life, I never left a gift unopened under the tree. How crazy would that be? When I was a kid we'd wake up at dawn on Christmas morning to unwrap gifts. Even as a grownup I still get excited about unwrapping gifts! I can't imagine leaving one unopened under our tree and keeping it on the living room floor long after the tree is gone. People might stumble over it, step on it, or just kick it out of the way. Besides, how would I know what's inside? What if it were something really special? Something I needed?

Some people do this very thing with God's gift of eternal life. They don't open it and accept it. They know it's there, but for different reasons they leave it unopened.

God's gift of eternal life is waiting for you today—but it won't sit there unopened forever. When Jesus returns someday, He will be coming for those who have accepted the gift.

Jesus came as a baby the first time to give His life. And He'll come the second time to give *us* life! Unlike the first time when just a few witnessed His coming in the manger, the second time everyone will see Him and hear Him! Revelation 1:7 says, "See! He is coming in the clouds. Every eye will see Him" (NLV). And 1 Thessalonians 4:16 says, "For the Lord Himself will descend from heaven with a shout, with the voice of an archangel, and with the trumpet of God. And the dead in Christ will rise first" (NKJV).

Isn't that incredible? The One who came as a helpless baby will come again with enough power to raise the dead! It won't matter how they died or how long they've been dead—they will be resurrected. Verse 17 goes on to say what will happen to those still living at His coming: "After that, we who are still alive and are left will be caught up together with them in the clouds to meet the Lord in the air. And so we will be with the Lord forever" (NIV).

When you think about it, it doesn't really matter whether we're dead or alive when Jesus comes. The end result will be the same: we will be with the Lord *forever*! His gift to you this Christmas is a gift that keeps on giving.

This Christmas, don't leave the greatest gift you'll ever receive unopened. Salvation is a gift, and you receive it by giving back—by giving your life to Jesus. What better gift could you give Him on the day that we celebrate His birth?

DECEMBER 6

Cold Feet, Warm Hearts

I pray that God will take care of all your needs with the wonderful blessings that come from Christ Jesus! Philippians 4:19, CEV.

It was Christmas Eve, and Sylvia wasn't going to miss out on caroling. A foot of snow lay on the ground, and her family couldn't afford boots for her. But she went in her tennis shoes!

After about two hours of going door-to-door, Sylvia was freezing! Then they came to a little house with no decorations in the yard and not even a car in the driveway. But there was a single string of lights lying flat in the front window.

"This will be our last house," Silvia's dad declared.

They sang "Hark, the Herald Angels Sing" first because it's loud and cheerful and would bring people to the door. But no one came. Then they sang "Joy to the World." Still no one.

They were starting to walk away when they heard from inside the house, "Wait! Don't leave!" So Sylvia and her family stopped and sang "Silent Night." A very unkempt elderly woman opened the door, smiling from ear to ear. After they finished singing, she invited them in to warm up. That's when they noticed that the home didn't even have any living room furniture.

The elderly woman explained that she and her husband had been in the attic making Christmas taffy, so it had taken her awhile to get to the door. "It's been a very hard year for us," she told Sylvia's family, "but we still wanted to celebrate. So my husband and I brought out this one string of lights for Christmas Eve and made one batch of taffy."

While Sylvia's dad and brother went up to the attic to see how taffy was made, her mom chatted with the woman. The woman said she'd always wanted a Bible, so Mom promised to try to get her one. Sylvia's family enjoyed some delicious taffy and then headed home, happy.

A few days later Sylvia's mom returned with some generous friends who had donated a chair, a couch, a lamp, blankets, and a Bible. The couple was thrilled!

As they were leaving, the elderly woman said to one of the visitors, "I sure hope you can do the same for the little girl with frozen feet in her little tennis shoes!"

A few days later Sylvia received her own gift: a pair of boots *and* a pair of shoes! She told me, "That year was the poorest we had ever been, but God provided. It's a Christmas I will always remember."

A New Reason to Celebrate

So it was, that while they were there, the days were completed for her to be delivered. And she brought forth her firstborn Son, and wrapped Him in swaddling cloths, and laid Him in a manger, because there was no room for them in the inn. Luke 2:6, 7, NKJV.

For years I didn't celebrate Jesus' birth, even though He had saved my life. For the first nine years of my life, Jesus wasn't a part of our family Christmas celebrations. Instead, the focus was on Santa, Rudolph, and Frosty. Little did we know that we were missing a chance to celebrate the greatest birth this world has ever known!

But then Jesus came into our hearts and into our home. They say a baby changes everything—and He did! The ornament on top of our Christmas tree was replaced with an angel. The family stereo played less of "Santa Claus is coming to town" and more of "Joy to the world, the Lord is come!" We prayed before Christmas dinner. And before we opened the gifts under the tree, Dad read the story of Jesus' birth in Luke 2.

Our hearts were touched when Dad first read the Christmas story from his Bible. We were in awe of such a miracle—such love! And we felt a sense of sadness that so many years had gone by when we hadn't put Christ in Christmas.

Many years have passed since my first Christmas as a new Christian. Celebrating Jesus' birth means more to me every year! I celebrate His *first* coming, and I also celebrate as I look forward to His *second* coming.

How can I be sure that Jesus will come a second time? Here's how: Some 700 years before His birth, the prophet Isaiah predicted that Jesus would come the first time—*and He did come.* If He kept His promise the first time, I know that He'll keep His promise the second time. Why would He be born to live and die for us if He wasn't planning to return for us?

After the disciples watched Jesus go up to heaven, two angels said to them: "Men of Galilee, . . . why do you stand here looking into the sky? This same Jesus, who has been taken from you into heaven, will come back in the same way you have seen him go into heaven" (Acts 1:11, NIV). This is just one of the many promises that Jesus will come again.

The birth of Jesus saved my life. It made me a better person. It gave me hope. Looking back on that first Christmas, I see that it changed my life forever. And it can change yours, too.

DECEMBER 8

Christmas Tree Makeover

Create a pure heart in me, O God,
and put a new and loyal spirit in me. Psalm 51:10, TEV.

Karen was miserable. She was supposed to be singing in the Christmas program. Instead, she lay at home on the couch trying to resist the urge to scratch. Her mom lathered goopy pink lotion on her sores to help stop the itching. Can you guess what she had? *Chickenpox!* She was sick with the chickenpox at Christmas. To make matters worse, her brother had it too.

Karen's dad decided to cheer them up by getting a Christmas tree. He came back from town with what seemed to be a huge tree for their little living room. Once it was secured in the stand, he stood back to see how it looked. It looked uneven on one side, so he quickly snipped off a branch and stood back to take another look. Now it seemed lopsided, so he snipped off a branch on the other side.

Karen lay on the couch watching her dad snip branch after branch, trying to shape the perfect tree. In the end there was a huge pile of evergreen branches on the living room floor—and one very small tree!

When Karen's mom walked into the room, the look on her face was priceless. Karen and her brother couldn't help but burst out laughing. It was the funniest thing to watch as their mother made herself very clear: Dad was to clean up the mess and go get another tree.

Sometimes we do with ourselves what Karen's dad did to their tree. We think we'd look better if we made a few changes here and there.

A girl might look in a mirror and think, *I'm not very pretty.* Then comes the snipping: "If I could get highlights, maybe my hair wouldn't look so dull." "If my parents would let me wear eye makeup, maybe I'd look older." "If I could lose 20 pounds, maybe boys would notice me."

A boy might look in a mirror and think, *I don't look very cool.* Then comes the snipping: "If I could grow my hair long, I'd look awesome." "If I could wear designer athletic shoes, I'd fit in." "If I could drink protein shakes, I'd be muscular."

I think that letting God "snip" here and there in our hearts is what will make us feel better about ourselves. Today's text is a prayer by King David, asking God to make his heart pure. Every time I've prayed that prayer, God has shown me something that I need to snip out of my own life. Why not give it a try? Then go look in the mirror. I think you'll like who you see.

A Season to Surrender

Then the angel said to her, "Do not be afraid, Mary, for you have found favor with God. And behold, you will conceive in your womb and bring forth a Son, and shall call His name Jesus." . . . Then Mary said, "Behold the maidservant of the Lord! Let it be to me according to your word." And the angel departed from her. Luke 1:30-38, NKJV.

Mary wasn't much older than many of you when God chose her to be Jesus' mom. Before that day, she probably had her own hopes and dreams for her life, just as any young girl would. Maybe when you daydream about your future you think about a career you'd like, the places you want to travel to, or the state or country you want to live in.

Mary's plan was to marry Joseph, be a carpenter's wife, and raise a family. But God's plans were different. An angel appeared and basically said, "God's plans are not your plans. You've been chosen to be the mother of the Messiah!"

She could have complained or even refused. She could have said, "But Lord, what will Joseph say? But Lord, my parents won't understand. But Lord, people will talk. But Lord, I planned my life another way. But Lord . . ."

Instead she said, "I am the Lord's servant! Let it happen as you have said" (Luke 1:38, CEV). How could she so willingly surrender? How could she, in a moment's time, give up her plans for God's plans? I think the answer is that she trusted. Her faith in God was strong enough to believe that His plan was better than hers, so she willing surrendered her own.

Before we can surrender our plans to God, we need to start with the basics and surrender our whole lives to Him. Have you done that? If not, you can do it through a simple prayer like this: "Here I am, Lord. I want to give my entire life to You—not just part of it."

I've known people who want to give only part of their lives to God, because they still want to be in control of certain areas. But they can't get the full benefits of being a Christian that way. They miss out on trusting a God who knows their lives from beginning to end.

It was easy for me to surrender my life to Jesus when I was 10. But it hasn't always been as easy to surrender certain plans or people to Him. Sometimes I want to hold on too tight! But when I finally do surrender, I never regret it. I realize that He always knows best.

You can trust that He knows what's best for your life, too. He's got your back.

DECEMBER 10

The Beggar's New Home

So if the Son sets you free, you are truly free. John 8:36, NLT.

The little boy was orphaned at age 7. His parents had been killed in the war for independence in Bangladesh, and he had been on his own for two years. He did the one thing he knew to do to survive—he became a beggar at the railway station nearby.

Hundreds of travelers came and went through that station every day, passing the boy lying there on his bamboo mat and begging for coins. On good days he would get enough money to buy some food. On bad days he went hungry. His mat was not just a place where he lay to beg. It was his bed at night, too. So he lived a very depressing and lonely life.

Of all the beggars at the station he was the most pitiful, because he had a growth on his left thigh that was as big as a cantaloupe! It held him captive. He couldn't run or play.

Then one day an American missionary doctor walked by and noticed him. The boy looked utterly miserable lying there in the hot sun.

The doctor stopped and asked him, "What is your name? Where are your parents? Where is your home?" But the boy just stared at the ground. So the doctor asked the shop owners nearby, and they told him that the boy didn't have any family—that the station was his home.

Feeling great pity for the boy, the doctor scooped him up in his arms and basically kidnapped him! The little guy was terrified, of course, not knowing what was going to happen.

The doctor took him straight to a hospital. There they removed the growth from his leg. Soon he would be able to run and play again! But that was only the beginning. The kind doctor took him to his own home for several weeks, got him some badly needed glasses, and enrolled him in the local Adventist boarding school. Suddenly the boy had a good home and a huge new family! At the school he learned about Jesus and became a Christian. What a story!

This is what the birth of Jesus did for our whole world. He saw that we were prisoners to sin. And in one great swoop of love He came to this earth to live and die and set us free.

When Isaiah predicted Jesus' birth, he said that Jesus would come "to bring good news to the poor, to heal the broken-hearted, to announce release to captives and freedom to those in prison" (Isaiah 61:1, TEV). What a story! And what a gift! The most amazing gift in the history of the universe.

One Snowy Night

And suddenly there was with the angel a multitude of the heavenly host praising God and saying: "Glory to God in the highest, and on earth peace, goodwill toward men!" Luke 2:13, 14, NKJV.

I almost missed the moment. If I had left the department store a minute sooner or a minute later I would have missed it.

It was the night before Christmas Eve and I was doing some last-minute shopping. I usually love the hustle and bustle of a store filled with holiday shoppers, but this year it felt like a chore. My knee had been injured, and the pain was taking away the fun of shopping. I had to walk up and down the store's stairs taking baby steps. I felt self-conscious and discouraged. I was tired of hurting. And yes, I was feeling a bit sorry for myself.

As I walked out onto the snow-covered sidewalk, I looked across the street and saw a young man struggling to steer his wheelchair through the snow. If that weren't enough to get me thinking, limping toward me on the sidewalk came a man with an artificial leg. And here I had been complaining about knee pain! The man with the artificial leg would have traded me places in a heartbeat. And I'm sure the young man in the wheelchair would have gladly traded places with the man with the artificial leg—just to be able to walk again.

Maybe, like me, you've been feeling sorry for yourself this Christmas. Maybe your best friend got to play Mary in the school Christmas program, and you got stuck as a shepherd. Maybe your grandparents can't come this year, and you've always celebrated with them. Maybe you broke your ankle and can't go sledding or ice skating with your friends. Maybe you have to split Christmas between your dad's and mom's places.

Whatever the case, I hope you can do what I did that snowy night. Look around you. Do you see other kids whose situations are worse than yours? Would your Christmas look pretty good to them? Take a look at your own life through their eyes and find things that you can be grateful for. Then do something nice for those kids. Buy them a simple gift, make them a card, or bake them some cookies. You'll feel so much better doing something kind for them!

Regardless of your situation or mine, this holiday is really about celebrating Jesus. When we focus on that, we're not focusing on what we wish was different. And that makes all the difference.

DECEMBER 12

Spread the News!

An angel of the Lord appeared to them, and the glory of the Lord shone around them, and they were terrified. But the angel said to them, "Do not be afraid. I bring you good news that will cause great joy for all the people. Today in the town of David a Savior has been born to you; he is the Messiah, the Lord. This will be a sign to you: You will find a baby wrapped in cloths and lying in a manger." Luke 2:9-12, NIV.

You just got a new puppy. You aced the science test. You found $10 in your coat pocket. You got a new snowboard. You're going to Disneyland next summer. Your relatives are coming for Christmas. What do you do when you have good news to share? You tell everyone! You call your best friend. You put it as your Facebook status. You tell your class the next day. You just can't keep the good news to yourself!

That's how the angels must have felt when they had good news to share. Jesus had been born! Heaven couldn't possibly keep quiet. There was a birth announcement to be made! And notice who the angels chose to hear it. Not a king. Not a rich person. Not the town social queen. They chose shepherds. Humble shepherds. And they announced that they had "good news" that would bring great joy to everyone.

What exactly was that good news? To put it bluntly, we deserved to die, but Someone had been born who would one day die in our place! Romans 6:23 says, "For the wages of sin is death, but the free gift of God is eternal life through Christ Jesus our Lord" (NLT). I like those words "free gift." Eternal life is free. Eternal life is a gift—to anyone who chooses it!

Since you and I know this good news, too, what should we do about it? I think we should be like the angels and announce it. The world could use some good news now more than ever.

How do we share it? Most important, through the way we live. Here are just a few ideas for you and your family and friends: bake and share Christmas cookies; go caroling; adopt a grandparent; invite neighbors to your church's Christmas program; send out Christ-centered Christmas cards; collect canned foods for your town's food bank.

I always wanted to be in a Christmas pageant, but never got the chance. If I had, and if I could have chosen my role, I'd have wanted to be the angel who proclaimed the good news. But you and I don't need to merely play that role. We can share the good news in real life!

DECEMBER 13

Why Believe in God?

I am the Living One. I was dead, but look, I am alive forever. Revelation 1:18, NLV.

I'm always happy to see religious slogans in store windows and on church signs this time of year. Some of the more popular ones are "Jesus is the reason for the season" and "Keep Christ in Christmas." They remind us what this holiday is all about—celebrating Jesus' birth. And I think they can be a good witness to people who don't usually think about God.

A few years ago I read about some anti-Christmas slogans that made me very sad. They were talking about Someone I love very much, and what they said wasn't true. An organization had spent thousands of dollars to put signs on city buses that read, "Why believe in god? Just be good for goodness' sake."

Something inside of me wanted to walk the streets of that city and tell everyone who read the signs, "Why believe in God? I can tell you why I do. Believing in God gives me a fresh start every day. I know that when I mess up, He will forgive me because He died so I wouldn't have to. Believing in God helps me face the day-to-day struggles of this life, because I have a constant Friend whom I can talk to about anything. Believing in God gives me hope for a better future."

That same organization put anti-Christmas slogans on buses in another country, too. These read, "There's probably no God. Now stop worrying and enjoy your life."

Something inside of me wanted to walk the streets of that country and tell everyone who read the signs, "It's not true! There *is* a God, and that's *why* I enjoy my life! I know there's a God because I can't deny the change He made in my dad's life when I was 10 years old. I watched Dad break old habits and turn into a better man. I know there's a God because I can't deny the peace I felt in the middle of my grief when my brother died of cancer—peace that he was resting until God raises him from the dead one day. And I can't deny the joy I feel when I read something in the Bible that tells me just what I need to hear that very day."

It's hard to understand why some people, created by God, don't even believe that He exists. And some people, for whom Jesus died, act as if the event never even happened.

If you're ever tempted to doubt whether or not God is real, make a list of all the evidence around you. Let your slogan be: "I know God is real because . . ." and fill it in for yourself. The Son of God really was born in that manger in Bethlehem. And He *is* the reason for the season!

DECEMBER 14

Christmas Miracle

But thanks be to God! He gives us the victory through our Lord Jesus Christ. 1 Corinthians 15:57, NIV.

Some say that Christmas is a season of miracles. Here's one Christmas miracle story about a man whose heart was as cold and hard as stone—until he heard the story of Jesus' birth.

Sean had been a slave to hatred since he was a young boy, and Christmas was his *least* favorite holiday. His dad had been an angry, abusive alcoholic, and he had ruined every single Christmas of Sean's life. There was not even one happy memory of a childhood Christmas. Each year something would happen that would set his dad off, and the abuse would begin. Even years later, after his dad had died, Sean held on to his anger and would not forgive his father.

Then one December evening Sean showed up at my dad's church. They were having a special Christmas Communion service, and Dad told the sweeping story of Jesus' love for us from the cradle to the cross. That night Sean heard the Christmas story as he'd never heard it before. The love and sacrifice of Jesus touched his bitter heart.

After the service he approached Dad and said, "If Jesus did all that for me, just so He could live and die for my sins, then I can forgive my father for all the terrible things he did to me and to our family through the years." Though all of Sean's former Christmases had been ruined by abuse, that Christmas he gained the victory over hatred.

What better time of year than this to heal a relationship? Jesus was born to live and die in order to freely offer us forgiveness. How can we offer less to anyone else?

It's important to Jesus that we forgive each other. Paul said in Ephesians 4:32, "You must be kind to each other. Think of the other person. Forgive other people just as God forgave you because of Christ's death on the cross" (NLV). Some injustices done by others can do a lot of damage—we might need the help of a counselor or a pastor so we can forgive and move on. But most are grudges we carry from little things: having a fight with a friend, getting in a battle of the wills with our parents, or trading harsh words with a sibling.

This Christmas you can have your own miracle of forgiveness. It's a gift that you give not only the other person, but also yourself. And you make Jesus proud, because when you forgive, you are imitating Him.

My Best Gift Ever

Thank God for his gift that is too wonderful for words! 2 Corinthians 9:15, CEV.

My husband and I were talking about Christmas the other day when he asked me, "What's the best Christmas gift you ever received?"

"It has to be the gift I received my sophomore year of college," I said.

It was Christmas morning, and my family was sitting around the tree opening gifts. My parents always got us each one main gift and maybe two smaller gifts. But I suddenly realized that all the gifts had been opened, and I had come up short! I kept looking around, trying to see if my main gift had accidentally been pushed aside. Dad and Mom always tried to be very fair in their giving to us kids, but for some reason this year was different. And although I was 20, I'll have to admit that I felt a little sad!

I didn't want to make my parents feel bad, so I didn't say anything. *Maybe they somehow forgot my main gift,* I reasoned to myself. *I'm sure it was an oversight.*

We all helped clear the floor of wrapping paper and ribbon, and Dad asked me to take the big garbage bag out to the garage. When I opened the door to the garage and turned on the light, there it was! My gift! A shiny blue used car to take back to college—complete with a bow on top! My whole family had been in on the surprise. Little did I know that my gift had been there all along, waiting for me on the other side of the door. I just had to open the door!

Now that I think about it, that car wasn't my best Christmas gift after all. My greatest gift was given to me 2,000 years before I was even born!

Jesus is the gift "on the other side of the door," so to speak. But He doesn't force His way in. He knocks. And He waits for you to open and invite Him in. He said in Revelation 3:20, "Look! I stand at the door and knock. If you hear my voice and open the door, I will come in, and we will share a meal together as friends" (NLT).

What better time than now—during the season when we celebrate Jesus' birth—to give your life to Him for the first time, or to renew your commitment to Him. Take some time to read about His birth in Luke 2:1-20. Then maybe suggest that your family read it together. It will remind you of the Gift that's on the other side of the door. He's knocking, and He's waiting with anticipation, hoping like everything that you will open and find out what you've been missing.

DECEMBER 16

An Unforgettable Christmas

This is my last gift to you, this example of a way of life:
a life of hard work, a life of helping the weak,
a life that echoes every day those words of Jesus
our King, who said, "It is more blessed
to give than to receive." Acts 20:35, Voice.

Want to have a Christmas you'll never forget? *Do something kind for someone else.* Kevin will tell you that. He's a grown-up now with a child of his own, but he told me that he'll never forget a particular Christmas when he was not much older than you readers.

"One thing I remember as clearly as yesterday," he told me. "It's the overwhelming gratitude of the people we helped. They were a Russian family, new to our town. Some of us kids got together and fund-raised so that we could give them a nice first Christmas in America.

"When we paid them a surprise visit, we couldn't believe how small and bare their house was, but we all packed in there. We couldn't speak each other's language, but I still remember their smiles. And they did manage to say thank you over and over.

"The dad was a big bear of a man, and he enveloped me in a huge hug. That's not difficult to do, considering I wasn't—and still am not—a big person. But I remember that hug as one of the warmest, most genuine hugs I've ever received.

"Christmas is normally for kids, and the kids were fascinated by the gifts we'd brought them. But now I think the parents must have been even more grateful because their kids got to have a special Christmas, and they felt loved and welcomed. The parents had probably been wondering how their kids would take to this strange but exciting country, and it must have been wonderful to have strangers welcome them and give them a special evening.

"I remember leaving their house feeling warmth and the love from the people, and also feeling like we had done something really meaningful. I knew what it was like to be a stranger—I'd moved with my family to that town not long before, so I knew the uncertainty and, quite frankly, the fear of being in a new place. The kids I'd done the fund-raising with had given me a warm welcome. And now I was able to give these people (who would have felt even more like strangers, having moved to a country halfway around the world) that same feeling of welcome and warmth that I had felt just a few months before.

To this day, I still have a special place in my heart for strangers and foreigners.

DECEMBER 17

The Spirit of Christmas

When you give to the poor, it is like lending to the Lord, and the Lord will pay you back. Proverbs 19:17, TEV.

Here are two stories about giving at Christmas that I hope will warm your heart and give you the "giving bug."

When my friend Joy was about your age, her family lived in the mountains of Colorado, where her mom taught the K-3 class. Each Christmas Joy's mom would choose a student's family to help. And the neat thing is that the students did the giving! They were asked to bring things from their own homes to help the family in need. No one but Joy's mom knew who the gifts would go to. One particular year her mom chose to help Grace's family. Grace was a third grader who had four younger sisters. She owned only three dresses.

For several days the kids brought in canned foods, toilet paper, soap, and clothes. On the last day of the collection drive, Grace brought in her own donation—one of her three dresses. And not just the oldest, most worn dress. She brought her newest dress to give away! Knowing that Grace's family was the one in need that year, and witnessing Grace's unselfish heart, Joy's mom burst into tears—although the class had no idea why.

You can imagine Grace's surprise when the teacher delivered the basket of gifts to her house that night. Her generosity was rewarded when she got her own dress back!

The second story happened in that same Colorado mountain town, and Joy was there to witness another giving. On Christmas Eve her family went caroling from door to door, asking for donations to send to needy people in other countries.

Joy knocked on the door of one fancy house. When the door opened, she saw about 20 people inside opening gifts—all of them dressed in expensive-looking clothes. They heard the singing and came to the door, smiling. But all of them said no when asked to give.

Then a 5-year-old boy in the house yelled, "Wait!" He ran back to the pile of presents and brought back a beautiful box that had a $5 bill in it.

The adults protested, "No! That is meant for you to start your first bank account!"

But the boy insisted, and gave away his first savings. Although he lived in a fancy house full of selfish people, he gave something that they could not: love, kindness, and generosity.

DECEMBER 18

The Bush People

"What kind of deal is it to get everything you want but lose yourself? What could you ever trade your soul for?" Matthew 16:26, Message.

"I'll let the Mrs. eat first; then I'll eat the leftovers," the homeless man told my sister.

So she gave him the food and drove away. That was the first time Debi shared food with the homeless couple, but not the last.

It all started one day as she was driving through town behind an expensive car when it stopped along the road. A well-dressed woman got out and carried a box of food toward some overgrown bushes. A homeless man came out to meet her, took the box, and disappeared.

The next time Debi passed the area, she slowed down and peered into the bushes. What she saw was someone's home: two sleeping bags, a backpack, and a shopping cart. She could see a man and woman in their 60s sitting inside. Debi drove her own car home to her warm three-bedroom house with carpet, a fireplace, beds, and lots of food in the cupboard.

She couldn't get the couple off her mind. They weren't out on the side of the road with a sign begging for food or money. They were just sitting there inside the only home they had with the only possessions they had. The next day she stopped by a fast-food restaurant and bought a couple of meals. She drove to the bushes, rolled down her window, and hollered, "I have food for you!" Both walked out in their dirty, tattered clothes and gladly took the food.

Debi then started giving them homemade food. This went on for months until the Christmas season came. She and her family decided to invite the couple to Christmas dinner along with other people in their church who had no place to go. So she went to the familiar bushes, but this time she parked her car and walked over to them.

"We'd like to invite you to our home for Christmas dinner," she said.

"Oh, we can't do that!" they said. "We can't leave our spot and our cart. Someone else might take them."

They couldn't be convinced, so Debi took them each a full plate of food on Christmas day. The next time she was able to go back was the first of January. To her shock, the bushes had been trimmed, and there was no sign of the couple. They had disappeared. But Debi says she'll never forget them, and what it was like to help Jesus care for the hungry and the homeless.

DECEMBER 19

Ugly Black Shoes

A grasping person stirs up trouble, but trust in God brings a sense of well-being. Proverbs 28:25, Message.

Kyle didn't mean to be selfish. And it never occurred to him that he was, until he made a discovery later that day.

He and his mom had gone back-to-school shopping to get him ready for fifth grade. It should have been fun, but this year money was pretty tight, making their choices harder.

When it came time to find some school shoes, Kyle knew exactly what he wanted, and he spotted them immediately. They had black polished leather uppers, thin soles, and pointed toes—the kind that the cool guys would be wearing that year.

But then his mom spotted the kind *she* thought he should get. They *were* black, but they had big, thick soles and wide, rounded toes—exactly the opposite of the ones he wanted. They were just plain ugly to him! Of course his mom knew that the popular shoes wouldn't last very long, and the "practical" ones—well, they'd last the whole school year!

Kyle argued hard for the ones he wanted, but in the end his mom had to stand her ground. They left with the ugly black shoes. All the way home Kyle sulked, thinking how totally embarrassed he would be to have to wear those shoes to school the next day.

When they got home, Kyle headed straight for his room. But on the way by his parents' bedroom, something shiny caught his eye. Going back for a closer look, he first saw just his mom's nursing uniform and slip laid out on the bed as usual. Then he saw what had caught his eye. It was a shiny safety pin reflecting light from the window. It was holding the strap of his mom's slip together. She had worn the slip for so long that the strap had worn clear in half.

Suddenly he felt very ashamed. Here he'd argued with his mom and made her feel bad that they couldn't afford the "cool" shoes, and all the while she was having to pin her own worn-out clothes together so she could buy his school clothes. How could he have been so selfish? He vowed then and there that he would never be selfish again.

This Christmas you may not get everything that's on your wish list. But I hope you can learn from Kyle's story and be thankful for what you *do* get. Whatever your parents give, they'll give it out of love, and love makes any gift a good one.

DECEMBER 20

Christmas Half a World Away

If you mistreat the poor, you insult your Creator;
if you are kind to them, you show him respect. Proverbs 14:31, CEV.

My husband, Keith, and his best friend, Ron, took a year off from college to serve as student missionaries in Bangladesh. Just months before they arrived, three million people had died in a civil war, and another half million had been swept out to sea during a massive storm.

When Christmas came, they took a break from building houses for war refugees and went to a missionary's home. What a meal! Mashed potatoes and gravy, gluten steaks, stuffing, and homemade apple pie! It was almost like being home, and they ate till they were stuffed!

Just two hours later they boarded a relief flight taking tons of flour to a starving village 20 minutes away by air. The pilot was very angry that he had to work on Christmas. He grumbled, "Why can't those people take the day off from starving on Christmas?"

When the plane landed in a bare field, village men began unloading the sacks of flour into trucks below the plane. Then Keith noticed them—a whole line of village children standing as close as they dared, watching eagerly. Their bellies were bulging over skinny legs, and their eyes were sunken—signs of malnutrition. In their hands were empty little bowls and baskets. They stood there hoping to get enough flour so they wouldn't go to sleep hungry.

At first Keith was thrilled to think that his country, America, was feeding these poor children. Then a wave of sadness washed over him, and the sadness turned to anger as he realized how terribly unfair this world is. Here he and Ron had just finished a huge Christmas meal, and they would have another one that night. But these kids were starving! And he and Ron had the power to fly away in "silver birds" to a country that seemed like heaven to these children—to America—to escape all this. But these children would never be able to leave.

As soon as the plane was empty and the loaded trucks moved away, the children rushed in to scrape up the spilled flour. Soon the plane took off and circled back by. Keith looked down at the village. The children looked as small as ants, and soon they disappeared completely.

Keith recently told me, "The eyes of those hungry children still haunt me. They remind me that life won't ever be *fully* good for any of us until it is *finally* good for all of us. Until then, I want to live my life the way Jesus did—helping people every way I can."

Thousands of Stars

Those of us who are strong and able
in the faith need to step in and lend a hand to those who falter,
and not just do what is most convenient for us. Strength is for service,
not status. Each one of us needs to look after the good of the people
around us, asking ourselves, "How can I help?" Romans 15:1, 2, Message.

In December 2012 there was a shooting at an Oregon mall near my parents' house. They had been there just an hour before, but then they'd had a change in plans and left early.

Several days after the shooting, my family and I went to the mall to shop for Christmas gifts. I didn't know what to expect when we walked through the doors, but nothing looked different. There were still Christmas decorations, stores full of merchandise, and busy holiday shoppers. But something just didn't feel quite right. It felt eerie to be in a place that just days before had been the scene of panic and death.

But when I reached the food court area where the shooting took place, the eerie feeling changed to a feeling of peace. All along the glass-panel railing were shiny cutout stars. Not dozens or hundreds of stars—but *thousands* of them! On the stars were notes that mall visitors had written to the family members of the victims and to the community. Messages like:

"Never Give Up."

"I could never say how sorry I am for your loss."

"Dear People, I am so sorry you got hurt. From Haley, age 4."

"Jesus Christ is our living and only hope."

"Day by day, hour by hour, minute by minute, we will get stronger."

"Trusting in God's goodness, even in the midst of this tragedy."

"He sees your tears. He fights your fears."

Look at today's text. What strengths do you have that could help someone this Christmas? Are you physically strong so you can help an elderly person? Is baking your strength so you can cheer people with your cookies? Is music your strength so you can sing or play in a Christmas program? Are words your strength so you can encourage someone who's sad this Christmas? Whatever your strength is, let it shine this Christmas. Let it shine like a star in this sometimes very dark world.

DECEMBER 22

Best-kept Secret

Here's another way to put it: You're here to be light, bringing out the God-colors in the world. God is not a secret to be kept. We're going public with this, as public as a city on a hill. If I make you light-bearers, you don't think I'm going to hide you under a bucket, do you? I'm putting you on a light stand. Now that I've put you there on a hilltop, on a light stand—shine! Keep open house; be generous with your lives. By opening up to others, you'll prompt people to open up with God, this generous Father in heaven. Matthew 5:14-16, Message.

The problem with Calvin was that he pretty much did whatever he wanted to. The problem with Dominic was that he always followed. Calvin was popular, and Dominic felt lucky to be his friend. Calvin was street-smart and always had something cool to say.

These unlikely friends attended the same school from fifth to seventh grades. I call them unlikely friends because they were so very different—and they weren't good for each other.

Calvin liked living on the edge. He pulled pranks and even had several brushes with the law. He thought it was funny to egg houses in their neighborhood and loved any chance to pick fights with the neighborhood boys. Dominic knew that the daring things Calvin did were wrong, and he never participated. He was an "innocent bystander," you might say. But he never said anything to try to talk Calvin out of his antics.

When they were in seventh grade, Calvin started hanging out with some kids from the big city. His behavior went from bad to worse. At the end of the year he transferred to another school, and Dominic lost track of him for over a year—until one day when he saw him unexpectedly. "I was riding in a car downtown," Dominic told me, "when I saw a kid being handcuffed and put in the back of a police car. *That's Calvin!* I said to myself. I'll always regret that I didn't try to help him by telling him that what he was doing was wrong, and by offering something else to do for fun. I'll never forget that image of him getting into the police car . . ."

When the angels announced that Jesus had been born, they didn't do it quietly. There was a bright light, an announcement, and an angelic choir! They weren't ashamed of their good news.

You have good news to tell your friends too. Don't keep it quiet. If you have a friend headed the wrong way like Calvin, talk to them. Show them Jesus by standing up for what you believe in and by showing them a better way to live. Spare them, and yourself, the regrets.

DECEMBER 23

Christmas Eve Visit

I have told you these things while I am still with you. The Helper is the Holy Spirit. The Father will send Him in My place. He will teach you everything and help you remember everything I have told you. Peace I leave with you. My peace I give to you. I do not give peace to you as the world gives. Do not let your hearts be troubled or afraid. John 14:25-27, NLV.

It was Christmas Eve, and we'd just finished celebrating with my side of the family. We now had a four-hour trip home as soon as we made a quick stop at the mall. But at the mall we ran into a friend who gave us some shocking news: a dear family friend, Alf, had been diagnosed with terminal cancer and was in the hospital. He had only a short time to live.

I looked at my husband and said, "We have to go to the hospital before we head home." He understood why.

Alf had been more than a close family friend. Six years before he had been our family's pastor when my brother faced his own terminal cancer. Alf was a constant presence—at the hospital, in our homes, staying in touch through phone calls and e-mails when he couldn't be there in person. Even after the funeral he was there for us.

When I walked into his hospital room, Alf was sitting up in bed with a big smile and twinkling eyes. He held his arms open for a hug. Then he said seriously, "Well, Nancy, we saw Dan through this. And now it looks like it's my turn." I nodded. My heart ached.

Alf didn't look like someone who had only a short time to live. And he certainly didn't act like it. His voice was cheery. He still had that contagious smile. He asked about every member of my family before he talked much at all about his own diagnosis.

How could he act this way while facing his own death? I wondered to myself. Then he said something I'll always remember, and it answered my question.

"I know that I'll be healed," he told me. "What I don't know is whether it will happen on this side of the curtain or on the other side."

In other words, Alf believed that he served a God who could and would heal. And healing would happen either in this life or at the resurrection. He trusted God to choose.

Because Jesus was born, died, and was raised from the dead, Alf will someday live again. And I will see him on the other side of the curtain.

DECEMBER 24

The Perfect Gift

For to us a child is born, to us a son is given, and the government will be on his shoulders. And he will be called Wonderful Counselor, Mighty God, Everlasting Father, Prince of Peace. Isaiah 9:6, NIV.

Our Christmas Eve celebration was interrupted by a phone call from the local hospital. A girl who had been attending Dad's church had tried to end her life. Since I was an older teen at the time, Dad asked me to go to the hospital with him.

I asked myself on the way to the emergency room, *Why would she do this at Christmas? It's supposed to be the most wonderful time of the year!*

Dad left me alone in the room with her for a while. I pulled up a chair next to her bed, placed my hands in hers, and looked straight into her eyes as we talked.

God helped me bring hope to this girl who had none. I told her that hope for her troubled world had arrived some 2,000 years ago in the form of a Baby. That Baby grew up to be a Wonderful Counselor, Mighty God, Everlasting Father, and Prince of Peace to the world.

If your own world feels troubled this Christmas, the gift of Jesus offers you the same help. Here's what He wants to be for you:

Wonderful Counselor: Do you have a problem and need someone to talk to? Jesus is a wonderful counselor! His words all through the Bible are full of answers and comfort. He'll listen when you talk to Him. Even with the whole universe to manage, He's not too busy for you.

Mighty God: Are you afraid of something? You have a mighty God who will come to your rescue. He is strong. He fears nothing. Nothing you face is too big for Him.

Everlasting Father: If your dad is physically or emotionally absent, Jesus wants to be your everlasting father. That means He'll be there for you forever. If an earthly parent has disappointed you, your heavenly one won't. He's everything you've ever wanted in a parent.

Prince of Peace: If you're anxious, He'll give you peace. He'll give it to you through His Word as you search the Bible and as you talk to Him about everything that worries you.

This Christmas you're not alone. You've been given a Wonderful Counselor, a Mighty God, an Everlasting Father, and a Prince of Peace. His name is Jesus, and He's God's perfect gift to you.

Merry Christmas!

Instructed by the king, they set off. Then the star appeared again, the same star they had seen in the eastern skies. It led them on until it hovered over the place of the child. They could hardly contain themselves: They were in the right place! They had arrived at the right time! They entered the house and saw the child in the arms of Mary, his mother. Overcome, they kneeled and worshiped him. Then they opened their luggage and presented gifts: gold, frankincense, myrrh. Matthew 2:9-11, Message.

Christmas day is finally here! I hope that in whatever way your family chooses to celebrate, today will be a special day for you. Whether you're reading this in the morning, afternoon, or night, I'd like to remind you of what's worth celebrating—the birth of Jesus!

The three Wise Men in today's text make up an important part of the Christmas story, and they remind us of a very important aspect—giving. Not only giving to each other, but also giving to Jesus.

I know a family who once celebrated Christmas in a way that I'd never heard of. The parents and four kids had lived without God all their lives, and they felt an emptiness. So they began attending evangelistic meetings that my husband, Keith, was involved in. When the meetings were over they wanted to study the Bible more, and Keith met with them every week. God's love for them and His offer of eternal life were irresistible! They made the decision to be baptized as a family.

That first Christmas, they understood what it was all about and wanted to celebrate Jesus' birth. Keith went to visit them just before Christmas, and there, painted in huge letters across their front window for the whole neighborhood to see, was: HAPPY BIRTHDAY, JESUS! They even made a birthday cake in His honor and ate it on Christmas day.

Although you and I might not celebrate in this way, the beautiful part of their story is that this was their gift to Jesus, and they were not ashamed of it.

What gift might you give Jesus today? First, you can give Him yourself. Then you can give to someone else, because the Bible says that when you give to others, you're giving to Him, too. So in a way you're giving Him two gifts!

Wishing you a Merry Christmas!

DECEMBER 26

Free, but Not Cheap

So, what do you think? With God on our side like this, how can we lose? If God didn't hesitate to put everything on the line for us, embracing our condition and exposing himself to the worst by sending his own Son, is there anything else he wouldn't gladly and freely do for us? Romans 8:31, 32, Message.

Sometimes we just don't get it. Maybe it's because so much of what we get in life we have to earn. How do you earn allowance? You do your chores. How do you earn an A? You do your homework well. So when it comes to salvation, sometimes it's hard to accept that it's free—that we can't earn it.

Salvation doesn't come through the point system. Can you imagine what it would be like if God was adding up points in heaven and you had to earn 100 before you could be saved? Even if you earned 99 by the Second Coming, you'd still miss out! What if God gave you a point every time you obeyed and subtracted a point every time you disobeyed? We'd be in trouble!

Although salvation is free, it wasn't cheap for Jesus to purchase it for us. *It cost Him His life.* And we don't want to take that for granted like spoiled, wealthy kids who get everything they want, thinking that they can disobey and still get their parents' gifts.

Another reason salvation isn't cheap is that it costs *us* something. It costs total surrender to Jesus. He said in Luke 9:23-25, "If any of you want to be my followers, you must forget about yourself. You must take up your cross each day and follow me. If you want to save your life, you will destroy it. But if you give up your life for me, you will save it. What will you gain, if you own the whole world but destroy yourself or waste your life?" (CEV).

To "forget about yourself" means that you're not "top dog," because Jesus comes first. To take up your cross means to be willing to suffer for Him—like when my three best friends temporarily dumped me after I became a Christian. Do you think the cost of following Him sounds too high? I don't. Because nothing is too much to give the One who died in our place.

How would it make you feel if you owned everything in the world? Pretty powerful, huh? But verse 25 asks, What good would that do if, in the end, you were lost? I'd rather have Jesus than the whole world any day. The world doesn't offer you anything that lasts. Jesus offers you everything! He gave His life to offer it, and I hope you will give Him yours in return.

What's God Like?

When you come looking for me, you'll find me. Yes, when you get serious about finding me and want it more than anything else, I'll make sure you won't be disappointed. Jeremiah 29:13, 14, Message.

Before my family became Christians, Mom was an atheist. She didn't believe that God existed. She learned evolutionary theory at her public school, and she just accepted that her ancestors had been monkeys. She also thought that when a person died, that was it, and their loved ones would never see them again. She did try going to church once with a relative, but the picture they painted of God was really scary! A "repent or you'll burn in hell!" type of scary.

But years later, when Dad started reading the Bible, she became curious. After he'd left for work one day, she picked up his Bible and randomly opened it. She read an Old Testament story about some bloody battle! Mom quickly closed the book and decided she didn't want anything to do with it. But in her words, "Something kept drawing me back." So she tried two more days, with similar results.

Then came the day when she opened Dad's Bible and read about Jesus' death on the cross. "I sat there and cried so hard!" she told me. "I was amazed that Someone could love the world that much."

A few days later she read 2 Peter 3:8, 9, where Peter is explaining why Jesus hasn't returned: "Dear friends, remember this one thing, with the Lord one day is as 1,000 years, and 1,000 years are as one day. The Lord is not slow about keeping His promise as some people think. He is waiting for you. The Lord does not want any person to be punished forever. He wants all people to be sorry for their sins and turn from them" (NLV).

Mom told me, "Reading that just really touched me. I couldn't get it out of my mind that God was so loving that He wants everyone to be saved. It softened my heart, and that night I gave my life to God."

Maybe you've had an experience like Mom's. Maybe certain people have painted a picture of God that you don't like. If you want to know what He's really like, you need to search for yourself, the way Mom did. And don't give up until you discover the God who is kind, compassionate, forgiving, joyful, patient, and good. Because that's what God is really like.

DECEMBER 28

Why Be Baptized?

That's what baptism into the life of Jesus means. When we are lowered into the water, it is like the burial of Jesus; when we are raised up out of the water, it is like the resurrection of Jesus. Each of us is raised into a light-filled world by our Father so that we can see where we're going in our new grace-sovereign country. Romans 6:3-5, Message.

"I don't know why I need to be baptized. Jesus knows that I love Him. Isn't that enough?" Whenever I'm asked this question I go to the story of Nicodemus in John 3:1-7.

Jesus told Nicodemus that no one could enter heaven unless they are born again. Nicodemus was confused. He asked Jesus how someone could be born again when they're already old. How could a person possibly go back inside their mom and be born again?

This is how Jesus answered him: "I assure you, no one can enter the Kingdom of God without being born of water and the Spirit. Humans can reproduce only human life, but the Holy Spirit gives birth to spiritual life" (verses 5, 6, NLT).

Jesus was talking about a spiritual rebirth—a rebirth of our hearts and minds. And baptism is a ceremony that symbolizes this. Being lowered into the water is a symbol of being buried to our sins and our old way of life. Coming up out of the water is a symbol of beginning a new life. A life with Jesus!

I asked a few kids your age why they want to be baptized. They said:

"I want to be baptized so I can make it known that I love Jesus."—Breanna.

"I'm going to be baptized because I want Jesus to be my best friend!"—Lynnie.

"I want to be baptized so that I can get closer to God."—Henry.

"I want to be baptized so I can give my life to God and be committed to Him."—Josie.

"I want to be baptized so I can show people how much I love Jesus."—Makayla.

"I want to be baptized because I love Jesus and want Him in my life forever."—Elliott.

"I want to be baptized because I think God is very important. I don't want to just go to Sabbath school and church. I want to study the Bible and be a missionary someday."—Larissa.

If you've been baptized, take a moment to remember that day, and do a checkup to see how you and God are doing. If you haven't been baptized, I hope you'll consider it. It will be the highlight of your life! A decision that you will never regret.

DECEMBER 29

Be That One

We show our love for God by obeying his commandments, and they are not hard to follow. Every child of God can defeat the world, and our faith is what gives us this victory. No one can defeat the world without having faith in Jesus as the Son of God. 1 John 5:3-5, CEV.

When my brother Dan asked the doctor how bad his cancer was, the doctor answered, "No one has ever survived this type of cancer." Dan was devastated! The nurse was watching him, and when the doctor stepped away from the examination table, she whispered in Dan's ear: *"You be that one."*

Her words gave Dan a glimmer of hope. He tried his hardest to "be that one" and win his battle over cancer. But in the end the cancer could not be beaten.

I've often thought about the words of that nurse. We're all in our own kind of battle. Not against cancer, but against the evil in this world that tries to separate us from God. But we can win that battle! So I want to pass the nurse's words on to you: *You be that one.*

You be that one who leaves when the party turns wild.

You be that one who stops someone from being bullied.

You be that one who studies hard for the math test rather than cheating.

You be that one who obeys your parents because God asks you to respect them.

You be that one who says, "Let's listen to music that doesn't have bad language."

You be that one who says, "No way. I'm not touching that stuff."

You be that one who says, "Let's play a video game that doesn't have a bunch of killing."

How will you know when to "be that one?" If you daily connect with God, the Holy Spirit will tell you. That's His job! He will guide you, and He will speak to you. Not in a voice you can actually hear, but in a voice you can hear in your conscience. Isaiah 30:21 says, "And if you leave God's paths and go astray, you will hear a voice behind you say, 'No, this is the way; walk here' " (TLB).

Have you heard that voice before? It's the Holy Spirit, whom Jesus sent after He went to heaven. He promised that the Holy Spirit would be with you always, telling you what's right and what's wrong. But even with His help, it's still your choice. You choose whether or not to get back on the right path. You choose whether or not to "be that one."

DECEMBER 30

Sacrifice Your Pet?

Dear friends, God is good. So I beg you to offer your bodies to him as a living sacrifice, pure and pleasing. Romans 12:1, CEV.

We all knew that it was just a skit, but we were so overcome by Jesus' loving sacrifice that we couldn't hold back our emotions. There we were—I, a grown-up, with several college students—crying in front of the kids during children's church.

That particular week the theme was Jesus' sacrifice. So we presented a skit that we thought would help the kids understand what His sacrifice really meant.

In the skit we were acting out a kids' church service. I played the pastor, and the college students played the kids. I was explaining that in the Old Testament, when people sinned, they had to sacrifice their innocent animals.

As planned in the skit, we "ran out of time," so I said to the actors, "Come back next week, and I'll tell you how the New Testament changed things."

But as the skit went, the actors pretended that they somehow didn't catch that last sentence. The skit went on to show that each one committed some sin during the week. Thinking that the Old Testament laws about sacrifice were still in effect, they acted heartbroken. They believed that now they would have to sacrifice their own pets!

In the final scene, the actors are gathered in the church, each holding an imaginary pet to be sacrificed—hugging them, crying, and saying goodbye. Then one boy lays his pet on the altar.

"I'm so sorry I sinned, Buddy!" he cries as he raises a butcher knife above his head.

"WAIT!" I yell, running into the room. "What are you guys doing here with all your pets? And why are you about to sacrifice Buddy?"

The actors all tell me that they sinned and now need to sacrifice their pets—just as I taught them the week before.

"That isn't the end of the story!" I tell them. "In the New Testament, Jesus came to sacrifice *Himself*—once and for all—for the sins of everyone! Your pets don't have to die!"

The "kids" in the skit are relieved! And you and I should be, too. Jesus, the Son of God, made Himself the sacrifice. Not just for innocent pets, *but for you and me*. That's how much He loves you. He gave His all. And all He wants in return is all of you.

DECEMBER 31

New Year's Eve Goodbye

Such a large crowd of witnesses is all around us! So we must get rid of everything that slows us down, especially the sin that just won't let go. And we must be determined to run the race that is ahead of us. We must keep our eyes on Jesus, who leads us and makes our faith complete. He endured the shame of being nailed to a cross, because he knew that later on he would be glad he did. Now he is seated at the right side of God's throne! So keep your mind on Jesus, who put up with many insults from sinners. Then you won't get discouraged and give up. Hebrews 12:1-3, CEV.

It's hard to believe that a whole year has gone by and our time together is over! There hasn't been a day in this past year when you, the reader, have not been on my mind. I've wondered where you live and what life is like for you. And I've prayed for you, that you would choose Jesus and stand strong for Him.

Last summer I was out walking one evening when a family on bicycles rode by. I looked behind me and saw a girl who was trying to catch up with them. As she rode by, I could see beads of sweat on her face and hear her huffing and puffing while she pedaled as fast as she could.

"You can do it!" I called out as she rode by me.

And that's what I want to say to you on this last day. *You can do it!* Whatever life throws at you between here and heaven, you can do it. You can make it through.

I don't know if you have any New Year's resolutions to make tonight, but the best commitment you can ever make is to choose Jesus and never leave Him. Life will have its ups and downs while you're growing up. It may even get really tough at times. But if you don't quit—if you don't give up on Jesus—two wonderful things will happen: you will have Him to help you through the tough times, and in the end He will take you to your new home in heaven.

When I look back on my life—from when I was your age until now—I can honestly say that I wouldn't trade life with Jesus for anything. If I could go back to the day when I was 10 and decide whether to give my life to Jesus or to see if life might be more exciting without Him—I'd choose Jesus again. In a heartbeat.

Don't give up, because when you get to heaven and look into the face of Jesus, you'll know it was all worthwhile. You can make it! You're not alone. *He's got your back.*

NOTES:

NOTES:

NOTES: